D1488548

Social Research to Test Ideas

Social Research
to Test Ideas

SELECTED WRITINGS OF

Samuel A. Stouffer

WITH AN INTRODUCTION BY *Paul F. Lazarsfeld*

The Free Press of Glencoe

Library of Congress Catalog Card Number: 61-9174

To Ruth, Dear Wife

GLENDOWER: *I can call spirits from the vasty deep.*

HOTSPUR: *Why, so can I, or so can any man; But will they come when you do call for them?*

—King Henry IV, first part, Act III, Scene 1

□ ☒ □ □ □ *Contents*

 *Preface*

In 1960, as these papers are compiled, mankind faces its grimmest peril or its most glorious opportunity. The press of a button, drunkenly or soberly, can destroy life on earth. But, if vouchsafed continuity, the human spirit has, thanks in part to modern science and technology, seemingly illimitable possibilities for understanding and mastery.

For the better understanding of man's relations to man, we have had for centuries the records of history and the insights of philosophers and poets. For only a few decades have we attempted also to study society with the theoretical and empirical tools of science and the results are small and tentative, when compared with the accumulated wisdom of the ages.

Too much has been promised, too fast, by some social scientists, especially by those unchastened by the arduous, meticulous, and often unrewarding labor of empirical testing of ideas. Overexuberance generates a predictable reaction, which is probably wholesome even when the reaction extends to sharp attacks on the basic strategy of studying man with the tools of science.

The most effective response to critical essays will not be more and better critical essays. Rather, it will be demonstration, by patient example, of what social science can do. At this point in man's adventure with destiny, such demonstrations are unlikely to be very dramatic. But as these efforts are modestly multiplied by scholars throughout the world, the evidence of and for social science will speak with increasing force. This book is one such effort. It is a selection from the research done by a student who is one of those struggling to put ideas about man's relations to man to an empirical test.

In the division of labor among social scientists there are numerous roles. The product illustrated in this book represents primarily activity in two of these roles—as a maker and tester of limited propositions that seem of some significance to sociology and social psychology and as a contributor to the improvement of the tools needed in the testing.

Some of the contents are programmatic—the opening essay, for example, the brief essays with which Parts One and Two conclude, and a few others. But most of the book's pages represent examples of concrete research with as much original data as space allows. By following the arguments and observing the fit or lack of fit of the data, others may learn how to do such research better in the future. Part One is mainly substantive. Part Two is mainly methodological.

Several of the papers included involve collaboration of others in the research and the writing. Without their efforts much here reported might not have seen the light of day. No words of the compiler of this volume can adequately express his sense of personal indebtedness.

Special notes of acknowledgment are due also to the publisher, Mr. Jeremiah Kaplan, whose importunities led to the bringing together of this collection of disparate efforts; to a number of academic colleagues who have encouraged the enterprise; and to my secretary, Mrs. Shirley M. Atkinson, who has assembled, sometimes from dusty archives, the papers from which the present selection is made and has seen this book in all stages to the printer.

SAMUEL A. STOUFFER

 *Introduction*

by *Paul F. Lazarsfeld*

For four decades the German poet, scientist, and statesman, J. W. Goethe, dominated the cultural life of his country. Trying to explain the reasons for his prominence, he said modestly that he and Germany grew up together. A similar statement could have been made by Samuel A. Stouffer. His academic life coincided with the development of empirical social research in the United States. As a graduate student he participated in the flowering of the Chicago school that set the stage for the application of sociological concepts to the empirical study of human affairs. When he returned from a fellowship in England, where he had worked with Karl Pearson and R. A. Fisher, he participated in and greatly strengthened the introduction of precise statistical methods into social inquiry. When sociologists felt strong enough to attack major social problems through empirical inquiry, he became director of the Social Science Research Council studies on the social effects of the depression; and, parenthetically, a few years later he played an important role in Myrdal's study of the Negro in the United States. By the time that World War II broke out, attitude surveys had acquired scientific validity, but they were mainly used for commercial purposes. Stouffer's monumental work on the American soldier established the link between the revolutionary technique and academic sociology. In the course of this enterprise he inaugurated one trend and became deeply involved in another that dominate the social research scene at this moment: the use of mathematical models and the integration of empirical data with social theory. Just before his death, he was preparing a large-scale project of applied sociology for the Population Council.

The present set of papers is, therefore, not only the record of a man's work: it symbolizes the growth of a science. A few months before his death,

Stouffer himself made the selection and classified the chapters in their present order. Nothing could or should be added to the editorial structure he decided upon. But what he did not say, and in his modesty might not even have realized, was that this collection provides for a new generation of students a coherent series of cases through which they can understand the development and the present state of empirical social research. It is this use of the volume which my introduction shall try to reinforce. To this end, I propose to comment on the papers in the biographical order in which they were originally written, simultaneously singling out a number of major ideas that underlie their continuity.

THE EARLY YEARS

Among Stouffer's first publications are the three on correlation analysis now combined in Chapter 13. Section C shows his knowledge of matrix algebra at a time when no one could predict how crucial it would become in the application of mathematics to the social sciences. Section A shows his ability to broaden traditional statistical formulas into new forms adapted to the specific problems of the sociologist. The really astounding paper in this group is Section B. Correlation techniques were developed first in connection with biological and later psychometric problems. Stouffer doubted whether they would be appropriate in their conventional form to the new type of material sociologists began to work with, a doubt that the experience of the last thirty years has more than justified. His criticism is especially directed against the use of partial correlation:

We may find that within groups I and II, a partial correlation between juvenile delinquency and the percentage of foreign born and Negroes is high, holding the other factors constant; while within groups III and IV the partial correlation may be low. This difference may be very important; yet it would be averaged out if all the data were analyzed in a single correlation scheme (page 268).

Here we find clearly formulated the difference between contingent and partial correlation. This distinction was seen only much later by others; it has finally become the cornerstone of what is now usually called "survey analysis."

The paper is also remarkable for its early insight into the notion of "validity." Up to quite recently, most textbooks dealt with this matter as if one could decide whether or not an index corresponded to objective reality. In 1934, few people, if any, defined the problem correctly: "Is (the index) really describing what we think it is describing?" (page 265) This relation between the index and the *intention of the investigator* is now much discussed under the heading of "construct validity." Finally, Section B foreshadows a concern that, as we shall see, was never far from Stouffer's mind: the difference between statistical and causal relations.

Some of the ideas in this expository paper were put to the test in his comparative study of fertility among Catholics written in 1935 and now included in Chapter 8. At the time the birth rate was still declining; Stouffer was able to show that, while Catholics had a higher birth rate than non-Catholics, the *decline* among Catholics was markedly more rapid. He made sure that no spurious factors, such as age, occupation, nationality, and residence, interfered with his findings. Stouffer's desire to take into account as many factors as possible is reflected in most of his later papers and is now accepted as indispensable for social research. The paper, incidentally, is interesting from still another point of view: it is a very early longitudinal study. The social characteristics of husband and wife were established by going back to the marriage records kept in city halls, information on the subsequent number of births was obtained by questionnaires sent to the married couples at the time of the study, and the main finding was checked separately for differing stages of his respondents' marriages.

Stouffer never lost his interest in problems of research technology, as evidenced by his work on the H-technique of scaling, published in 1952 and included here as Chapter 14. (The reader should not overlook the large number of empirical tests condensed in the modest lines of the last two paragraphs of that paper.) But, in the main, the emphasis of his life's work was a substantive one, on "social research to test ideas." His basic philosophy is summarized in the last chapter of the present collection. How it developed step by step and with an ever-broadening scope the following pages will try to trace.

STUDIES IN SOCIAL EFFECTS

Around 1934 there was much talk about studying the effects of the depression by extending the *Recent Social Trends*. But financial support was not forthcoming, so the Social Science Research Council decided to do the best it could without carrying out original research. A committee under Ogburn's chairmanship was asked to organize a series of monographs using available sources to trace the effects of the depression on various sectors of American society; the mandate included sketching out feasible research ideas that might be carried out at a later time. Stouffer became staff director and kept in close touch with all the authors for the various monographs. For himself he chose the topic of the family. The resulting monograph appeared in 1937, and two selections are included in the present volume as Chapter 6.

Section B of Chapter 6 shows a crucial broadening of Stouffer's thinking, again of a kind that antedates similar efforts by others in the field. He starts out by making systematic speculations about what the depression might have done to the American family. His anchor point is the general sociological observation that, over the years, the institution of the family had become less traditionally woven into the whole texture of society and was more likely to reflect the personal needs of two contracting partners. Did the depression accentuate this trend? From an armchair, both a negative and a positive answer seem plausible. (Stouffer repeatedly showed in his monograph how such contradictory expectations could be equally well justified.) Obviously, facts were needed. But how could facts be related to a complex series of speculations? First, the concepts involved had to be analyzed more carefully. Thus, for instance, he pointed out that a less traditional marriage would be more "impulsive." Now, it is possible to describe quite convincingly an impulsive marriage, and Stouffer does so in this monograph. But he adds: "Such a description, essentially psychological, is unworkable statistically. Some indexes must be sought with the hope that they may have some relationship to the intangibles."

Let us remember that the rule of the game on this occasion prohibited collection of new data; we then begin to appreciate the ingenuity with which Stouffer unearthed some pertinent material. Drawing upon the image of an impulsive marriage, he proposed three indicators: the proportion of marriages performed outside the residence of either the bride or bridegroom, whether the ceremony was carried out by a magistrate or a religious officer, and the divorce rate at a given period after the marriage. Stouffer argued convincingly for all three indicators, always reminding his readers of their possible limitations. Marriages performed in "Gretna Greens" rather than in the residence of the parents are notoriously impulsive, and the absence of a minister indicates almost by definition the weakening of tradition. Early divorce is a retroactive indicator that again, incidentally, shows Stouffer's sensitivity to the advantages of longitudinal material. Undoubtedly, one could think of other indicators to characterize an impulsive marriage; the choice Stouffer made was dictated partly by the availability of data. But this interplay between conceptual analysis and operational considerations is in itself a characteristic feature of empirical research guided by systematic thinking. In this sense, Section B of Chapter 6 sets the stage for a style of work that we shall repeatedly encounter in this review. And let us not overlook the impressive command of sources: Australia, Canada, and several of our states converge to provide tentative evidence. Incidentally, Section A of Chapter 6 discusses in general terms the pitfalls in the use of trend data for the purpose of discovering the effect of a specific social event. The recently increasing interest in historical sociology will give this piece of logical caution a renewed value.

In introducing Chapter 6, Stouffer emphasizes that, at the time that the monographs on the depression were planned and written, few considered the possibility of using attitude surveys. But they were soon to come, and Chapter 7 is a rather dramatic signpost at the almost sudden moment of transition. In 1937 the Rockefeller Foundation began its support of a series of studies into the effects of radio on various facets of American society. The two selections included in Chapter 7 were among Stouffer's contributions to one of these projects. Section B bears a close similarity to his work on the effect of the depression. Again the paper starts with some general speculations from which specific expectations are derived. They in turn are tested by particular data. At one point Stouffer is led to "expect the circulation of newspapers to increase more or to decline less . . . in the immediate trade area of the city than in the outlying one." He unearthed circulation figures for a large number of newspapers, and his corroborative evidence consists of the four figures reported in Table 7-2. Its apparent simplicity should not conceal the sophistication behind it. The units of analysis are 181 cities. They are characterized according to whether the aggregate circulation of their newspapers in 1937 was larger or smaller than in 1929; a further subdivision compares this change for central and outlying areas. Thus, for each city six pieces of information are needed to place it into a cell of a fourfold table, while usually only two such pieces are used to this end. Another type of analysis is introduced when minute fluctuations in circulation are related to external events such as elections or critical moments on the international scene. Notice again in Figure 7-2, it is not the circulation itself but the ratio of circulation on corresponding days in 1938 and 1937 that provides the pertinent information.

Section A of Chapter 7 deals with a new type of material. In a public opinion survey made available to Stouffer, people had been asked whether they preferred radio or newspapers as a source of news. Here for the first time he was confronted with the kind of attitude material that he handled so masterfully in subsequent years; from the beginning he brought his own style to this kind of analysis. He starts out with a general question: what advantages do the two media offer? For instance, radio delivers the news more quickly, but the newspaper provides more details. From there he proceeds to a second step: for which kinds of people would each of these advantages be relevant? Only then does he begin to present figures on the preferences of respondents classified by sex, social and economic status, and size of city of residence. Thus, Table 7-1 becomes not a descriptive record but a test of an interlocking series of hypotheses showing consistencies in many directions.

THE THEORETICAL INTERPRETATION OF EMPIRICAL DATA

This mode of thinking grew into the achievement of *The American Soldier.* In 1940 Stouffer became research director for the Information and Education Branch of the United States Army. He organized several hundred attitude surveys among soldiers all over the world. At the end of the war, the Carnegie Corporation made a grant to a committee under the chairmanship of the former Chief of the Branch, General Osborn, that permitted Stouffer to retain some of his collaborators and to summarize their work in four large volumes. It is most fortunate that Stouffer included here a number of shorter selections from this work, which was so extensive that it did not lend itself easily to use by teachers. Now at last students will be able to ponder what is still, fifteen years after its publication, the best example of survey research available in the literature.

The specific items that Stouffer chose for inclusion in Chapter 2 are characteristic of his own development as well as of the trends discernible among the sociological avant-garde. After the war, as those who knew Stouffer will remember, the relation between social theory and empirical research became his central preoccupation. In all his postwar writings, he started out with a piece of theory, developed either by others or by himself, and inquired how it could be tested. In *The American Soldier* this sequence was, of course, not possible. The original studies were carried out to answer practical morale problems with which the Army was confronted. In the final publication Stouffer showed in innumerable places that even such applied research had, in fact, theoretical implications. The selections of Chapter 2 highlight this point of view. All are related to one central concept—the notion of relative deprivation, which "would seem to have a kinship to and, in part, include such well-known sociological concepts as 'social frame of reference,' 'patterns of expectations,' or 'definitions of the situation'" (page 17). There is no need for me to elaborate on this point. In a paper read to the American Association for the Advancement of Science and included here as Chapter 1, Stouffer himself selected the concept of relative deprivation as his main example to illustrate the strategy of the social sciences. There he summarizes succinctly the theoretical considerations that link together the four selections of Chapter 2.

Two technical remarks may help to relate Chapter 2 to other parts of this book. For one, the consistency of what I previously called Stouffer's analytical style should be noted. Perhaps the best example is Section B. The basic material here is quite simple: soldiers were asked whether they were satisfied with the promotion opportunities they found in the Army. Stouffer's main thesis was that their answers would depend very much on the kind of group with which they compared themselves. He then speculated which comparisons were likely to occur. The soldiers knew, by and large, that educated men were promoted more quickly; as a result, among soldiers of the same rank the more poorly educated men were less likely to be dissatisfied, because they expected less. And again within the same rank, men who have been in the Army only a short time should be more optimistic, because they have not yet seen many others getting ahead of them. After these expectations are spelled out, sophisticated multivariate data are presented to show that each of these factors (rank, longevity, and education) does indeed play the independent role assigned to it on the basis of theoretical considerations (Figure 2-2, page 23). The formal similarity with the discussion of media preferences in Section A of Chapter 7 is striking, and yet there is a new element: the discussion of media preferences started with a list of various advantages attributed to the radio and newspaper, respectively; the study of attitudes toward promotion opportunities goes back to a single, more fundamental concept—that of relative deprivation.

The substantive examples taken from the promotion study may seem paradoxical. By and large, they show that if a class of soldiers had little chance to be promoted, then its individual members were more satisfied than were those in another class in which the objective chances were greater. Stouffer showed this not only by comparing statistical classes, such as educated and uneducated soldiers, but also by comparing whole Army units. The table of organization in the Air Force provided for more promotions than did that of the Military Police. Nevertheless, the members of the former were, on the average, more dissatisfied with their opportunities. Of course, within each unit the individuals who were promoted were more satisfied than those who were not. This emphasis on comparisons within collectives and between collectives is another point deserving special attention. Individual and ecological correlations have often been distinguished. Thus, for instance, in early political studies, if one wanted to assess the effect of income on voting, the units of analysis had to be the voting precinct because the only information available was the voting records of precincts; since the advent of polls, it is possible to relate the vote of individual persons to their income. As far as I know, Stouffer was the first to realize that the two types of relations can lead to very different results and that the difference can be of great theoretical importance. Within a unit, individual promotion is positively related to satisfaction. Between units the promotion opportunities and the average satisfaction are negatively correlated. The bridge between the two results is found in the complex of ideas developed around Stouffer's notion of relative deprivation.

This aspect of Stouffer's work has had great influence on the research of the younger generation of sociologists who wanted to move from the atomistic approach introduced by the flourishing of surveys to that done in an organizational context. It is impressive to see that the whole line of thought was obviously in Stouffer's mind long before his work for the Army provided relevant data. In the study of Catholic fertility (Chapter 8) Stouffer dealt with individual as well as with ecological correlations. As discussed above, his main data were obtained from individuals living in Wisconsin. At the end of the paper (pages 181–184) he asks if his findings could be extended to the whole United States. The only available data were of an ecological nature: the correlation between the proportion of Catholics and the decline in the number of children over two census periods for a large number of American cities. He did indeed find a positive correlation; but, with characteristic caution, he added the following reservation: how can we tell that the proportion of Catholics in an area is paralleled by a sentiment favorable to the teachings of the Catholic church? Perhaps in an area, split fifty-fifty between Catholics and Protestants, the average anti-Catholic feeling is stronger than at either of the two ends of the ecological continuum, where there are very few or a large majority of Catholics. Since 1935 the insight that statistical rates require and permit contextual sociological interpretation has helped much to bridge the gap between theorists and empiricists.

THE EMPIRICAL TESTING OF SOCIAL THEORY

All the findings in Chapter 2 have one characteristic in common. The concept of relative deprivation is used as an interpretive device; at no point is an effort made to measure it directly. This is, in principle, the problem to which Stouffer turned after the completion of *The American Soldier*. He began to ask himself whether some of the basic concepts in sociological theory would be amenable to direct assessment; for a major test he chose the notion of "role." Social theorists had for some time stressed that an individual's conduct is affected by the expectations of others. Obviously, Stouffer reasoned, if these expectations are to be effective, they must be known to the actor. Why not really investigate what people thought was expected of them and how these expectations influenced them? This crucial turning of the problem led to the two papers on role conflict included here in Chapter 3. They are so compact in their presentation, so characteristic of Stouffer's interests in the last ten years of his life, and so important for anyone concerned with the relation between theory and research that they require somewhat extended discussion.

The translation of the concept of role into empirical research procedures requires at least three specifications:

1. A concrete sphere of action must be selected. Stouffer decides on an example in which a student-proctor finds a student cheating during an examination; what should the proctor do?

2. The idea that "society" holds expectations is too vague: different groups may hold different expectations regarding a specific role. Stouffer distinguishes between the friends of the proctor and college authorities, who might not agree regarding what the proctor should do.

3. It is not really the objective expectations of these two groups that matter. Stouffer brings into the focus of attention the expectations that the proctor imputes to the others.

This last point is the crucial one. The study centers around a sample list of actions the proctor could take; these are ranked in order of punitiveness: stop the examination and report the student to the authorities at one extreme, not taking notice of the cheating at the other. Thus are created the first three variates: what the respondent himself would do and what he thinks the student body and the school authorities would want him to do. We are not surprised to learn that the proctor thinks the school authorities will expect greater punitiveness than the students (Figure 3-1), but Stouffer directs our attention to a different aspect of this expectation variable. The respondents agree that the administration will want them to be harsh with the cheater. But expectations imputed to students are much more diversified: not only do the respondents themselves vary greatly in their opinion; they also feel that the student body is not homogeneous in their expectations. Thus, the *range* of expectations imputed to the students is much broader than that imputed to the administration. Turning the notion of expectation into an empirical variable made it quite natural to inquire not only into its average value but also into its standard deviation. Then Stouffer could turn around and ask how this standard deviation fits into the conceptual scheme. He found, for instance (see Table 3-7, page 51), that a proctor who thinks that the students have definite expectations will act according to them regardless of whether or not the school authorities knew his choice. But if the proctor thinks that student opinion spreads more widely and therefore gives him some elbow room, then the visibility of his choice makes a difference: he would comply with the imputed requirements of authorities in a public decision, but would conform more to imputed student standards in a private act.

To subsume Stouffer's main idea under current terminology: the translation into an empirical operation "feeds back" into the conceptual discourse and enriches it, in this case by creating the notion of "social slippage" (page 52). (Today he might call it "normative leeway.") In addition the paper demonstrates how a simple questionnaire can reproduce a very complex phenomenon. At the core of the study there are three variables: the severity of action the proctor himself can take and the expectations he imputes to two reference groups—the administration and the students. Stouffer adds an element of risk due to a variation in visibility: the respondents are asked to compare their probable behavior according to whether or not the authorities are likely to learn about it. And finally, the nature of the culprit is introduced as a variate: in one case he is described as a close friend of the proctor and in another case as a student toward whom the proctor feels indifferent. As a result, the study is a polyphony of five variables that appear in various combinations and at different levels of complexity in each of its tables and charts.

At the end of the paper, Stouffer raises a further question. If the proctor thinks that the expectations of others leave him considerable freedom of action, what would further determine his behavior? The assumption is that a sixth variable, some psychological characteristic of the proctor, would have to be introduced. In a subsequent paper (Section B) this new element is further explored, drawing upon Parsons' distinction between universalistic and particularistic social relations. A variety of situations are brought up, in which a respondent can either follow strict objective standards or act in a slightly dishonest way to help a good friend in difficulty. By combining four such situations, each respondent can be classified into one of five levels of "particularism" according to how often he would bend his position in favor of a friend. Stouffer then reintroduces the proctor-cheating situation and analyzes whether the general tendency helps to account for the specific choices he has investigated before. While he does not reintroduce all five variables covered in the previous paper, he provides enough links (Figure 3-3, page 64) to show that, by this new procedure, he has indeed made progress toward identifying the psychological variable that was previously missing.

Some of the programmatic essays included here as Chapter 11 argue along the lines of the studies in role conflict. In Section D, for instance, Stouffer makes the point that notions such as reference groups are usually introduced only inferentially for the sake of interpreting existing data; there is need to develop techniques by which we can find out directly what reference groups people have in mind when they act in concrete situations. Public opinion polls can provide such information on a large scale and therewith contribute to sociological theory. Section A starts out with the observation that many children with very high I.Q.'s do not go to college. Lack of money is not a sufficient explanation. Stouffer feels that it should be possible to characterize the motivational climate of families in which it is not "in the cards" to send children to college. This paper, incidentally, again makes outstanding use of longitudinal data. He asks at what point in an educational career the road to college is blocked off. School grades collected from children in the eighth grade and again at the end of high school show that, even in a small sample, clearly distinct patterns can be found (Table 11-3, page 229).

THE DEVELOPMENT OF A FORMAL THEORY

Translating conceptual constructs into research operations was only one way in which Stouffer looked at the relation between theory and research. A second avenue he explored was the direct formulation of a theory in mathematical terms. As a proving ground, he selected a problem of migration. In terms of time and labor invested, this was probably the largest effort he made in the later part of his life.

From his Chicago days on, Stouffer was always very much interested in population theory. Repeatedly he advised governmental and private agencies on demographic research. During the period in which he helped Myrdal organize the data for *The American Dilemma*, he felt that the Negro migration from South to North should have been given more attention. (What he had in mind is clearly described in Section B of Chapter 11.) It is, therefore, not surprising that he chose a migration problem for his main effort to set up and test a piece of formal theory. The two papers on intervening opportunities now combined in Chapter 4 show how his thinking on this matter developed. They are not easy to read, and the second one, published in the *Journal of Regional Sciences*, was addressed to an audience trained specifically in demographic analysis. Still, as Stouffer points out, his general approach has implications for many sociological problems, such as selection of marriage partners, the choice of colleges, and utilization of leisure time (page 91). Students of sociology will need help to understand the type of work that occupied

Stouffer for a period of twenty years. The best procedure seems to be to compare the two papers and thereby partition them into smaller units, each of which encompasses a specific move in Stouffer's strategy.

The basic purpose of the model is to "account for much of the observed movement of population in space. The idea is that the number of people going a given distance from a point is not a function of distance directly but . . . of the spatial distribution of opportunities" (page 91). The basic data are the number of people who move from one point (the origin) to any other points (targets). In the target area there are a certain number of opportunities suitable for the purposes of the specific migrants. Between the origin and the target there are a cumulative number of opportunities that the migrant passes by. The number of people who move from a specific origin to a specific target will be given by the following fraction:

$$\frac{\text{Opportunities in target area}}{\text{Cumulative opportunities between origin and target}}$$

The basic formula states: The number of people moving between two places will be larger the more opportunities there are in the target area and the fewer opportunities are interposed between it and the origin. For actual computation this fraction must be multiplied by a constant scale factor to adjust for the specific measure of opportunities that is introduced in an empirical study.

In both papers the opportunities themselves are assessed in an indirect way. Instead of counting directly the opportunities available in a given area, Stouffer counts the total number of people moving into this area: obviously, if the attractiveness of the locality is high, the number of immigrants will be large. In the more refined treatment this measure is corrected by its complement, the number of people who leave the area.

In an offhand remark, he points out that the basic logic of his procedure is quite similar to the idea underlying chi-square analysis (footnote 27, page 94). This remark is so helpful for expository purposes that it deserves a brief elaboration. Suppose a county has six towns, all of which are located on a single road. They are numbered in the order of their place on the road. We know how many people migrated to and from these six places, and we put our knowledge into the following scheme:

		Target of migration						
		1	2	3	4	5	6	Total emigration
Origin of migration	1							300
	2					w		100
	3			x				100
	4				y			100
	5					z		100
	6							300
Total immigration		100	200	200	100	300	100	

The last row and the last column in the scheme, the marginals, give the total emigration and immigration for the six towns. (The figures are, of course, fictitious.) Stouffer wants to develop *a theory that would make it possible to fill in the internal cells of the scheme, knowing only the marginal figures.* Much depends upon the definition of opportunities. We chose an oversimplified index that Stouffer, of course, never used, but that is in line with his thinking: the difference between the number of all the immigrants to and of all the emigrants from a given town. Suppose then that the task is to fill in the cell that indicates the number of people who would move from town 2 to town 5. According to Stouffer's theory, we would first compute the attractiveness of area 5, which would be $z = (300 - 100) = 200$. We would then add together the attractiveness of areas 3 and 4, which people have to pass by on the way from area 2 to 5. These intervening opportunities would be $x + y = (200 - 100) + (100 - 100) = 100$. The model would then require that we fill in the box (2–5) by the figure

$$w = \frac{az}{x+y} = \frac{200a}{100}$$

(The constant a would be determined by the fact that the sum of all boxes would have to add up to the total number of 1,000 cases.) The content of Stouffer's two papers is an ever-increasing refinement of this basic idea. The following four points embrace the core of his argument:

1. The migrations move on a two-dimensional plane, not a one-dimensional road. The two papers differ in the way they take care of this point. In the first, Stouffer just drew a circle around a point of origin, with the target lying on the circumference; everything within the circle contributes to the measure of intervening opportunities. At the end of the first paper Stouffer stresses that this model lacks *directionality.* Any target area at the same distance from the origin has the same intervening opportunities. The second paper provides the answer: the notion of "intervening" is now restricted to a narrower path between origin and target. Two targets at equal distance from the origin but lying in different directions may now have different denominators in the basic equation. This is the meaning of Figure 4-5. The area of circle A symbolizes the old, the area of circle B the new definition of "intervening." Obviously, for different points on the circumference of A, the corresponding circle B could provide different cumulative opportunities.

2. Once directionality is introduced, the "attractiveness of the target area" can also be refined. In the first paper it was just the number of people who moved into a specific section S of a town in a recent number of years. For any other area of origin, the section S had the same attractiveness, providing the same numerator in the basic equation. In the new paper it is possible to introduce the notion of *relative attractiveness.* A target can be more attractive for one origin than for another. Migration from St. Louis to Denver,

for example, is the result of two factors: the attractions which *pull* people to Denver and the disadvantages which *push* them away from St. Louis. His measure of the opportunities which Denver holds for people in St. Louis is, therefore, but for a scaling factor, the product of the total migration *to* Denver times the total migration *from* St. Louis. In our oversimplified example, the numerator of the basic equation would now use for each cell marginal data about both cities, the origin and the target. The real computations in Stouffer's new model are shown in Part 2, Section B, of Chapter 4.

3. In the first paper it is assumed that the migration is inversely proportional to the intervening opportunities. In the second paper it is *inversely proportional to some power, b,* of this factor: the value of b can be established from empirical data. Note the similarity of this to the lively discussion among astronomers a few decades ago. Newton had assumed that the attraction between two celestial bodies is inversely proportional to the square of their distance. Refined measurements showed that the motion of some planets could not be accounted for in this way, and various efforts were made to establish what power of the distance would best reflect the empirical data. The issue was not settled by curve-fitting but by a fundamental reformulation of theory that made the Newton law valid in specific cases. At the end of his second paper Stouffer himself expects that the next step in the kind of work he inaugurated will come from the "exploration, testing, and modification of still broader theoretical conceptions" (page 112). Here it is advisable, even for the mathematically untrained reader, to compare Equation 1 of Section A with the corresponding new Equation 1 of Section B; all the differences have been accounted for by the three points just mentioned.

4. One more difference between the two papers shows up in the way the two models are tested. In the first paper the number of people who, according to the theory, should move between any two tracts is computed and then compared with the actual data. (See Tables 4-1 and 4-3, pages 75 and 80, and the corresponding graphs.) The same test is applied in the second paper (Table 4-20, pages 106–108). But a different idea of testing is added and highlighted in the second round. The new equation contained two basic constants. One is the scaling factor that must be applied to the push-pull figure; the other is the power to which the measure of intervening opportunities has to be raised. (They correspond to the coefficients a and b in Equation 1, page 49.) Now, if the scheme is to be a really general theory, these two constants should have the same value *irrespective of which two cities are being studied and regardless whether attention is focused on migration from city 1 to city 2 or on migration in the opposite direction.* It so happens that by some arithmetical transformation this test can be made by inspecting visually Figure 4-7(*a*) (page 97). (The arithmetical details are worked out on the pages preceding this graph and need no discussion here.) The essence of the test is the requirement that all the dots of Figure

4-7(*a*) lie on the same line. Actually, they do as far as pairs of cities go but not when it comes to the direction of migration: in the specific example, migration *to* St. Louis is continuously underestimated.

In Part 3 of Section B, Chapter 4, Stouffer develops a *third model*, introducing the concept of "competing migrants." The basic idea is as follows: A city, say, St. Louis, may have many immigrants just because it is easily accessible from many other cities. The migration from Denver to St. Louis should be assessed not absolutely, but relative to the latter's general accessibility.

The push-pull between the two cities was computed by multiplying *all* migrants from Denver and *all* migrants to St. Louis. This could overestimate the specific movement from Denver to St. Louis. Stouffer therefore introduces a correction to eliminate the factor of general accessibility, or, as he calls it, "competing migrants." This correction is made by drawing a circle around the *target* city and counting the cumulative migration from the circled area into this city. The push-pull figure between origin and target is now taken relative to the attractiveness of the target for the whole area as far as or nearer than the origin (Figure 4-8, page 98). The final formula of this third model then reads as follows:

$$\frac{\text{Push-pull between origin and target}}{\begin{array}{l}\text{(directional intervening oppor-} \\ \text{tunities between the two cities)}\end{array} \times \begin{array}{l}\text{(correction for general accessi-} \\ \text{bility of target to cities as} \\ \text{near as or nearer than origin)}\end{array}}$$

Equation 5 is the real equation, and it contains, of course, the scaling factor, *a*, and the power exponent, *b*, explained above in comparison 2. The effect of this improvement is vividly exemplified in Figure 4-7(*b*). The empirical data permit a computation of the constants *a* and *b*, which are practically the same for migration to as well as from St. Louis relative to the three other cities. Stouffer points with pride to Figure 4-7(*b*), where now all the dots lie practically on one line. The end of the paper, Part 4, is essentially given over to various specific tests, showing how this third and final model fits the data surprisingly well (Table 4-19) and furnishes additional information not provided by the other models.

While Section B of Chapter 4 contains step-by-step refinements of the original model, Section A has a feature that deserves further attention. The material available for the city of Cleveland comes from a real property inventory reporting how many people moved into a certain tract during a recent period. But Stouffer wants to study mobility of different racial and socioeconomic subgroups. The division by race is accomplished fairly easily by singling out tracts that are predominantly white or Negro and submitting them to separate analysis. But from a socioeconomic point of view, most of the tracts in Cleveland are mixed, and it is therefore necessary to estimate what proportion of the recent immigrants belong to each social stratum. Stouffer draws on a considerable number of additional sources to arrive at interesting conjectures regarding differential social mobility between the Cleveland tracts. These pages are best read in conjunction with the similar efforts at using inferential data that characterized his work for the monograph on the depression. The two papers are in themselves a lesson in the philosophy of science. From one move to the next, concepts are refined: physical distance becomes intervening opportunities, the new variable is refined by adding directionality, and then, in turn, this notion is improved upon by correcting for accessibility. Each new step is motivated by empirical tests that show shortcomings in the previous one and is justified by a better match between theory and data.

THE USES OF SOCIOLOGY

The remaining papers in the present collection reveal Stouffer's interest in applied sociology. The most direct application is included here as Chapter 8. One of the great practical achievements of the Army research was the development of the point system according to which soldiers were returned from overseas duty at the end of the war. The original studies, reported in the second volume of *The American Soldier*, are not included in the present selection; but it seems that after the system had been adopted by the Army, some doubts were raised and Stouffer was asked to recheck his conclusions. Chapter 8 reproduces the reports he wrote to General Marshall about this recheck. I think that it is included here for two reasons. For one, Stouffer wanted to show that, by and large, American soldiers approved of the system he had developed. But in addition, he wanted to give an example of how complex research material could be succinctly summarized in a form understandable to laymen. He always felt that a research man should have two skills: (1) he should be trained in detailed analysis of the kind characteristic for most of his papers; but (2) he should also be able, if need be, to extract quickly the main points essential for practical decisions. Chapter 8 is certainly an interesting exhibit of this second kind of skill.

The two selections on tolerance and nonconformity included in Chapter 5 derive from Stouffer's work for the Fund for the Republic. His study on Communism, conformity, and civil liberties was carried out at the height of the McCarthy period. As a result of his work, he became convinced that a Fascist threat would meet with resistance among the American people; but most of all he wanted to argue that tolerance to nonconformist ideas is likely to increase in this country. Section B supports this conviction. It is an interesting sequence of empirical data. They show first that, in all age groups, people are more tolerant the better educated they are. Because of the rapid rise in the level of education, twenty years hence a fifty-year-old person will be more hospitable to unconventional ideas than one who is fifty years old today. But Stouffer did not want to leave the matter on this purely descriptive level. He singles out and develops measures for a number of crucial attitudes, such as the tendency to categorize people into good and bad or to subscribe to an authoritarian type of education. He then shows that these characteristics are negatively related to education on the one hand and positively to tolerance on the other (pages 124–132). In this way, he suggests the links intervening between education and tolerance; this intimation makes the social processes in which he believes much more understandable and plausible.

Section A of Chapter 5 is addressed to a more general audience. Stouffer refers to some of the data just mentioned and adds one more argument. It is possible, he says, that social and vertical mobility create anxieties and might make some people look for scapegoats. But stronger than that, he thinks, is the intellectual flexibility created by new social and geographical contacts. At this point he adds new data showing that the larger cities and the higher social strata toward which people in this country tend to move are the more tolerant (pages 118–120).

One more chapter belongs with these applied studies, although in a somewhat remote sense. Chapter 10 is entitled "Attitudes as Related to Subsequent Behavior." No one should expect that what people feel about a future situation can predict their behavior precisely: as a matter of fact, the discrepancies are themselves an important object of study in which Stouffer was always interested. Still, the degree to which attitudes actually do predict behavior is in itself a matter of obvious importance. The two selections of Chapter 10 contribute knowledge on this point; they are clear-cut and do not require any lengthy comment. One should note, however, that in Section A the double approach of individual and group analysis reappears. The problem is whether soldiers who, during training, expressed high morale in paper-and-pencil tests were also more likely to perform well in actual combat. In one study, the morale score of individual soldiers is correlated with their performance ratings provided by officers after battle. In the other study the average morale score of whole units is correlated with a characteristic that is applicable only to a collective—the proportion of soldiers in each unit who had a nervous breakdown during battle. The scope of the study, however tragic its setting, is certainly unparalleled in social research anywhere. Parenthetically, the relation between attitude and subsequent behavior appears also in Section A of Chapter 2: soldiers who, during a survey, protested the legitimacy of their being drafted subsequently had a variety of difficulties more often than did those who, from the beginning, expressed their willingness for military service (page 16).

These, then, were the main themes in Stouffer's work. This is not the place to trace the development of these themes in the further work of his collaborators and students. But we can see the character of this intellectual influence

by turning only to three books dedicated to him: the study of school superintendents by Neal Gross and Associates, which took off from Stouffer's work
on role conflict; the major publication of the Bush-Mosteller learning model,
which was influenced by Stouffer's conception of precise theory; and the report
of the Columbia University voting studies, which profited from his skillful
procedures of survey analysis. To take only one other instance of the influence:
the impressive series of studies in attitudes and communications, directed by
the late Carl Hovland at Yale during the last fifteen years, extended the work
he and Stouffer had organized during the war and in turn stimulated new
inquiries elsewhere.

Stouffer disliked telling people what to do or enunciating principles of research. When he had an important idea he developed it so that it would
enter into the collective stream of scholarly work. As in all art, what he did
has meaning on many levels. The papers in this collection will give the careful
reader leads to interesting problems, an extension of technical training, and
insight into the strategy of social research.

Columbia University
November, 1961

Social Research to Test Ideas

I

☐ ☒ ☐ ☐ ☐ *Sociology and the Strategy of Social Science*

Among various essays and lectures attempted by the author of this topic over the years, this one expresses about as succinctly as any the frame of reference that dominates this volume. This paper was read before the American Association for the Advancement of Science in September, 1948. Actually, it is a rewrite of some remarks made by the author in a "debate" with Professor Percy Bridgman, Nobel Laureate in Physics, that was staged by a joint committee of graduate students in the natural sciences and the social sciences in the New Lecture Hall at Harvard earlier that year, with President James B. Conant presiding. Professor Bridgman was, in fact, responsible for some, but not all, of the criticisms of social science which are singled out for discussion in this paper.

While I feel that the accumulation of research in the twelve years since the paper was written would enable me to make a somewhat more effective case, most of the remarks, especially the notes of caution, are applicable today. Perhaps this circumstance only goes to show that in sidereal time twelve years are but an instant.

"Sociology and the Strategy of Social Science," paper read before the American Association for the Advancement of Science, September 16, 1948. Published in *Centennial*, Washington, D.C., September 13-17, 1948. Washington, D.C.: American Association for the Advancement of Science, 1950.

Social science, and especially sociology, is in its early adolescence. Like a fourteen-year-old boy, it suddenly finds itself growing at the rate of a foot a year and looks wistfully into a mirror to see whether that faint down on the upper lip gives promise of turning into whiskers. As kindly elders, wise scientists from fields of physics and chemistry, look at this gangling lad with a certain tolerant amusement, some of them are inclined to say, "No son, those ain't whiskers yet."

From writings and from conversations of my colleagues in the older sciences, I have heard a number of well-intended but on the whole rather disparaging remarks. With some I agree, and with others I disagree. Today I should like to select a few for frank discussion, illustrating my comments mainly from the field of sociology. For example, it is said that:

1. Social sciences are too much in a hurry to get practical results before the groundwork has been sufficiently laid in understanding.

2. Theories in social science are not susceptible to crucial verification, because social behavior is not predictable.

3. The human organism is exceedingly complex and until we have spent a few centuries in studying the individual, we will not be ready to tackle the study of groups of individuals or of society.

4. Values cannot be a subject of detached and scientific study.

5. Measurement and controlled experiments, which have played such an important role in the older sciences, are unsuited to social science problems.

First, let me discuss a criticism with which I agree, namely, that social scientists are all too eager, with inadequate equipment in theory or techniques, to try to solve the great practical problems of the day. It should be said at once that social scientists are divided on this issue. Some feel very deeply their obligation to be of immediate practical help whether they build a science or not. For example, a recent presidential address of the American Sociological Society closes on this note, and I quote:

The circumstances under which we live do not any longer allow the saints to sit in their ivory tower while burly sinners rule the world. . . . [Our] subject matter is the life of man in society and the heart of that subject matter today is the understanding of the processes through which consensus on a world scale is created. Unless we solve that problem, and solve it soon, there will be no opportunity to work on any of the others on which our minds or our hearts are set.

Now words like these are very moving. They appeal not only to many social scientists, but also to laymen, including the powerful laymen on the boards of great foundations who control the major purse strings for research. It is true that many of these laymen may be skeptical of what social science has accomplished, but still they feel that the urgency of the world crisis compels them to take large risks. Who knows, maybe social science can save the world in the next five or ten years—it may be a one-in-one-thousand shot, but it is worth taking. In consequence, social science is getting financial backing such as it has never known before, and—I say this soberly and earnestly—social science is in grave danger of being ruined thereby.

Why do I say this? Because much of the support now pouring in upon social science is based upon a false conception of what social science is able to deliver, and, unless those of us who see this threat have the vision and courage to reply resourcefully, our best talent will be drawn off, bribed if you will, to work on big, spectacular practical problems that social science as such is not now equipped to solve. I know what these pressures are. Faced with a choice of spending 100,000 dollars on a big study to improve race relations tomorrow or 100 dollars on a "trivial" laboratory experiment on the displacement of aggression which a generation from now might even be looked back on as a small but critical step in analyzing the behavior called prejudice, the young social scientists is tempted to spend the 100,000 dollars. And of course he must write a book, which if it is not to disappoint his sponsors, must contain pages of big generalizations about society and also, perhaps, a lot of statistics and charts to make the work look scientific. It will be helpful too if the theories in the book are spiced with academic jargon—there is prestige in a little, though not too much, incomprehensibility.

The dilemma facing the social scientist is all the more difficult because a plausible case can be made for both sides.

Let us take the "Save the world now" school of thought. If you will accept the premises of some who hold this view, the conclusion is almost unassailable. Different proponents start from different premises. Let us examine three of them:

1. Society as we know it may have only a few months or years to live; in this crisis there is no place for the long view. If a ship is sinking, an expert in hydraulics who is a passenger on the ship is not expected to go on speculating about a new equation in hydraulics, but is expected to do anything practical he is asked to do. When his house is on fire, a chemist may have to man a hose, not continue to putter around with chemical formulas which a generation hence may yield a better fire extinguisher. Obviously, if we refuse to admit the probability that society will exist fifty years from now, there is not much use contemplating a fifty-year research program.

But there are many who are not panicked by the imminence of the end of the world, and who yet reach the same conlusion as to what social scientists should be doing. Consider this position:

2. Social science as such is not much good and probably never will be. But it does attract some very bright men, and in the course of their social science training they learn something about history and statistics and they acquire some useful academic habits of detachment that enable them to view practical social problems more clearly and wisely than men without this discipline. It is doing society a service to bribe these men to use their talents

in big, practical problems instead of wasting them in academic cells and laboratories where their puttering will be futile.

Curiously, from exactly the opposite premise a similar conclusion is drawn:

3. Social science is just wonderful. It has given us laws of psychology—see Freud. It has given us laws of society—sociology and anthropology already know many of the answers to current problems if the educators and politicians and newspaper men will just listen to them. Therefore, the main duty of the young social scientist is to use his energies to put these laws to work. This is not a caricature. There are a good many sociologists, social psychologists, and economists who themselves believe this. When their claims are put before laymen who have strong will to believe—especially if the alleged scientific principles provide the cure for war, poverty, race prejudice, crime, or marital unhappiness—they are all but irresistible.

To sum up at this point. We who would take the long view on basic social research must assume that there is a betting chance that Armageddon can be deferred and, in addition, must assume that, while social science does not have an impressive apparatus of tested concepts awaiting application to the world's troubles, there is a chance that such an apparatus in the long run can be constructed.

At the same time, I do not think it is either necessary, desirable, or indeed possible for us to take an extreme position of withdrawal from practical application. There are three reasons. One, we are citizens as well as social scientists, and we have an inescapable obligation to society in our citizenship role. Second, financial support of long-term research will not be forthcoming unless what might be called the engineering applications of that research can be shown to have manipulable consequences. Third, efforts to deal with practical problems can sometimes, though not always, help sensitize basic research to the location of strategic variables.

Now when we talk about the long-range what should we be talking about? What is the strategy that long-range research in social science should pursue? You will get different answers from different social scientists. There are some who think that the main energies should be devoted to collecting large bodies of facts with a minimum of a priori theorizing. They cite the value of historical monographs, of ethnological studies, and of empirical analysis of economic and social statistics either as published by the government or obtained by field interview, as by public opinion polls. A recent illustration of this type of contribution is the Kinsey report—a biologist exploring human behavior in order to get the facts, not to test any explicit hypotheses.

Then there are other social scientists who emphasize the importance of developing large and inclusive conceptual schemes. Some of them are impatient of any theorizing that does not attempt to encompass all of society or all of human nature in terms of great universal principles, and it's understandable if such men regard the fact-finders with considerable scorn. It is, I think, regrettable that so much of social science has tended in the past to polarize about one or the other of these two extreme viewpoints. Both positions can be defended, but neither represents—at least some of us believe— the only road or even the main road to developing an effective social science.

Some of us think that the progress of social science depends on the development of *limited theories*—of considerable but still limited generality—from which prediction can be made to new concrete instances. These theories must be stated in operational language which permits empirical verification or disproof. Most theories in social science are not like this; you can neither verify them nor disprove them, as stated, and their authors, like slippery wrestlers, can elude every hold we clamp upon them. But we do not need to agree with skeptics who say that our theories cannot be otherwise.

Perhaps we in the social sciences can profit from the history of medicine. For a century after Newton the students of disease were beguiled by the search for a great principle of disease which would be medicine's theory of gravitation. Dr. Benjamin Rush of Philadelphia thought he had it, a century and a half ago, in his theory of convulsive action. One enthusiastic disciple suggested that statues to this master be erected in all the world by a grateful humanity. We now know, of course, that not one grand conceptual scheme, but many limited generalizations, were to mark the conquest of many of mankind's scourges. Germ theories are useful for certain diseases, deficiency theories for others, psychosomatic theories for still others. Some day a synthesis of these theories may be found, but the ideas of Pasteur have been rather fruitful for research and for the saving of lives in the absence of that synthesis.

But there are those who are skeptical about even limited generalizations in social science. Let us consider some of the bases of skepticism. One is the belief that social behavior is simply not predictable. It would be folly to deny the numerous and lamentable failures in prediction made by statesmen, for example, or even those made by husbands and wives about each other. But let us not overlook the fact that much of the time all of us do predict correctly. So much of our social behavior is routinized, even though no formal laws or rules may enforce it, that we manage to make hundreds of little predictions in the course of a week and we are ordinarily aware only of the exceptional cases.

Our success in prediction, at the common-sense level, is, of course, mainly due to the existence of cultural uniformities. And we may be even more successful in predicting about an institution as a whole than about an individual. When the A.A.A.S. issues a program of its annual meeting, one can predict with a high degree of confidence that most of the papers announced will actually be given. It is quite true, as some natural scientists warn us, that people are complex, but I suspect that there are large areas of social behavior where prediction is much more accurate than, say, the predictions of the meteorologist.

But science, of course, is not just an aggregate of unrelated ad hoc predictions. There is a search for propositions or general rules from which deductions can be made as to a wide variety of expected empirical behavior. And it is in its success in finding such useful rules that social science must eventually be judged. Progress has been modest, but there is progress.

Because of the uniformities of behavior, sociologists, for example, are able to specify some rather useful concepts. To illustrate: there seems to be on the part of members of a social group a strain for conformity to the central values of the group. One of the great contributions of anthropology has been to report this phenomenon as it occurs throughout nonliterate as well as literate cultures, and social scientists have studied the informal as well as formal social controls which enforce conformity. In enforcing conformity, it has been pointed out, a lifted eyebrow may be more potent than a squad of policemen. In complex cultures like ours, however, most individuals have roles in not one but in several social groups. If, as so often happens, these social groups have different central values and if these different values are incompatible, tensions arise in persons who have roles in both groups. This concept of multiple roles seems to have rather wide generality. Those of you here today who grew up in a home of first-generation immigrants will know vividly what this means.

This way of looking at a problem is quite at variance with many common-sense viewpoints. For example, in a few urban slum areas it was found that almost all boys were juvenile delinquents. The codes or values to which they conformed and which were sanctioned by their adult role models happened to be at variance with those of the larger society. The better integrated a boy was with his gang and the more isolated he was from the larger society, the less conflict of values he experienced. It is little wonder that psychologists and physiologists studying such boys could find no marked anomalies in their psychological and physiological measurements. Indeed, the boys most needing psychiatric treatment in those particular slum areas may have been those who were loosely integrated with their gangs or were actually nondelinquents! Such findings have implications for social action. Treatment of gang members as individual behavior problems was certain to be ineffective; what was required was a restructuring of group values, particularly by stimulating organized cooperation of adult role models who, even though themselves shady characters, did not want their children to be.

Or take the matter of fixed opinions, which, when we don't like them, we call prejudice. It is sometimes thought that prejudice is a psychological defect in an individual, which may, in fact, have some physiological basis. One biochemist would approach it through a study of basal metabolism. But on the basis of the concept of roles, a sociologist or anthropologist should feel safe in predicting, for example, not only that white natives of a Mississippi village would be hostile to any Negro who stepped out of his place, but also that a white resident born and reared in the village who had exceptionally democratic attitudes toward such a Negro would be a queer person from the psychological standpoint and might be the one man in the village most in need of psychiatry. This prediction is, however, a guess, not yet a research finding.

If the theory of roles is correct, it follows that changes in values are likely to take place most rapidly when an individual becomes identified with multiple social groups whose values conflict. Hence, the breakdown of isolation, as a result of technological inventions like the automobile and as a result of internal migration, promotes changes in values, just as, of course, does formal education in the public schools and colleges when it supports values in conflict with those of a family or friendship group.

Attention should be called to the fact that ideas like these can be formulated without explicit reference to individual psychology, just as one can study other aspects of culture, a people's grammar, for example, without necessarily examining the idiosyncrasies of all the individuals using it. This is a fact which is sometimes overlooked by critics of the social sciences who know how terribly complicated the human organism is and who feel that until the individual has been explored in all his intricacy, we cannot proceed with efforts at conceptualizing uniformities of social behavior. Yet the kinetic theory of gases did not attempt, I believe, to account for the behavior of each individual molecule.

Part of the confusion between what we might call a sociological or what we might call a psychological frame of reference arises from the fact that we go to the individual for information about the cultural uniformities we are studying. An anthropologist constructs the grammar of a Polynesian tribe by talking with individuals of the tribe; he constructs the value system of the tribe in precisely the same manner. Informants tell him whether this or that behavior with respect to cross-cousin marriage is proper; if his informants agree, he is likely to assume that his map at this point is filled in correctly.

One of the most significant advances in social research has been the development of new tools for eliciting this kind of information in a complex culture like our own. The systematic study of attitudes by methods permitting accurate statistical tabulation is a relatively recent innovation. Because of some of the older scientists' concern about the difficulties of measurement in social science, I think it is worth while to dwell briefly on this development.

Just as research in medicine has depended on the invention of instruments like the thermometer and microscope, so the new social research depends and will increasingly depend on what some people deprecatingly call gadgets. A questionnaire or an attitude test is such a gadget. When you think of all the amateurish and stupid questionnaires you have filled out, you may be a little cynical at this point. But attitude testing is coming of age. During World War II, a War Department research unit with which I happened to be associated studied the attitudes of half a million American soldiers all over the world. Sometimes some quite important Army policies were based on these studies. For the benefit of those who think (*a*) that behavior is unpredictable and (*b*) that complex attitudes cannot be measured, may I offer just one illustration? Before D-Day we surveyed the attitudes of men in 108 rifle companies of four divisions in England. All these companies landed in Normandy on D-Day or within the next four days. From the daily morning reports of these companies in the first two months in France, it was possible to account for each man among those making the invasion. Then we could compute for each company a nonbattle casualty rate—the number of nonbattle casualties (many, if not most of which were psychiatric or psychosomatic cases) divided by the average daily strength. What did we find? We found that, if in a given regiment with nine rifle companies, we picked out those three companies with the worst attitudes before D-Day, these three companies were destined to have a 60 per cent higher nonbattle casualty rate in France, on the average, than the three companies in the same regiment with the best attitudes.

The attitude studies made during the war were crude, indeed, as compared with what the future holds. Just as World War I gave impetus through the Alpha test to a new and highly fruitful attack on the measurement of mental abilities, so World War II may prove to have stimulated a comparable development in socio-psychological measurement. Think of how far we have progressed in mental measurement in one generation, and note the interrelationship between measurement and theory. It was only yesterday that psychologists were debating the constancy of the I.Q. and the extent to which it was alterable by education. We now know from empirical studies based on the mathematical models of factor analysis, utilizing matrix algebra and *n*-dimensional geometry, that there is probably not just one mental abililty but that there are several mental abilities. Having isolated some of them (there is still no complete agreement about them), we can set up controlled experiments in the public schools to see which of these abilities are educable and to what extent. Preliminary studies suggest that some of the abilities may be rather easily amenable to improvement; others may be less so. In attitude measurement we still have far to go. For example, we need to measure the intensity of an attitude as well as its general direction. There are at present several rather promising mathematical models for the measurement of various aspects of attitudes; current research projects are making important progress in reconciling three of these models, logically with mathematical reasoning and empirically with actual data.

Perhaps the greatest single difference between the social science of an older era and the new social science is the difference in tools for empirical verification of theory. If time permitted, I would like to dwell further on this point. But may I just say in passing that the controlled experiment is also coming into its own? In World War II, more than thirty controlled experiments were made deliberately to change attitudes and to analyze experimentally the conditions under which changes did or did not take place. It is quite possible to develop simple models that permit isolation and manipulation of some of the relevant variables. There are several universities that are now conducting such experiments with encouraging results.

Now when, earlier in these remarks, I spoke of the concept of multiple roles, I deliberately chose that example, rather than somewhat more maturely developed examples from economics, social psychology, or even sociology, because I hoped it would be instructive on several counts.

One point is that one can conceptualize uniformities in social behavior and expect some success in prediction. Another is that values, and nonrational behavior in general, which some scientists seem to be worried about, can be an object of detached and scientific study. A third point is that the tools for such a study, especially techniques for the measurement of attitudes, are undergoing rapid development. A fourth point is that controlled experiments are not precluded. Finally, I should like to point out that, in contrast with some of the earlier theorizing in social science, a concept like that of multiple roles, while apparently useful in focusing attention on relevant variables in a wide variety of social situations, is not offered as a nostrum to explain everything. It is so far quite inadequate to explain certain types of deviant behavior. It is tentative. Better formulations, particularly as our better measuring instruments begin to yield us more accurate observations, are to be expected. In particular, we need better conceptual tools than we now have for predicting what alternative happens when an individual finds himself having simultaneous roles in groups with conflicting values. We know that there are several possibilities:

1. He may drop some values, often at the price of disengaging himself from groups holding them, and cling to others.
2. He may attempt to cling to conflicting values, sometimes, though not always, at the price of considerable psychological tension.
3. He may become cynical about all or most values, although such anarchy, which is traditionally an occupational disease of some sophomores, is apparently not a state which can be endured long by individuals in any society.

I am confident that, upon application of the new tools we are forging for measuring attitudes, abstract propositions which are brought forward to help us specify the conditions under which 1, 2, or 3 will occur, at least with a fairly high probability, can be tested empirically.

In these remarks, less, than justice, I fear, has been done to the very great importance of the labors of those in social science who are primarily interested not in the verification of limited generalizations, but rather in adding to our body of factual knowledge, or mainly in applying now the knowledge we have, even though the applications, notably in business and government, often involve enlightened common sense rather than deductions from tested theory. There is room for much division of labor in our social science enterprise, but I do think that in our strategy for the future we can and should emphasize far more than in the past the kind of approach I have sought to represent today.

We have been warned that the job of social science is a hard one. Of course it is. And there are so few of us working at it—at least at the formulation and testing of the implications of the kind of limited generalizations social science most needs. All the published papers of all the sociologists in the world in a year do not number more than a few hundred; economists and psychologists are little more productive. Compare this with 25,000 separate papers cited annually in *Biological Abstracts*.

A change, I think, is coming. The new graduate students in sociology and other social sciences are, perhaps, more tough-minded and resourceful than their predecessors. Several in my own department, for example, have come in with a background of rigorous undergraduate training in mathematics, physics, chemistry, or biology. The National Research Council has recognized the value of interdisciplinary training by creating fellowships for advanced students of natural science to study the problems and methods of social science, and vice versa. Other students are bringing from a background in the humanities a knowledge of great literary insights which sensitize them to the nuances of some of the problems we are studying. Some of the new generation of graduate students are impatient with mere fact-finding, impatient with global generalization. Their names are unknown today, but if they have the vision to follow the gleam undeterred by the tempting rewards for concentrating on the immediate practical problems of the day, some of their names may be enrolled among the pioneers of the new social science.

Yes, the job is difficult. We of this generation perhaps will not have accomplished very much. Those of the next generation will accomplish more. Our work and their work will be cumulative. By developing limited theories, testable and tested empirically, by being modest about them and tentative, we can, I think, make a small but effective contribution toward an ultimate science of society whose engineering applications will help regulate the complex civilization wrought by physical science and technology. In that spirit we shall try.

Part One

2

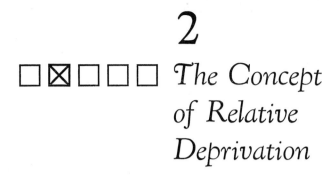 *The Concept*
of Relative
Deprivation

The American Soldier, in two volumes, contains selections of research done in the American Army during World War II by the Research Branch, Information and Education Division of the War Department, in which the author was director of the professional research staff. These works, together with books on *Experiments in Mass Communication* and *Measurement and Prediction*, constituted a four-volume series of *Studies in Social Psychology in World War II*. Since these volumes are readily available in most libraries, only limited excerpts from them are used in the present compilation.

It may be of value, however, to bring together in one place a part of the actual empirical research which throws light on a concept which has had some influence on subsequent theory and research quite crucial for sociology. The concept, as introduced in *The American Soldier* is that of *relative deprivation* or its symmetrical counterpart, *relative gratification*.

In the volume, *Continuities in Social Research: Studies in the Scope and Method of The American Soldier*, Merton and Kitt summarized the research findings with respect to relative deprivation and sought systematically to relate these findings to the concept of reference groups or reference collectivities. Following this theoretical essay, Merton has deliberated much further on the subject, as is evidenced by a searching new theoretical chapter in his revised *Social Theory and Social Structure*.

Further considerations about the theory of reference systems, to which sociologists and social psychologists have contributed, have led to a valuable distinction between reference groups or collectivities which essentially serve the purposes of *comparison* groups and those which, while in some cases also serving as comparison groups, have the power of positive or negative sanctions over a member or expiring member. The latter may be called *sanctioning* groups.

It now seems that the cases cited in *The American Soldier* and illustrated below belong largely in the category of comparison groups. Year by year, further research is leading to sharpening the conceptualization of this important type of subgrouping within the social system, a recent paper by Davis being particularly notable for its theoretical freshness and clarity.

Further comment on *sanctioning* reference groups or collectivities will be made subsequently in this volume, in connection with the author's studies of role conflict.

Of the four studies utilized below, the second one, dealing with promotion opportunities, has considerably the strongest empirical grounding, primarily because it was possible to replicate on an armywide basis the essential idea which first turned up in the form of an unexpected anomaly in a comparison of promotion opportunities in two branches of the service. Some of the interpretations in the other papers are more speculative, but it could be of interest to read the papers as a group because of the applicability of a single concept in the elucidation of such a wide variety of problems.

A. *Willingness for Military Service*

Previously in this work we have seen that on items reflecting personal *esprit* and personal commitment the following relations held:

The better educated tended to be *more* favorable than the less educated.
The married tended to be *less* favorable than the unmarried.

The men twenty-five and over tended to be *less* favorable than the men under twenty-five in personal commitment, and the age differences on personal *esprit* were inconsistent.

"Willingness for Military Service," from Chapter 4, pp. 122-127, *The American Soldier: Adjustment during Army Life*, Vol. I, by Stouffer, Suchman, DeVinney, Star, and Williams. Princeton: Princeton University Press, 1949.

In order to study such patterns more intensively, let us look at a cross section of soldiers in the United States in February, 1944, and focus on one query; namely, how did men feel about being drafted when they entered the Army?

First, we shall see that responses to a question about the fairness of induction distinguished between the cross section of soldiers and two groups of deviants—AWOL's and psychoneurotics.

Second, we shall see that when the cross section is broken down, it also reveals consistent differences in attitudes toward induction by education, age, and marital condition.

The question, with its check-list categories, is as follows:

At the time you came into the Army did you think you should have been deferred?

- ☐ I was not drafted, the question does not apply to me.
- ☐ No, I did not think I should have been deferred.
- ☐ Yes, because of dependents who needed my support.
- ☐ Yes, because of the importance of my job.
- ☐ Yes, because of my health or physical condition.
- ☐ Yes, because of some other reason.

In evaluating responses to this question, one must remember that volunteering, in many instances, meant merely entering the Army one step ahead of draft-board action. Nevertheless, Table 2-1 shows that, if we combine the proportions who said they volunteered and who said they should not have been deferred, we find 74 per cent among the cross section, 53 per cent among the psychoneurotics, and 41 per cent among the AWOL's. Among the psychoneurotics, 35 per cent gave health as a "reason" that they should have been deferred; the AWOLs' "reasons," on the other hand, divided mainly between "dependents who need my support" (26 per cent) and "health" (20 per cent).

Table 2-1. Attitudes toward Being Drafted and "Reasons" Given Why One Should Not Have Been Drafted (United States, September, 1943, and January, 1944)

QUESTION: "AT THE TIME YOU CAME INTO THE ARMY DID YOU THINK YOU SHOULD HAVE BEEN DEFERRED?"	PERCENTAGE GIVING INDICATED RESPONSE		
	Cross Section*	Psychoneurotics*	AWOL's†
I was not drafted—this question does not apply to me.	25	17	25
No, I did not think I should have been deferred.	49	36	16
Yes, because of:			
Dependents who needed my support.	7	5	26
The importance of my job.	5	3	4
My health or physical condition.	9	35	20
Some other reason. (Includes no answer.)	5	4	9
	100	100	100
Number of cases	3,729	613	218

*Cross section and NP's from S-99, January, 1944.
†AWOL's from S-74, September, 1943.

While this question belongs primarily in the general area of personal commitment, responses to it also reflect personal *esprit* at the time of response. This is shown by the fact that among men in the cross section who were highest in personal *esprit* as determined by a cross tabulation of the "good spirits" item and two other related items, 90 per cent said either that they volunteered or that they should not have been deferred. The responses to this question are not, however, *merely* a reflection of state of mind at the time of response. When asked of new recruits, whose report on their feelings about induction could not be colored by months or years of subsequent Army experience, the question discriminated significantly between recruits who *later* become psychoneurotics and other men. For example, in Volume II, Chapter 9, of *The American Soldier*, it is shown that among seventy-three new recruits studied soon after they entered the Army and found later to have been diagnosed as psychoneurotics within a period of six months *after* the attitude

Table 2-2. Willingness for Service, by Marital Condition on Entering the Army, Education, and Age

PERCENTAGE IN CROSS SECTION WHO SAID THEY VOLUNTEERED OR SHOULD NOT HAVE BEEN DEFERRED

	UNMARRIED WHEN ENTERED ARMY		MARRIED WHEN ENTERED ARMY	
	Not H.S. Graduates	H.S. Graduates	Not H.S. Graduates	H.S. Graduates
30 and over	68 (320)	77 (157)	59 (193)	64 (128)
25 to 29	72 (323)	89 (289)	60 (124)	70 (146)
20 to 24	73 (572)	85 (719)	67 (144)	76 (105)
Under 20	79 (200)	90 (217)	. .	. .

Number of cases is shown in parentheses. For source of data see Table 2-1.

survey, 32 per cent gave reasons why they should not have been drafted. This was a response to a question worded somewhat differently from that in Table 2-1. By contrast, in a sample of 730 "normal" recruits—equated with the psychoneurotics for education, age, and marital condition—who were part of the original sample to which the subsequently diagnosed psychoneurotics belonged, only 12 per cent gave reasons why they should not have been drafted. As with the psychoneurotics in Table 2-1, health was the predominant "reason" for deferment given by the pre-psychoneurotics.

Attitudes toward induction among new recruits also were positively associated with *subsequent* promotion, although this relationship, discussion of which is found in Section V, Chapter 4, Volume I, of *The American Soldier*, is complicated by a countervailing tendency of older men to have the worst attitude toward induction but better objective chances of advancement.

Now let us see how willingness for service varied by education, age, and marital condition. The results, for the same Army cross section shown in Table 2-1, are given in Table 2-2. The range in proportions saying either that they volunteered or that they should not have been deferred was from 59 per cent among the married men over thirty years old who had not gone through high school to 90 per cent among the unmarried high school graduates under twenty years of age. Quite consistently, Table 2-2 shows, the favorable responses go up as age goes down, are higher for the unmarried than married in corresponding age and educational groups, and are higher for high school graduates than others in each age group by marital condition. This table—which can be replicated from other studies—makes it quite unmistakable that the older married men and the less educated were more inclined to express reluctance about being in the Army than were other soldiers and thus more nearly resembled the AWOL's and psychoneurotics in their responses.

To help explain such variations in attitude, by education, age, and marital condition, a general concept would be useful. Such a concept may be that of relative deprivation, which, as we shall see, is to prove quite helpful in ordering a rather disparate collection of data. . . . The idea is simple, almost obvious, but its utility comes in reconciling data, . . . where its applicability is not at first too apparent. The idea would seem to have a kinship to and in part include such well-known sociological concepts as "social frame of reference," "patterns of expectation," or "definitions of the situation."

Becoming a soldier meant to many men a very real deprivation. But the felt sacrifice was greater for some than for others, *depending on their standards of comparison.*

Take one of the clearest examples—marital condition. The drafted married man, and especially the father, was making the same sacrifices as others plus the additional one of leaving his family behind. This was officially recognized by draft boards and eventually by the point system in the Army which gave demobilization credit for fatherhood. Reluctance of married men to leave their families would have been reinforced in many instances by extremely reluctant wives whose pressures on the husband to seek deferment were not always easy to resist. A further element must have been important psychologically to those married men who were drafted. The very fact that draft boards were more liberal with married than with single men provided numerous examples to the drafted married man of others in his shoes who got relatively better breaks than he did. Comparing himself with his unmarried associates in the Army, he could feel that induction demanded greater sacrifice from him than from them; and comparing himself with his married civilian friends, he could feel that he had been called on for sacrifices that they were escaping altogether. Hence, the married man, on the average, was more likely than others to come into the Army, with reluctance and, possibly, a sense of injustice.

Or take age. Compared with younger men—apart now from marital condition—the older man had at least three stronger grounds for feeling relatively greater deprivation. One had to do with his job—he was likely to be giving up more than, say, a boy just out of high school. Until the defense boom started wheels turning, many men in their late twenties and early thirties had never known steady employment at high wages. Just as they began to taste the joys of a fat pay check, the draft caught up with them. Or else they had been struggling and sacrificing over a period of years to build up a business or profession. The war stopped that. Second, the older men, in all probability, had more physical defects on the average than younger men. These defects, though not severe enough to satisfy the draft board or induction station doctors that they justified deferment, nevertheless could provide a good rationalization for the soldier trying to defend his sense of injustice about being drafted. Both of these factors, job and health, would be aggravated in that a larger proportion of older men than of younger men got deferment in the draft on these grounds—thus providing the older soldiers, like the married soldiers, with ready-made examples of men with comparable backgrounds who were experiencing less deprivation. Third, on the average, older men—particularly those over thirty—would be more likely than youngsters to have a dependent or semi-dependent father or mother—and if, in spite of this fact, the man was drafted, he had further grounds for a sense of injustice.

The concept of relative deprivation may seem, at first glance, not to be applicable to the educational differentials in attitude toward being drafted, as it is to differentials by age and marital condition. Indeed, it is plausible that differentials in comprehension of the nation's military requirements and feelings of personal responsibility concerning them may have accounted for some part of the educational differentials in all attitudes reflecting personal commitment. Some evidence supporting this view is presented in Chapter 9, Volume I, of *The American Soldier*, on "The Orientation of Soldiers toward the War." However, the same types of factors that would seem to vary with age may also have varied with education, age and marital condition constant.

Take health. It would not be unreasonable to surmise that the better educated, *on the average*, were healthier than the less educated. Education and income are quite highly correlated, and it is likely that men from homes of relatively higher income were more likely to have had better nutrition as children, better medical and dental care, less venereal disease, and better protection against the hazards of insanitation. Consequently, such men, on the average, would be less likely to have real physical grounds for feeling that an injustice had been done in inducting them and also would have, on the average, relatively fewer friends who were classified 4-F.

Or take jobs. The less educated soldiers may have made no greater sacrifice on this score than the better educated, but when they compared themselves with their civilian friends, they may have been more likely to feel that they were required to make sacrifices which others like them were excused from making. The two great classes of work which accounted for most exemptions on occupational grounds were farming and skilled labor, predominantly work done by men who have not finished high school. The great mass of professional, trade, and white-collar occupations were not deferable, although there were important exceptions in some managerial and engineering fields. The average high school graduate or college man was a clear-cut candidate for induction; marginal cases on occupational grounds probably occurred much more often in groups with less educational attainment. On the average, the non-high school man who was inducted could point to more acquaintances conceivably no more entitled to deferment than himself, who none the less had been deferred on occupational grounds. As Research Branch data show, the soldier who was a non-high school graduate was more likely than the better educated to report that he actually tried to get deferred and was turned down. Finally, the better educated (still keeping age and marital condition constant) would on the average have somewhat less anxiety about dependent fathers or mothers, since their parents would on the average be in relatively more secure income groups.

As is discussed in detail in Chapter 9, Volume I, of *The American Soldier,* "The Orientation of Soldiers toward the War," the informal as well as formal social pressures in the civilian community demanded military service where deferment was not clearly indicated. It is likely, too, that the positive social pressures were felt more keenly by some classes of the population than others. Thus, the healthy youngster, the man without a family, and especially the man who was concerned about his future civilian status in his community or in the larger society, would be most vulnerable to these social pressures. The man with future status aspirations, in particular, could not afford to jeopardize them. This situation could serve to counteract, to some extent, feelings of deprivation which might otherwise have been stronger, particularly among the better educated, who, by and large, would represent the majority of those with high social aspirations.

B. Who Were the Most Critical of the Army's Promotion Opportunities?

Data from research surveys to be presented will show, as would be expected, that those soldiers who had advanced slowly relative to other soldiers of equal longevity in the Army were the most critical of the Army's promotion opportunities. But *relative rate of advancement can be based on different standards by different classes of the Army population.* For example, a grade school man who became a corporal after a year of service would have had a more rapid rate of promotion, compared with most of his friends at the same educational level, than would a college man who rose to the same grade in a year. Hence,

"Who Were the Most Critical of the Army's Promotion Opportunities?" from Chapter 6, pp. 250-258, *The American Soldier: Adjustment during Army Life,* Vol. I, by Stouffer, Suchman, DeVinney, Star, and Williams. Princeton: Princeton University Press, 1949.

we would expect, at a given rank and a given longevity, that the better edu-cated would be more likely than others to complain of the slowness of pro-motion. The facts, as we shall see, tend to bear this out. The better educated, in spite of their superior chances of promotion, were the most critical.

A similar phenomenon appeared to operate between different branches of the service. This tendency, along with the differentials by rank and education,

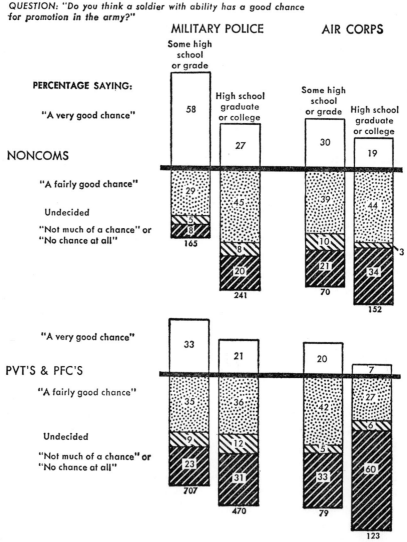

Figure 2-1. *Opinions about promotion opportunity—comparisons by education and rank between Military Police and Air Corps (white enlisted men in the Army one to two years, continental United States). Military police data from special survey of a representative cross section of MP's, S-107, March, 1944. Air Corps data are a segment from representative cross section of all white EM in United States, S-95, January, 1944.*

is illustrated in Figure 2-1. Here the responses of Military Police to the question, "Do you think a soldier with ability has a good chance for promotion in the Army?" are compared with responses of Air Corps men, in early 1944. Longevity is held roughly constant by taking only men who had been in the Army one to two years. It will be noted that more of the less educated, among both privates and noncoms in both branches, had favorable opinions than did the better educated. For example, among privates and Pfc.'s in the Military Police, 33 per cent of the less educated said that a soldier with ability had a very good chance for promotion, as compared with 21 per cent of the better educated privates and Pfc.'s. Finally, it will be seen, among both privates and noncoms in each educational group, that the Air Corps men tended to take a dimmer view of promotion opportunities for men of ability in the Army than did the Military Police.

Without reference to the theory that such opinions by soldiers represent a relationship between their expectations and their achievements relative to others *in the same boat with them,* such a finding would be paradoxical, indeed. For chances of promotion in the Military Police were about the worst in any branch of the Army—among this sample of men in the Army one to two years, only 24 per cent of MP's were noncoms as compared with 47 per cent of the Air Corps men. The MP's felt, too, that as a *branch* the Military Police had been discriminated against in getting ratings, two-thirds of them saying in answer to another question that MP's do not have as good a chance for promotion as men in other branches.

But consider a high school graduate or college man in the Military Police with Army longevity of one to two years. The chances of his being a noncom were 34 out of 100, based on the proportions of noncoms in this sample at this time. If he earned the rating, he was one of the top third among his fellows of equal educational status. If he failed to earn the rating, he was in the same boat with two-thirds of his fellows with equal schooling. Contrast him with the Air Corps man of the same education and longevity. The chances of the latter's being a noncom were 56 in 100, based on the proportions in this sample at this time. If he had earned a rating, so had the majority of his fellows in the branch, and his achievement was relatively less conspicuous than in the MP's. If he had failed to earn a rating, while the majority had succeeded, he had more reason to feel a sense of personal frustration, which could be expressed as criticism of the promotion system, than if he were one of two-thirds in the same boat, as among the MP's.

The process would work in the same way among the less educated. In both the Military Police Branch and the Air Corps, the promotion chances of the less educated were inferior to the chances of others. In the MP sample, only 17 per cent of the less educated were noncoms; in the Air Corps sample, the corresponding figure was 47 per cent. An MP who did not complete high school would feel unusually rewarded compared with others in his outfit in becoming a noncom; one who remained a private had so much company that he hardly could view discrimination against him as a reflection on his personal competence. In the Air Corps, those with ratings had almost as much company as those who remained privates—with less room for personal satisfaction over comparative achievement and more room for dissatisfaction over comparative failure to climb the status ladder.

While the psychological mechanisms seem to operate as described above in producing the pattern of opinions about promotion possibilities, we must not lose sight of the fact that on the average those with ratings had more favorable opinions about promotion than those without. Nor must we jump to the conclusion that men who were critical of promotion policy were necessarily dissatisfied with their Army jobs. True, cross tabulation, within a particular subgroup, of opinions about promotion and expressions of job satisfaction will almost invariably show that men who were most critical about promotions were also least satisfied with their jobs. But that is *within* a given subgroup. As between subgroups, the relationship may vanish or reverse itself. In the case of the comparison of the Military Police and the Air Corps, it reverses itself. Although the Air Corps men were more critical of promotion, they also were more likely than the MP's to be satisfied with their Army job. For example, 36 per cent of the Air Corps men in this sample said they would *not* change to some other Army job if given a chance, whereas only 21 per cent of the MP's gave this response. Promotion opportunity was only one of many factors in job satisfaction, as Chapter 7, Volume I, of *The American Soldier* shows in detail. Other elements, such as the chance to learn something useful in civilian life, entered in, as did informal status factors such as the general prestige of the branch to which assigned. In general, Air Corps was a high-prestige branch, Military Police a low-prestige branch. One of the elements which contributed to making the difference in prestige was, no doubt, the difference in T/O[1] opportunities for social mobility.

The illustration presented in Figure 2-1 was based on a special cross-section survey of Military Police in March, 1944, and the Air Corps segment of a cross-section survey of the Army at the nearest available date—namely, January, 1944. These data were especially selected to exhibit the structure of opinion on two sharply contrasting groups with respect to promotion opportunities in the Army. It is desirable to see whether the same general pattern holds up on a broader basis, where there is less contrast between groups.

The findings of a study based on a representative cross section of white enlisted men in continental United States in June, 1943, are shown in Figure 2-2. Here is charted, in a given vertical bar, the percentage distribution of response to the same question about promotion opportunity as was portrayed in the previous chart. Instead of MP's and Air Corps, we now compare Ground Force branches, Service Force branches, and Air Corps. The same educational groups are shown as in Figure 2-1. Five ranks are shown, from private to top three grades, and three longevity periods—under six months, six months to one year, and one year or over.

1. Table of Organization. This specified the number of grades authorized for the organization.

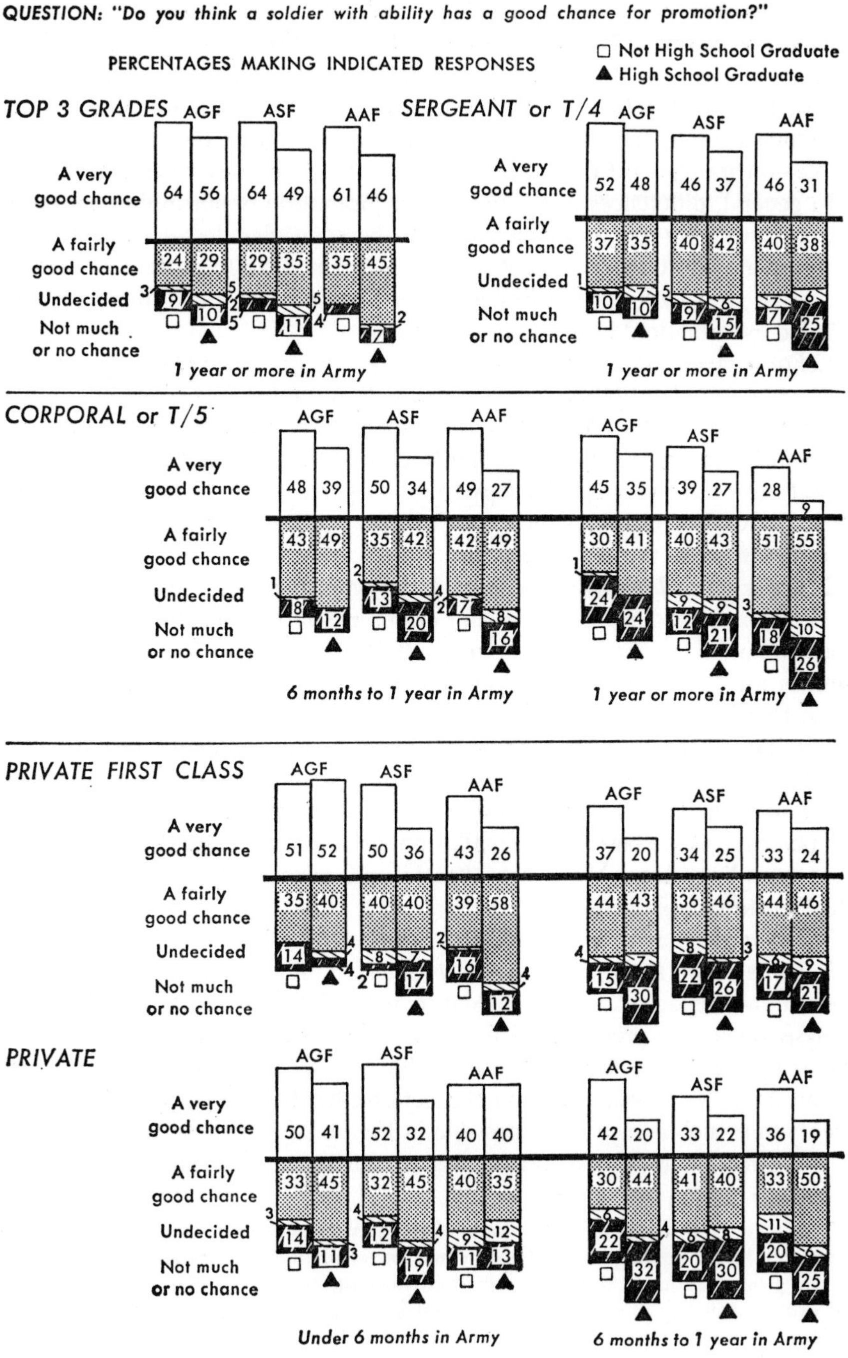
QUESTION: "Do you think a soldier with ability has a good chance for promotion?"
PERCENTAGES MAKING INDICATED RESPONSES
□ Not High School Graduate
▲ High School Graduate
TOP 3 GRADES
SERGEANT or T/4
CORPORAL or T/5
PRIVATE FIRST CLASS
PRIVATE
AGF
ASF
AAF
A very good chance
A fairly good chance
Undecided
Not much or no chance
1 year or more in Army
6 months to 1 year in Army
Under 6 months in Army

Figure 2-2. Opinions about promotion opportunities by force, according to rank, longevity, and education (United States white cross section, July, 1943, S-63 and S-64).

The number of cases on which an individual bar is based is in many instances very small. No comparison is shown if the numbers in the sample for a particular rank, longevity, and education group fell below thirty for any one of the three Army Forces. Nevertheless, no particular inference should be drawn from a single pair of comparisons. It is rather on the *pattern as a whole*—on its regularities and irregularities—that we must focus attention.

In general, differences in opinion about promotion opportunities are rather small, tending in any individual case to be somewhat less striking than in the extreme illustration presented earlier, but a definite pattern is present, as can be seen by a general inspection of Figure 2-2 and confirmed by more detailed examination. Four findings emerge:

1. *For a given rank, the shorter the longevity, the more favorable tends to be the opinion about promotion.* Compare, for example, less educated Ground Force privates in the Army less than six months with those in the Army six months to one year. The proportion of men who say that promotional opportunities are very good drops from 50 per cent to 42 per cent, respectively. A total of eighteen such comparisons can be made in Figure 2-2, and all eighteen are in the same direction.

2. *For a given longevity, the higher the rank, the more favorable tends to be the opinion about promotion.* For example, consider less educated Ground Force men in the Army a year or more. The number who say that opportunities are "very good" is 64 per cent among the top three grades, and it drops to 52 per cent among buck sergeants, and to 45 per cent among corporals. Thirty comparisons are possible between any two grades in Figure 2-2. Of these, twenty-five show the tendency indicated, one shows no difference, and four show the reverse tendency. (It must be remembered that many of the percentages are based on a small number of cases and are thus subject to a large sampling error. Moreover, the tie and reversals are all found in the Pfc.-Private comparisons.)

3. *For a given rank and longevity, the less the education, the more favorable tends to be the opinion about promotion.* This, as are the two conclusions above reported, is in accordance with the expectation based on the analysis previously presented. Take Ground Force top three grades with over a year in the Army. Among the less educated, 64 per cent rated promotion opportunity "very good"; among the better educated, 56 per cent. There are twenty-four such comparisons possible in Figure 2-2. Of these, twenty-two are in the direction indicated, one shows no difference, and one is a tie.[2]

2. In view of the possibility that some of the apparent difference between the less educated and better educated conceivably could be attributable to an artifact—namely, a slightly greater tendency of the less educated than the better educated to check the first and extreme category in a list of responses—it is worth noting that when comparisons are made in Figure 2-2 after combining the responses of "very good chance" and "fairly good chance," the conclusion is essentially unaltered. The less educated still were more favorable than the better educated in eighteen out of twenty-four comparisons, with six reversals.

4. *For a given rank, longevity, and educational level, the less the promotion opportunity afforded by a branch or combination of branches, the more favorable the opinion tends to be toward promotion opportunity.* This, again, is in accord with our previous discussion. On the average, promotion opportunity was very much better in the Air Corps than in either Service Force or Ground Force branches. It was somewhat better in Service Forces than in Ground Forces. Consider privates first class with less than high school education and less than six months in the Army. In Ground Forces, 51 per cent rated promotion opportunities "very good," in Service Forces 50 per cent, in Air Forces 43 per cent. Between Ground Forces and Air Forces, sixteen such comparisons can be made in Figure 2-2, and of these fourteen are in the direction indicated and two are reversals. Of the sixteen comparisons between Air Forces and Service Forces, thirteen are in the direction indicated with one tie and two reversals. Of the sixteen comparisons between Ground Forces and Service Forces, the Ground Force men are more favorable in eleven, the Service Force men more favorable in four, and in one comparison both are the same. These patterns of difference are statistically significant,[3] but the picture tends to become less decisive if looked at from some other viewpoints. For example, we know that promotion opportunities were best in Air Forces, intermediate in Service Forces, and least in Ground Forces. But in only ten of the sixteen comparisons do the proportions "very favorable" come out in exactly the reverse order. And the results, though still in the same direction, tend also to be statistically indecisive if comparisons between any two forces are made by combining the "very favorable" and "fairly favorable" categories. To be conservative, we should limit our conclusion by saying that a force with relatively fewer promotion chances tended to have a larger proportion of men speaking very favorably of promotion opportunities than another force with greater promotion chances.

As in our earlier discussion of the Military Police and the Air Corps, a caution must be sounded against assuming from these findings that a liberalization of promotion policy—which might reduce rather than raise the relative self-gratification of the successful men and increase rather than reduce the sense of defeat of the unsuccessful—would increase job satisfaction. What actually would happen we do not know, because this could be determined

---

Because of the extremely skewed nature of the overall distribution of responses, 80 per cent of the entire sample checking either "very good" or "fairly good," comparisons on the basis of the "very good" category alone are preferable, as long as the educational response bias is not more serious. An educational response bias would not likely apply, of course, to other comparisons, for example between rank groups, as education is at least broadly controlled in these comparisons.

3. Assuming, as a null hypothesis, that a positive difference was equally as likely as a negative difference and calling ties failures, the likelihood of getting twelve or more successes by chance, in sixteen comparisons, would be less than 0.04. The likelihood of getting thirteen or more successes would be 0.01 (using the point-binomial distribution).

only from controlled experiments, which were never made. But it is relevant to point out that job satisfaction was highest in the Air Forces, intermediate in Service Forces, and lowest in Ground Forces—reversing exactly the direction seen in attitudes toward promotion. This is discussed at length in the chapter on job satisfaction, Chapter 7, Volume I, of *The American Soldier.* For example, using the question, "How satisfied are you with your Army job instead of some other Army job?" for the same men as shown in Figure 2-2, Army Air Force tends to have, in almost all subgroups, a larger proportion of men who say they are very satisfied with their job. Air Forces exceed Ground Forces in all sixteen comparisons and exceed Service Forces in fourteen out of sixteen comparisons, with one tie and one reversal. Service Forces exceed Ground Forces in thirteen out of sixteen with one tie and two reversals.[4]

The strong role of status in job satisfaction is reflected in the fact that in thirty comparisons which may be made between job satisfaction of men at a given rank level with men at the next higher rank level (holding education, force, and longevity constant) twenty-seven show the greater proportion of satisfied men among men with the higher rank.[5]

It has been possible to repeat the analysis shown in Figure 2-2 in other samples and at other periods in the war. No unusual or significant divergencies from the pattern there revealed of attitudes toward promotion have been observed. From one survey made in the Pacific, it was possible to compare the results from two questions, somewhat different in manifest content, which were asked on the same questionnaire. One was, "Do you think a soldier with ability has a good chance for promotion in the Army?"—the same question with the same check list of responses as was used in Figure 2-2. The other was, "Do you think a soldier with ability has a good chance for promotion in your outfit?" As might perhaps be anticipated, for a given longevity, differences by rank were sharper with the latter question than the former, as were differences by longevity for a given rank. But with respect to education and branch, the pattern of differences was the same with either question. Consistently, using either question and holding rank and longevity constant, the less educated tended to look more favorably on promotion opportunities than the better educated. Likewise, the men in Air Forces tended to look less favorably on promotion opportunities than men in Service Forces and, in turn, the latter tended to be less favorable than men in Ground Forces.

4. Based on the proportions answering "very satisfied" to the question on job satisfaction. If the "satisfied" are added to the "very satisfied," Air Forces exceed Ground Forces in fifteen out of sixteen comparisons, Air Forces exceed Service Forces in fourteen out of sixteen, and Service Forces exceed Ground Forces in fourteen out of sixteen. There were no ties.

5. Again based on those answering "very satisfied." If the "satisfied" are added, the men of higher rank are more likely to express satisfaction in twenty-eight out of thirty comparisons.

C. Attitudes toward Officers

Perhaps the most significant findings, from the standpoint of a conceptualization of the leadership problem, are those which show that overseas attitudes toward officers were most favorable in the front lines and least favorable in the rear areas. These findings may be illustrated by Figure 2-3. Here it is shown that responses to items reflecting attitudes toward officers were most favorable among men in infantry rifle and heavy weapons companies (81 per cent of whom said they had been in actual combat), intermediate among

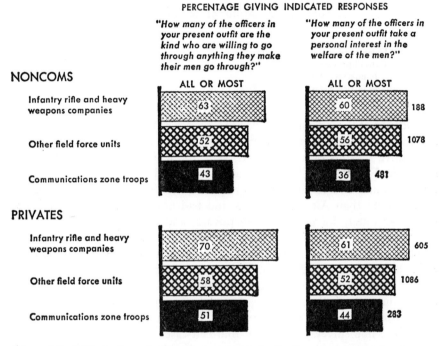

PERCENTAGE GIVING INDICATED RESPONSES

"How many of the officers in your present outfit are the kind who are willing to go through anything they make their men go through?"

"How many of the officers in your present outfit take a personal interest in the welfare of the men?"

NONCOMS

ALL OR MOST | ALL OR MOST

Infantry rifle and heavy weapons companies — 63 | 60 — 188

Other field force units — 52 | 56 — 1078

Communications zone troops — 43 | 36 — 481

PRIVATES

Infantry rifle and heavy weapons companies — 70 | 61 — 605

Other field force units — 58 | 52 — 1086

Communications zone troops — 51 | 44 — 283

Figure 2-3. Attitudes toward officers among troops in the European theatre, by closeness to the fighting. Data from S-223, April, 1945. The numbers following the bars are the numbers of cases on which percentages are based.

men in other field force units (48 per cent of whom said they had been in combat), and least favorable among men in the communications zone (only 17 per cent of whom said they had been in combat).

The proportions among front-line infantrymen responding favorably on these two questions were higher than was ever found in a survey in the

"Attitudes toward Officers," from Chapter 8, pp. 365-374, *The American Soldier: Adjustment during Army Life*, Vol. I, by Stouffer, Suchman, DeVinney, Star, and Williams. Princeton: Princeton University Press, 1949.

United States using these two items, except among recruits with less than three months' service in the Army.

Strictly comparable data are not available on a sufficient sample of Air Forces combat flying personnel overseas to permit reporting comparisons, though there is little reason to doubt that the same phenomena would be present. In a study made in 1945 at a B-29 training base, just before a B-29 group embarked for combat in the Pacific, the percentages of enlisted men who responded to the question, "How many of your present officers are the kind that always try to look out for the welfare of enlisted men?" by saying "all" or "most" are shown in Table 2-3.

Table 2-3. Attitudes toward Officers

	Percentage Giving Favorable Response
Flying personnel in B-29 group	33 (1,153)
Ground personnel:	24 (1,134)
In bomber group	30 (477)
In service group	28 (362)
In base unit	13 (295)

Evidence of the type summarized in Chapter 5, Volume I, of *The American Soldier*, which illustrates the relatively low esteem in which officers were held in inactive theaters overseas, as well as in the rear areas of active theaters, is shown in Figure 2-4. These data are for enlisted men in the Army one to two years and two to three years, respectively, who were in branches of the service other than Air and Infantry and had not been in combat. Data are shown separately for noncoms and privates and for two educational groups. The troops in the United States are compared with those in six overseas theaters or departments. The question is: "How many of your officers take a personal interest in their men?" The percentage saying "all" or "most" is higher among troops in the United States than among those overseas in thirty-four out of the thirty-eight matched comparisons available in this chart. For noncombat Air Corps men, fourteen comparisons are available from the same surveys, and in all fourteen cases the soldiers at home made higher percentages of favorable responses than soldiers overseas. The same kind of picture is obtained from responses to other questions reflecting attitudes toward officers. As the summaries in Chapter 5, Volume I, of *The American Soldier*, made clear, there can be little doubt that attitudes toward officers were lower in such overseas areas than at home or among troops at the front. It will be noted that the studies reported in Figure 2-4 were made at a midpoint in the war—long before the swelling chorus of criticism, arising at the end of the war, reached the public's ears and motivated the Army to appoint a board of investigation headed by Lieutenant General Doolittle to review the problem of officer–enlisted man relationships.

Even if the behavior of officers had been a model of self-denial and concern for the welfare of the enlisted men, it is reasonable to expect that the leadership would have been a target for aggression. Army life, for most civilian soldiers, was a succession of deprivations and frustrations, and it is not surprising that the blame should have been personalized and focused on those in authority. The fact that combat soldiers had more favorable attitudes than others toward their officers could be attributed in part to the opportunity to discharge their aggression directly against the enemy. But this would be much too simple a view of the matter. Among combat troops, whether air or ground, officers and enlisted men shared the common experiences of deprivation, danger, and death. Social differentiations and special

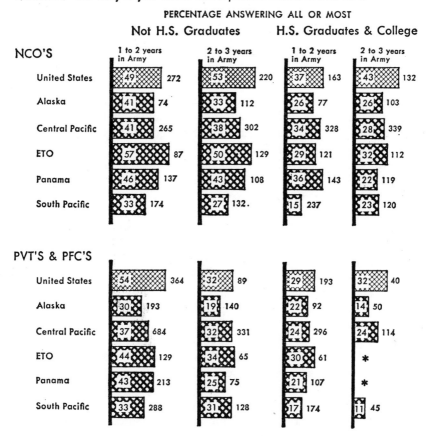

QUESTION: "How many of your officers take a personal interest in their men?"

PERCENTAGE ANSWERING ALL OR MOST

Not H.S. Graduates   **H.S. Graduates & College**

NCO'S

	1 to 2 years in Army	2 to 3 years in Army	1 to 2 years in Army	2 to 3 years in Army
United States	49 — 272	53 — 220	37 — 163	43 — 132
Alaska	41 — 74	33 — 112	26 — 77	26 — 103
Central Pacific	41 — 265	38 — 302	34 — 328	28 — 339
ETO	57 — 87	50 — 129	29 — 121	32 — 112
Panama	46 — 137	43 — 108	36 — 143	22 — 119
South Pacific	33 — 174	27 — 132	15 — 237	23 — 120

PVT'S & PFC'S

United States	54 — 364	32 — 89	29 — 193	32 — 40
Alaska	30 — 193	19 — 140	22 — 92	14 — 50
Central Pacific	37 — 684	32 — 331	24 — 296	24 — 114
ETO	44 — 129	34 — 65	30 — 61	*
Panama	43 — 213	25 — 75	21 — 107	*
South Pacific	33 — 288	31 — 128	17 — 174	11 — 45

*Not enough cases in sample.

Figure 2-4. *Attitudes toward officers in the United States and various overseas theaters among enlisted men in branches other than Air Corps and infantry—winter and spring of 1943–1944. Source: United States, S-95 (February, 1944); Alaska, S-133 (April, 1944); Central Pacific, S-125 (February, 1944); ETO, S-92 (November, 1943); Panama, S-115 (January, 1944); South Pacific, S-124 (March, 1944). The numbers following the bars are the number of cases on which percentages are based.*

privileges were at a minimum. In rear areas and inactive theaters and, to a lesser extent, in the United States, the privileges enjoyed by the officer class were so much out of line with democratic tradition and so unjustified in the eyes of the men that a smoldering resentment, which was to burst into flame with the end of the war, probably was inevitable.

Why was the criticism of officers even more acute in inactive theaters and in rear areas of active theaters than in the United States? The most plausible hypothesis seems to turn on the concept of *scarcity*. If the supply of attractive women, liquor, or entertainment is severely limited, as was the case in many overseas areas, the problem of equitable distribution is much more acute than if there is plenty to go around. The charge which enlisted men repeated in theater after theater was that the officers used their rank to monopolize these desired objects. This was not expressed merely in indictments of particular officers, although some were more conspicuous in giving offense than others. It was an indictment of a *system*—a system by which a privileged minority acquired, through their authoritarian position, a preponderant share of the scarce objects which were craved by others.

The principal source of information on this subject is the free comments written by men all over the world on the margins and at the ends of their Research Branch questionnaires. By way of illustration, let us look at a single area, the Persian Gulf Command, in which a survey was made in October and November, 1943, of 1,793 enlisted men constituting a representative cross section of the command.

In this survey, about three-fifths of the men took the trouble voluntarily to add written comments in their own words at the end of the questionnaire. As is always the case with such comments, almost all represented specific complaints, rather than complimentary remarks about the Army.

When the free comments were classified, it was found that well over half the comments concerned officers and officer–enlisted man relations and almost all were unfavorable. Of the criticisms of officers, only one out of six charged incompetence. The overwhelming majority of the criticisms dealt with special privileges of officers, their concern for their own prerogatives and welfare, and their indifference to the deprivations of enlisted men. Many of the criticisms not classified under the heading of criticisms of officers probably belonged in the same category. For example, complaints about a town being placed off limits for enlisted men were classified as criticisms of officers only if officers were specifically blamed for it or if invidious comparisons were made about officers' access to such a town as compared with enlisted men's.

The following quotations from free comments from the Persian Gulf Command are representative of the range of criticisms on the score of special privilege and indifference to enlisted men's needs:

The officers in this command are the most selfish egotistical people I've ever come across. They never think of the men but they get very angry when things do not go right for themselves. A good illustration is the incident where the officers' club was built before the hospital. Another example of the officers' selfishness occurs practically daily in the PX. They are allowed to enter the PX at all hours for the ridiculous reason that it is beneath them to wait their turn to get served. After all, we do belong to the greatest democracy the world has ever known but you would not know it after being stationed in the Persian Gulf Service Command.

When we first came to this camp our barracks was just below the officers' club and we heard that it was built while work was stopped on our hospital. Well, we had no place to go, no facilities for entertainment, etc., we were practically restricted to the camp. Every place was out of bounds to us while it wasn't to the officers and then at nites we could sit on our bunks in the darkness and hear music, laughter, loud drunken voices coming to us from the officers' club. They were having a good time. Dances every Saturday nite. The colored orchestra was up there a couple nites each week. It didn't help our morale any to see that go on. Then the officers had beer (our canned beer) for several months before we ever got any.

Our roofs on our barracks leaked right through the first rain. The officers immediately had their roof tarred—even tho they had tin under their mud roofing while we had straw. It seems to me that the officers should think of their men first, but instead they think of themselves first and never think of us at all.

Only today I saw an officer with a carton of Luckies, some Fig Newtons, and a new cigarette lighter, all three of which our PX has been out of for days. Pabst beer, supposedly the better of the two kinds available here, is always stocked at the officers' PX, and seldom at ours. Because of the time wasted during working hours is the reason for throwing that PX off limits to us. Officers who draw many times more pay are therefore costing the government much more in the time they waste during working hours. And yet, our PX is open to them at any time, and they can barge right up to the counters for immediate service. The officers' mess serves fresh eggs any morning they want them, chicken several times a week, and far greater quantities of fresh fruits and vegetables than we ever see, yet the officers and men are supposed to be rationed equally. If whoever reads this were to talk to every enlisted man in this camp, I think the opinion would be basically the same as mine. We have become bitter at the many injustices imposed on us and don't care who knows.

Officers are too much concerned about themselves having a good time and everything they want. It is nothing more than just selfishness they are showing with rank to back it up. One very good example of what I am trying to say is this. In the desert district I have seen a few officers take an ice box unit for an officers' club that rightly belonged to a mess hall that ran day and night and fed around 800 to 900 men, who had to do without cool drinks just so a few officers could have ice water and cold drinks. That's god damn near just like the *German* army.

The distinction made between officers and men is so great that it spoils any attempt to raise our morale by movies and footballs. All we ask is to be treated like

Americans once again. No "out of bounds," no different mess rations, and no treating us like children.

Why should we, as tax payers, after the war pay for that $75,000 officers' Club they built? And the Colonel with his $15,000 home. If we are "in the field," let's all be in the field. Why do we have an *enlisted men's* service club with reservations for *officers?* I am not the company's "griper," either. You wanted my honest opinion, so there it is.

Recreation hall is called enlisted men's recreation hall yet best seats are reserved for officers in movie hall. Half of seats reserved for officers at USO shows and enlisted men outnumber at least 10 to 1. Officers have own club, own bar much more expensive than enlisted men's yet they still utilize men's service club. Colonel moves into expensive cottage of stone with two screen porches while men live in mud barracks without screen doors.

I was told one night that only Chelsea and Twenty Grand cigarettes were available, and while I was still at the counter this same clerk sold Philip Morris to officers. I asked the clerk if I might trade for a carton of Philip Morris and he refused me. This was at the hospital PX at Khorramshahr.

I think they are spending far too much money for officers' clubs and quarters and for their personal enjoyment. How about spending some of that on enlisted men? Also I think they should have built the hospital before the officers' club.

Why must the enlisted man be confined to camp as though he were in a concentration camp, when the officers can go where they dam please? The officers go to town, the officers get the few available women; there are several social affairs given from time to time for officers but nothing for the enlisted man unless it be an exciting bingo party. My pet peeve—to see a commissioned officer out with a girl, flaunt her in front of enlisted men, who cannot go out with nurses.

The Polish camp is "out of bounds" to enlisted men and still I have seen American officers go right into this camp and pick up women. I am of Polish descent and I believe those boys who can speak the Polish language should be given the privilege of associating with those people right in their camp.

We, as enlisted men, are not allowed to go into the better restaurants, but yet we often stand by and see our superior officers entering such places with nothing less than street walkers.

Too much discrimination between officers and enlisted men in town. "Out of bounds" signs would be a scandal in the U.S.A.

The officers are getting American whiskey and we are not. I do not think it's fair.

The practice of putting every decent nightclub "out of bounds" causes much resentment among EM. In fact we do not believe it would be tolerated in the States.

The operation of the PX in this command is something the responsible officer should be ashamed of. The Exchange that is best stocked and more convenient is out of bounds to enlisted men. Officers may purchase from a much larger assortment of stock. This condition has certainly not helped the morale of the men. The reason given is that men were buying things during working hours. Now the men are working and the officers are keeping the place busy.

There is nothing to do around here but read. Reading is good but it really gets boresome. We have no place to go or anything to do. Everything that is worth while is "off limits." Officers have it as nice as they do in the States. Big club and all the American women they want to date.

We in motor transport have many problems which would be straightened out with a little officer interest. We have the pleasure of seeing the side curtains from our trucks on an officer's jeep which sits outside his quarters all night while we are on the road shivering with the cold. When they have an accident they take our trucks and we stay with theirs often as much as twelve hours without food. These are only a few of our troubles.

We see our side curtains and tops on the officers jeeps which are parked outside of their quarters. Meantime we drive on the road with none and make our run shivering with the cold.

I understand that different units of assorted magazines are supposed to be sent for use of the men. I know for a fact that one of these units arrived at our Battalion headquarters where they were immediately appropriated for the officers—none of them ever reached the men.

There is no more flagrant violation of the individual soldier's rights than in this command. One of the first things that most men learn upon induction are these rights. Furthermore, most men realize some of the privileges they must forego when coming into the Army and as Americans they are glad to do so, for they cherish their privileges as civilians. With so many officers I have met I have noted a "privileged class" attitude toward the men. This the men resent very much, for many of them in civilian life have had positions of equal or higher responsibility than some of the officers over them. We are fighting a war to stamp out a clique system and yet we find it in our midst. In this command, officers in authority still consider it necessary to teach military discipline and courtesy. I feel that there are all too many officers who should respect their knowledge a bit more. As a matter of fact I know some Generals and Colonels who need a little training also. If you can't make this a two-way proposition—stop it.

Too many officers have that superior feeling toward their men. Treat them as if they were way below them. Many of the men have just as good an education, if not better, than many officers and also have come from just as good families. What's the matter with us enlisted men, are we dogs?

It is said that the American soldier is fighting for freedom and justice and equality. Somehow the army ways represent the very things we are fighting against. Such as: Everything is special for the officer (as if their bodies are more genteel or fragile than ours); a nurse is frowned upon if she associates with an enlisted man;

even the Non Coms are urged to stay in a station above the "common herd." Better establish a little justice and equality.

There is no basis for thinking that the irritations caused by the special privileges enjoyed by the officers were fewer in other theaters (outside the actual fighting zones) than in the command from which the above excerpts were drawn. It would be easy to multiply the above quotations—differing only in specific detail—many-fold from all over the world.[6]

The significant point is not that individual officers took undue advantage of their rank in certain circumstances, but rather that the Army's aristocratic tradition, described in the chapter, "The Old Army and the New," of Volume I of *The American Soldier*, sanctioned and encouraged a *system* of special privilege. A case also can be made for the hypothesis that the American enlisted man, with his democratic civilian background, resented not so much the fact that superiors could *afford* certain privileges as the denial of his own *right* to enjoy them. As one enlisted man in the Persian Gulf Command put it, "Back in the states, if a private had the price, he could go to the same place that a general could. I bet the people back home don't know the conditions here." In America economic inequalities result in inequality of consumption, but, except for certain minority groups, there is generally no such pattern of denial of the *right* to consumption as was represented in the system of special privilege in the American Army overseas and, to a lesser extent, in the Army at home.

In spite of the criticism, in all theaters, of excessive special privileges for officers, there were always some enlisted men who found little or nothing to criticize in the general practice. This should be borne in mind, lest the practically complete unanimity of critical comments among men volunteering comments on the subject lead to a misconception. In May, 1945, in answer to the question, "Considering their responsibilities, how do you feel about the privileges officers get compared with those enlisted men get?" 18 per cent of the enlisted men in ETO replied that officers "get about the right number of privileges" or "too few," as did about 12 per cent in MTO. Further breakdown of the answers showed, however, that the largest contribution to the approving responses was made by men in front-line combat units. In November, 1945, when a cross section of troops in the United States was questioned, the proportion who thought officers "get about the right number of privileges" or "too few" was 14 per cent—the men with short service who had not been overseas being those most likely to give this response.

6. To cite one other specific example, detailed tabulation was made of free comments at the end of the questionnaires in a survey in February and March, 1944, of a cross section of enlisted men (2,353) in the China-Burma-India theater. As in the case of the Persian Gulf Command, over half the men took the trouble to write free comments, and the most frequent topic was criticism of officers and officer–enlisted man relations. Complaints about special privileges accorded to officers headed the list of criticisms.

D. *Negro Soldiers in Northern and Southern Camps*

The evidence thus far reviewed . . . shows the comparative extent of Negro dissatisfaction with being stationed in the South instead of the North and cites as illustrations of the roots of that dissatisfaction the attitudes toward two factors in the culture widely regarded as symbols of race discrimination—justice as administered by the local police and segregation as practiced in public transportation facilities.

It must not be concluded, however, that Negroes stationed in the South were generally more poorly adjusted to the Army than were their Negro comrades in the North. About two-thirds of the Negroes stationed in the South came from the South, and nearly two-thirds of these southern Negroes preferred their southern location for reasons, as we have seen, of proximity to their homes, being used to the South, and preferring the climate there. Moreover, more than three-fifths of the Negroes stationed in the North also came from the South, and while these southern Negroes were much more likely than those stationed in the South to prefer a camp in the North (48 per cent versus 14 per cent), a good many of them (29 per cent) still preferred a southern camp. This preference on the part of many southern Negroes to be stationed in the South, together with the size of the proportion of Negroes in the Army who came from the South, had the effect of keeping the differential in discontent about location between those stationed in the North and in the South from being as large as might have been expected. While about three out of ten (31 per cent) Negroes stationed in the South reported an explicit preference for a northern location, approximately two out of ten (21 per cent) Negroes stationed in the North were equally definite about preferring to be in the South.

In addition to the obvious factors mentioned by the men themselves as accounting for the preference of many southern Negroes for being stationed in the South, it seems likely that both northern and southern Negroes may have been considerably influenced in their overall adjustment by other psychological compensations in being stationed in the South, which can be understood if we look at their situation as one of *relative status*.

Relative to most Negro civilians whom he saw in southern towns, the Negro soldier had a position of comparative wealth and dignity. His income was high, at least by general southern standards. Moreover, in spite of the Army carryover of many civilian practices of segregation, the Negro soldier received treatment more nearly on an equality with the white soldier than the treatment of the Negro civilian in the South as compared with the white civilian. Officially, the Army policies always insisted upon equality of

"Negro Soldiers in Northern and Southern Camps," from Chapter 10, pp. 562-566, *The American Soldier: Adjustment during Army Life*, Vol. I, by Stouffer, Suchman, DeVinney, Star, and Williams, Princeton: Princeton University Press, 1949.

treatment of the races, even when this meant separate treatment, and throughout the war repeated though often unsuccessful efforts were made by the War Department to translate these policies into practice and to enforce them even against the private wishes of some white commanding officers.

Consider, on the other hand, the northern Negro stationed in the North. The differential in income and status between soldier and civilian was not the same as that in the South. The industrial earning power of one's northern Negro civilian acquaintances was at an all-time high, very often far exceeding that of the Negro soldier. Moreover, the contrast between the racial practices of the Army and the racial practices of northern civilian society was, frequently, the reverse of the contrast in the South. Although the northern Negro was accustomed to countless irritations and instances of discrimination in northern civilian life, he was not confronted to the same extent with the official policies of racial segregation that existed in the Army.

Putting it simply, the psychological values of Army life to the Negro soldier in the South *relative to the southern Negro civilian* greatly exceeded the psychological values of Army life to the Negro soldier in the North *relative to the northern Negro civilian.*

How generally applicable the foregoing analysis is cannot be established from data of the Research Branch, but such an analysis might account for a part of the preference of some Negro soldiers for a Southern location in spite of their criticism of Southern camps and for the relatively good adjustment to the Army of other Negroes in the South in spite of their preference for the North. In any event, the Negro soldiers stationed in the South tended in general to show no less favorable attitudes reflecting general adjustment to the Army than Negro soldiers stationed in the North.

Drawing upon the three United States surveys cited in the section of Chapter 10, Volume I, of *The American Soldier*, on general adjustment to the Army, we have the following examples of Negro responses, by camp location: [7]

In general, how would you say you feel most of the time, in good spirits or low spirits? [8]

Percentage answering "I am usually in good spirits":

	Northern camps	Southern camps
March, 1943	32	38
August, 1944	28	28
June, 1945	22	25

7. Numbers of cases were: Northern camps, March, 1943, 850; August, 1944, 1,690; June 1945, 248; Southern camps, March, 1943, 2,150; August, 1944, 2,988; June, 1945, 805.

8. In March, 1943 the question read "satisfied and in good spirits."

In general, what sort of time do you have in the Army?
Percentage answering "I have a pretty good time":

	Northern camps	Southern camps
March, 1943	29	26
June, 1945	17	15

Are you ever worried or upset?
Percentage answering "I am hardly ever worried or upset":

	Northern camps	Southern camps
March, 1943	22	23
June, 1945	20	24

In general, do you think you yourself have gotten a square deal in the Army?
Percentage answering "Yes, in most ways I have":

	Northern camps	Southern camps
August, 1944	33	28
June, 1945	24	26

How interested are you in your Army job?
Percentage answering "Very much interested":

	Northern camps	Southern camps
March, 1943	71	73
August, 1944	54	63

How do you feel about the importance of the work you are doing right now as compared with other jobs you might be doing in the Army?
Percentage answering "It is as important as any other job I could do":

	Northern camps	Southern camps
August, 1944	51	54
June, 1945	48	52

Do you usually feel that what you are doing is worth while or not?
Percentage answering "I usually feel it is worth while":

	Northern camps	Southern camps
March, 1943	68	69
August, 1944	70	72

Would you change to some other Army job if given a chance?
Percentage answering "No":

	Northern camps	Southern camps
August, 1944	18	27
June, 1945	23	25

Do you feel proud of your company?
Percentage answering "Yes, very proud":

	Northern camps	Southern camps
March, 1943	54	57
August, 1944	40	43

If it were up to you to choose, do you think you could do more for your country as a soldier or as a worker in a war job?
Percentage answering "As a soldier":

	Northern camps	Southern camps
March, 1943	22	29
June, 1945	15	13

Almost all the differences shown above between responses of Negroes in northern and southern camps are small, and they are not consistently in either direction. Further breakdowns, holding education and region of origin constant, do not alter the general conclusion, namely, that the Negroes in southern camps made no worse a general adjustment to Army life than those in northern camps. When we take into account not only the large number of Negroes who lived in the South and wanted to be near home but also the previously discussed point about relative status—that the Army gave Negro soldiers in the South relatively higher position than southern society gave to Negro civilians, while the contrast was much less or even reversed in the North—it may even be surprising that the Negro soldiers in southern camps were not actually much better adjusted to the Army than Nego soldiers stationed in the North. But we also have seen how general was the resentment against southern policies and practices of differential treatment of whites and Negroes—as seen, for example, through attitudes toward civilian and military police and toward bus transportation. Whatever psychological compensations they may have found in experiencing in the South a status superior to that of civilians of their own race, many Negro soldiers still preferred life in the North.

3

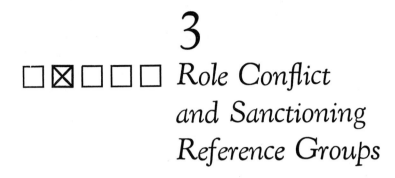 *Role Conflict and Sanctioning Reference Groups*

Two papers are included in this chapter. The first, *An Analysis of Conflicting Social Norms*, seeks quasi-experimentally to investigate responses to a hypothetical situation in which the subject is faced with expectations from two reference groups, each of which possesses sanctioning power. To the author, one of the most important findings of this study was the evidence of the degree of variability with which subjects defined the social norms in question, leading him to the suggestion that it may be precisely such ranges of permissible behavior which most need critical examination and measurement.

In the second paper, *Role Conflict and Personality*, an effort is made to examine further the nature of this variability and particularly to see to what extent it can be accounted for as a personality trait or characteristic of the individual. Thus, the paper seeks to provide a link between sociological studies of social structure and psychological studies of personality, suggesting that in any given empirical situation both types of theory need to be taken into account.

The pursuit of such problems subsequently has been quite extensive by many sociologists and psychologists. Particularly interesting as sharpening our conceptual framework is the work by Gross, Mason, and MacEachern, *Explorations in Role Analysis*. Illustrating their thinking with empirical data obtained from school superintendents, they develop and document a theory of role-conflict resolution that postulates (1) that action in a conflict situation will depend on balancing the relative *legitimacy* and *sanctions* of the competing reference and groups (2) that a further personality variable (defining *moral-expedient orientation*) must be introduced to predict behavior in situations where one set of pressures is perceived as low in legitimacy and high in sanctions, while the conflicting pressures are perceived as high in legitimacy and low in sanctions.

A. An Analysis of Conflicting Social Norms

This paper illustrates an empirical procedure for studying role obligations, with particular reference to simultaneous role obligations which conflict.

The writer became especially interested in the problem when considering the strains to which the noncommissioned officer in the Army was subjected. On the one hand, the noncom had the role of agent of the command, and in case the orders from above conflicted with what his men thought were right and necessary, he was expected by his superiors to carry out the orders. But he also was an enlisted man, sharing enlisted men's attitudes, often hostile attitudes, toward the commissioned ranks. Consequently, the system of informal controls was such as to reward him for siding with the men in a conflict situation and punish him if he did not. There was some evidence that unless his men had confidence that he could see their point of view, he was an ineffective leader; on the other hand, open and flagrant disobedience by him of an order from above could not be tolerated by the command.[1]

The general theoretical viewpoint behind this paper involves several propositions:

1. In any social group there exist norms and a strain for conformity to these norms.
2. Ordinarily, if the norms are clear and unambiguous, the individual has no choice but to conform or take the consequences in group resentment.
3. If a person has simultaneous roles in two or more groups such that simultaneous conformity to the norms of each of the groups is incompatible, he can take one of only a limited number of actions, for example:
    a. He can conform to one set of role expectations and take the consequences of noncomformity to other sets.

"An Analysis of Conflicting Social Norms," *American Sociological Review*, 14 (December, 1949), pp. 707-717.

This study was made at the Harvard Laboratory of Social Relations, in connection with research sponsored by the RAND Corporation under Air Force Project RAND.

1. Stouffer, Suchman, DeVinney, Star, Williams, *The American Soldier*, Vol. I, Chapter 8.

b. He can seek a compromise position by which he attempts to conform in part, though not wholly, to one or more sets of role expectations, in the hope that the sanctions applied will be minimal.

It need hardly be pointed out that conflicts of role obligations are a common experience of all people, especially in our complex Western society. The foreman in industry, like the noncom in the Army, is an obvious example; the "marginal man," as represented by the second-generation foreign-born, for example, has been much studied. But role conflicts are not limited to such situations. Every adolescent is certain to experience situations in which his family and his peer group are in conflict, such that conformity to the norms of the one is incompatible with conformity to the norms of the other. Most adults are subject to strains to conformity to norms incompatible from one group to another, although, often enough to make life tolerable, either the conflicts do not arise simultaneously or there is a broad enough range of tolerated behavior to provide some flexibility.

In any authoritarian situation, it is axiomatic that adherence to the rules prescribed by the authority depends to no small extent on the compatibility of the rules with dominant values of those who must obey them. It is likely, in most social situations, that the compatibility is not absolute but a matter of degree. There may be variability among members of the group in the extent to which a given value is held in common. The existence of such variability is a factor that should weaken the sanctions against any particular act and facilitate compromise solutions.

With respect to any social value, there are at least two classes of variability which need to be distinguished:

1. Each individual may perceive a narrow range of behavior as permissible, but for different individuals the ranges, though small, may constitute different segments of a continuum.

2. Each individual may perceive a rather wide range of behavior as permissible, even though there is considerable consensus as to the termini of this range.

It is the viewpoint of this paper that the *range* of approved or permissible behavior as perceived by a given individual is an important datum for the analysis of what constitutes a social norm in any group, and especially for the analysis of conflicting norms.

In order to illustrate some of these concepts and to make some preliminary attempts to define them so that statistical operations could be performed with them, an empirical study was made of conflicting role expectations in a sample of 196 Harvard and Radcliffe students, mostly undergraduates. Since the concern was wholly methodological, no effort was made to obtain a random or representative sample of the student body, and the data here reported cannot necessarily be regarded as typical of how a properly drawn sample would respond. The students were all taking the same course, Social

Relations 116. The data were collected on the first day of the course, without any explicit prior discussion of the theoretical problems involved.

Each student filled out a brief questionnaire, anonymously. He was told first:

Imagine that you are proctoring an examination in a middle-group course. About halfway through the exam you see a fellow student openly cheating. The student is copying his answers from previously prepared notes. When he sees that you have seen the notes as you walked down the aisle and stopped near his seat, he whispers quietly to you, "O.K. I'm caught. That's all there is to it."
You do not know the student. What would you as proctor do?

Table 3-1

CHECK ONE IN EACH VERTICAL COLUMN

POSSIBLE ACTIONS	My Most Likely Action (Check One)	My Next Most Likely Action (Check One)	My Least Likely Action (Check One)	My Next Least Likely Action (Check One)
A. Take away his notes and exam book, dismiss him and report him for cheating	☐	☐	☐	☐
B. Take away his notes, let him finish the exam, but report him for cheating	☐	☐	☐	☐
C. If he can be led to withdraw from the exam on some excuse, do *not* report him for cheating; otherwise report him.	☐	☐	☐	☐
D. Take away his notes, but let him finish the exam, and *not* report him for cheating.	☐	☐	☐	☐
E. Act as if nothing had happened and *not* report him for cheating.	☐	☐	☐	☐

If you knew that, *except for your action,* there could be very little chance that either the authorities or your student friends would hear about your part in the incident, which of the following actions (*see Table 3-1*) would you as proctor most likely to take? Next most likely? Least likely? Next least likely? [2]

After he had finished checking these questions, he was presented with a new complication, as follows:

Now, assume that *except for your action,* there could be very little chance that your student friends would hear about your part in the incident. But assume that, for some reason, there is a good chance, whatever you do, of the authorities finding out about it. Which of the following actions would you as proctor be most likely to take? Next most likely? Least likely? Next least likely? [2]

2. The questionnaire also contained a parallel set of answer categories for the situation where he was asked:

Now assume that, *except for your action,* there could be very little chance that the authorities would hear about your part in the incident. But also assume that there is a good chance that whatever you do your student friends would hear of it. Which of the following actions would you as proctor be most likely to take? Next most likely? Least likely? Next least likely?

However, only the situations indicated above will be used in the present paper.

This was followed by exactly the same check list as before.

Next the respondent was asked to fill out the following check list:

A. Suppose now that a proctor's action would be: *Take away his notes and exam book, dismiss him, and report him for cheating.*

How would the university authorities feel if they knew you as proctor did this? (check one)
☐ Would expect one to do something like this
☐ Would not necessarily expect one to do this, but would not disapprove
☐ Would disapprove
☐ Would not tolerate it

How would your friends in the student body feel if they knew you did this? (check one)
☐ Would expect one to do something like this
☐ Would not necessarily expect one to do this, but would not disapprove
☐ Would disapprove
☐ Would not tolerate it

B. Suppose that a proctor's action would be: *Take away his notes, let him finish the exam, but report him for cheating.*

C. Suppose now that a proctor's action would be: *If he can be led to withdraw from the exam on some excuse, do not report him for cheating; otherwise report him.*

D. Suppose now that a proctor's action would be: *Take away his notes, but let him finish the exam, and not report him for cheating.*

E. Suppose now that a proctor's action would be: *Act as if nothing had happened and not report him for cheating.*

(For B, C, D, and E, the same check lists were used as for A, but are here omitted to save space.)

Next the respondent was confronted with what it was hoped, for the methodological purposes of this illustrative study, would be more of a dilemma. He was told:

Now suppose the facts in the case in which you as proctor see a fellow student are exactly the same as in the first case, except for one difference. The student you as proctor see cheating is *your own roommate and close friend.* You know that your roommate is a hard working, though not a brilliant, student and desperately needs a good grade in this course.

If you knew that, *except for your action,* there could be very little chance that either the authorities or your student friends would know about your part in the incident, which of the following actions would you as proctor be most likely to take? Next most likely? Least likely? Next least likely?

The check list was the same as in the ordinary case presented first. This was followed by:

Now assume that *except for your action,* there could be very little chance that your student friends would hear about your part in the incident. But assume that, for some reason, there is a good chance, whatever you do, of the authorities finding out about it. Which of the following actions would you as proctor be most likely to take? Next most likely? Least likely? Next least likely?

Again the check list was the same.

Finally, the identical series of questions about expectations on the part of authorities and students was repeated for this roommate-friend situation.

The five actions described were designed to constitute, from A to E, an ordered sequence along a dimension of *degree of punitiveness*. That they were so perceived generally by the respondents can be shown easily. To illustrate: If a person said that the authorities, for example, would expect or approve more than one act, it is necessary for unidimensionality that the two or more acts be contiguous (for example, A and B, or B and C, or A, B, and C, but not A and C only). Actually, as we shall see, most students reported at least two acts that would be either expected or approved by the authorities; likewise, most reported at least two acts that would be either expected or approved by their friends in the student body. In all, there were four chances for each respondent to designate such ranges. Of the 744 responses designating ranges of two or more, the acts checked were entirely contiguous in all but 41; in other words, 95 per cent of the responses were consistent with the perception of the sequence of acts as a continuum.[3]

Attention should be called to the likelihood that the responses as to the approval or disapproval of the authorities or of one's friends in the student body to a given act have an intrinsic merit that for our purposes could be superior to the merit of the estimates of one's own probable action in a hypothetical case. In any social situation, we have some kind of awareness of the group expectations as to an act affecting the group. We can verbalize those, and these responses when tabulated are *primary data* as to the agreement among group members concerning such expectations. On the other hand, a guess as to what one would do oneself in a particular hypothetical conflict situation has a more "iffy" quality, which, though possibly quite highly correlated with actual behavior, need not necessarily be so correlated. The main stress in the present paper, it will be seen, is on the reported *role expectations*. The hypothetical personal action is introduced mainly to suggest how concepts like role expectations, when adequately measured, can be applied in the study of an individual's behavior in that role. Ideally, in place of the individual's hypothetical behavior we would like to substitute actual behavior, either in a natural or experimental situation, or reported past be-

---

3. To simplify the subsequent presentation, the inconsistencies are here treated as checking errors, although in some cases the respondent may actually have perceived an act as not fitting into an ordered sequence. (For example, when he said A and C would be approved, but B would be disapproved, he may really have viewed B in a different way from other respondents.) Fortunately, the inconsistencies were so few that it is possible to edit them without appreciable effect one way or another, except to simplify the ensuing presentation materially.

havior. Studies may be devised in the future with such improvements, but in any case the basic sorting variables would be the reported role expectations as perceived by different group members.

Figure 3-1 is a picture of social norms, as perceived and reported by the respondents in this study. At the left, we see (heavy line) that almost all of the respondents thought the authorities would approve acts A and B, about a fifth thought the authorities would approve act C, and almost nobody thought the authorities would approve acts D and E.[4] Also at the left we see

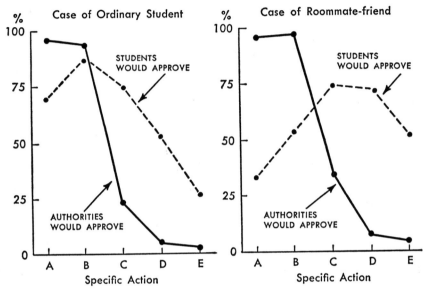

Figure 3-1. Percentage saying that a specific action as proctor would be approved by authorities and by fellow students, respectively.

(dotted line) that the majority of the respondents felt that their friends in the student body would approve the most punitive acts, namely, A and B. But, in addition we see that three-fourths of the respondents thought act C would be approved and a bare majority said the same for act D. Only a few felt E would meet student approval. In other words, if a proctor took action consistent with the authorities' expectations, he would not be in conflict with student expectations, although the range of expectations is wider for students than for the authorities.

The left diagram in Figure 3-1 portrayed the estimate of the situation where the offender was an ordinary student. By contrast, the right-hand dia-

4. To simplify the presentation, "approval" is here taken to mean that the respondent checked either of the following categories:
☐ Would expect one to do something like this
☐ Would not necessarily expect one to do this, but would not disapprove

gram shows far less overlap in expectations imputed to authorities and students, respectively. The offender in this case was one's roommate and friend. Feelings that the proctor in punishing an ordinary offender was behaving consistently with the long-range interest of the students are now overshadowed by the obligations involved in codes of personal friendship: "You can't rat on a friend; you can't let a friend down."

In the case of the friend, the respondents perceived the authorities' position to be about the same as in the case of the ordinary student, except that about a third now thought the authorities might let the proctor get away with C in view of the proctor's personal dilemma. But only a third of the respondents

Table 3-2. Percentage Who Attribute Given Role Expectations on the Part of Authorities and/or Students with Respect to Each Specific Act

	A	B	C	D	E	All Actions
PERCENTAGE DISTRIBUTION FOR EACH SPECIFIC ACTION						
CASE OF ORDINARY STUDENT						
Think given action would be approved by:						
Authorities only	28	12	3	..	..	9
Both authorities and students	68	81	19	4	2	35
Students only	1	6	55	48	24	27
Neither authorities nor students	3	1	23	48	74	29
	100	100	100	100	100	100
CASE OF ROOMMATE-FRIEND						
Think given action would be approved by:						
Authorities only	63	44	9	1	..	24
Both authorities and students	33	53	25	6	4	24
Students only	..	..	49	66	48	33
Neither authorities nor students	4	3	17	27	48	19
	100	100	100	100	100	100

N = 196

thought the students would approve act A. The modal acts are C and D. About half believed that the least punitive of all, E, would be approved by most of the students.

In Table 3-2 each act (separately for the case of the ordinary student and the friend, respectively) is broken down according to the percentage who think it would be approved by (*a*) the authorities only, (*b*) both the authorities and students, (*c*) students only, and (*d*) by neither the authorities nor students.

Let us now examine the relationship between these role expectations and the respondent's own hypothetical behavior as proctor. It will be recalled that in both the case of the ordinary student and the roommate-friend, the respondent was asked what he personally would do under two hypothetical conditions: (1) if neither the authorities nor his student friends would hear about his part in the incident and (2) if there could be very little chance that the authorities would hear about his part in the incident.

In Table 3-3 we have a percentage distribution of the acts which each student said he would be *most* likely to choose in the given situation. In the case of the ordinary student, as Table 3-2 shows, the majority of respondents say they would be most likely to employ acts A or B, the most punitive. There is not a large difference between the hypothetical behavior in private or in public (public only in the restricted sense that the authorities would hear about it in any case, though students need not). The main difference is a small increase, from a private 21 per cent to a public 30 per cent, in first choices for the most severe act A. However, the hypothetical behavior in the roommate-friend case shows a very different pattern. As can be seen in Table 3-3, nearly two-thirds of the respondents elect acts D or E as their first preferences in private action, and only 16 per cent say they would employ as

Table 3-3. Percentage Distribution of Hypothetical Actions Which the Respondents Say They Would Be Most Likely to Take as Proctor

ACTION	IN CASE OF ORDINARY STUDENT		IN CASE OF ROOMMATE-FRIEND	
	Private*	Public†	Private*	Public†
A	21	30	4	6
B	47	48	12	34
C	16	13	18	31
D	15	7	38	18
E	1	2	28	11
	100	100	100	100

N = 196

*"If you knew that, *except* for your action there could be very little chance that either the authorities or your student friends would hear about your part in the incident."
†"If you knew that, *except* for your action there could be very little chance that your student friends would hear about your part in the incident, but that there is a good chance, whatever you do, of the authorities finding out about it."

first choice punitive acts A or B. But if the authorities were sure to find out about it, the picture changes. Less than a third would elect D or E as first choice and 40 per cent would prefer A or B. Yet this is still only about half as large as the proportion who would prefer A or B in comparable circumstances in the case of the ordinary student.

Table 3-3, while of a good deal of interest in itself, is subject to the caveats entered earlier in this paper against taking reports on such hypothetical behavior too literally. But the main purpose for introducing the material in Table 3-3 is to enable us to see how such hypothetical behavior is related to the reported perceptions of authorities' and students' expectations, respectively, of proper behavior from a proctor. The data in Table 3-3 are, therefore, next broken down according to the categories used in Table 3-1. Here we see in Table 3-4, as we doubtless would expect to see, that most students who chose acts A or B as their first preference if they themselves were proctors, also tended to perceive such acts as one which *both* the authorities and students would approve. But that tended to be true of several of the respondents who would take less punitive action—they had a different perception of

**Table 3-4. Respondents Whose Own Most Likely Hypothetical Action as
Proctor Is as Indicated, Broken Down by Expectations Attributed
to Authorities and/or Students**

		WOULD BE APPROVED BY			
		Authorities Only	Both Authorities and Students	Students Only	Neither
CASE OF ORDINARY STUDENT					
(Private act)	A	6	35	. . .	. .
	B	3	86	3	. .
	C	. .	13	17	1
	D	. .	5	21	4
	E	. .	. . .	2	. .
		9	139	43	5
(Public act)	A	9	50	. . .	. .
	B	5	87	3	. .
	C	. .	13	13	. .
	D	. .	4	9	1
	E	. .	. . .	2	. .
		14	154	27	1
CASE OF ROOMMATE-FRIEND					
(Private act)	A	1	7	. . .	. .
	B	2	20	. . .	1
	C	. .	14	17	5
	D	. .	4	62	9
	E	. .	3	39	12
		3	48	118	27
(Public act)	A	2	10	. . .	. . .
	B	14	50	. . .	2
	C	4	21	30	5
	D	. .	4	29	3
	E	. .	4	15	3
		20	89	74	13

expectations and thus thought they were avoiding conflict. In the case of the
ordinary student, only 43 of the 196 respondents indicated a private action
which was perceived to be acceptable to students only, and only 27 a public
action. Contrast this with their hypothetical behavior when the offender
was a roommate-friend. Of the 196 respondents, 118 preferred a private action
tolerated by the students only. This number was reduced to 74 who would
still stick by their friend even if they knew the authorities would find out
about their action, or rather, inaction.

Figure 3-1, it will be recalled, indicated quite a marked range of tolerance
in imputed student expectations, especially in the roommate-friend situation.
But it is not possible to tell directly from Figure 3-1 the extent to which this
is due to (*a*) different respondents visualizing different role expectations,
or to (*b*) respondents generally agreeing that a wide range of role expectations existed. Let us now look at Table 3-5, where the frequency with which

Table 3-5. Frequency with Which Various Ranges of Acts Are Perceived as Approved by Authorities and Students, Respectively

RANGE		CASE OF ORDINARY STUDENT ACTS APPROVED BY		CASE OF ROOMMATE-FRIEND ACTS APPROVED BY	
		Authorities	Students	Authorities	Students
1	A	13	4	4	3
	B	5	1	4	3
	C	...	...	...	2
	D	...	3	...	2
	E	...	...	...	4
		18	8	8	14
2	A	134	37	120	12
	BC	3	10	2	10
	CD	...	7	...	14
	DE	...	5	...	26
		137	59	122	62
3	ABC	33	42	52	20
	BCD	...	14	...	18
	CDE	...	7	1	42
		33	63	53	80
4	ABCD	5	27	8	11
	BCDE	...	14	1	11
		5	41	9	22
5	ABCDE	3	25	4	18
	Total	196	196	196	196

each range of expectations was indicated is shown. We see here quite clearly the degree of consensus among respondents as to what the authorities would approve. Among the 196 respondents, 134, or two-thirds, checked A, B identically for the case of the ordinary student; 120 checked A, B for the case of the roommate-friend. The majority of the remainder checked A, B, C in both cases.

Far different is the picture from Table 3-5 in the case of imputed student expectations. The majority settled for a range of either two or three acts in both of the situations, but within a given range there were all possible variations. For example, in the roommate-friend situation there were 80 who indicated a range of student approval covering three acts, but of these, 20 perceived the range as A, B, C; 18 perceived it as B, C, D; and 42 as C, D, E. Clearly, there is an absence of consensus here, and it is not a mere uniform coverage of the whole range of possibilities by all individuals.

If we take, for illustration, the 120 respondents who perceived the range of acts approved by the authorities in the case of the roommate-friend as A, B, and order the ranges approved by students, according to these same respondents, we see in Table 3-6 the ways in which these different specific ranges are related to one's personal hypothetical behavior as proctor. Here we show for *each pattern* of role expectation the hypothetical private and

Table 3-6. An Illustration of Hypothetical Actions of Respondent as Proctor, as Related to Specific Ranges of Student Approval in Case of Roommate-Friend

RANGE OF STUDENT APPROVAL	PRIVATE BEHAVIOR							PUBLIC BEHAVIOR						
	A	B	C	D	E	Total Frequency	Average Rank*	A	B	C	D	E	Total Frequency	Average Rank
A	1	..	..	..	..	1	1.0	1	..	..	..	..	1	1.0
AB	2	3	2	2	2	11	2.9	2	6	2	..	1	11	2.3
B	..	..	1	..	1	2	4.0	..	1	..	..	1	2	3.5
ABC	2	5	4	2	2	15	2.7	5	4	4	1	1	15	2.3
BC	..	..	3	2	..	5	3.4	..	3	2	..	..	5	2.4
ABCD	..	1	3	3	1	8	3.5	1	3	4	..	..	8	2.4
C	..	..	2	..	..	2	3.0	..	2	..	..	..	2	2.0
BCD	..	4	1	8	..	13	3.3	..	9	3	1	..	13	2.4
ABCDE	..	3	1	7	3	14	3.7	..	9	2	1	2	14	2.7
CD	1	..	1	4	2	8	3.8	1	..	4	3	..	8	3.1
BCDE	..	1	1	3	1	6	3.7	..	3	1	1	1	6	3.0
CDE	..	1	1	10	9	21	4.3	..	6	9	4	2	21	3.1
DE	..	..	..	6	7	13	4.5	..	2	2	4	5	13	4.0
E	..	..	..	..	1	1	5.0	..	..	..	..	1	1	5.0
Total						120							120	

*A, B, C, D, E ranked 1, 2, 3, 4, 5, respectively.

public behavior, respectively. For convenience, these hypothetical acts A, B, C, D, E have been ranked 1, 2, 3, 4, and 5, respectively, and average ranks computed.

As we move from role expectations A to E, we see how the average ranks of the students' hypothetical behavior increase. It is interesting to note that, at least in the present example, this progressive increase seems to depend more on the midpoint of the range than on the termini. For example, if the expectation is BC, the average rank of the hypothetical behavior is just about the same as when the expectation is A, B, C, D. In some cases the pattern with the longer range has higher average rank than its counterpart with the same midpoint but shorter range; in other cases the reverse is true. The number of cases available in the present data is, however, exceedingly small for this kind of comparison.

While the average rank of hypothetical acts did not tend to differ consistently when we compared two or more ranges with the same midpoint in Table 3-6, there is a hint that differences in the *range* of hypothetical acts vary with the *range* of role expectations that have the same midpoint. It doubtless would be expected that if a respondent perceived the range of approved behavior to be B, C, D, he would be more likely to choose *either* B or D for his own act than if he perceived the range to be only C. Take the following from Table 3-6:

	A	B	C	D	E	
C	..	..	2	..	..	2
BCD	..	4	1	8	..	13
ABCDE	..	3	1	7	3	14

Most of the other examples in Table 3-6 are less neat than this, and the number of cases is distressingly few, but if we form other tables like Table 3-6 for other values of the range of expected approval by the authorities and take all possible matched comparisons thus available (for example, authorities ABC; students BC versus ABCD), we obtain a rather convincing overall result, in the roommate-friend situation: [If students impute to their colleagues a narrow range of expectation, then they are very likely to act themselves within the same range, irrespective of whether their own decision will be publicly known or not. If the imputed expectations have a wider range (but the same midpoint), then the decisions of the responding actors

Table 3-7

	STUDENT EXPECTATIONS THAT HAVE IDENTICAL MIDPOINTS BUT DIFFERENT RANGES	
	Those with Minimum Range	Those with Greater than Minimum Range
PRIVATE ACT		
Own behavior more severe than any act within the *minimum* range of student expectation	2	12
Own behavior within *minimum* range	31	20
Own behavior less severe than any act within *minimum* range	8	34
	—	—
	41	66
PUBLIC ACT		
Own behavior more severe than any act within the *minimum* range of student expectation	5	29
Own behavior within *minimum* range	32	21
Own behavior less severe than any act within *minimum* range	4	16
	—	—
	41	66

will themselves vary more widely; and what they will do is quite different according to whether they visualize public knowledge or not (Table 3-7).*]

The same tendency is also seen, though somewhat less strikingly, in the case of the ordinary student.

While interpretation of such a finding should be indulged in only with caution, the results are sufficient to suggest the importance of taking into account not only the midpoints of a given range of role expectations, but the magnitude of the range as well.

We have now completed the analysis of the present data except for one further observation which has implications for further research.

In such a study as this, it would be interesting first to differentiate individuals into types according to the way they perceive conflicting role expectations and then to ask how these different types of persons vary according to other social and psychological characteristics. Information of the latter

---

* The interpretation of this table is missing in the original publication. The sentences in brackets are a reconstruction by the editors.

type was not collected in the present study. However, the foregoing analysis has suggested how typologies could be set up and related to such outside variables. To take a simple illustration from the roommate-friend situation:

One could classify most of our respondents into three main types according as they perceived the role conflict.

Type I. Those who thought the range of approved acts identical from the point of view of authorities and students (21 cases). For such respondents the problem of conformity in their own hypothetical acts could not have been difficult.

Type II. Those who thought the range of acts approved by the authorities did not overlap in any way with the range of acts approved by the students (56 cases). For them simultaneous conformity to both was impossible. It is noteworthy, parenthetically, that 51 of the 56 said their own private act would be one conforming to student expectation, though 16 of these 51 shifted their act to a nonstudent position in the public situation.

Type III. Those who perceived a difference in the range of authorities' and students' expectations but who found at least one act which would be tolerated by both (119 cases). Privately, only 36 of these individuals would take an action satisfactory to both. Publicly, however, 73 out of the 119 were able to find in an act perceived to be mutually acceptable the basis for their own hypothetical solution.

Why did these three types differ so markedly in their definition of the situation? Why, within these types, did different subtypes prefer different solutions? These are the kinds of questions that subsequent research can explore. But first we must have a way of defining and classifying the role expectations relevant to our problem, and the purpose of the present study is to illustrate a technique for accomplishing this first step.

From the theoretical standpoint, the most important implication of this paper may stem from its stress on variability. In essay writing in this field, it is common and convenient to think of a social norm as a point, or at least as a very narrow band on either side of a point. This assumption probably is quite unrealistic as to most of our social behavior. And it may be precisely the ranges of permissible behavior which most need examination if we are to make progress in this realm which is so central in social science. For it may be the very existence of some flexibility or social slippage—but not too much—which makes behavior in groups possible.

B. *Role Conflict and Personality*

A convenient way to examine the informal social controls operating in a given institution is through the study of role conflict. In an earlier statistical analysis of an example of role conflict, stress was laid on the concept of variability and implications for the theory of role of different classes of variability.[5]

The present paper also is concerned with role conflict. But it seeks to provide a link between the study of social norms, with which the former paper was primarily concerned, and the study of personality. Specifically, when there is a lack of consensus in a group as to the "proper thing to do" in a morally conflicting situation, is there a tendency for some individuals to have a predisposition or a personality bias toward one type of solution and for other individuals to have a predisposition toward another type of solution? If such a predisposition exists, there should be a tendency to carry over certain types of behavior from one role conflict to another with some consistency.

An especially common role conflict is that between one's institutionalized obligations of friendship and one's institutionalized obligations to a society. The obligations of friendship in western culture, to use the terminology of Parsons, are particularistic rather than universalistic, affectively toned rather than affectively neutral, and diffuse rather than specific.[6] A universalistic obligation is applicable to dealings with anybody (e.g., obligation to fulfill a contract); a particularistic obligation is limited to persons who stand in some special relationship to one (e.g., the obligation to help a relative or a close friend or neighbor). Diffuseness of particularistic obligations provides flexibility in the definition of these roles. That is, the content of an individual's particularistic obligations (toward a friend, a brother, a grandchild) depends in part on the intimacy of the relationship itself. The greater the affection, the greater the sense of obliga-

Samuel A. Stouffer and Jackson Toby, "Role Conflict and Personality," *American Journal of Sociology*, 56 (March, 1951), pp. 395-406. Copyright 1951 by the University of Chicago.

The research here reported was conducted with the assistance of the Laboratory of Social Relations, Harvard University. Special acknowledgment is due to Paul F. Lazarsfeld, Talcott Parsons, and Gordon W. Allport. Professor Lazarsfeld proposed the applicability of a new form of latent distance structure and himself carried out the computations reported in the note appended in this paper. A pretest of the present study was the subject of a paper by the authors at the American Sociological Society in December, 1949, at which the paper's discussion by Professor Leonard S. Cottrell contributed to the present formulation.

5. Samuel A. Stouffer, "An Analysis of Conflicting Social Norms," *American Sociological Review*, XIV (December, 1949), 707-17. (See also Section A of this chapter.)

6. See, e.g., Talcott Parsons, *Essays in Sociological Theory* (New York: Free Press, 1949), chap. viii.

tion. On the other hand, universalistic obligations are defined more rigidly, for they regulate behavior toward all human beings—regardless of affective involvement. Hence, in any specific situation involving conflict between duty to a friend and duty to society, we would expect that some individuals are more prone to regard the particularistic obligation as taking precedence than others because there is variability from individual to individual in the intimacy of friendships. That is, respondents tend to project into the hypothetical situations *reference* friendships drawn from their own experience. A description of an institutionalized social norm not only must take into account, then, the beliefs and behavior of a modal member of the group but must also observe the individual variability in the perception of obligations. This variability—or "social slippage"—was a major concern in the paper previously cited.

In the present paper we shall deal with several situations involving conflicts between obligations to a friend and more general social obligations. If, as our conception of the intrinsic variability of particularistic obligations would lead us to expect, some people are more likely than others to choose the particularistic horn of the dilemma rather than the universalistic in a variety of situations, we should be able to devise a scale to measure such a tendency. With such a scale, people should be ranked along a single dimension according to their probability of possessing the attribute or predisposition of choosing one type of solution rather than the other.

What we have to present here is only a crude beginning, indeed, only a classroom example. Yet it should prove instructive in a number of respects to those who may wish to carry on further research with needed refinements. Our data are based on a short pencil-and-paper questionnaire completed by 648 undergraduate students at Harvard and Radcliffe in February, 1950. No claim is made for the representativeness of the sample, since almost all were members of a single class, "Social Relations 1A."

Four little stories were presented, as follows:

1. You are riding in a car driven by a close friend, and he hits a pedestrian. You know he was going at least 35 miles an hour in a 20-mile-an-hour speed zone. There are no other witnesses. His lawyer says that if you testify under oath that the speed was only 20 miles an hour, it may save him from serious consequences.
    What right has your friend to expect you to protect him?

Check one:
☐ My friend has a definite right as a friend to expect me to testify to the lower figure.
☐ He has some right as a friend to expect me to testify to the lower figure.
☐ He has no right as a friend to expect me to testify to the lower figure.

What do you think you'd probably do in view of the obligations of a sworn witness and the obligation to your friend?

Check one:
☐ Testify that he was going 20 miles an hour.
☐ Not testify that he was going 20 miles an hour,

2. You are a New York drama critic. A close friend of yours has sunk all his savings in a new Broadway play. You really think the play is no good.

What right does your friend have to expect you to go easy on his play in your review?

Check one:

- ☐ He has a definite right as a friend to expect me to go easy on his play in my review.
- ☐ He has some right as a friend to expect me to do this for him.
- ☐ He has no right as a friend to expect me to do this for him.

Would you go easy on his play in your review in view of your obligations to your readers and your obligation to your friend?

Check one:

- ☐ Yes
- ☐ No

3. You are a doctor for an insurance company. You examine a close friend who needs more insurance. You find that he is in pretty good shape, but you are doubtful on one or two minor points which are difficult to diagnose.

What right does your friend have to expect you to shade the doubts in his favor?

Check one:

- ☐ My friend would have a definite right as a friend to expect me to shade the doubts in his favor.
- ☐ He would have some right as a friend to expect me to shade the doubts in his favor.
- ☐ He would have no right as a friend to expect me to shade the doubts in his favor.

Would you shade the doubts in his favor in view of your obligations to the insurance company and your obligation to your friend?

Check one:

- ☐ Yes
- ☐ No

4. You have just come from a secret meeting of the board of directors of a company. You have a close friend who will be ruined unless he can get out of the market before the board's decision becomes known. You happen to be having dinner at that friend's home this same evening.

What right does your friend have to expect you to tip him off?

Check one:

- ☐ He has a definite right as a friend to expect me to tip him off.
- ☐ He has some right as a friend to expect me to tip him off.
- ☐ He has no right as a friend to expect me to tip him off.

Would you tip him off in view of your obligations to the company and your obligation to your friend?

Check one:

- ☐ Yes
- ☐ No

The problem is: Do the answers to these questions indicate the existence of a unidimensional scale, along which respondents can be ordered as to the degree to which they are likely to possess a trait or bias toward the particularistic solution of a dilemma? For simplicity, we label for a given item the response "My friend has a definite right . . ." as particularistic, the response "He has no right . . ." as universalistic. If he marks "He has some right . . . ," we label the response particularistic if in the second part of the question he says he would favor the friend in action; universalistic if he says he would not favor the friend.

There was a considerable spread among the four items in the percentage giving particularistic responses:

Item 1	(car accident)	26
Item 2	(drama critic)	45
Item 3	(insurance doctor)	51
Item 4	(board of directors)	70

Such frequencies suggest the hypothesis of a distance or cumulative scale.

Following Louis Guttman's scalogram method, the responses to all the items were cross-tabulated and scale patterns arranged according to nearest scale type, as shown in Table 3-7. While the reproducibility (0.91) and the distribution of cutting points suggest the admissibility of the hypothesis that these items form a Guttman scale, the items are too few in number for us to speak with confidence, especially in the presence of two sets of rather numerous nonscale responses (+ − + + and − + − +). Rigor would require ten or more items to start with, in order to determine scalability, although we might in the end select fewer items for subsequent use.

The pure Guttman model can be viewed as the limiting case of a more general latent-distance model which Paul F. Lazarsfeld has introduced.[7] It seems worth while, therefore, to examine the applicability to these data of the Lazarsfeld latent-distance model, which postulates a latent continuum with as many ordered classes as there are items, plus one. The model assigns to each item a probability that a positive (e.g., particularistic) response to that item assigns the respondent to a particular segment of the hypothetical latent continuum.[8]

For reasons of space, the arithmetic in testing the applicability of the latent-distance model to our data will not be exhibited here. However, a brief technical summary of the results appears as an appendix to this paper. Although the procedure used is still too new to have developed wholly satisfactory acceptance standards, the outcome was quite encouraging.

Actually, an additional precaution was taken. Experience with projective

7. Stouffer, Guttman, Suchman, Lazarsfeld, Star, and Clausen, *Studies in Social Psychology in World War II*, Vol. IV: *Measurement and Prediction* (Princeton: Princeton University Press, 1950). Guttman's theory and procedures are described in chaps. ii-ix, Lazarsfeld's in chaps. x and xi. Chapter i provides an introduction to both methods.

8. Latent-structure theory postulates that all the relationship between any two manifest items can be accounted for by the joint correlation of the items with the latent structure. In other words, within any segment of the latent structure the correlation between two manifest items is zero.

material has taught us to expect considerable differences when we ask, "What do you think about something?" from results if we asked, "What do you think somebody else would think about something?" Especially, when we are seeking by crude question-and-answer procedures to learn something about social norms, it is very important to know what, if any, differences are produced by such shifts imposed on the point of view of the respondents. Hence, only a third of our 648 respondents were asked questions in the form exhibited above.

For a third of the subjects the stories were rewritten so that the friend of the respondent, not the respondent himself, faced the role conflict. To illustrate with the motorcar example:

Your close friend is riding in a car which you are driving, and you hit a pedestrian. He knows that you were going at least 35 miles an hour in a 20-mile-an-hour zone. There are no other witnesses. Your lawyer says that if your friend testifies under oath that the speed was only 20 miles an hour, it may save you from serious consequences.

What right do you have to expect him to protect you?

Check one:

☐ I have a definite right as a friend to expect him to testify to the lower figure.
☐ I have some right as a friend to expect him to testify to the lower figure.
☐ I have no right as a friend to expect him to testify to the lower figure.

What do you think he would probably do in view of his obligations as a sworn witness and his obligation as your friend?

Check one:

☐ Testify that you were going 20 miles an hour.
☐ Not testify that you were going 20 miles an hour.

For still another third of the respondents, a third version was presented. In this case neither the respondent nor his friend faced the dilemma but two hypothetical people, Smith and Smith's friend, Johnson. Again to illustrate with the motorcar example:

Smith is riding in a car driven by his close friend, Johnson, and Johnson hits a pedestrian. Smith knows that his friend was going at least 35 miles an hour in a 20-mile-an-hour zone. There are no other witnesses. Johnson's lawyer says that if he testifies under oath that the speed was only 20 miles an hour, it may save Johnson from serious consequences.

What right does Johnson have to expect Smith to protect him?

Check one:

☐ Johnson has a definite right as a friend to expect Smith to testify to the lower figure.
☐ He has some right as a friend to expect Smith to testify to the lower figure.
☐ He has no right as a friend to expect Smith to testify to the lower figure.

If Smith were an average person, what do you think he would probably do in view of his obligations as a sworn witness and his obligation to his friend?

Check one:

☐ Testify that Johnson was going 20 miles an hour.
☐ Not testify that Johnson was going 20 miles an hour.

Table 3-8. Scalogram Pattern for Respondents to Four Items on Role Conflict

SCALE TYPE	SCALE PATTERN 1 2 3 4	PARTICULARISTIC RESPONSE TO ITEM NO.				UNIVERSALISTIC RESPONSE TO ITEM NO.				"ERRORS"
		1	2	3	4	1	2	3	4	
5	++++	66	66	66	66	...	...	...	...	0
	+-++	52	...	52	52	...	52	...	...	52
	++-+	15	15	...	15	...	...	15	...	15
	+++-	8	8	8	...	...	...	...	8	8
	+-+-	5	...	5	...	...	5	...	5	10
	++--	6	6	...	...	...	...	6	6	12
4	-+++	...	95	95	95	95	...	...	...	0
	-++-	...	16	16	...	16	...	...	16	16
3	--++	...	...	80	80	80	80	...	...	0
	--+-	...	...	14	...	14	14	...	14	14
2	---+	...	...	...	71	71	71	71	...	0
	-+-+	...	66	...	66	66	...	66	...	66
	+--+	13	...	...	13	...	13	13	...	13
1	-+--	...	21	...	...	21	...	21	21	21
	+---	6	...	...	...	...	6	6	6	6
	----	...	...	...	...	114	114	114	114	0
Total		171	293	336	458	477	355	312	190	233

Reproducibility $= 1 - [233/(4 \times 648)] = 0.91$

The different forms of the questionnaires were interleaved and handed out at random. In testing for the goodness of fit of the latent-distance scale, separate tests were applied to each of the three types of items. The model seemed to fit about equally well in all three cases, and the rank order assigned to particular scale patterns was very much the same, except for a few scale types containing a negligible number of cases. As would be expected, the rank-order grouping derived from the latent-distance model is very close to the rank-order grouping obtained by scoring to nearest scale type in scalogram analysis.[9] For purposes of subsequent analysis, the rank groupings for each of the three forms were constituted as in Table 3-8. The extent to which the three forms agreed with one another can be seen from Table 3-9. The principal discrepancies are due to differences in frequency of responses to Items 2 and 3, respectively, but the groupings shown at the bottom of Table 3-8 do not differ from one form to another more than would be expected by

9. In scoring to nearest scale type by scalogram procedure, the objective is to arrange the scale patterns to minimize "error." Thus + + − + is grouped with + + + +, on the assumption that the response to the third item only is an error. If it were grouped with − + + +, we should have to assume two errors, in the first and third items, respectively. However, there are some items which might be grouped in different ways with the same amount of error. For example, − + − + would be grouped with − + + + if we assumed that the third item was an error, but would be grouped with − − − + if we assumed that the second item was an error. Such doubtful cases are resolved by the latent distance analysis, which in the present example usually gave clear and consistent information.

Table 3-9. Scale-pattern Groupings Shown Separately for Three Forms of Questionnaire

Scale Type	Scale Pattern 1 2 3 4	Form A (Ego Faces Dilemma)	Form B (Ego's Friend Faces Dilemma)	Form C (Smith Faces Dilemma)
5	$+\ +\ +\ +$	20	20	26
	$+\ -\ +\ +$	9	23	20
	$+\ +\ -\ +$	6	4	5
	$+\ +\ +\ -$	2	3	3
	$+\ -\ +\ -$	2	3	0
	$+\ +\ -\ -$	1	3	2
4	$-\ +\ +\ +$	38	25	32
	$-\ +\ +\ -$	7	6	3
3	$-\ -\ +\ +$	24	29	27
	$-\ -\ +\ -$	6	5	3
2	$-\ -\ -\ +$	23	31	17
	$-\ +\ -\ +$	25	15	26
	$+\ -\ -\ +$	4	4	5
1	$-\ +\ -\ -$	6	6	9
	$+\ -\ -\ -$	1	2	3
	$-\ -\ -\ -$	42	37	35
	Total	216	216	216
	Reproducibility	0.92	0.91	0.90

Totals

		Form A	Form B	Form C
5		40	56	56
4		45	31	35
3		30	34	30
2		52	50	48
1		49	45	47
		216	216	216

chance, according to the chi-square test. Incidentally, it is of some interest to note that the reproducibility of each form is in the neighborhood of 0.90.

This is, of course, much too small a set of items about which to make any serious claims either to rigorous scalability or to generality, but the results encourage one to believe that we can develop good measures of individual predisposition to a bias in a particularistic or universalistic direction. We must note that a scale such as this is not an unequivocal measure of *particularism-universalism*. Since friendship obligations are diffuse and affectively toned as well as particularistic and societal obligations are specific and affectively neutral as well as universalistic, we have scaled a predisposition for diffuse, affectively toned over specific, affectively neutral obligations as well as a predisposition for particularistic over universalistic obligations. But this fusion of variables in our situations *does* seem to generate a unidimensional scale, the dimension involved being the degree of strength of a latent tendency to be loyal to a friend even at the cost of other principles. The rank groupings would represent ordered degrees of probability of taking the friend's side in a role conflict.[10]

Ideally, having assigned each of the 648 individuals to one of five scale types or rank groupings, we would like to see how these groupings relate to behavior in a new, nonverbal situation of role conflict. Such a design would be very costly and complicated but must be carried out sooner or later if we are to have full confidence that our scale is not an artifact—for example, that it does not arise merely from differences in imaginative ability, a possibility which was suggested by Leonard S. Cottrell in his discussion of the first draft of our paper. As a simple but decidedly inferior procedure, we investigated the relationship between the scale and other verbal responses relative to role conflict.

We selected some academic situations not too far removed from the experience of college students. The problem was to see whether respondents who were near the particularistic end of the scale, for example, tended to have a higher probability of giving particularistic responses in these academic situations than other respondents. (The scale itself involved no academic situations.)

You are employed by Professor X to mark examination books in his course. Your close friend makes somewhat under a passing grade. If you give him a special break, you can boost him over the passing line. He needs the grade badly.

What right does your friend have to expect you to give him a special break?

Check one:

☐ He has a definite right as a friend to expect me to do this for him.
☐ He has some right as a friend to expect me to do this for him.
☐ He has no right as a friend to expect me to do this for him.

Would you give him this special break in view of your obligations to the university and your obligation to your friend?

Check one:

☐ Yes
☐ No

The same scoring system was used as in the scale items. Among those with Scale Type 1, only 7 per cent responded particularistically in this situation, the percentage rising to 49 among those in Scale Type 5:

Scale Type	Per Cent
5	49
4	25
3	31
2	30
1	7

10. Of course, we shall eventually be interested in finding out whether a more abstract scale—for example, one of universalism-particularism alone—would stand up and, if it did, more about its genesis.

Another situation presented was the following, scored similarly to the others:

You are in charge of the reserve desk at a library. A certain reserve book is in heavy demand. A close friend is pressed for time and can use the book only at a certain hour. He has suggested that you hide the book for a while before his arrival so that he will be sure to get it. He needs it badly.

What right does your friend have to expect you to hide the book?

Check one:

☐ He has a definite right as a friend to expect me to hide the book for him.
☐ He has some right as a friend to expect me to do this for him.
☐ He has no right as a friend to expect me to do this for him.

Would you hide the book for him in view of your obligations to the library and your obligation to your friend?

Check one:

☐ Yes
☐ No

Variation in proportions responding particularistically was from 16 to 70 per cent:

Scale Type	Per Cent
5	70
4	55
3	58
2	46
1	10

The following story, almost identical with that used in the paper previously cited in the *Review*, also was presented and scored as were the other items quoted in the present paper.

You are proctoring an examination in a middle-group course. *You are the only proctor* in the room. About halfway through the exam you see a fellow-student, who is also your close friend, openly cheating. He is copying his answers from previously prepared crib notes. When he sees that you have seen the notes as you walked down the aisle and stopped near the seat, he whispers quietly to you, "O.K., I'm caught. That's all there is to it."

Under these circumstances, what right does he have to expect you not to turn him in?

Check one:

☐ He has a definite right as a friend to expect me not to turn him in.
☐ He has some right as a friend to expect me not to turn him in.
☐ He has no right as a friend to expect me not to turn him in.

Under these circumstances, what would you probably do in view of your obligations as a proctor and your obligation to your friend?

Check one:

☐ Report him.
☐ Not report him.

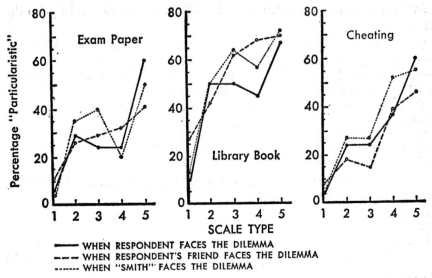

Figure 3-2. *Scale scores as related to the proportion "particularistic" in certain academic situations.*

Variation was from 6 to 50 per cent, in proportions responding particularistically:

Scale Type	Per Cent
5	50
4	35
3	28
2	25
1	6

These items, like the items included in the scale, were asked in three alternate forms. A respondent, for example, who had the "Smith-Johnson" form of the scale items also had a "Smith-Johnson" form of the new academic items. There was considerable variability in patterns of relationship, but the upward progression was present on all forms on each item, as is shown in Figure 3-2.

An important element of a friendship relationship is what Parsons calls an "other-orientation" rather than a self-orientation, such as is institutionalized in our society in a business transaction. Though other-orientation is institutionalized, it is probably not an absolute value. While the individual is supposed to subordinate his own interests to those of his friends under many circumstances, there are limits to the sacrifices which one may legitimately expect of a friend. These limits tend to be vague and undefined, perhaps so that they may vary with the intimacy of the friendship. This introduces another source of behavorial variability: the respondent's perception of the risk to himself by defying universalistic norms and coming to the friend's aid. It was of interest, therefore, to vary the cheating situation by asking the respondent to imagine an analogous setting with much greater risk to the proctor:

Consider the same cheating situation as above, with an *additional* element. Suppose now *there is another proctor (an extremely conscientious fellow!) in the examination room with you* and that you would be running a fifty-fifty risk of personal exposure by him to the authorities for failing as proctor to turn in a cheater.

(Check list the same as before)

How the increase in risk reduced the particularistic responses is shown in Table 3-10.

Table 3-10. Percentage "Particularistic" When Risk Varies

Scale Type	In Both Situations	In Situation of Low Risk Only
5	20	30
4	16	19
3	10	18
2	11	14
1	2	4

We hoped to make a further study of high and low risk to see how differences in predispositions might be related to other factors in this specific cheating situation, such as students' perceptions of the severity of penalties, of fellow-students' attitudes, and of the cheater's own probable reactions. Questions were designed on these points, but they were not satisfactory. The main problem that emerged, however, and that negated much further intensive cross-tabulation, was that sizable differences in response occurred depending on whether we asked the cheating question involving little risk to the proctor *prior to* or *after* the cheating question involving risk to the proctor. Actually, in a random half of the cases the little-risk situation was presented first; in the other half the risk situation was presented first.

For each form (ego as proctor, ego's friend as proctor, Smith as proctor) we have, then, two reports. There are six replications in all. Results are graphed in Figure 3-3. The reader will observe that the form in which ego is proctor stands up well. We get about the same picture, irrespective of the order of presentation of the low-risk and high-risk situations, respectively. But the results are chaotic for the forms in which ego is the cheater or in which the actors are third persons.

The reasons for this result are not immediately obvious. Further trials and study are required before reaching a conclusion. One plausible suggestion is that a paper-and-pencil test like this requires a good deal of imagination on the part of a respondent and that the act of imagination is made easiest when ego himself is pictured as confronting the dilemma. By increasing the salience, one reduces the temptation for casual or careless checking. However,

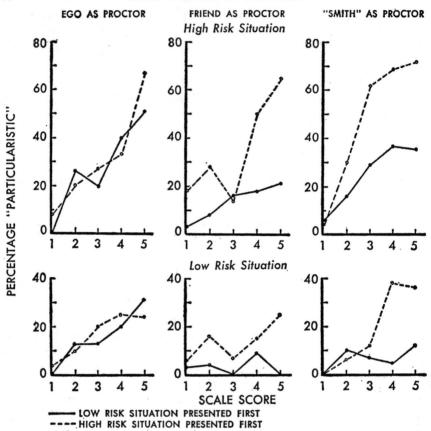

Figure 3-3. *Scale scores as related to the proportion "particularistic" in the cheating situations, showing variations related to different forms of questionnaires.*

this speculation is inadequate to explain why, on the two aberrant forms, the prior presentation of the high-risk situation produced a *higher* particularistic response to the two items than did the prior presentation of the low-risk situation.

The systematic study of the extent to which identification, salience, ego defenses, etc., modify questionnaire responses is still in its infancy. Hence, the superior results shown in Figure 3-3 on the form in which ego himself faced the dilemma should not tempt us to hasty conclusions. After all, (1) as Table 3-9 shows, all three forms yielded about the same pattern of distribution of scale types, and (2), as Figure 3-2 shows, all three scales showed about the same general relationship in the specific academic situations, including the cheating situation.[11]

11. In the high-risk cheating situation (not shown in Figure 3-2), when the two sequences of presentation are combined, there is also relatively little difference among the three forms, all showing a definite correlation with the scale types.

Our study suggests that it is possible to classify people according to a predisposition to select one or the other horn of a dilemma in role conflict. As more studies are made—not only with pencil-and-paper tests, but also with role-playing in experimental and real-life situations and with other procedures —information exceedingly important to social science can be derived. We must anticipate the possibility, as Edward A. Suchman of Cornell has suggested in a letter to the writers, that tendencies of a respondent to adopt more stereotyped roles in hypothetical than in real-life situations will complicate prediction.

Studies in this field will help sociologists in developing theories of institutionalization and social psychologists in developing theories of personality and, indeed, can serve as a crucial link between the two bodies of theory. The importance of such a link, employing such variables as particularism-universalism, affectivity-neutrality, specificity-diffuseness, self-other, has been in the forefront of the thinking of Talcott Parsons and associates, who have been working on a new schema looking toward unification of social science theory.[12] The immensity of the technical task involved in making such concepts amenable to measurement in the years of patient work that lie ahead is at least suggested by the experience of our present study. Indeed, one of the most important values of this paper should be its service as a brake on the enthusiasm of those who may anticipate quick and easy progress in moving from highly abstract concepts in social science to empirical operations.

Such studies as ours can also be applied in practical research if sustained effort is devoted to technical developments. Leadership, for example, involves skill in the solution of role conflicts. Classic examples are the foreman in industry or the noncommissioned officer in the army. If such thoughtful observers as Chester I. Barnard are correct, skill in handling role conflicts is also a *sine qua non* at the high executive levels.[13] Eventually, we may have role-playing situational tests, involving nonverbal as well as verbal behavior, that will be useful in the selection and training of leaders. The present study represents only a primitive effort to formulate some of the problems of definition and measurement.

NOTE ON LAZARSFELD'S LATENT-DISTANCE SCALE AS APPLIED TO ROLE-CONFLICT DATA

In *Measurement and Prediction*, chapter xi,[14] the reader will find a numerical example of a latent-distance analysis carried out in full, on Research Branch data on psychoneurotic symptoms. That analysis used only one computed parameter

12. Talcott Parsons and Edward Shils, eds., *Toward a General Theory of Action*, (Cambridge: Harvard University Press, 1951).

13. Chester I. Barnard, *The Functions of the Executive* (Cambridge: Harvard University Press, 1938), esp. chap. xvii.

14. Stouffer, *et al., op. cit.*, pp. 441-447.

Table 3-11

LATENT CLASS	ITEM			
	1	*2*	*3*	*4*
I	a_1	a_2	a_3	a_4
II	b_1	a_2	a_3	a_4
III	b_1	b_2	a_3	a_4
IV	b_1	b_2	b_3	a_4
V	b_1	b_2	b_3	b_4

for each item. In the present example on role-conflict data, Lazarsfeld, who kindly made the analysis, introduced more flexibility by computing two parameters for each item. The latent structure is set up as shown in Table 3-11. Each value of *a* tends to be a large fraction, and each value of *b* tends to be small. (The example in chapter xi added the restriction that $a_i = 1 - b_i$. In the perfect Guttman scale each $a = 1$ and each $b = 0$.) The algebra and arithmetical routine involved will be presented by Lazarsfeld in a separate paper. Final results, however, are shown here as Table 3-12, using as illustration, for reasons of space, only the form in which ego faces the dilemma. In this table the scale patterns are ordered as in Table 3-8 and do not follow precisely the rank order they would have in Lazarsfeld's schema. The most serious discrepancy between the ordering indicated by the Lazarsfeld model and by the scalogram procedure of scoring to the nearest scale type is with respect to pattern + − − + based on only four cases (see Table 3-12). The Lazarsfeld procedure would place this pattern within the top group. By scalogram procedure, to assign this pattern to the top group would be to imply that respondents made two "errors," in both Items 2 and 3, which, indeed, may have been the case. The present assignment implies only one error, on Item 1. The reader will note that two-error patterns + − + − and + + − −, with two cases and one case, respectively, that could have been assigned variously by scalogram methods, belong, by the Lazarsfeld model, just where they have been put.

Table 3-12. Illustrative Results of Fitting Latent-Distance Structure (Data for Form in Which Ego Faced Role Conflict)

ITEMS	PERCENTAGE OF EACH PATTERN IN EACH LATENT CLASS					TOTALS		
1 2 3 4	*I*	*II*	*III*	*IV*	*V*	Total	Fitted	Actual
+ + + +	95.9	4.0	0.1	....	....	100	19.1	20
+ − + +	94.8	3.9	0.2	0.2	0.9	100	10.0	9
+ + − +	91.7	3.7	3.0	0.3	1.3	100	6.5	6
+ + + −	95.7	4.3	....	....	....	100	2.5	2
+ − + −	96.7	3.3	....	....	....	100	1.3	2
+ + − −	92.3	5.1	2.6	....	....	100	0.8	1
− + + +	0.9	95.6	3.0	0.3	0.2	100	39.9	38
− + + −	0.8	87.7	2.7	0.4	8.4	100	5.7	7
− − + +	0.9	88.9	2.7	4.8	2.7	100	22.2	24
− − + −	0.3	34.8	1.2	1.7	62.0	100	7.4	6
− − − +	0.3	25.3	19.9	34.7	19.8	100	25.4	23
− + − +	0.5	52.3	41.2	3.8	2.2	100	23.7	25
+ − − +	86.2	3.6	2.4	4.8	3.0	100	3.6	4
− + − −	0.3	23.1	18.4	1.6	56.6	100	6.9	6
+ − − −	33.9	1.8	....	1.8	62.5	100	1.2	1
− − − −	....	2.1	1.6	2.8	93.5	100	41.0	42

The picture presented in Table 3-12 is analogous to the picture presented in *Measurement and Prediction*, chapter xi, Table 13, but it must be remembered that it has involved a more flexible basic design.

The last two columns of Table 3-12 show good agreement between the fitted and actual totals. Approximately as good a fit was obtained with the other two forms of the questionnaire, and the rank ordering of the scale patterns on the basis of the percentage of a given pattern in each latent class is not markedly different. Much further study is needed of the latent-distance model used here, especially with respect to reliability of small frequencies and, as has been mentioned earlier, to the testing of acceptance standards. The concept of a latent structure is theoretically quite appropriate to data of the type we are likely to assemble in subsequent investigations of role, and of informal social norms generally.

4

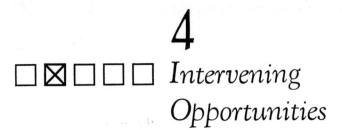 *Intervening Opportunities*

Here are two attempts to construct and test conceptual models that might account for the distribution of migrants over space. The first paper is called *Intervening Opportunities: A Theory Relating Mobility and Distance*. The empirical fit was moderately satisfying to the author at the time, even though there were some serious loose ends. With varied success, others replicated the work on other populations. It was suggested in the original paper, "Even where numerical data are inadequate for direct application of the theory of intervening opportunities, the general idea may be useful as a basic organizing principle in accounting for the *tendency* toward certain types of spatial patterns of population." Included might be such phenomena as spatial propinquity to the selection of marriage mates, relationship between certain types of crime and the residence of criminals, the choice of colleges, and the utilization of leisure and vacation time. Some such uses have been made, and the concept seems to have some interest to geographers as well as to sociologists.

As in almost any ideal model, of course, the necessary simplifications have led to failures to predict important aspects of the behavior studied. One of the major difficulties was in a failure to take into account *direction*. This is a defect which the author's model shares in common with those of a number of others, such as those of Zipf, Stewart, and Dodd, that were published subsequently.

Therefore, a study was undertaken leading to the second paper, entitled *Intervening Opportunities and Competing Migrants*. Here intervening opportunities are redefined. Moreover, account is taken of the fact that if a person wishes to go from a particular origin to point A or B, his choice will depend in part upon the numbers of potential migrants who are closer than he is to A or B, respectively. In this second paper, after working out an example in detail for a small set of cities for which previous models failed hopelessly, the author seeks to show that the revision handles these stubborn data quite well and then goes on to apply the concepts more widely.

Because of the heavy computation involved, it did not seem likely—certainly at the time the first paper appeared—that the ideas, however attractive theoretically, would receive very much empirical treatment. That situation has now changed, thanks to the ease with which problems like this can be handled on the new electronic computers, and it will be interesting to see what kind of follow-up research, if any, the second paper generates. This paper was published in 1960, although a preview of it was presented four years before at the American Sociological Society.

A. *Intervening Opportunities: A Theory Relating Mobility and Distance*

The movement of people in space is a basic subject of sociological inquiry. Since the classic work of Ravenstein a half-century ago, numerous studies have demonstrated a close relationship between mobility and distance. Most people go a short distance; few people go a long distance.[1]

"Intervening Opportunities: A Theory Relating Mobility and Distance," *American Sociological Review*, 5 (December, 1940), pp. 845-867.

This study was financed, in part, by the Social Science Research Committee, University of Chicago. Special recognition is owed to the writer's research assistant, Severn Provus, who contributed criticisms and suggestions as well as careful statistical work. Among others, particular acknowledgment is due to Frieda Brim, Robert Winch, Patricia Burt, and Richard Bair, University of Chicago. The present research grew out of a discussion with C. E. Lively of the University of Missouri, who has been making intensive studies of rural mobility. Preliminary unpublished papers by the writer, which were presented at the 1938 and 1939 annual meetings of the American Sociological Society, have been incorporated in the present paper.

1. E. G. Ravenstein, "The Laws of Migration," *J. Royal Statist. Soc.* 48: 167-235, June 1885; 52: 241-305, June 1889. A comprehensive annotated bibliography of modern studies is available in Dorothy S. Thomas, *Research Memorandum on Migration Differentials*,

Distance is such an important factor that it needs more explicit study than it has received. Whether one is seeking to explain "why" persons go to a particular place to get jobs, "why" they go to trade at a particular store, "why" they go to a particular neighborhood to commit crime, or "why" they marry the particular spouses they choose, the factor of spatial distance is of obvious significance.

Recently, the writer listened to a conversation between two educators who were talking about a survey made on students' reasons for choosing a certain small college. One educator asked the other to guess the most important reasons. A half dozen were suggested. "You have missed the most important," was the reply. "It is simply proximity." Yet, in the extensive literature, there has been little effort to analyze the ways in which distance operates to determine the distribution of population movements. Concepts like "push" and "pull" are used frequently, but it is not likely that their analysis can be very fruitful until the distance component in "push" and "pull" is conceptually and empirically isolated. If we say that Chicago has more "pull" on people from Iowa than does New York and that New York has more "pull" on people from Massachusetts than does Chicago, it is clear that we must deal with the distance factor in any analysis of the attraction of the two cities.

This paper seeks to make an addition to sociological theory by proposing a conceptual framework for attacking the problem of distance. The theory is offered as a key which may open at least an outer door, although like any simple abstract theory it may require considerable elaboration and modification if it is to explain a wide variety of actual events. The writer believes that what sociology most needs is basic theories that can be so stated that verification in particular cases is possible. Therefore, painstaking effort has been made to test the theory in a particular case. If other studies confirm the success of this initial effort at verification, we have here a modest formulation of a new sociological law. The ultimate utility of the abstract theory will be determined by the variety and abundance of concrete situations in which it proves helpful in providing at least an initial ordering of thinking and of data. As will be illustrated subsequently, a systematic numerical application is not likely to be easy. Data collected for other purposes may rarely be suitable. Even when quantitative data are inadequate or unavailable, the theory may have its uses in contributing to a logical framework for analyzing *tendencies*.

Social Science Research Council Bulletin No. 43, New York, 1938. Studies in which distance appears as an explicit factor are indexed in Thomas's monograph, pages 420-421. An important study, published too late to be listed in the monograph, should be cited: H. Makower, J. Marschak, and H. W. Robinson, "Studies in Mobility of Labor: A Tentative Statistical Measure," *Oxford Economic Papers*, Oct. 1938; see also two recent articles by the same authors, "Studies in Mobility of Labor: Analysis for Great Britain, Part I," *Oxford Economic Papers*, May 1939, 70-97, and same title and journal, Part II, Sept. 1940, 39-62.

The theory here proposed and studied empirically assumes that there is no necessary relationship between mobility and distance. Instead, it introduces the concept of *intervening opportunities*. It proposes that *the number of persons going a given distance is directly proportional to the number of opportunities at that distance and inversely proportional to the number of intervening opportunities*. Another way of stating the same hypothesis is that the number of persons going a given distance is directly proportional to the percentage increase in opportunities at that distance. Symbolically, let

Δy = number of persons moving from an origin to a circular band of width Δs, its inner boundary being $s - \frac{1}{2}\Delta s$ units of distance from the origin or center of the circle and its outer boundary being $s + \frac{1}{2}\Delta s$ units from the origin (Distance may be measured in units of space, or even of time or cost.)

x = number of intervening opportunities, that is, the cumulated number of opportunities between the origin and distance s (Opportunities must be precisely defined in any employment of the theory. The particular operational definition appropriate will depend on the type of social situation investigated. This is the hardest problem in any practical application. In the main body of the paper, a precise definition, appropriate to the concrete study here made, is developed.)

Δx = number of opportunities within the band of width Δs

Then, we postulate

$$\frac{\Delta y}{\Delta s} = \frac{a}{x}\frac{\Delta x}{\Delta s} \qquad (1)$$

This mathematical formulation has the virtue of precision and, with the aid of operational definitions of distance and opportunities, lends itself to verification. Actually, it merely says in symbols what is said more picturesquely and less precisely in the statement: A basic concept in handling movement and distance is the ratio of opportunities in the promised land to the intervening opportunities.

The main part of this paper is devoted to a verification of Equation 1 in a particular case. Before we proceed, however, some consideration of its implications may be desirable. Equation 1 does not specify a direct and invariant relation between mobility and distance. Rather it postulates a direct relation between mobility and opportunities. The relation between mobility and distance may be said to depend on an auxiliary relationship that expresses the cumulated (intervening) opportunities as a function of distance. This latter relationship may take any form, subject, of course, to the intrinsic limitation that it never decreases with increasing distance. It is not necessary to assume that it is a continuous function. Actually, the distribution of opportunities over space is the result of a multitude of historical, geographic, economic, political, and social factors and will vary from situation to situation. The distribution of opportunities in farming would radiate from an Indiana township quite differently from the way in which it would from a Texas township. The distribution of opportunities for stenographers or nurses would be different from the distribution of opportunities for unskilled laborers or Negro sharecroppers. If the theory embodied in Equation 1 holds, we should eventually be able to account for some of the observed differentials in the distance moved by members of different types of occupational groups, perhaps by sex and age. It is to be hoped that the new mobility data collected by the 1940 United States Census will be helpful in such a future investigation. Even where full numerical data are missing, the abstract theory presented here should, if it stands up under further research, serve to provide a cue for predicting the tendency of different types of specific population groups to assume certain types of spatial patterns in their mobility. Equation 1, as formulated, also has some interesting mathematical and psychological implications.

If we assume the existence of some continuous function

$$x = f(s) \tag{2}$$

and if we substitute differentials in Equation 1, giving

$$\frac{dy}{ds} = \frac{a}{x} \frac{dx}{ds} \tag{3}$$

we have, upon substituting (2) in (3) and integrating,

$$y = a \log f(s) + c \tag{4}$$

Equation 4 enables one to formulate the theory in somewhat different words. It will be understood that, in Equation 4, y is the cumulated number of movers between the origin and a circle of radius s and $f(s)$ is the cumulated number of opportunities within that circle. Thus, Equation 4 says that the total number of movers who stop *at any point within the circle* is directly proportional to the *logarithm* of the number of opportunities within the circle.

It may be asked why Equations 1 or 3 could not have been set up in such a form that Equation 4 would show the total number who stop at any point within the circle to be some function, other than the logarithm, of the number of opportunities within the circle. The answer is, of course, that this could have been done. However, there is at least some good common-sense basis for the type of equation chosen, apart from its great virtue of simplicity. It is unlikely that a person will have the same detailed knowledge of each far-distant opportunity that he has of the nearby opportunities. Let us call the opportunities of which he is aware *apparent* opportunities and denote them by the symbol z, in contrast with x, the *actual* opportunities. Let us then postulate that y_i, the number of persons who will move somewhere within distance s_i, is directly proportional to z_i, the number of *apparent* opportunities within the distance s_i. We now have

$$y_i = kz_i \tag{5}$$

But z_i is some function of x_i, such that as x_i increases, z_i increases more slowly. If we were dealing here with a simple problem in perception, the relationship between z_i and x_i, the *apparent* and *actual* number of opportunities, could be represented by the equation

$$z_i = m \log x_i + c' \tag{6}$$

the well-known Fechner law. This would be too simple a postulate to represent the actual socio-psychological situation. There is good reason to suspect, however, that the net effects of the complex actual factors, whatever they may be, would produce an equation closely analogous to Equation 6. It is unlikely that data exist at the present time enabling one to test a hypothesis involving an equation containing more parameters than those in Equation 6. Hence, there is no hesitation, as a first approximation, in substituting (6) in (5) and obtaining (4).

One further implication of Equation 4 may be noted. In an ideal special case, in which opportunities are distributed continuously throughout an area with a distribution function $x = ks^b$, Equation 4 would take the form

$$y = a' \log s + c' \tag{7}$$

This special case would be, as indicated, an ideal situation, probably never realized in experience, except possibly within a very short distance from the center of out-movement.

TEST OF THEORY ON CLEVELAND RESIDENTIAL MOBILITY DATA

We now proceed to a direct empirical investigation of Equation 1. The data selected are data on residential mobility in Cleveland, Ohio.[2] They are probably unique in the United States in their detail. Each year, for the three years 1933–1935, Howard Whipple Green obtained the addresses of all families moving within the Cleveland Metropolitan District. In a table, containing 321×321 cells, he tabulated the number of families moving from each census tract to every other census tract.

If Equation 1 holds, and if we can control enough disturbing factors, we should be able to use Green's data as a test of the theory of intervening opportunities, as applied to residential mobility in one metropolitan city. Specifically, we should be able to distribute theoretically the families mov-

2. H. W. Green, *Movements of Families within the Cleveland Metropolitan District*, Report No. 7 of the Real Property Inventory of the Metropolitan District, Cleveland, Ohio, 1936.

ing from dwellings within a given census tract to their places of future dwelling within the Cleveland Metropolitan District, and this expected spatial distribution should tend to agree with observations.

First, we report the results of applying Equation 1 to the movers from twelve census tracts inhabited by white persons. Of these tracts, seven are on the west side of Cleveland, five on the east side.

Figure 4-1(*a*), based on Table 4-1, summarizes the expected and actual frequency distribution of all moves according to distance from the twelve

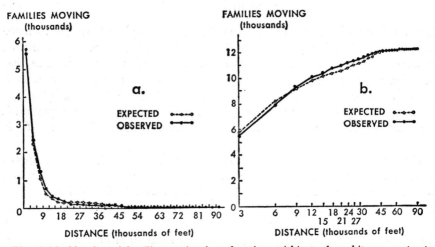

Figure 4-1. *Number of families moving from locations within twelve white census tracts, by intervals of distance. Comparison of expectation from Equation 1, with actual distribution. Cleveland, Ohio, 1933–1935. The data in a are taken from Table 4-1. Part b is a cumulative distribution of the data in a, with distance in logarithmic measure.*

tracts combined, during the three-year period. A more detailed discussion will be given later. The open circles connected by a dotted line represent the theoretical distribution, predicted by Equation 1; the black circles connected by a solid line the actual distribution. In general, it will be seen that the theory of intervening opportunities represented in Equation 1 agrees closely enough with observation to be encouraging. Many of the discrepancies are too large to attribute to chance, but a closer fit hardly would be expected, in view of the assumptions and approximations, presently to be discussed, which were involved in the processing of the data.

Figure 4-1(*b*) uses the same data, but presents the results in different form. Here we have a cumulative distribution of families moving. On the vertical axis is plotted the number moving a given distance or less. On the horizontal axis is plotted the logarithm of the distance. As in Figure 4-1(*a*), the expected numbers are shown by open circles and dotted lines, the observed by black circles and solid lines.

Figure 4-1(*b*) portrays, as does Figure 4-1(*a*), the general agreement between theory and observation, but it reveals more adequately an interesting discrepancy in the early middle distances. This discrepancy, as will be pointed out in more detail later, reflects the effect of a directional factor in the movement that could be only partly taken into account with the available data. In general, the excess movements to middle distances represent movements toward the edge of the city, westward if the tract lay west of the business section, eastward if the tract lay east of the business section.

Table 4-1. Number of Families Moving from Locations within Twelve White Census Tracts, by Intervals of Distance. Comparison of Expectation from Equation I with Actual Distribution, Cleveland, Ohio, 1933-1935

Distance in Thousands of Feet	Expected	Observed	Distance in Thousands of Feet	Expected	Observed
(1)	(2)	(3)	(4)	(5)	(6)
0– 2.9	5834	5585	48–50.9	57	30
3– 5.9	2332	2471	51–53.9	46	39
6– 8.9	1065	1313	54–56.9	39	31
9–11.9	563	737	57–59.9	27	17
12–14.9	355	431	60–62.9	17	12
15–17.9	217	320	63–65.9	8	5
18–20.9	214	217	66–68.9	6	3
21–23.9	223	178	69–71.9	6	4
24–26.9	204	172	72–74.9	7	4
27–29.9	207	125	75–77.9	1	2
30–32.9	196	137	78–80.9	..	2
33–35.9	175	106	81–83.9	..	2
36–38.9	157	85	84–86.9	..	2
39–41.9	133	102	87–89.9	..	..
42–44.9	111	102	90–92.9	..	1
45–47.9	78	57			
			Total	12,278	12,292

The long distances represent movements across the city to the edges on the opposite side, and such movements, except at the most extreme distances, were slightly less numerous than were predicted.[3]

A more detailed graphic comparison of the agreement between expectation and observation appears in Figure 4-2. Here, for each of the twelve census tracts, the expected number of families moving within a given distance band is plotted on the *x*-axis and the observed number on the *y*-axis.

3. Figure 4-1(*b*) is also of interest as showing how the theory based on Equation 1 and the observations *agree* in their uniform departure from what we postulated would have been the distribution in the ideal case represented by Equation 7. If the opportunities actually had been homogeneously distributed, the data in Figure 4-1(*b*) should have formed a logarithmic straight line ($y = a' \log s + c$). Both lines clearly curve, reflecting the fact that the empirical distribution of cumulated opportunities increased rapidly in the early and middle distances and then, with considerable abruptness, began to slow up, eventually becoming asymptotic.

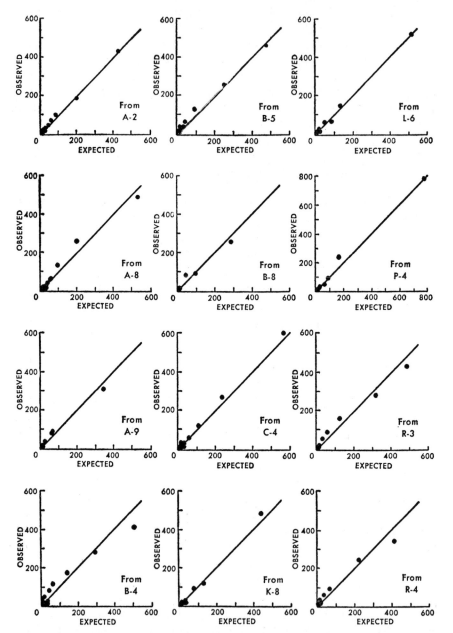

Figure 4-2. Number of families moving from locations within each of twelve white census tracts, by intervals of distance. Comparison of expectation, from Equation 1, with actual distribution. Cleveland, Ohio, 1933–1935. Data are from Table 4-2.

The data are taken from Table 4-2. If the theory represented by Equation 1 predicted the observations perfectly, the data would all lie on the diagonal. For example, we predict that 431 families will move within a distance of 3000 feet from their home in A2. The observed number is 440.

It was thought that a particularly interesting test of the theory would be provided by applying it to Negro tracts because of the barriers erected against free mobility. Therefore, ten tracts extending through the heart of the Black Belt were chosen and an effort made to predict the intratract and intertract movements by Equation 1. The results are shown in Figure 4-3, the data appearing in Table 4-3. As in Figure 4-2, the observed data are plotted against the actual data and perfect agreement would be represented by all points lying on the diagonal. For example, we predict that in Table 4-3, 70 would leave Tract H9 for Tract M8. Actually, the observed number was 65. As we inspect Figure 4-3, we see, as in the white tracts, a rather satisfactory agreement. The tracts nearer the center of the city, such as H9, I7, and I8, tended to receive slightly fewer in-movers than expected and the tracts farther from the center of the city, such as M3, M4, and M5, slightly more, indicating, as in the white tracts, the operation of a directional factor that data and technique did not permit taking fully into account. The general pattern of agreement between expectation and observation is, however, unmistakable.

DESCRIPTION OF THE TECHNIQUE USED IN TESTING THE THEORY

The first problem is to formulate an operational definition of opportunities. If a person moves from Tract X to a house or an apartment in Tract Y, there must have been previously created in Tract Y a vacancy which he could occupy. The particular vacancy which he occupied and similar vacancies anywhere in the city which he might have occupied but did not, we will call *opportunities*. Similar vacancies which are closer to his former residence in X than the dwelling he occupied in Y we shall call *intervening opportunities*.[4]

But this is not enough. What do we mean by *similar vacancies?* Since no two vacancies are exactly alike, we must select certain relevant characteristics. One might be the economic character of the dwelling, as measured by the rental. For example, if he pays 50 dollars per month for his new dwelling, the similar opportunities would be limited to vacancies at about the same rental value. Another characteristic might depend on whether he is moving to a rented dwelling or buying a house. If the latter, the similar opportunities would be limited to purchasable residences at about the same value. Other characteristics might be determined by the direction, the newness of the

4. In studying some other kind of mobility, different definitions of opportunities would be needed, of course; for example, job openings or farms available.

Table 4-2. Number of Families from Locations within Each of Twelve White Census Tracts, by Intervals of Distance. Comparison of Expectation from Equation 1 with Actual Distribution, Cleveland, Ohio, 1933-1935

DISTANCE IN THOUSANDS OF FEET	A2		A8		A9		B4		B5		B8		C4		K8		L6		P4		R3		R4	
	Exp.	Obs.	Exp.	Obs.	Exp.	Obs.	Exp.	Obs.	Exp.	Obs.	Exp.	Obs.	Exp.	Obs.	Exp.	Obs.	Exp.	Obs.	Exp.	Obs.	Exp.	Obs.	Exp.	Obs.
(1)	(2)	(3)	(4)	(5)	(6)	(7)	(8)	(9)	(10)	(11)	(12)	(13)	(14)	(15)	(16)	(17)	(18)	(19)	(20)	(21)	(22)	(23)	(24)	(25)
0– 2.9	431	440	513	493	349	311	508	410	485	473	288	253	572	609	452	483	528	536	793	784	491	442	424	351
3– 5.9	199	187	194	258	60	78	296	280	253	258	98	92	242	260	125	122	146	153	172	250	287	229	229	246
6– 8.9	80	97	88	118	64	81	141	173	91	126	46	84	105	120	77	94	86	74	87	97	130	156	70	93
9–11.9	54	73	54	57	25	40	66	112	43	72	15	22	59	56	27	27	51	66	73	52	92	92	40	68
12–14.9	44	50	35	43	21	21	47	77	30	35	9	15	32	38	29	18	28	23	36	33	56	56	16	22
15–17.9	26	30	13	17	7	17	22	50	12	35	15	17	24	37	19	9	29	27	28	18	36	56	32	32
18–20.9	17	19	19	17	11	13	21	49	16	13	15	22	26	21	17	8	26	14	23	33	22	26	13	8
21–23.9	22	27	18	17	14	8	13	18	24	14	11	11	34	14	25	13	22	13	19	16	17	22	9	19
24–26.9	19	14	18	14	13	10	16	21	22	21	15	8	30	26	18	11	22	14	23	15	21	9	8	6
27–29.9	24	20	26	14	16	8	12	11	28	10	11	13	30	17	17	13	11	4	22	21	12	13	13	5
30–32.9	23	19	17	3	13	6	17	21	14	9	14	13	31	21	25	14	10	4	17	17	8	10	8	4
33–35.9	17	14	19		9	7	23	12	15	11	13	13	21	17	18	11	8	8	22	14	9	4	5	8
36–38.9	20	8	18		11	3	28	15	23	10	6	3	21	10	6	12	6	10	13		7	10	6	4
39–41.9	18	14	13	12	6	3	19	10	14	12	9	4	14	14	8	6	6	8	12	8	11	12	8	7
42–44.9	15	13	13	3	3	4	16	10	12		6	3	7	8	6	6	4	4	8	2	6	4	7	3
45–47.9	8	8	5		2	3	12	5	5	1	1	1	5	6	5	5	5	2	5	3	6	7	4	2
48–50.9	4	8	4		1	4	6	4	4	4		2	5	2	2	2	4	10	7	4	8	9	5	4
51–53.9	4	4	4			2	6	5	3		2		2	2	1	1	6	4	5	3	7	9	5	2
54–56.9	3	1	3		2		5	6	3	1	2	2	4	2	1	2	3	2	4	5	6	10	8	5
57–59.9	1		2	1	2		3	2	2	1	2		5	2		1	2	3	3	5	6	12	7	2
60–62.9	1	1	2			2	1	2	2	1		1	2		1	2	4	7	2		4	10	6	4
63–65.9							1	2	2	2		2	2			2	3	9		1	3	9	5	3
66–68.9			2				1		3	4		2	2		1	1	2	7	3		2	4	4	2
69–71.9			2					1					2	2		1	3	4	5	3	7	7	7	3
72–74.9	1												2		1		4	9	5	5	4	4	4	4
75–77.9	1												2	2			2	10	3	1	5	3	2	5
78–80.9							1									1			1		2			
81–83.9						2		1		2		1					2	3	1		1	1	2	2
84–86.9																								
87–89.9				1				1												1		1		
90–92.9																								1
Total	1,032	1,034	1,114	1,113	633	634	1,316	1,316	1,116	1,118	551	552	1,274	1,273	843	845	990	991	1,345	1,349	1,771	1,172	893	895

neighborhood to which he moved, or the nationality composition. Thus, an area zoned against Negroes would not provide any opportunities for Negroes, or an area settled solidly by Italians would provide few opportunities for members of other ethnic groups, unless it were an area in transition.

Actually, in the present study only two of the criteria of similarity sug-

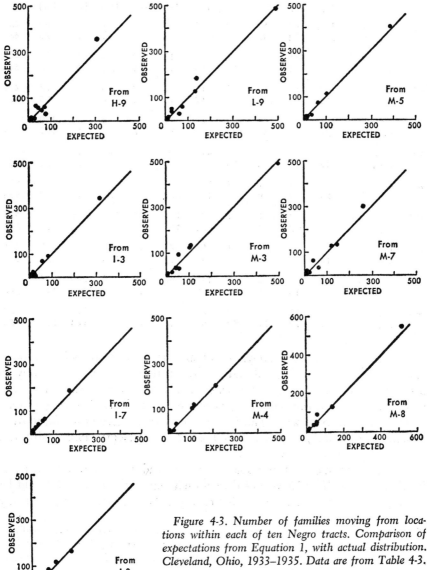

Figure 4-3. Number of families moving from locations within each of ten Negro tracts. Comparison of expectations from Equation 1, with actual distribution. Cleveland, Ohio, 1933–1935. Data are from Table 4-3.

Table 4-3. Number of Families Moving from Locations within Each of Ten Negro Tracts, by Tract of New Location. Comparison of Expectation from Equation I with Actual Distribution, Cleveland, Ohio, 1933-1935

TRACTS FROM WHICH FAMILIES MOVED	COMPARI-SONS	TRACTS TO WHICH FAMILIES MOVED										TOTALS
		H9	I3	I7	I8	L9	M3	M4	M5	M7	M8	
(1)	(2)	(3)	(4)	(5)	(6)	(7)	(8)	(9)	(10)	(11)	(12)	(13)
H9	Observed	351	49	52	62	50	9	11	7	32	65	688
	Expected	303	54	45	40	54	25	11	11	75	70	688
I3	Observed	93	336	69	21	16	13	2	6	10	18	584
	Expected	88	310	59	22	25	15	9	...	23	33	584
I7	Observed	68	60	191	45	11	3	3	5	12	27	425
	Expected	68	62	172	43	17	12	6	6	14	25	425
I8	Observed	94	26	49	169	22	15	4	8	28	120	535
	Expected	78	23	69	174	24	15	6	8	28	109	534
L9	Observed	32	12	4	5	489	189	50	48	123	52	1004
	Expected	59	15	13	16	487	140	31	32	138	72	1003
M3	Observed	14	2	1	4	132	481	131	96	38	34	933
	Expected	23	9	9	9	117	499	114	53	48	52	933
M4	Observed	5	3	1	1	45	121	208	119	9	13	525
	Expected	11	7	6	5	31	117	211	102	15	21	526
M5	Observed	7	3	...	1	26	77	111	407	11	12	655
	Expected	14	...	5	6	37	65	102	383	18	24	654
M7	Observed	37	5	10	7	118	64	19	19	300	134	713
	Expected	69	13	11	23	120	43	12	11	264	148	714
M8	Observed	51	18	9	42	82	36	18	29	132	552	969
	Expected	61	22	21	58	66	47	16	17	143	519	970

gested have been used, namely, rental and race. The following working definition of opportunities, determined by restrictions of data presently to be discussed, was adopted: *For a white family leaving a dwelling in rental group K in Tract X, the number of opportunities in Tract Y is proportional to the total number of white families, whatever their place of origin, moving to dwellings in rental group K within Tract Y.* For a Negro family, substitute Negro for white in the above definition.[5]

Even the necessary information on rental and race, however, was not directly available. The Cleveland data do not report the new rental paid by a family moving from A2 to A1, for example. Nor do the data report any

---

5. At first glance, this definition may seem to favor the hypothesis unduly; actually, it does not, because it says nothing about the origin of those moving. It simply postulates that the number of opportunities in an area is proportionate to the number of families moving to dwellings within the area. These families merely may have moved from next door or may have come long distances. The theory then attempts to account for the number moving from a *particular origin* to this area.

other characteristics of this family. They simply report the total number of families moving. The first problem which had to be solved then, was how to infer the characteristics of the family indirectly.

Another publication,[6] based upon a real property inventory in 1934, opened the road to an approximation. First, it showed that such a large proportion of the movement was to rented dwellings that for all practical purposes movements to newly purchased residences could be ignored. Second, it gave for each tract a frequency distribution by broad class intervals of rental of the dwellings occupied less than one year by their tenants. This

Table 4-4. Data for Two Census Tracts to Illustrate Method of Allocating the Observed Data to Rental Groups

					RENTAL				
ITEMS	TRACT	Under $10	$10 -14	$15 -19	$20 -29	$30 -49	$50 -74	$75 and Over	TOTAL
(1)	(2)	(3)	(4)	(5)	(6)	(7)	(8)	(9)	(10)
Percentage distribution of rented homes occupied	A1	. . .	0.5	3.8	19.6	52.4	19.0	4.7	100.0
less than one year (1934)	A2	0.2	0.9	15.6	42.6	33.9	0.8	. . .	100.0
Number of families moving	A1	(. . .)*	(15)	(113)	(583)	(1,559)	(565)	(140)	2,975
to census tract (1933-1935)	A2	(2)	(85)	(191)	(522)	(415)	(10)	(. . .)	1,225
Number of families moving from census tract (1933-1935)	A2	(2)	(71)	(161)	(441)	(351)	(8)	(. . .)	1,034

* Figures in parentheses are estimates, made by applying percentages in the first two rows to observed totals. Thus, 0.038 × 2,975 = 113, 0.069 × 1,225 = 85, 0.069 × 1,034 = 71. For source, see text.

could be converted into a percentage distribution as in illustrative Table 4-4. The total number of people moving to tract A1 at any time in the three-year period, namely, 2,975, was assumed to be distributed, by rental, in the same proportions. Similar calculations were made for A2 and for all other tracts.

From Table 4-4, we estimate, for example, that in the three-year period, 565 families moved to locations within A1, renting at 50 to 74 dollars. It is evident, however, that these vacancies could not constitute opportunities for many movers from A2, since only ten of the dwellings vacated by residents of A2 and reoccupied rented for 50 to 74 dollars. Unless those vacating dwellings in A2 stepped up decidedly in rental, there could have been almost no movement from A2 to the 50- to 74-dollar dwellings in A1. Since the higher rental tracts as a whole did not gain by migration appreciably more than the lower rental tracts, and vice versa, it is probable that the change in economic

6. H. W. Green, *Standards of Living in the Cleveland Metropolitan District*, Special 1935 Report of the Real Property Inventory of Metropolitan Cleveland, Cleveland, Ohio, 1935.

conditions between 1933 and 1935 was not marked by any substantial average movement upward or downward in the rental scale.[7]

Therefore, we can simplify our task if we divide the families leaving A2 into separate economic strata and conceive each group as moving, on the average, within its own respective stratum. Actually, 1,034 families moved out from dwellings inside of A2. We assume that, on the average, they were distributed in new dwellings in the same rental groups as the newcomers replacing them in A2. Thus, if, from Table 4-4, 15.6 per cent of the new-comers to A2 occupied dwellings renting from 15 to 19 dollars, we assume that 15.6 per cent of the 1,034 families leaving a location in A2, or 161 families, moved into dwellings renting from 15 to 19 dollars. In other words, we define, for each of these 161 families, "opportunities" as constituting those *available* dwellings anywhere in the Cleveland Metropolitan District which had rented within the past year for 15 to 19 dollars. From Table 4-4, column 5, we see that there were 113 such opportunities in A1. By extending Table 4-4 to include all tracts in the city, it was possible to estimate the number of opportunities, corresponding to 113 in A1, in each tract.

The next step was to construct a spot map of Cleveland on which all opportunities in the rental group 15 to 19 dollars were recorded. This step introduced another major problem in procedure, in addition to the inferring of the characteristics of the family by the above indirect means. We did not have the exact addresses of these dwellings. Therefore, their approximate location within a tract had to be estimated. This was done with the aid of maps giving assessed valuations for the Cleveland Metropolitan District,[8] and with the generous assistance of Robert Winch, a graduate student at the University of Chicago. He also is a resident of Cleveland and knows the city well. For each rental group, a spot map was made of the Cleveland Metropolitan District, by census tracts, the dots being located as accurately as possible on the basis of the above knowledge. It was found by empirical test that errors in the spotting of dwellings or "opportunities" would not appreciably affect the results when considered in relation to a tract of out-movement which was at a distance of over a mile or two. However, when the tract of out-movement considered was one close to the tract providing the opportunities, small changes in the location of the dots made relatively

7. From tracts with 1930 median rental under 40 dollars, 23,251 families moved out and 25,446 families moved in at some time during 1933–1935. From tracts with median rental over 40 dollars, 27,115 families moved out and 30,834 families moved in (computed from data in *Movements of Families within the Cleveland Metropolitan District, op. cit.*, p. 4). Objection may be raised that the procedure employed would not be applicable if there were great upward mobility, that is, if most movers shifted to better homes; or vice versa. However, a numerical adjustment could have been made with relative ease to take care of this situation. The application of the theory is not limited to a relatively static economic time interval.

8. *The Principles of Land and Building Appraisals as Scientifically Applied in Cuyahoga County*, published in 1932 by the Board of County Commissioners, Cuyahoga County, Ohio.

greater difference. In the latter case, plotting errors were minimized if the tracts were small and densely populated, but errors were probably larger in sparsely populated tracts, owing to the difficulty in accurately centering the dots.

To reduce the subsequent labor (which required several months of clerical work), class intervals were used in spotting. Thus, in the rental group 15 to 19 dollars, one dot represented fifty opportunities, except in tracts far distant from those selected for out-movement investigation. In the distant tracts, a number was entered to represent the number of dots which might have been plotted.

Imagine then a spot map of the Cleveland Metropolitan District showing the opportunities available within each tract at rental 15 to 19 dollars. The next step may be understood by reference to Figure 4-4, which reproduces a very small segment of this map surrounding Tract A2. This map is drawn to

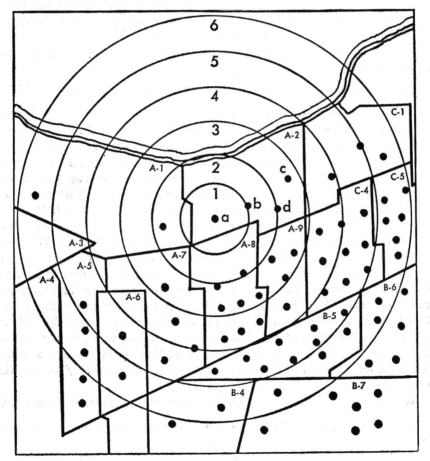

Figure 4-4. Segment of map of Cleveland, Ohio, with dots and circles to illustrate method of calculating the distribution of "opportunities" (see pages 82-86).

the same scale as Green's map of Cleveland.[9] Consider the dot in A2 here labeled *a*. A sheet of transparent paper, ruled in concentric circles, was laid on the map, with the center of the circles at *a*. The intervals between the circles represent 1,000 feet on Green's map. We now count the number of dots lying within one interval of *a*, two intervals, three intervals, etc., and record the tract in which they lie. For example, for a family leaving a dwelling in the region of spot *a*, *there was one* (times 50, of course) opportunity[10] in the first interval of distance, lying within A2; three opportunities in the second interval of distance, of which one was in A2, one in A1, and one in A8; ten opportunities in the third interval, of which two were in A2, one in A1, four in A8, and three in A9, and similarly for other intervals of distance. When these data were recorded, the map was shifted to center the circles at dot *b*, and similarly at *c* and *d*.

When the data for *a*, *b*, *c*, and *d* were added, a table similar to illustrative Table 4-5 was constructed. The sum of the columns gives Δx for this rental group, where Δx is proportional to the number of opportunities within a given distance band. The values of Δx were cumulated and x, the intervening opportunities, determined by linear interpolation on the cumulative distribution. Thus,

$$x_2 \text{ at the second interval of distance} = x_1 + \tfrac{1}{2}\Delta x_2 = 8 + (\tfrac{1}{2})(14) = 15$$

Next we calculate the ratios $\Delta x/x$ that appear on the bottom row of illustrative Table 4-6. In Equation 1, it will be remembered $\Delta x/x$ represents the ratio of opportunities in a given distance band to the intervening opportunities. (Actually, $100\,\Delta x/x$ was calculated, to avoid decimals.) Each of these ratios was then broken down and distributed among the various tracts in the same proportions as the opportunities in each tract (as shown in Table 4-5). In the third column of Table 4-5, for example, 1/14 of the opportunities were in A1. In Table 4-6 in the thrid column of the row opposite A1, therefore, we enter $(1/14)(100\,\Delta x/x) = (1/14)(93) = 7$. When we add across the rows, we have for each tract an expected number of movers to it from all points in A2 that should be proportional to the actual number. For example, the sum for A1 is 12. Such sums are shown in the next-to-last column of Table 4-6 and have a total of 764. But the total in rental group 15 to 19 dollars who left a dwelling in A2 we estimated earlier (Table 4-4) at 161 families. Therefore, by multiplying the individual values in the next-to-last column by 161/764, we have our expectation of the number who left Tract A2 for all tracts in the metropolitan area. The ratio 161/764 is *a*, the constant of proportionality, in Equation 1.

We still cannot check these numbers against observation, because, it will

9. H. W. Green, *Census Tracts of Greater Cleveland*, map published by Cleveland Health Council.

10. For each family in the neighborhood of dot *a*, there would be fifty opportunities, or possibly more strictly, $50 - 1 = 49$.

Table 4-5. Section of Work Sheet Illustrating Method of Tabulating Opportunities Available to Movers from 15 to 19-dollar Locations within Tract A2

TRACT IN WHICH OPPORTUNITY OCCURRED	DISTANCE FROM LOCATION IN A2 (THOUSANDS OF FEET)													*	78–80.9
	0–0.9	1–1.9	2–2.9	3–3.9	4–4.9	5–5.9	6–6.9	7–7.9	8–8.9	9–11.9	12–14.9	15–17.9	18–20.9	*	78–80.9
(1)	(2)	(3)	(4)	(5)	(6)	(7)	(8)	(9)	(10)	(11)	(12)	(13)	(14)	*	(15)
A1		1†	1	1	1	1	1	2						*	
A2	8	5	3											*	
A3							3	4	5	4				*	
A5					1	3	6	6	3	1				*	
A6					1	3	3	1						*	
A7			1	3	7	4	1							*	
A8		1	11	14	5	1								*	
A9		3	10	3										*	
B4						1	4	5	4	2				*	
B5			2	29	8	1								*	
B6				6	14	15	4	1						*	
B7					4	12	9	3						*	
C1		2	2	5	2	1								*	
C2					1	3	2	1	1					*	
C4		2	11	16	6	1								*	
C5			10	15	10	5								*	
C6				1	8	8	6	4	1					*	
C8					5	8	10	6	3					*	
*	*	*	*	*	*	*	*	*	*	*	*	*	*	*	*
Other tracts							2	20	48	140	124	60	44	*	8
Δx	8	14	39	54	75	67	71	68	75	151	124	60	44	*	8
ΣΔx	8	22	61	115	190	257	328	396	471	622	746	806	850	*	3,006
x	4	15	42	88	153	224	293	362	434	547	684	776	828	*	3,002

* Omitted to save space. This is an illustrative table.

† The entry 1, opposite A1 in column headed 1–1.9 means that the opportunities in A1 at this distance from A2 were 1 (times 50).

be remembered, our observations of families actually moving from A2 to, say, A1 are not broken down by rental groups. Therefore, we repeat for all other rental groups the procedure described above with respect to rental group 15 to 19 dollars. Then we form Table 4-7. The third column of numbers in this table, it will be observed, is the same as the last column of Table 4-6, and the other columns are analogous for other rental groups. Adding the entries in a given row, we have a sum that represents the expected number moving from all points within A2 to the tract represented in that row. This sum is entered in the next to last column of Table 4-7, and the observed number is entered in the last column. For example, to Tract A1, we estimated that 3 families would go in rental groups 15 to 19 dollars, 13 in group 20 to 29 dollars, and 41 in group 30 to 49 dollars. Total, 57; actually, 70 went. To points within Tract A2 itself, we estimated that 329 would go; the actual number was 373.

Because of the crudities of the procedure, particularly the errors intro-

Table 4-6. Section of Work Sheet Illustrating Method of Applying Equation 1 to the Data in Table 4-5

TRACT IN WHICH OPPOR-TUNITY OCCURRED	DISTANCE FROM LOCATION IN A2 (THOUSANDS OF FEET)																ADJUSTED TOTAL†
	1	2	3	4	5	6	7	8	9	10–11.9	13–15	16–18	19–21	*	78–80.9	Total	
(1)	(2)	(3)	(4)	(5)	(6)	(7)	(8)	(9)	(10)	(11)	(12)	(13)	(14)	*	(15)	(16)	(17)
A1		7	2	1	1				1					*		12	3
A2	200	33	7											*		240	51
A3						1	1	1	1					*		4	1
A5					1	1	2	2	1					*		7	1
A6					1	1	1							*		3	1
A7			2	3	5	2								*		12	3
A8		7	26	16	3									*		52	11
A9		20	24	3										*		47	10
B4						1	1	1						*		3	1
B5				2	19	4								*		25	5
B6					4	6	5	1						*		16	3
B7					2	4	2	1						*		9	2
C1		13	5	6	1									*		25	5
C2					1	1	1							*		3	1
C4		13	26	18	4									*		61	13
C5				11	10	4	2							*		27	6
C6					1	4	3	2	1					*		11	2
C8						2	3	3	1	1				*		10	2
*	*	*	*	*	*	*	*	*	*	*	*	*	*	*	*		
Other tracts							1	6	11	26	18	8	5	*	0	197‡	42‡
100 Δx/x	200	93	93	61	49	30	24	19	17	28	18	8	5	*	0	764	163§

* Omitted to save space.
† The procedure is to redistribute 100 Δx/x from Table 4-5 within each column in the same proportion as individual cell entries in Table 4-5 bear to Δx. The final column (17) is the expected numbers leaving a location within A2 for each specified new location within rental group 15 to 19 dollars.
‡ Actually, separate figures were calculated for tracts, within each interval of distance.
§ From illustrative Table 4-4, the number leaving a location within Tract A2 for locations renting at 15 to 19 dollars is estimated at 161. The discrepancy between 163 and 161 is due to rounding. The figures in column 17 were obtained by multiplying those in column 16 by 161/764.

duced by the use of broad class intervals and arbitrary spotting, there is bound to be considerable inaccuracy in predicting the movement to individual tracts. If more detailed data had been accessible, many of these errors might have been avoided. Therefore, it is preferable to make a final grouping of tracts into broader intervals. This was done by taking intervals of 3,000 feet and assigning each tract in its entirety to that interval of distance from A2 in which the majority of the opportunities occurred. Thus, A8 and A9, as well as A2 itself, fall in the first interval, A1, A7, B5, C1, C4, and C5 in the second interval, etc. The sum of the expectations in the first interval is 431; of the observations, 440. The sum of the expectations in the second interval is 199; of the observations, 187.

These are the data appearing in Table 4-2 and Figure 4-2 for movements from each of the twelve white tracts studied. Table 4-1 is formed by summing Table 4-2 for each interval of distance.

Table 4-7. Section of Consolidation Sheet Illustrating Method of Combining Estimates from Last Column of Work Sheets Like Table 4-6 to Obtain Final Estimate of Number of Families Leaving a Location within A-2 to Other Locations

TRACT OF DESTINATION	EXPECTED NUMBER OF FAMILIES MOVING, BY RENTAL GROUPS				EXPECTED NUMBER OF FAMILIES MOVING	OBSERVED NUMBER OF FAMILIES MOVING
	$10–14	$15–19	$20–29	$30–49		
(1)	(2)	(3)	(4)	(5)	(6)	(7)
A1	..	3	13	41	57	70
A2	24	51	141	113	329	373
A3	..	1	5	7	13	31
A5	..	1	7	6	14	28
A6	..	1	4	2	7	15
A7	..	3	13	9	25	22
A8	3	11	25	17	56	47
A9	3	10	22	7	42	18
B4	..	1	9	5	15	10
B5	2	5	8	3	18	8
B6	2	3	3	...	8	3
B7	1	2	4	...	7	2
C1	2	5	9	5	21	37
C2	..	1	1	...	2	3
C4	9	13	28	6	56	43
C5	3	6	8	3	20	7
C6	2	2	3	2	9	4
C8	1	2	2	...	5	1
To other tracts*	19	42	137	130	328	312
Expected	71	163	442	356	1,032	....
Observed†	73‡	161	441	359§	....	1,034

* Actually, separate figures were calculated for tracts within each interval of distance.
† The total of the observed, 1,034, is known. (See Table 4-4.) The distribution of the observed, by rental, is estimated by the procedure illustrated in Table 4-4.
‡ Includes two families from rental <10 dollars.
§ Includes eight families from rental 50–74 dollars.

Actually, one other restriction was made in the operational definition of opportunities as described above. Since, except in a few transitional census tracts, a dwelling vacated by a Negro would not be sought by a white person and vice versa, it was necessary to make separate estimates of opportunities for Negroes and whites. In the absence of direct information on mobility by race, an indirect method was required. This method is illustrated in Table 4-8, for Tract M4. First, the percentage of Negroes living in each rental group (for rented dwellings only) was calculated from data in the Real Property Inventory. In rental group 20 to 29 dollars, for example, the percentage was 91.5. Second, the percentage in each rental group reported as living in rented dwellings less than one year was arbitrarily divided into white and Negro by multiplying by this percentage. In Table 4-8, the percentage 27.6 (column 6) on the second line was multiplied by 0.915, giving new percentages, 2.3 for whites and 25.3 for Negroes, which were entered on lines 3 and 4, respectively. From the mobility volume, as in illustrative Table 4-4, we known that 980 families moved at some time within the three-year period into a dwelling in Tract M4. We distribute this number by race according to rental, in lines 6 and 7 of Table 4-8 by multiplying it by the

Table 4-8. Data to Illustrate Method of Allocating Observed Data by Race, According to Rental, for Census Tract M4

ITEMS	LINES	RENTAL					TOTAL
		Under $10	$10 –14	$15 –19	$20 –29	$30 –49	
(1)	(2)	(3)	(4)	(5)	(6)	(7)	(8)
Percentage of Negro families among families living in rented dwellings (1934)	(1)	77.4	86.4	86.2	91.5	91.5	. . . .
Percentage distribution of rented dwellings occupied less than 1 year (1934)	(2)	5.9	21.1	32.9	27.6	12.5	100.0
Whites (estimated)	(3)	1.3	2.9	4.5	2.3	1.1	
Negroes (estimated)	(4)	4.6	18.2	28.4	25.3	11.4	
Number of families moving to M4 (1933-1935)	(5)						980
Whites (estimated)	(6)	13	28	44	22	11	
Negroes (estimated)	(7)	45	179	278	248	112	
Number of Families leaving M4 for other locations in Cleveland metropolitan district (1933-1935)	(8)						866
Whites (estimated)	(9)	11	25	39	20	9	
Negroes (estimated)	(10)	40	158	246	219	99	

respective percentages in lines 3 and 4. Similarly, we know that 866 left dwellings in Tract M4 for some other point in the Cleveland Metropolitan District. We distribute these 866 families by race according to rental by multiplying 866 by the percentages in lines 3 and 4 and record the numbers in lines 9 and 10.

The opportunities for movers from the white tracts, therefore, were defined as limited to the numbers in line 6. These numbers, not the totals for both races, were plotted on the maps for calculating opportunities for families moving from the twelve white tracts.

A completely new set of maps was required, in addition, for calculating the movements from the ten Negro tracts reported earlier in Figure 4-3 and Table 4-3. These maps showed Negro opportunities only, such as defined for M4 by line 7 of Table 4-8. In other words, for the Negro tracts, twice as many operations were required as for the white tracts, since separate and independent estimates had to be made of the movements of Negroes and whites within these tracts. Thus, for movement from a Negro tract, we had two tables corresponding to Table 4-7 and then combined the figures in the last column. However, the task was lightened by the fact that the Negro population is so heavily concentrated in a rather small area.

A word should be said about the problem of spotting Negro and white opportunities on the map for tracts containing both races. This was necessarily rather rough, but it was facilitated by the courtesy of the Bureau of the Census. Leon E. Truesdell furnished a special tabulation for each mixed tract of the 1930 population by enumeration districts according to race, and Clarence E. Batschelet supplied photostats of maps showing enumeration district boundaries. Some allowance was made, in plotting, for probable shifts in racial composition between 1930 and 1935.

CONCLUDING COMMENTS

The detailed description of the operations has doubtless been tedious to the reader, but there is no other way of making explicit and objective the mold in which the definitions adopted had to be shaped. The definition of opportunities, given in italics on page 80, is a general verbal formulation, but the definition as used cannot be completely understood except in terms of the unfolding statistical operations.

We have shown, then, in Figures 4-1, 4-2, and 4-3 and accompanying tables, that the agreement between expectation and observation is encouraging. The principal discrepancies arise, as would be expected by anyone familiar with the process of city growth, because the opportunities, *as defined*, take no account of *direction* of movement. Extend a line from the center of the city through Tract X. Actually, a dwelling in rental group K lying on or near this line farther from the center of the city than X is likely to be more attractive, *on the average*, to a mover from X than a dwelling in rental group K lying nearer the center of the city than X and the same distance from X as the outlying dwelling. Indeed, if this bias had not appeared in Figures 4-1, 4-2, and 4-3, we should have been surprised and puzzled. It would be quite possible, however, to subsume this directional factor within the theory here presented. Just as we divided our universe into two racial groups and again into several rental groups, we could make one further subdivision, as follows: (*a*) those to whom direction is irrelevant and (*b*) those for whom opportunities comprise only dwellings of rental group K *in a certain general direction* from Tract X. The entire study could be done in duplicate by applying Equation 1 to each of these two groups, (*a*) and (*b*), and the results pooled at the end. There would be a difficult empirical problem of determining the relative total numbers assignable to (*a*) and (*b*), respectively. (This also was difficult with respect to race and rental.) Empirically, as a first approximation, one might go through the operations as in the present study, determine the total excess of the observed to expected in a given direction, and use this excess as a basis for estimating the relative size of (*b*). Then, considering only opportunities in the one direction, one could redistribute the excess by a reapplication of Equation 1. The point to be made here is that the directional factor involves no more *logical* difficulties with our theory than the racial or economic factor.

Still another factor, not explicitly considered in the present operations, is the nationality (other than racial) factor. Again, logically, this involves no insurmountable difficulties. Practically, however, because of lack of data it was not possible to deal with it as neatly as was the case with Negroes. To a considerable extent, the control by rental seemed to take care of ethnic differences, but not entirely. The influence of the ethnic factor (other than Negro-white) may be seen, for example, in the movements from the east-side tracts studied. At the eastern edge of Cleveland, where the city merges into East Cleveland, was the largest concentration of Jewish population in 1930. Tracts P5 and P6 were Jewish areas with moderately high rentals. From Tract P4, also a Jewish tract, the observed movement to P5 and P6 was 257, as compared with only 156 as estimated by Equation 1 using a definition of opportunities which ignored the ethnic (other than Negro-white) factor. From Tracts K8, L6, R3, and R4, containing relatively few Jewish families, the observed movement to P5 and P6 was 142, as compared with 170 estimated. Similarly, some of the discrepancies in movement from Tract A2 on the west side may be attributable to a large Italian population in part of the tract. A redefinition of opportunities to take direct account of the ethnic factor was not attempted for lack of data on the individual families moving. There would be special difficulties, since members of an ethnic group might fall into two types in their movement, namely, those who follow the trend of movement within their nationality group and those who deliberately seek to dissociate themselves from their group. Here is an intriguing problem for further study. The application of Equation 1 some-what as in the present study, might serve, as a first approximation, to permit a rough estimate of the relative numbers in the two types; and as a second approximation, the equation could be reapplied to each type, separately, using for each type separate universes of opportunities.

A word should be said as to the application of the theory, not to all move-ments, as in the present study, but only to the net movement after a lapse of several years. The 1940 Census will provide data on place of residence April 1, 1940, and place of residence five years earlier. Some persons will have moved several times during this interval. It follows necessarily from the theory that after several moves persons will be more widely dispersed in space than after one move. If the general spatial pattern of opportunities remains relatively constant during a time interval, the expected distribution after *t* years could be estimated by successive applications, year by year, of Equation 1. Practically, this would be exceedingly laborious. Introducing some short-cut approximations, Severn Provus, research assistant to the writer, is attempting this for Chicago physicians with Loop offices whose changes of residence for several years can be traced.

There is one class of mobility to which it would be rather easy to make a direct application of Equation 1, namely, movements of farmers to other farms. Here, the place of work and place of residence coincide, while in residential mobility the place of work may introduce restrictions on place of residence accounting for some variation from expectation of the theory as here expressed in simple form. In defining opportunities in connection with the movement of farmers, care must be taken to hold constant the type of farming involved. Thus, ordinarily, cotton farmers might be more likely to move a long distance to another cotton farm than a short distance to a stock farm. Such tendencies are fully consistent with the theory here introduced and can be adequately handled statistically if appropriate definitions of opportunity are laid down.

In conclusion, we should like to repeat what was said in the beginning, namely, that even where numerical data are inadequate for direct application of the theory of intervening opportunities, the general idea may be useful as a basic organizing principle in accounting for the *tendency* toward certain types of spatial patterns of population. It may be found that there are certain types of mobility which cannot be subsumed within the present theory—for example, the importation of a trainload of Mexicans from southern Texas to a northern industry. At the same time, it may be found that other sociological phenomena, such as the relationship of spatial propinquity to the selection of marriage mates, the relationship between certain types of crime and the residence of criminals, the choice of colleges, and the utilization of leisure time in vacation travel, may be illuminated by application of the general theory.

B. *Intervening Opportunities and Competing Migrants*

1. INTRODUCTION

The aim of this paper is to make a contribution toward theory in human ecology and sociology. In 1940 the writer[12] introduced the concept of intervening opportunities to provide a simple model accounting for much of the observed movement of population in space. The idea is that the number of people going a given distance s from a point is not a function of distance directly but rather a function of the spatial distribution of opportunities. More specifically, it was postulated that the number of people going s distance from a point is directly proportional to the number of opportunities on the perimeter of a circle with radius s and inversely proportional to the number of opportunities on or within that circle. After operational definitions of "opportunities were made," it was possible to demonstrate empirically that the model provided a quite promising description of the actual residential mobility between census tracts in metropolitan Cleveland. Subse-

"Intervening Opportunities and Competing Migrants," *Journal of Regional Science*, 2 (Spring, 1960), pp. 1-26.

12. Stouffer, Samuel A., "Intervening Opportunities: A Theory Relating Mobility and Distance," *American Sociological Review*, 5, December, 1940, pp. 845-867. (See also Part A of this chapter.)

quent studies by Bright and Thomas,[13] Isbell,[14] Strodtbeck,[15,16] and others have applied the model to other populations, in America and abroad, with considerable success. Recently an interesting use of the concept of intervening opportunities in the geographical interpretation of commodity flow has been proposed by Ullman.[17]

The writer pointed out in his original paper that the model as presented was inadequate in handling marked directional drifts where the uneven distribution of opportunities *within* the circle might facilitate greater movement in one direction from the starting point than in an opposite direction. Nor are models involving distance, alone, of any help in such a case. Equations such as proposed by Zipf,[18] Stewart,[19-21] Dodd,[22] and others take no account of the distribution of intervening populations. A discussion by Anderson,[23] and Iklé,[24] which appeared while the present paper was in preparation, emphasized the need for further study.

Consider migration from St. Louis to New York, Denver, and Los Angeles, respectively. Between St. Louis and New York are most of the large population centers of the country. Between St. Louis and Denver or between St. Louis and Los Angeles are few population centers. We seek a model which will take that fact into account. The concept of intervening opportunities in the form originally presented by the writer, does not. New York is only

13. Bright, Margaret, and Thomas, Dorothy S., "Interstate Migration and Intervening Opportunities," *American Sociological Review*, 6, December, 1941, pp. 773-783.

14. Isbell, Eleanor C., "Internal Migration in Sweden and Intervening Opportunities," *American Sociological Review*, 9, December, 1944, pp. 627-639.

15. Strodtbeck, Fred, "Population, Distance and Migration from Kentucky," *Sociometry*, 13, May, 1950, pp. 123-130.

16. Strodtbeck, Fred, "Equal Opportunity Intervals: a Contribution to the Method of Intervening Opportunity Analysis," *American Sociological Review*, 14, August, 1949, pp. 490-497.

17. Ullman, Edward L., *American Commodity Flow; a Geographical Interpretation of Rail and Water Traffic Based on Principles of Spatial Interchange*. Seattle, Washington: University of Washington Press, 1957.

18. Zipf, George K., *Human Behavior and the Principle of Least Effort: an Introduction to Human Ecology*. Reading, Massachusetts: Addison-Wesley Press, 1949.

19. Stewart, John Q., "An Inverse Distance Variation for Certain Social Influences," *Science*, 93, 1941, pp. 89-90.

20. Stewart, John Q., "A Measure of the Influence of a Population at a Distance," *Sociometry*, 5, 1942, pp. 63-71.

21. Stewart, John W., "Demographic Gravitation: Evidence and Applications," *Sociometry*, 11, 1948, pp. 31-57.

22. Dodd, Stuart C., "The Interactance Hypothesis: A Gravity Model Fitting Physical Masses and Human Groups," *American Sociological Review*, 15, April, 1950, pp. 245-256

23. Anderson, Theodore R., "Intermetropolitan Migration: A Comparison of the Hypotheses of Zipf and Stouffer," *American Sociological Review*, 20, June, 1955, pp. 287-291.

24. Iklé, Fred Charles, "Comment on Theodore R. Anderson's 'Intermetropolitan Migration: A Comparison of the Hypotheses of Zipf and Stouffer,'" *American Sociological Review*, 20, December, 1955, pp. 713-714.

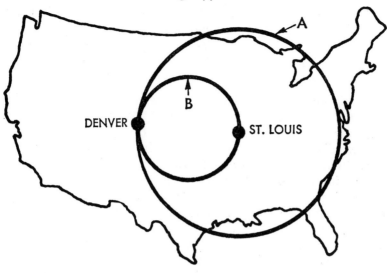

Figure 4-5

slightly farther from St. Louis than Denver. Hence, a circle with center at St. Louis will show almost as many intervening opportunities between St. Louis and Denver as between St. Louis and New York. And it will show even more between St. Louis and Los Angeles.

2. A REDEFINITION OF INTERVENING OPPORTUNITIES

We first propose a redefinition of intervening opportunities as follows:

1. Connect any two cities with a straight line.
2. Draw a circle with this line as a diameter.
3. Count the opportunities on or within this circle. This circle, shown as Circle B in Figure 4-5, can be contrasted with Circle A, which has St. Louis as its center and the distance St. Louis–Denver as its radius.

The construction of B as a circle is arbitrary; it is selected for its simplicity. An ellipse might turn out to be more appropriate or even a pie-shaped wedge with apex at St. Louis and angle whose optimum magnitude could be determined only empirically.[25]

Now let us examine some empirical data. From the 1940 Census of Population, in the volume, *Internal Migration 1935 to 1940, Color and Sex of Migrants*, Table 16, we find the reported number of migrants from each city

25. In constructing circles such as B for any two cities for the present paper, the writer arbitrarily extended all diameters to a point approximately 75 miles on the map beyond each of the two cities to allow for the influence of large population centers which otherwise might be just outside the range and which it seemed imprudent to ignore.

of 100,000 or over to each other such city. From St. Louis to Los Angeles, Denver, and New York [26] the figures are as follows:

Los Angeles	3,945
Denver	462
New York	1,269

The total migrants from St. Louis to all cities of 100,000 or over are 24,000.

We define opportunities in a given city as total number of migrants to that city from all other cities of 100,000 or over, except from that city's suburban satellites.[27] These data are totaled in the census volume referred to above. From the same source we have also the data on the number of migrants leaving a given city for all other cities of 100,000 population or over (less those going to the city's suburban satellites).

We now draw three Circles A around St. Louis as a center, with radii Los Angeles, Denver, and New York, respectively, and count the total number of opportunities in all cities lying approximately on or within each circle. Likewise, we draw three Circles B as described above and count the total numbers of opportunities therein. We obtain the data in Table 4-9.

Table 4-9

	Total Migrants to Given City (Thousands)	X_D, Distance from St. Louis (Miles)*	X_A, Intervening Opportunities (Circles A) (Thousands)	X_B, Intervening Opportunity (Circles B) (Thousands)	Y, Migrants from St. Louis to Given City
Los Angeles	139.4	1,901	743	288	3,945
Denver	11.6	878	456	58	462
New York	83.7	965	547	444	1,279

*Highway driving distances, as given in *Rand McNally Reference and Road Atlas*, 1953.

If we let X_M equal the product of all migrants from St. Louis and of all migrants to a given city, we have for X_M, in thousands,[28]

Los Angeles	3,345.6
Denver	278.4
New York	2,008.8

Consider now the intervening-opportunities model as originally stated: [29]

$$Y = \frac{aX_M}{X_A^b} \tag{1}$$

26. All cities of 100,000 or over lying within the metropolitan area of a major center are treated as part of the central city in this paper. Moreover, cities like Minneapolis–St. Paul or San Francisco–Oakland are combined and treated as one.

27. At first glance, our definition of opportunities may seem to involve "circularity." It does not. There is even less "circularity" in its use in the present paper than would be the use of marginals in a contingency table in determining association among the individual internal cells of the table.

28. For example, $24.0 \times 139.4 = 3,345.6$. Clearly, both factors must be taken into account. The product, instead of some other relationship, is used because of simplicity, especially in view of subsequent operations.

29. Stouffer, *op. cit.*

where $b = 1$. Let us allow b to be determined empirically. In logarithms we can write

$$\log Y - \log X_M = \log a - b \log X_A \qquad (2)$$

which is a straight line with a slope of b.

Our new intervening opportunities model substituting X_B for X_A, *for which we make no a priori postulate about b*, becomes the straight line.

$$\log Y - \log X_M = \log a - b \log X_B \qquad (3)$$

The model based on distance irrespective of intervening opportunities can be written as a straight line:

$$\log Y - \log X_M = \log a - b \log X_D \qquad (4)$$

The logarithms are in Table 4-10.

Table 4-10*

	$(\log Y - \log X_M)$	$\log X_A$	$\log X_B$	$\log X_D$
To Los Angeles	1.08	2.87	2.46	3.28
To Denver	1.22	2.66	1.76	2.94
To New York	0.80	2.74	2.65	2.98

*To keep these values positive, for convenience, we express X_M in terms of *tens of thousands*. Thus, for Los Angeles, $\log X_M = \log 334.56 = 2.52$; $\log Y = 3.60$; $\log Y - \log X_M = 1.08$.

The data are plotted on the top row of Figure 4-6. Figure 4-6 (*a*) is based on the concept of intervening opportunities as originally presented, and the picture is hopelessly bad, since New York falls far short of what would be expected if Denver and Los Angeles fit the model. Figure 4-6(*b*) is based on the distance model. It is no better. On the other hand, Figure 4-6 (*c*), based on the new intervening-opportunities idea, alone of the three charts puts the points in correct rank order, although not in a perfect straight line.

Now a model has value only if it has some generality. Let us see how the three concepts order the data when the reverse migration movements are considered—*to* St. Louis. Here the ecology is very different. Our Circles A are now drawn around Los Angeles, Denver, and New York, respectively, with circumferences passing through St. Louis. There is sparse population within the Los Angeles and Denver circles as compared with the New York circle. The population within Circles B will differ only slightly from that in the previous Circles B.[30]

The observed data are given in Table 4-11. Total migrants to St. Louis from all cities of 100,000 or over are 11,800, whence values of X_M, the product

30. Actually, the only difference is illustrated by the procedure that the intervening population in the St. Louis to Los Angeles case includes within it the total number of migrants to Los Angeles, though, of course, excluding migrants from St. Louis itself, while the intervening population Los Angeles to St. Louis includes the total number of migrants to St. Louis, excluding migrants from Los Angeles.

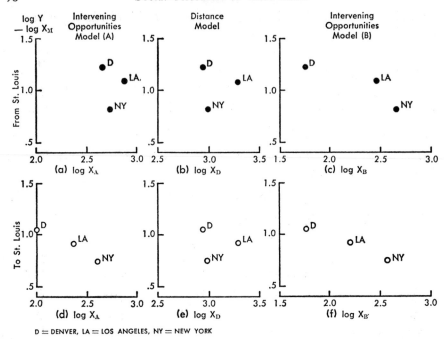

Figure 4-6. *Predictability compared of three models of migration from and to St. Louis.*

Table 4-11

	Total Migrants from Given City (Thousands)	X_D, Distance to St. Louis (Miles)	X_A, Intervening Opportunities (Circle A) (Thousands)	X_B, Intervening Opportunities (Circle B) (Thousands)	Y, Migrants to St. Louis from Given City
Los Angeles	47.8	1,901	229	160	452
Denver	14.7	878	99	59	197
New York	106.7	965	405	372	702

of all migrants from Los Angeles times all migrants to St. Louis, etc., are
as follows:

Los Angeles	564.0
Denver	173.5
New York	1,259.1

Table 4-12

	$(\log Y - \log X_M)$	$\log X_A$	$\log X_D$	$\log X_B$
From Los Angeles	0.91	2.36	3.28	2.20
From Denver	1.05	2.00	2.94	1.77
From New York	0.75	2.61	2.98	2.57

The logarithms are given in Table 4-12. These data are plotted in the lower
half of Figure 4-6. In this case, both of the intervening-opportunities models

order the data in correct rank order and also with rather satisfying linearity. The distance model fails again.

At this point we see that only the new intervening-opportunities model 2(*f*) has correctly ordered both sets of data, involving migration both from and to St. Louis. But if the new model is to have the kind of generality we seek, these two sets of three points should not only each lie approximately on straight lines, but also should lie on the *same* straight line.

In Figure 4-7(*a*) we superimpose on the same graph the data charted on Figures 4-6(*c*) and 4-6(*f*). Consistently, *the migration from St. Louis is somewhat overestimated as compared with the migration to St. Louis.*

What is happening? What plausible modifications of our model might take it into account?

3. INTRODUCING THE CONCEPT OF COMPETING MIGRANTS

We seek some factor which is asymmetrical as between two cities—sheer distance and, to a large extent, our new concept of intervening opportunities are not. In the present instance, it should be a factor which makes opportunities in Los Angeles or Denver relatively more attractive to St. Louis migrants than the reverse.

One such factor could be what we shall call *competing migrants*. Consider the map. Migrants from almost any city in the United States are closer to St. Louis initially than are migrants from Los Angeles to St. Louis. On the other hand, St. Louis emigrants are closer to Los Angeles than are the majority of big-city emigrants in America.

Is it not plausible to suggest that, everything else being equal, the attractiveness of City Y for migrants from City X will depend, at least to some

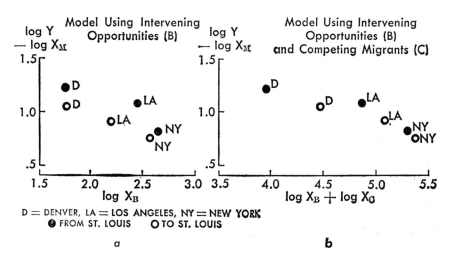

Figure 4-7. Migration to and from St. Louis superimposed on the same chart.

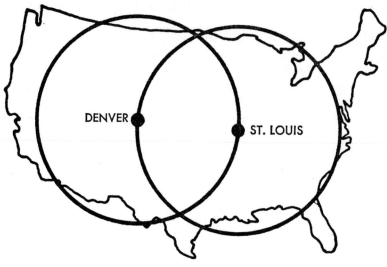

Figure 4-8

extent, on how many potential migrants are closer to Y than are the potential migrants in X?

Let us define the number of competing migrants as X_C *the total number of persons leaving cities as close or closer to Y than the migrants in* X. We draw two Circles C around Denver and St. Louis, respectively, in Figure 4-8, with radii St. Louis–Denver. From the same census source we find that the total number of emigrants from cities of 100,000 or over within the circle centered at Denver is 160,000, the number of emigrants from cities within the circle centered at St. Louis is 512,000. Similarly, we compare two Circles C with radius St. Louis–Los Angeles and two Circles C with radius St. Louis–New York (Table 4-13). In each case the competition is greater when move-

Table 4-13

	Thousands of Migrants Competing for	Thousands of Migrants Competing for St. Louis
Los Angeles	259	782
Denver	160	512
New York	452	625

ment is in the direction of St. Louis than when movement is in the reverse direction.

Let us now try a new model, involving both our revised concept of intervening opportunities X_B and our new concept of competing migrants that we will call X_C, and for simplicity we treat X_B and X_C as multiplicative:

$$Y = \frac{KX_M}{(X_B X_C)^b} \qquad (5)$$

Table 4-14

	(log Y − log X_M)	log X_B	log X_C	(log X_B + log X_C)
FROM ST. LOUIS				
To Los Angeles	1.08	2.46	2.41	4.87
To Denver	1.22	1.76	2.20	3.96
To New York	0.80	2.65	2.66	5.31
TO ST. LOUIS				
From Los Angeles	0.91	2.20	2.89	5.09
From Denver	1.05	1.77	2.71	4.48
From New York	0.75	2.57	2.80	5.37

This, if a good fit, should order all six points (log Y − log X_M) on a negatively sloped linear function of (log X_B + log X_C) as in Table 4-14. The data are plotted in Figure 4-7(b). There can be little doubt that the fit is improved, and most, though not quite all, of the systematic discrepancy in the graph of Figure 4-7(a) is now removed.

Because of its simplicity, this model seems preferable, at least initially, to one which logically might be even more attractive in that it would attempt directly to weight each intervening city's contribution to a cumulated intervening opportunity total by a figure proportional to that city's competing migrants (or some power of this figure). At present this operation would seem prohibitively laborious, but it might become feasible if programmed for one of the big computers.

4. A WIDER TEST OF THE MODEL INVOLVING BOTH INTERVENING OPPORTUNITIES AND COMPETING MIGRANTS

The construct introduced here could be effective, in the illustration given, merely because it accidentally corresponded to some other factors peculiar to St. Louis in relation to the other cities. If the model is to have generality, it must hold for other cities as well, and both X_B and X_C must be needed to do the job.

Therefore, we shall now study the migration to and from Los Angeles, Denver, Chicago, and New York from each of the sixteen American cities with more than 500,000 population in 1940.[31] This yields 116 intercity observations in all. The basic data, in logarithms, are shown in the first five columns of Table 4-15.

31. We shall continue to treat Minneapolis–St. Paul, San Francisco–Oakland, and Kansas City, Missouri–Kansas City, Kansas, as single cities. All cities of 100,000 or over in the metropolitan area of a large central city (e.g., Camden, New Jersey, in relation to Philadelphia) are treated as part of the central city.

Table 4-15. Data Used in Predicting Intercity Migration; Comparison of Observed Migration (log Y) with That Predicted by Intervening Opportunities and Competing Migrants (log Y'_{MBC}) and Predicted by Distance (log Y'_{MD})

	log X_M	log X_B	log X_C	log X_D	log Y	log Y'_{MBC}	log Y'_{MD}
TO LOS ANGELES FROM							
San Francisco	2.60	2.14	1.67	2.60	4.08	4.17	3.92
Denver	2.31	2.23	1.99	3.08	3.70	3.63	3.28
Kansas City	2.58	2.39	2.31	3.21	3.86	3.77	3.52
Minn.–St. Paul	2.48	2.40	2.46	3.30	3.71	3.58	3.35
St. Louis	2.52	2.46	2.41	3.28	3.60	3.62	3.41
Chicago	3.05	2.53	2.56	3.33	4.21	4.19	4.01
Milwaukee	2.20	2.57	2.62	3.34	3.15	3.09	2.98
Detroit	2.61	2.68	2.71	3.38	3.63	3.52	3.45
Cleveland	2.58	2.72	2.74	3.39	3.47	3.45	3.41
Pittsburgh	2.36	2.74	2.77	3.41	3.19	3.15	3.13
Buffalo	2.20	2.72	2.79	3.42	2.94	2.95	2.93
Baltimore	2.30	2.83	2.81	3.44	2.80	3.02	3.04
Washington	2.48	2.82	2.80	3.44	3.20	3.26	3.26
Philadelphia	2.62-	2.88	2.87	3.46	3.29	3.38	3.42
Boston	2.48	2.92	2.93	3.49	3.13	3.16	3.23
New York	3.18	2.84	2.89	3.46	4.28	4.09	4.09
FROM LOS ANGELES TO							
San Francisco	2.22	1.54	1.84	2.60	4.07	3.87	3.46
Denver	1.74	1.60	2.56	3.08	3.03	2.94	2.59
Kansas City	1.85	2.09	2.90	3.21	2.87	2 73	2 64
Minn.–St. Paul	1.84	2.09	2.92	3.30	2.80	2.71	2.58
St. Louis	1.75	2.20	2.89	3.28	2.66	2.57	2.48
Chicago	2.41	2.42	2.89	3.33	3.39	3.30	3.24
Milwaukee	1.60	2.39	2.92	3.34	2.37	2.29	2.26
Detroit	2.27	2.58	2.91	3.38	3.00	3.05	3.04
Cleveland	1.86	2.60	2.90	3.39	2.50	2.53	2.54
Pittsburgh	1.57	2.62	2.91	3.41	2.23	2.16	2.18
Buffalo	1.65	2.60	2.91	3.42	2.10	2.26	2.27
Baltimore	1.91	2.74	2.90	3.44	2.36	2.53	2.57
Washington	2.32	2.75	2.90	3.44	3.07	3.05	3.07
Philadelphia	1.99	2.80	2.90	3.46	2.81	2.61	2.66
Boston	1.81	2.85	2.90	3.49	2.53	2.36	2.42
New York	2.60	2.81	2.88	3.46	3.60	3.38	3.39
TO DENVER FROM							
San Francisco	1.53	2.25	2.63	3.11	2.59	2.38	2.32
Los Angeles	1.74	1.60	2.56	3.08	3.03	2.94	2.59
Kansas City	1.51	1.56	1.68	2.79	3.13	3.05	2.49
Minn.–St. Paul	1.40	1.60	2.11	2.93	2.56	2.71	2.27
St. Louis	1.44	1.76	1.20	2.94	2.66	2.65	2.31
Chicago	1.96	1.99	2.33	3.01	3.09	3.15	2.90
Milwaukee	1.11	2.15	2.37	3.02	2.10	2.01	1.87

Table 4-15 (Continued)

	log X_M	log X_B	log X_C	log X_D	log Y	log Y'_{MBC}	log Y'_{MD}
TO DENVER FROM							
Detroit	1.53	2.35	2.70	3.12	2.33	2.31	2.31
Cleveland	1.51	2.49	2.74	3.14	2.10	2.21	2.28
Pittsburgh	1.28	2.53	2.78	3.15	1.94	1.89	1.99
Buffalo	1.11	2.54	2.80	3.19	1.67	1.66	1.76
Baltimore	1.23	2.68	2.82	3.21	1.64	1.74	1.90
Washington	1.40	2.63	2.83	3.23	2.40	1.97	2.09
Philadelphia	1.54	2.75	2.85	3.24	2.06	2.09	2.25
Boston	1.40	2.78	2.95	3.31	1.92	1.86	2.04
New York	2.08	2.69	2.90	3.25	2.84	2.77	2.90
FROM DENVER TO							
San Francisco	1.71	2.31	2.10	3.11	3.18	2.80	2.54
Los Angeles	2.31	2.23	1.99	3.08	3.70	3.63	3.28
Kansas City	1.32	1.59	2.45	2.79	2.76	2.47	2.26
Minn.–St. Paul	1.32	1.63	2.55	2.93	2.26	2.41	2.18
St. Louis	1.24	1.77	2.71	2.94	2.29	2.18	2.07
Chicago	1.89	2.15	2.81	3.01	2.85	2.80	2.81
Milwaukee	1.08	2.14	2.81	3.02	1.72	1.79	1.83
Detroit	1.76	2.40	2.85	3.12	2.41	2.51	2.59
Cleveland	1.34	2.50	2.86	3.14	1.79	1.94	2.07
Pittsburgh	1.04	2.52	2.87	3.15	1.56	1.55	1.70
Buffalo	1.15	2.53	2.86	3.19	1.46	1.69	1.81
Baltimore	1.40	2.69	2.87	3.21	1.73	1.93	2.10
Washington	1.81	2.66	2.86	3.23	2.66	2.46	2.58
Philadelphia	1.48	2.76	2.86	3.24	1.74	2.01	2.18
Boston	1.30	2.78	2.86	3.31	1.78	1.77	1.92
New York	2.09	2.72	2.81	3.25	2.62	2.81	2.91
TO CHICAGO FROM							
San Francisco	2.20	2.60	2.90	3.34	2.80	2.96	2.98
Los Angeles	2.41	2.42	2.89	3.33	3.39	3.30	3.24
Denver	1.89	2.15	2.81	3.01	2.85	2.80	2.81
Kansas City	2.18	2.01	2.41	2.70	3.39	3.39	3.35
Minn.–St. Paul	2.08	1.84	2.29	2.61	3.49	3.38	3.29
St. Louis	2.11	1.86	2.00	2.47	3.55	3.54	3.41
Milwaukee	1.77	1.75	1.23	1.95	3.50	3.48	3.32
Detroit	2.20	1.97	1.85	2.43	3.56	3.67	3.54
Cleveland	2.18	2.23	2.18	2.54	3.32	3.38	3.45
Pittsburgh	1.94	2.29	2.36	2.67	3.09	2.99	3.08
Buffalo	1.79	2.29	2.45	2.73	2.73	2.76	2.87
Baltimore	1.88	2.47	2.52	2.84	2.57	2.77	2.91
Washington	2.08	2.40	2.54	2.84	2.95	3.04	3.15
Philadelphia	2.20	2.58	2.62	2.88	2.99	3.08	3.27
Boston	2.08	2.64	2.80	3.00	2.88	2.83	3.05
New York	2.76	2.53	2.70	2.92	3.83	3.77	3.92

Table 4-15 (Continued)

	log X_M	log X_B	log X_C	log X_D	log Y	log Y'_{MBC}	log Y'_{MD}
FROM CHICAGO TO							
San Francisco	2.44	2.58	2.56	3.34	3.47	3.41	3.27
Los Angeles	3.05	2.53	2.56	3.33	4.21	4.19	4.01
Denver	1.96	1.99	2.33	3.01	3.09	3.15	2.90
Kansas City	2.06	1.80	2.24	2.70	3.30	3.40	3.21
Minn.–St. Paul	2.05	1.48	1.94	2.61	3.51	3.64	3.25
St. Louis	1.97	1.48	2.00	2.47	3.35	3.52	3.24
Milwaukee	1.82	1.04	1.93	1.95	3.50	3.55	3.38
Detroit	2.49	1.91	2.20	2.43	3.74	3.90	3.89
Cleveland	2.08	2.12	2.29	2.54	3.17	3.27	3.34
Pittsburgh	1.79	2.17	2.48	2.67	2.77	2.80	2.90
Buffalo	1.89	2.18	2.66	2.73	2.78	2.85	2.99
Baltimore	2.13	2.41	2.73	2.84	2.86	3.02	3.21
Washington	2.54	2.39	2.73	2.84	3.38	3.54	3.70
Philadelphia	2.20	2.55	2.66	2.88	2.95	3.08	3.27
Boston	2.03	2.60	2.66	3.00	2.80	2.85	2.99
New York	2.82	2.56	2.58	2.92	3.94	3.88	3.99
TO NEW YORK FROM							
San Francisco	2.38	2.91	2.89	3.49	3.26	3.06	3.11
Los Angeles	2.60	2.81	2.88	3.46	3.60	3.38	3.39
Denver	2.09	2.72	2.81	3.25	2.62	2.81	2.91
Kansas City	2.36	2.68	2.72	3.08	2.92	3.20	3.34
Minn.–St. Paul	2.26	2.66	2.73	3.10	2.93	3.08	3.20
St. Louis	2.30	2.65	2.66	2.98	3.11	3.16	3.33
Chicago	2.82	2.56	2.58	2.92	3.94	3.88	3.99
Milwaukee	1.97	2.60	2.63	2.96	2.67	2.78	2.94
Detroit	2.38	2.43	2.45	2.80	3.37	3.44	3.53
Cleveland	2.36	2.36	2.34	2.70	3.41	3.49	3.57
Pittsburgh	2.15	2.32	2.23	2.57	3.52	3.29	3.40
Buffalo	1.98	2.20	2.25	2.57	3.22	3.12	3.19
Baltimore	2.08	2.19	1.92	2.28	3.48	3.39	3.49
Washington	2.26	2.12	2.04	2.35	3.93	3.60	3.67
Philadelphia	2.40	1.98	1.46	1.94	3.94	4.08	4.09
Boston	2.26	2.07	2.09	2.36	3.81	3.60	3.66
FROM NEW YORK TO							
San Francisco	2.57	2.89	2.88	3.49	3.59	3.30	3.34
Los Angeles	3.18	2.84	2.89	3.46	4.28	4.09	4.09
Denver	2.08	2.69	2.90	3.25	2.84	2.77	2.90
Kansas City	2.19	2.62	2.80	3.08	2.83	2.98	3.13
Minn.–St. Paul	2.19	2.59	2.78	3.10	2.92	3.00	3.12
St. Louis	2.10	2.57	2.80	2.98	2.85	2.89	3.09
Chicago	2.76	2.53	2.70	2.92	3.83	3.77	3.92
Milwaukee	1.94	2.51	2.74	2.96	2.68	2.74	2.90
Detroit	2.62	2.35	2.65	2.80	3.57	3.69	3.82
Cleveland	2.20	2.20	2.62	2.70	3.23	3.24	3.38
Pittsburgh	1.92	2.13	2.62	2.57	3.12	2.92	3.12
Buffalo	2.00	1.92	2.42	2.57	3.32	3.19	3.22
Baltimore	2.26	1.95	2.13	2.28	3.60	3.63	3.71
Washington	2.67	1.97	2.12	2.35	4.00	4.14	4.16
Philadelphia	2.33	1.52	1.89	1.94	3.82	4.00	4.00
Boston	2.16	1.67	2.01	2.36	3.63	3.67	3.54

We now fit to these data by least squares the following equation:

$$\log Y = \log K + A \log X_M + B \log X_B + C \log X_C \qquad (6)$$

We introduce the separate coefficients B and C in order to compare their relative magnitudes, and we introduce the coefficient A to allow for the possibility that sheer numbers of immigrants to and emigrants from a given city may have an exponential rather than linear effect on the movement between that city and another.

For purposes of comparison, we separately test the postulates of Zipf, Stewart, and others, involving sheer distance.[32] For this test we also give X_M the freedom to vary exponentially and leave the coefficient of X_D, distance, to be determined empirically. We have

$$\log Y = \log K' + A' \log X_M + D \log X_D \qquad (7)$$

By multiple regression analysis, the least-square constants in Table 4-16 are determined.

Table 4-16

Intervening-Opportunities and Competing-Migrants Model	Distance Model
log K = 2.5237	log K' = 2.3902
A = 1.2509	A' = 1.2047
B = −0.4195	D = −0.6157
C = 0.4238	

The values of $\log Y'_{MBC}$ and of $\log Y'_{MD}$ predicted from these two equations, respectively, are shown in the last two columns of Table 4-15.

It is interesting to note that the coefficients B and C are nearly alike— −0.4195 and −0.4238, respectively.

Also it is interesting to note that, in these cities, both A and A' are somewhat greater than unity, being 1.2509 and 1.2047 for the two models, respectively. This says that the attractive power of one city for another, either when intervening opportunities and competing migrants are held constant, or when distance is held constant, is best measured by raising X_M, the product of total in-migrants and total out-migrants, to the 1.2509 or 1.2047 power, respectively. This means that great centers like New York, Chicago, or Los Angeles draw from or export to other large centers exponentially more people than to or from smaller centers, or than do two small centers to or from each other. Analogous findings should be watched for in all further studies of intercity migration.

The multiple correlation coefficients (R) and standard errors of estimate (S) are given in Table 4-17.

32. Results using the original intervening-opportunities model A are omitted in the interest of brevity. Although fitting better, on the average, than the distance model, it possesses many of the same systematic errors.

Table 4-17

	Intervening-Opportunities and Competing-Migrants Model	Distance Model
R	0.9761	0.9332
S	0.1414	0.2299

While multiple correlations as high as these are unusual in sociological studies and gratifying, one must keep in mind the fact that there is a very wide range in the value of log Y. This can be seen by the fact that observed migrants varied all the way from 29 from Denver to Buffalo to 18,942 from New York to Los Angeles. The predicted value of Y could correlate very highly with the observed values and still differ by a substantial percentage error. Hence, in comparing the two models, the respective values of the standard errors are more informative in some respects than the correlation coefficients. As shown above, S, the standard error of estimate from the regression plane, is much larger for the distance model. The significance of this can be better appreciated if we look in Table 4-18 at S in terms of its antilogarithms, which represent the ratio of the observed to expected Y.

Table 4-18

	Intervening-Opportunities and Competing-Migrants Model	Distance Model
Upper band of standard error	1.38	1.70
Lower band of standard error	0.72	0.59

About a third of the time the observed migration is more than 38 per cent higher or more than 28 per cent lower than predicted from our intervening opportunities and competing migrants model. Unless these errors are systematic—within one type of region, for example, or for movement in one general direction—this discrepancy means that there are special local factors operating not covered in the theory, as we should expect. For example, the largest percentage error for any two cities was in the case of Washington, D.C., to Denver. One would not expect the movement to and from the nation's capital to follow closely either general pattern, except by accident. We observe 251 migrants from Washington to Denver but predict only 93. The discrepancy, which could be due to the transfer of an entire government office to Denver, is numerically small but very large in percentage.

The distance model, on the average, is far less satisfactory. In about a third of the cases the error exceeds 70 per cent, on the positive side, or 41 per cent, on the negative side.

Of course, much of the observed correlation in the case of each model is attributable to X_M. Let us, therefore, hold X_M constant and look at the residual correlations (see Table 4-19).

Table 4-19

	Intervening- Opportunities and Competing- Migrants Model	Distance Model
Partial correlation of X_B with Y, holding X_M and X_C constant	−0.59	
Partial correlation of X_C with Y, holding X_M and X_B constant	−0.57	
Combined partial correlation of X_B and X_C with Y, holding X_M constant*	0.91	Partial correlation −0.72 of X_D with Y holding X_M constant

*This measure may be unfamiliar to some readers. It is obtained by the formula

$$R_{Y \cdot X_B X_C \cdot X_M} = [1 - (1 - R^2_{Y \cdot X_B \cdot X_M})(1 - R^2_{Y X_C \cdot X_B X_M})]^{1/2}$$

which was introduced by the writer in 1936. As a multiple correlation, it cannot, of course, be assigned a minus sign. [Stouffer, Samuel A., "Evaluating the Effect of Inadequately Measured Variables in Partial Correlation Analysis," *Journal of the American Statistical Association*, 31, June, 1936, pp. 348-360.]

These findings are interesting for two reasons:

1. They show that, for the 116 intercity migrations here studied, the impact of competing migrants is approximately equally as effective as the impact of intervening opportunities. The partial correlations of −0.57 and −0.59, respectively, are each significant far beyond the 0.01 level. And this complementarity occurs in spite of the fact that the overall zero-order correlation between the measures of intervening opportunities and competing migrants is fairly high, namely, +0.74.

2. When X_M is held constant, the combined partial correlation of the two measures with the residuals of Y is a quite satisfactory 0.91, a measure that is substantially better than the comparable measure of 0.72 for distance alone. It can be shown further that the standard error of estimate of [log Y − f_Y (log X_A)] from [log X_D − f_D (log X_A)] is about two-thirds larger than the comparable standard error from the model using intervening opportunities and competing migrants.

Comparison of any two models should not rest alone on the over-all correlational comparisons. It is actually possible for one model to yield a higher correlation with observed data than another, on the average, yet still be inferior.

Why? Because, the errors in the one model could be highly systematic, while the errors in the other, though greater on the average, could be more or less at random. In developing theory, we are seeking maximum generality, and a model is unsatisfactory if it contains large systematic errors, that is, if it consistently overpredicts or consistently underpredicts for a substantial block of cases which are similar in their characteristics. For example, inland cities as a whole, or cities on either seaboard as a whole, or for one direction of migration as compared with another.

Let us now examine the two models for evidence of such systematic errors. Table 4-20, giving the anti-logs of the last three columns in Table 4-15, presents the observed and predicted values for all observations, arranged to enable easy observation of systematic error if present.

Study of Table 4-20 makes it very clear that the type of problem illustrated with the special case of St. Louis in the first part of this paper is no isolated phenomenon. The intervening-opportunities and competing-migrants concepts, taken together, do tend to erase large systematic discrepancies in the distance model, many of which are more drastic than the St. Louis illustration. Both models are sadly inadequate for some special cases, but our new measures order the data much better than the distance model for migration to and from Los Angeles, Denver, and Chicago and at least as well for migration to and from New York.

One way of summarizing Table 4-20 is to compare the relative performance of the two models in predicting migration (Table 4-21).

Table 4-20. Migrants Observed and as Predicted from Two Models; with Subtotals for Groups of Cities

	Observed	Predicted from Intervening Opportunities and Competing Migrants	Predicted from Distance		Observed	Predicted from Intervening Opportunities and Competing Migrants	Predicted from Distance
TO LOS ANGELES FROM				**FROM LOS ANGELES TO**			
San Francisco	11,667	14,479	8,318	San Francisco	11,934	7,414	2,884
Denver	5,032	4,266	1,905	Denver	1,083	871	389
	16,699	18,745	10,223		13,017	8,285	3,273
Kansas City	7,319	5,888	3,311	Kansas City	735	537	437
Minn.–St. Paul	5,103	3,802	2,239	Minn.–St. Paul	636	513	380
St. Louis	3,945	4,169	2,570	St. Louis	452	372	302
	16,367	13,859	8,120		1,823	1,422	1,119
Chicago	16,251	15,490	10,230	Chicago	2,441	1,995	1,738
Milwaukee	1,408	1,230	955	Milwaukee	234	195	182
	17,659	16,720	11,185		2,675	2,190	1,920
Detroit	4,261	3,311	2,818	Detroit	989	1,122	1,096
Cleveland	2,979	2,818	2,570	Cleveland	314	339	347
Pittsburgh	1,544	1,413	1,349	Pittsburgh	169	145	151
Buffalo	872	891	851	Buffalo	127	182	186
	9,656	8,433	7,588		1,599	1,788	1,780
Baltimore	635	1,047	1,096	Baltimore	231	338	372
Washington	1,582	1,820	1,820	Washington	1,173	1,122	1,175
Philadelphia	1,947	2,399	2,630	Philadelphia	643	407	457
Boston	1,354	1,445	1,698	Boston	336	229	263
	5,518	6,711	7,244		2,383	2,096	2,267
New York	18,942	12,300	12,300	New York	3,982	2,399	2,454

Table 4-20. (Continued)

	Observed	Predicted from Intervening Opportunities and Competing Migrants	Predicted from Distance		Observed	Predicted from Intervening Opportunities and Competing Migrants	Predicted from Distance
TO DENVER FROM				**FROM DENVER TO**			
San Francisco	391	240	204	San Francisco	1,511	631	347
Los Angeles	1,083	871	389	Los Angeles	5,032	4,266	1,905
	1,474	1,111	598		6,543	4,897	2,252
Kansas City	1,365	1,122	309	Kansas City	571	295	182
Minn.–St. Paul	364	513	186	Minn.–St. Paul	180	257	151
St. Louis	462	447	204	St. Louis	197	152	117
	2,191	2,082	699		948	704	450
Chicago	1,218	1,413	794	Chicago	714	631	647
Milwaukee	127	102	74	Milwaukee	53	62	68
	1,345	1,515	868		767	693	715
Detroit	214	204	204	Detroit	259	324	389
Cleveland	125	162	191	Cleveland	62	87	118
Pittsburgh	87	77	98	Pittsburgh	36	35	50
Buffalo	42	46	58	Buffalo	29	49	65
	473	489	551		386	495	622
Baltimore	44	55	79	Baltimore	54	85	125
Washington	251	93	123	Washington	453	288	382
Philadelphia	114	123	178	Philadelphia	55	125	151
Boston	83	72	110	Boston	60	59	83
	492	343	490		622	557	741
New York	686	589	794	New York	413	645	813
TO CHICAGO FROM				**FROM CHICAGO TO**			
San Francisco	635	912	955	San Francisco	2,928	2,570	1,862
Los Angeles	2,441	1,995	1,738	Los Angeles	16,251	15,490	10,230
Denver	714	631	647	Denver	1,218	1,413	794
	3,790	3,538	3,340		20,397	19,473	12,886
Kansas City	2,433	2,455	2,239	Kansas City	2,011	2,512	1,622
Minn.–St. Paul	3,058	2,399	1,950	Minn.–St. Paul	3,245	4,365	1,778
St. Louis	3,516	3,467	2,571	St. Louis	2,231	3,311	1,738
	9,007	8,321	6,760		7,487	10,188	5,138
Milwaukee	3,158	3,020	2,090	Milwaukee	3,187	3,548	2,399

Table 4-20 (Continued)

	Observed	Predicted from Intervening Opportunities and Competing Migrants	Predicted from Distance		Observed	Predicted from Intervening Opportunities and Competing Migrants	Predicted from Distance
TO CHICAGO FROM				**FROM CHICAGO TO**			
Detroit	3,606	4,677	3,467	Detroit	5,448	7,943	7,763
Cleveland	2,083	2,399	2,818	Cleveland	1,482	1,862	2,188
Pittsburgh	1,221	977	1,202	Pittsburgh	594	631	794
Buffalo	535	576	741	Buffalo	606	708	977
	7,445	8,629	8,228		8,130	11,144	11,722
Baltimore	368	589	813	Baltimore	730	1,047	1,622
Washington	882	1,096	1,413	Washington	2,383	3,467	5,012
Philadelphia	985	1,202	1,862	Philadelphia	895	1,202	1,862
Boston	757	676	1,122	Boston	636	708	977
	2,992	3,563	5,210		4,644	6,424	9,473
New York	6,790	5,888	8,318	New York	8,130	7,586	9,773
TO NEW YORK FROM				**FROM NEW YORK TO**			
San Francisco	1,828	1,122	1,288	San Francisco	3,857	1,995	2,188
Los Angeles	3,982	2,399	2,454	Los Angeles	18,942	12,300	12,300
Denver	413	645	813	Denver	686	589	794
	6,223	4,166	4,555		23,485	14,884	15,282
Kansas City	823	1,585	2,188	Kansas City	682	955	1,349
Minn.–St. Paul	856	1,203	1,585	Minn.–St. Paul	840	1,000	1,319
St. Louis	1,279	1,446	2,138	St. Louis	702	777	1,230
	2,958	4,234	5,911		2,224	2,732	3,898
Chicago	8,685	7,586	9,773	Chicago	6,790	5,889	8,318
Milwaukee	468	603	871	Milwaukee	481	550	794
	9,153	8,189	10,644		7,271	6,439	9,112
Detroit	2,356	2,575	3,389	Detroit	3,747	4,898	6,607
Cleveland	2,593	3,091	3,716	Cleveland	1,686	1,738	2,399
Pittsburgh	3,301	1,950	2,512	Pittsburgh	1,307	832	1,318
Buffalo	1,671	1,319	1,549	Buffalo	2,074	1,549	1,660
	9,921	8,935	11,166		8,814	9,017	11,984
Baltimore	3,009	2,455	3,091	Baltimore	4,011	4,266	5,129
Washington	8,562	3,982	4,678	Washington	10,003	13,800	14,460
Philadelphia	8,624	12,030	12,300	Philadelphia	6,620	10,000	10,000
Boston	6,500	3,982	4,571	Boston	4,306	4,677	3,467
	26,695	22,449	24,640		24,940	32,733	33,056

Table 4-21

	Intervening Opportunities and Competing Migrants Better	Same	Distance Better	Total
To Los Angeles	14	2	0	16
From Los Angeles	11	..	5	16
To Denver	15	..	1	16
From Denver	13	..	3	16
To Chicago	13	..	3	16
From Chicago	13	..	3	16
To New York	9	..	7	16
From New York	11	2	3	16
Total (less duplications)*	89	4	23	116

* For the reader's convenience, data of the type Los Angeles–Denver appear twice in Tables 4–15 and 4–20 (under both Los Angeles and Denver.) In computing the equations, of course, such data counted only as one observation.

The direction of systematic bias in the distance model and the extent to which it has been corrected can be seen graphically in Figures 4-9 and 4-10, where totals for cities grouped regionally are charted. For example:

The migration to Los Angeles, Denver, and Chicago from cities west of Chicago is systematically underpredicted by the distance model. The same is true of the reverse migration.

The migration from inland cities to New York is systematically overpredicted by the distance model, as is the migration from New York to these same cities.

In almost all such cases graphed in Figures 4-9 and 4-10, the utilization of measures of intervening opportunities and competing migrants narrows the gap, with the resulting errors now in one direction, now in another.

Both models are fairly free of systematic error for coast-to-coast movement, except in the case of movement involving New York. There is a large excess of migrants from New York to Los Angeles and San Francisco, reminiscent of the amusing "New Yorker's map of New York," on which Hollywood is a western suburb. Likewise, there is some excess of reverse migration from the West Coast to New York.

There are a few other special cases of discrepancies. Both models underestimate the short-distance migration to New York from Baltimore, Washington, Philadelphia, and Boston and overestimate the migration in the reverse direction. Both models (though the distance model is much worse) underestimate the migrants from Los Angeles to San Francisco and Denver. Reference to Table 4-20 will show that Washington, D.C., behaves erratically with respect to Denver and New York.

Nobody who contemplates the multiplicity of economic, political, social, and psychological factors that must enter into the personal contemplation of any prospective migrant would expect any simple model, using only two or three variables, to account for everything. The fact that the two concepts of intervening opportunities and competing migrants order so much of the phenomena so well may indeed be surprising to some readers, especially to psychologists, who may be predisposed to look first at an individual's motives and only secondarily, if at all, at the massive framework of ecological structure.

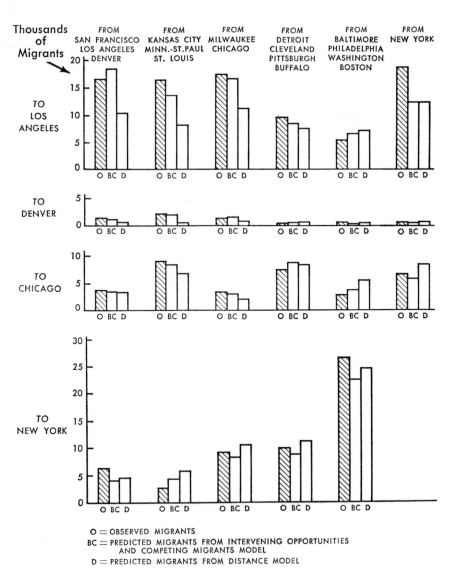

Figure 4-9. In-migrants, observed and predicted, to Los Angeles, Denver, Chicago, and New York.

5. CONCLUSION

It is the writer's hope that this present study, like his previous one, in which the concept of intervening opportunities was introduced, will stimulate further research. It may very well turn out that the notions of intervening

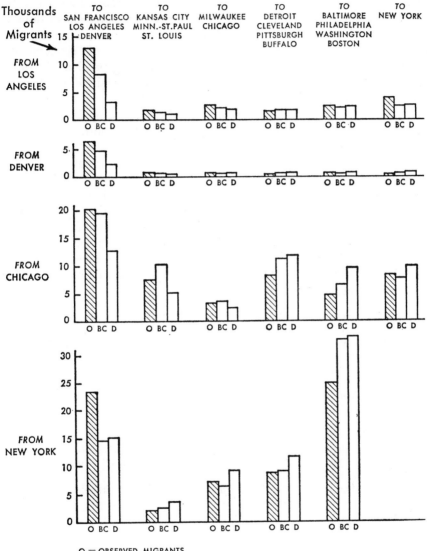

Figure 4-10. Out-migrants, observed and predicted, from Los Angeles, Denver, Chicago, and New York.

opportunities or competing migrants as here developed, are imperfect reflections of some other more effective concepts yet to be discovered. Moreover, the writer would be the last to suggest that the measurements used in this paper are the best possible. They are crude and arbitrary. Improvements in measurement may improve particular predictions.[33]

Especially, it should be noted that neither the distance model nor the model proposed in this paper requires necessarily a measurement of distance in terms of simple miles. A more sophisticated approach, in either case, might be to measure distance not in miles but in terms of "economic distance," based on transport costs. This is a challenging problem for future students. See discussion in papers by Harris,[34] Dunn,[35] and Nelson,[36] and in Chapter 11 in the book by Isard *et al.*[37]

In summary, this analysis contributes to migration theory by demonstrating the shortcomings of a mere mechanical use of physical distance and by demonstrating rather dramatically the advantages of a better model in the reduction *both* of average and systematic error. Whether or not the concepts of intervening opportunities and competing migrants long remain in their present formulation, they should stimulate theoretical and empirical analysis that will lead to further improvement in the theory of migration. And they should, of course, stimulate the exploration, testing, and modification of still broader theoretical conceptions of which those related to geographical mobility may be only a special case, such, for example, as are involved in Zipf's "Principle of Least Effort," Stewart's "Demographic Gravitation," or Dodd's "Theory of Dimensional Analysis."

33. The intervening opportunities and competing migrants concepts are especially cumbersome in application to two major centers with few or no cities intervening. For example, in defining intervening opportunities to include those in the target city as well as in those in between, we avoid the absurdity of possibly predicting an infinite number of migrants; but whatever result we get may be due in part to a variety of partly compensating errors. Similarly, in defining competing migrants to include those in the city of emigration.

34. Harris, Chauncey D., "The Market as a Factor in the Localization of Industry in the United States," *Annals of the Association of American Geographers*, Vol. 44, December, 1954.

35. Dunn, Edgar S., "The Market Potential Concept and the Analysis of Location," *Papers and Proceedings of the Regional Science Association*, Vol. II, 1956.

36. Nelson, Phillip, "Migration, Real Income and Information," *Journal of Regional Science*, 1, Spring, 1959, pp. 43-74.

37. Isard, Walter, *et al.*, *Methods of Regional Analysis*. New York: John Wiley & Sons, 1960.

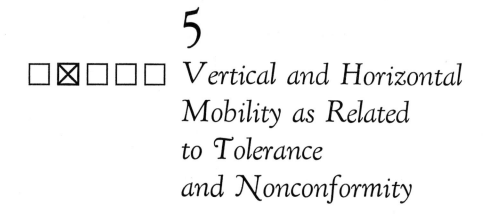

5

□ ☒ □ □ □ *Vertical and Horizontal Mobility as Related to Tolerance and Nonconformity*

At the time McCarthyism was at its height in the United States, I directed a survey of attitudes in a representative cross section of about 5,000 Americans and in a special sample of 1,500 local community leaders. Since the volume in which the findings appear, *Communism, Conformity, and Civil Liberties,* is readily available in libraries, no extensive excerpts will be made in the present compilation. Instead, I have chosen to include a paper read before the American Philosophical Society, *Needed Research on the Tolerance of Nonconformity,* which summarizes some theoretical expectations as to why vertical and horizontal mobility will lead, on the one hand, to an increase in tolerance and, on the other hand, to a decrease. In this paper, some empirical findings from the book are used illustratively to document my conclusion that the weight of evidence supports the viewpoint that such mobility tends basically to increase tolerance. This conclusion is not an obvious one and has been sturdily disputed. It is to be hoped that much more needed research will be done on this highly important topic.

In order to exhibit, in somewhat more detail than the first paper could provide, the empirical process that lies back of the conclusions, one excerpt is included from *Communism, Conformity, and Civil Liberties*, dealing with simultaneous relationship between age and education, on the one hand, and tolerance of nonconformity, on the other hand. For the operations which went into the construction of a scale of tolerance, the reader is referred to the book itself.

Although I believe that the data are remarkably consistent with the conclusion which I set forth, rather than with the opposite conclusions which have been so widely held, I would be more comfortable if some of the inferences I was obliged to make could be checked against more direct data. Particularly, it would be desirable to have a direct measure of vertical mobility based upon a comparison of the respondent's place in the social structure with that of his parents and a direct measure of horizontal mobility based upon information as to previous places and times of residence.

A. *Needed Research on the Tolerance of Nonconformity*

Some time ago the Fund for the Republic sponsored an extensive inquiry into public attitudes toward the internal Communist threat and toward reactions to this threat as they involved a disregard for civil liberties. A committee, aided by numerous expert advisers, planned a survey in which 500 interviewers from two national survey agencies discussed these problems with a cross section of about 5,000 representative Americans in all walks of life and, in addition, with a unique special sample of 1,500 community leaders. The interviews were long and searching, lasting from one to three hours each.

The data are drawn together in a book entitled *Communism, Conformity, and Civil Liberties* . . .

I do not propose to summarize the book or to regale you with voluminous statistics that better can be studied critically in the book itself by those scholars or laymen who are interested. Rather, as a sociologist, I desire to select a few rather general propositions about the topic of tolerance of nonconformists over which I have reflected while studying our current data and to urge the importance of carrying on further researches. For no one study in social science, however searching, can be expected to do more than open a window a few inches.

By tolerance of nonconformists, of course, we do not mean approval of their views. If we are tolerant of a Socialist or an atheist or even of a Com-

"Needed Research on the Tolerance of Nonconformity," *Proceedings of the American Philosophical Society*, 99 (August, 1955), pp. 239-243.

munist, it does not mean that we endorse Socialism, atheism, or Communism. Rather, it means that we will defend the right, within the law, for points of view of such people to be heard, discussed, and debated and for the legal privileges of such people as guaranteed in the Bill of Rights to be safeguarded.

It is not always easy to take the sober second thought about respecting the rights of those of whom we disapprove. But some people are more likely than others to take this sober second thought. The study just completed sought to find out what kind of people would draw a line where. Everybody has his limits of tolerance. Few, if any, would tolerate an admitted Communist in sensitive portions of our defense program or as a teacher in high school or college. But there are many who would purge a Communist's books from a public library or refuse him the right to speak in their town. And not only that. A large number would apply the same sanctions to a Socialist or a freethinker about religion, or even to a man whose loyalty had been criticized by a Congressional committee, though he denied under oath he was a Communist.

Who are the relatively tolerant people and who are the relatively intolerant? Our survey shows that the people more likely than others to take the sober second thought are the better educated people, including, it may be noted, a majority of the local community leaders, the younger people, and people who live in cities in contrast with those who live in small towns and on farms.

These empirical findings, which have been documented with many charts and tables, may take on a broader significance if we try to see them in the light of two great social forces in American life. One such force is described by sociologists by the concept of "vertical mobility," the other by the concept of "horizontal mobility."

When we speak of vertical mobility, we mean the process by which people born into homes of relatively low social economic status climb the ladder of achievement during their own lifetime. This has been possible in America to a degree not equaled elsewhere because our dominant value system has coincided with an expanding frontier of opportunity. Once this expanding frontier was geographical; today it is technological. Miracles of technology and economic organization are creating, directly and indirectly, millions of new jobs of a technical, managerial, and clerical nature—white-collar jobs for women as well as men—and the main gateway to these jobs is education.

Keeping pace has been the most spectacular progress in the education of the masses in all history. It can be illustrated from one of several pieces of evidence in our recent study. Of people over sixty in our representative national cross section, less than one in four had graduated from high school. Of adults under thirty, two out of three had graduated from high school. The proportion of these younger people with college education is double that of their elders of sixty and over; the proportion of younger people with only a grade school education is but a fifth of that among their elders. And the trend is continuing.

Now there are at least two theoretical expectations that would predict that America's unprecedented social mobility would produce an increase in *in*tolerance.

One is in terms of an increase in personal frustration. In a highly mobile society with a high level of aspiration on the part of so many people, there will be many who do not achieve goals that they set too high. The higher the level of aspiration, the larger the discrepancy between aspiration and achievement may become. Though one's success may be great by the absolute standards of the whole world, a person may have greater anxiety about failure relative to others than he would if he lived in a more static and less striving society. The principle here involved has been given the name of "relative deprivation."

If vertical mobility in America breeds relative deprivation in the sense described, the anxiety and frustration generated in the breasts of the relatively unsuccessful should produce a heavy load of aggression that such people would need to discharge on others. They cannot always discharge it on realistic targets; these must be "safe" targets; today there is no safer target than the American Communists or those who have been defined by demagogues as near equivalents. Hence, if we look for the people who are most intolerant of nonconformists, perhaps we should look in particular for people who have aspired but have been frustrated in their effort to realize the American dream.

There is a second reason, in addition to the operation of the principle of relative deprivation, that might led us to expect vertical mobility in America to be a bad sign for tolerance. This lies in the fact that the mobile person may have experienced two conflicting systems of values. One is the set of values learned in his childhood, in his home or neighborhood, and one is the values of the wider world imposed on him by school and college. Obviously, some strains are involved where a simple childhood picture of life in term of truth and falsehood, good and bad, reinforced by the sanctions of an infallible church or an infallible Bible, gets replaced in school or college by the tentatives of science and philosophy. Some people can handle such strain less easily than others, and the anxieties and frustrations thus produced can generate the same effects that psychological theories lead us to attribute to relative deprivation.

On two counts, then, of relative deprivation and conflict of values, we may be led to anticipate that vertical mobility as in the United States today can generate anxieties and frustrations that make people psychologically ripe for intolerance toward objects against whom it is relatively safe to have aggressive attitudes.

And there is another great social force in American life which can reinforce what we have just said—particularly with respect to the conflict of values. That factor is what sociologists call "horizontal mobility."

People in America are moving around increasingly. Fewer and fewer people, and those predominantly in the rural areas, live in the neighborhoods in which they grew up in childhood. Fast-changing technology, including the inventions of communication and transportation, has accelerated horizontal mobility. And the movement is mostly in one direction—from the farm and small towns to the cities and city suburbs. The transition from rural folkways to urban folkways involves breaks in custom and values which can be productive of psychological strain. Hence, horizontal mobility, like vertical mobility, by setting the stage for increased anxiety, can result in projections of that anxiety on others and an increased tendency toward intolerance of people whom it is safe to dislike.

That the mechanisms of anxiety and scapegoating that we have postulated do exist has been quite clearly established in clinical psychological studies. However, it is not too easy to establish directly the operation of these mechanisms either in experimental studies or in surveys like the study upon which we are reporting. At the conscious level, our study showed most of the population to be surprisingly optimistic about their personal future. Two-thirds of the people said they expected life to be better for themselves in the future than in the past, and only one person in seven thought life would be worse. However, the latter tended to be predominately people in their sixties, seventies, and over, some of whom were worried about failing health or lack of security. The general climate of optimism today perhaps should not be too much of a surprise, considering the level of employment and real wages in the country or considering the optimism indirectly evidenced by the sustained high birth rate. People who, though possessing today's knowledge of contraception, are having larger and larger families are not behaving as anxiety-ridden individuals. Nor has fear of atomic extinction taken possession of the public. In the first half hour or so of our interviews, we sought to probe, with as skillful nondirective techniques as we knew how to employ, for anxieties about war and the atom bomb and found few, indeed, who appear to be worrying about impending doom. Of course, the worries may be deep but suppressed, yet most of the evidence marshaled in this study is against such a likelihood, rather than in favor of it.

We do find, however, that the more optimistic people also tend to be more tolerant toward nonconformists like Socialists, atheists, or admitted Communists or toward suspected Communists. This may, indeed, account in part for our finding that people over sixty are more intolerant than younger people, for the finding as to age holds at every educational level.

But before we press the frustration-aggression hypothesis too far, let us consider some other facts.

First, may I give an impressionistic report? If you could sit down as I did and read the entire questionnaires of the most intolerant people in our study, containing masses of free comments taken down as nearly verbatim as possible, you might wonder whether another explanation of much of the intolerance were not even more plausible. Most of these people seemed to be good, wholesome Americans who were drawing logical inferences from incorrect premises. Consider, for instance, an ardent Protestant fundamentalist or

Catholic who has been told that freethinkers about religion are Communists or Communist dupes. If he believes—as is probably true—that secular colleges do weaken some religious certainties of students, it is not illogical for him to be as intolerant of the concept "freethinker" as of the concept "Communist" and put them in the same box. One hardly needs to postulate deep personal anxiety to account for this kind of anti-intellectualism.

And, indeed, most of the statistical data in our study, in my judgment, are not inconsistent with a rather simple cognitive level of explanation of the relationship between tolerance and vertical and horizontal mobility.

What does tolerance require, at the cognitive level? The first step in learning tolerance would seem to be learning that other people can have values different from mine and that what is different is not necessarily bad. Or, even if I don't like such people, I can live and let live. This may be only the first lesson, since a further requirement is to learn that it is a positive good for America to maintain a free market place of ideas, however unconventional and unpopular those ideas may be.

Now how do the social forces of vertical and horizontal mobility operate with respect to teaching at least the first of these lessons? Both would seem to favor it. Education, the main mechanism today of vertical mobility, is a process of exposure of youth to new and competing ideas. The higher one goes up the educational ladder, the more likely he is to encounter the unfamiliar and to learn how to cope with it. Of course, this encounter can produce its *Sturm und Drang*, but the encounter is made and without it tolerance might be less likely. Likewise, the person who lives all his life in the same rural community where he grew up is much less likely to encounter in his personal contacts people with values different from his own than is the person who migrates to the city. Again, as we have pointed out, strain can be produced among the latter, but there is something in city life which teaches that people can be different from me and not necessarily bad or that, even if I dislike them, I can live and let live. In the office, in the labor union, in the city neighborhood, as well as in the general anonymity of more casual contacts, these lessons can be learned.

The empirical data in our study give strong support to such an interpretation. Tolerance is highest among college graduates in metropolitan cities. It is lowest among grade school people on the farms. In each type of community in every region taken separately, it increases with education. For example, take middle western metropolitan cities. On a fifteen-item scale of tolerance of nonconformists, the percentages classed as "relatively more tolerant" vary as follows:

College graduates	64
Some college	59
High school graduates	42
Some high school	31
Grade school	18

The same pattern, though with different absolute level of percentages, holds in all other types of communities and all other regions. Or look at people at the same educational level, when compared by type of community. Take, for example, people in the Middle West who have finished grade school but not high school. Percentages classed as more tolerant on our scale are, by place of residence:

Metropolitan areas	31
Other cities	23
Small towns	17
Farm	13

Such data argue strongly for the proposition that education and city life each operate in the direction of tolerance, in spite of whatever strains which they may generate.

With respect to education, there are two further points to be made. First, as part of the process of learning that the different is not necessarily bad, one has to learn to make discriminations—for example, between the Communist and the freethinker, or between the risk of a Communist in a sensitive defense job and the risk of a Socialist making a speech in one's community. The better educated tend to make such discriminations; the less educated less so. We tapped the variable of "rigidity of categorization" by asking whether respondents agreed or disagreed with the statement, "People can be divided into two classes—the weak and the strong." The pattern of responses by education closely paralleled the pattern of responses to our scale of tolerance of nonconformists.

Second, there is evidence that the better educated people are less authoritarian in attitudes and more likely to favor independence training in child-rearing practices. For example, the patterns of responses by education closely paralleled the responses to the tolerance scale when we examined agreements and disagreements to the following two statements:

A child should never be allowed to talk back to his parents, or else he will lose respect for them.

If a child is unusual in any way, his parents should get him to be more like other children.

When we see, in addition, that it is not only the better educated, but also the younger among the better educated who are most likely to favor non-authoritarian and independence training, we may have a clue which will warn us not to asssume that intolerance is a function of aging alone. The present younger generation is a product of a school system which has been influenced to varying degrees by the independence training of progressive education. Likewise, the younger people of today are the products of far more permissive child-rearing practices in the home than are their elders. "Life with Father" may be a caricature, but if it ever existed, it probably is gone forever.

These forces in education, namely, greater independence training in child-rearing and in the school, may indeed be working in such a way that the young person of thirty, even if he has no more formal education than his parents, may be more tolerant when he is sixty than his parents were at sixty, everything else being equal. And since, as is indisputable, the majority of our younger people are actually getting far more years of schooling than their parents, the outlook should be anything but dismal.

To sum up at this point. On the one hand, I have suggested how conceivably vertical and horizontal mobility in America could generate strains and anxieties that could lead to intolerance, through the mechanisms of relative deprivation and conflict of values as they lead to projection of aggressions on others. On the other hand, I have suggested how vertical and horizontal mobility could teach lessons that are a necessary condition to tolerance by bringing one into contact with people and values different from one's own and paving the way for ultimate appreciation of the positive virtues of a free market place of ideas. As I read the evidence from our study, both sets of forces may be operating, but the latter seem to me far to outweigh the former. In other words, vertical and horizontal mobility on balance seem to promote tolerance of nonconformity in spite of strains that may be generated in an opposite direction.

It may be objected that in the years since World War II intolerance has risen at the same time that mobility has gone on apace. Granted. But never since the Copperhead conspiracy has there been such a provocation for the suspension of civil liberties. It takes time for the sober second thought of the nation to be mobilized in the face of such provocation. For a period a very small group of demagogues seemed to hold the stage with hardly a challenge. But there are many intimations that the rising tide of intolerance since the War is not a long-term trend, but rather a cyclical fluctuation around a trend. And the trend may be responsive to great social forces making in the long run for greater tolerance, unless new external provocations press too heavily against it.

Now I have entitled this paper "Needed Research on the Tolerance of Nonconformity." I did so with deliberation, although I cannot take the time to outline in detail the kinds of further research that are needed. I chose this title to emphasize the lack of knowledge, in contrast with the extent of knowledge.

While . . . *Communism, Conformity, and Civil Liberties* has added some new facts to our body of knowledge and has proposed some new ways of conceptualizing the problems, it has not produced definitive answers. Its most important contribution, if any, should be in the stimulation of further inquiry.

Fortunately, psychology and the social sciences have come sufficiently of age so that inquiry need not be limited to essays in the armchair or unsystematic clinical observations, however useful they may be. The psychological mechanisms we have postulated are capable of experimental study, with explicit tests in laboratory situations. Such investigations have been going on, in ever-increasing number, and they need to be further accelerated. Sociologists and anthropologists, through field surveys, with better and better instruments for measuring the crucial responses, are demonstrating that even such difficult and elusive subjects as social values can be studied with some objectivity and precision and that there are very significant relationships between what people say and what they do, even though by no means a perfect correlation. And we know how to draw good probability samples, thanks to the mathematical statisticians, and how to make appropriate tests of significance.

The most crucial studies in the future may not be the big ones. They may be small intensive inquiries designed to test narrow restricted hypotheses. And some of the most relevant of these hypotheses may seem at the moment far removed from the burning issues of the day. (If any foundation executives happen to be around, I hope they have listened with special attentiveness to this last sentence.)

The maps we have now, including the one I have sought to draw for you today, are as crude as the maps of the western world in the early sixteenth century. But galleons are sailing the Spanish main, and, if more and more can be dispatched, we shall fill the gaps in our knowledge.

If, in turn, such knowledge can help ever so little in the preservation of the ideals of freedom enshrined here in Independence Square, the effort will not have been in vain.

B. *The Younger Generation Has More Schooling—What Does This Fact Portend?*

There is one crucial fact which could support the prediction that as the younger generation ages, it will still be more tolerant than its elders—given more or less the same external conditions. This fact is *the greater schooling which the younger generation has received.*

In thirty years, America has seen an almost revolutionary uplift in the schooling of its population at both the high school and college levels. Consequently, if education, *independent of age*, makes for tolerance, the present younger generation, when it reaches later years, should be more tolerant than its elders are today.

In all surveys, including the Census, there is a tendency for people to report more schooling than they had actually had. Thus, some people who tell us they finished high school probably did not. And there is some inflation in the college group, although trained interviewers will keep on questioning in order to screen out trade schools which the interviewee may call college. For our present purpose, it is not necessary to take the educational levels with precise literalness. It is quite safe to assume that most people who reported some high school education had more schooling than most of the people who reported grammar school only.

Figure 5-1 shows how sharply education differs by age. In the complete cross section shown at the top of the figure, 64 per cent of the people over sixty reported only a grade school education, as compared with only 14 per cent of the younger people in their twenties. Among the more interested people shown in the lower half of the chart, the *pattern* is the same, but the educational level in each age group is higher.

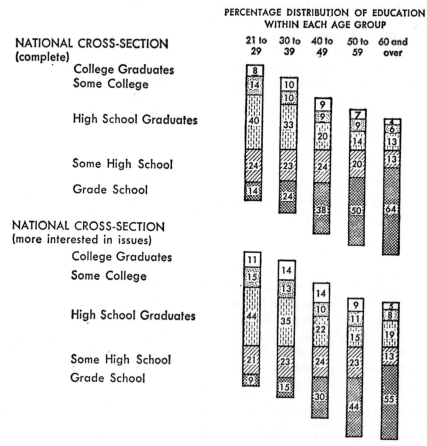

Figure 5-1. The older generation has much less education than the younger generation.

The question that we now ask of our data is important: *Among older people, as well as among younger people, by separate age groups, are the better educated more tolerant toward nonconformists?* If so, then one cannot say that aging alone will account for a difference between generations.

Figure 5-2 shows that in *all* age groups the better educated tend to be more tolerant than the less educated. The picture is quite decisive until we reach age sixty. Even among those sixty and over, those who have attended or graduated from college are more likely to be tolerant of nonconformists

PERCENTAGE DISTRIBUTION ON SCALE OF
WILLINGNESS TO TOLERATE NONCONFORMISTS

	LESS TOLERANT	IN-BETWEEN	MORE TOLERANT	
21 to 29				
College Graduates		23	77	60
Some College		28	69	78
High School Graduates	10	46	44	229
Some High School	15	53	32	109
Grade School	17	59	24	46
30 to 39				
College Graduates		22	75	96
Some College	8	36	56	88
High School Graduates	12	46	42	242
Some High School	15	50	35	154
Grade School	12	69	19	102
40 to 49				
College Graduates	7	29	64	86
Some College	9	38	53	64
High School Graduates	11	44	45	135
Some High School	17	49	34	146
Grade School	23	62	15	184
50 to 59				
College Graduates	10	33	57	40
Some College	14	42	44	48
High School Graduates	19	36	45	64
Some High School	18	59	23	97
Grade School	22	59	19	177
60 & Over				
College Graduates	8	61	31	26
Some College	19	54	27	41
High School Graduates	13	58	29	98
Some High School	20	65	15	69
Grade School	27	61	13	283

Figure 5-2. *The older generation and the less educated are less tolerant of nonconformists. Data are for "more interested" only. Numbers at right show size of sample.*

than those who have not completed high school, though the differences are smaller. Some bars in Figure 5-2 are based on too few cases to be decisive, but the over-all pattern is unmistakable.

We can say with some confidence, then, that older people are less tolerant not merely because they are older. As the educational level of those entering the older generation goes up decade after decade, we should expect our oldsters to be *increasingly tolerant*—unless external conditions change drastically.

At the same time, if we examine Figure 5-2 carefully, we observe that there is *also* a consistent tendency for the upper educational groups to become less tolerant as they get older. The percentages classed as "more tolerant" among college graduates goes down progressively on Figure 5-2 as age increases—77, 75, 64, 57, 31. A similar pattern, in spite of lower percentages throughout, exists for the "some college" group. The two high school groups and the grade school people show no very consistent tendency to become less tolerant with age, though all drop off somewhat in this respect by age sixty. This does not in the least invalidate the conclusion in the preceding paragraph. We may still, in effect, predict that a person, on the average, is likely to be more tolerant than his own parents. To this we must add: Although he is likely to be more tolerant when he reaches sixty than were his own parents at sixty, he may at the same time be less tolerant than he was in his own younger days.

In its implications for the future of the American scene, Figure 5-2 may have very considerable significance. Whatever may happen externally to stimulate greater or less tolerance, we now have a glimpse at the tendencies inherent in the changing structure of our population.

And we can improve that glimpse with the aid of further information from the survey.

SOME INTERESTING PSYCHOLOGICAL VARIABLES

Rigidity of Categorization. One of the aims of all education is to teach the importance of qualifying statements: for example, the concepts of true and false. In matters not immediately concerned with his daily life, the uneducated person sometimes has difficulty with statements such as, "This is likely to be true under such and such conditions; it is not so likely to be true under such and such conditions." Possibly, that is why education has somewhere been rather cynically defined as "a weakening of certainties." Moreover, one of the necessary conditions of tolerance of nonconformists would seem to be the ability to make distinctions—between the menace of a Communist in a key defense plant, let us say, and the risk to the community of a Socialist making a speech in a local hall. Rigidity of categorization—to use a rather clumsy though accurate phrase—would be expected among intolerant people in our sample.

How measure rigidity of categorization? We do not pretend to have a very good measure. Preferably we need a scale based on several internally consistent items. But one question was asked that sought, however imperfectly, to get at this factor. The interviewer read the following statement: *People can be divided into two classes—the weak and the strong,* and asked the respondent whether he agreed or disagreed with it.

Among "more interested" people, about a third disagreed and two-thirds agreed. Omitting 3 per cent who did not answer, we can cross-check the answers with the responses on the scale of tolerance toward nonconformists (Table 5-1).

Table 5-1. Rigidity of Categorization

	PERCENTAGE DISTRIBUTION				NUMBER OF CASES
	Less Tolerant	In Between	More Tolerant	Total	
"Disagreed"	9	42	49	100	940
"Agreed" (categorizers)	17	53	30	100	1,745

The "rigid categorizers," even though defined by a single, rather crude statement, are likely to be less tolerant of nonconformists than those who disagreed with the statement.

Now let us look at Figure 5-3. It shows that in each age group the better educated are more likely than others to disagree with the statement about two classes, the weak and the strong. The lower the educational level, the more numerous the rigid categorizers.

This finding must be regarded as suggestive rather than as proved. But the general pattern of relationships in Figure 5-3, which says nothing whatever about Communism or radicalism, is strikingly similar to the pattern in Figure 5-3, which was based on our scale of tolerance of selected types of nonconformists.

Authoritarian and Conformist Attitudes toward Child-Rearing. Now let us try two more statements to tap psychological dispositions. Both have to do with ideas about child-rearing. They are:

A child should never be allowed to talk back to his parents, or else he will lose respect for them.
If a child is unusual in any way, his parents should get him to be more like other children.

People who agree with the first statement are expressing what we might call an *authoritarian* attitude; those who agree with the second, a *conformist* attitude. In their extreme forms, both tendencies, like the previous one on categorization, contain a strong element of rigidity. (The wording of each question might be improved. In particular, there may be a legitimate objection to using the words, "talk back" rather than "differ." But these are old questions used in previous research, and, as will be observed, they seem to be discriminating.) We see in Table 5-2 that those who would be very strict

QUESTION: *People can be divided into two classes—the weak and the strong. Do you agree or disagree?*

PERCENTAGE "DISAGREEING" AMONG THOSE ANSWERING

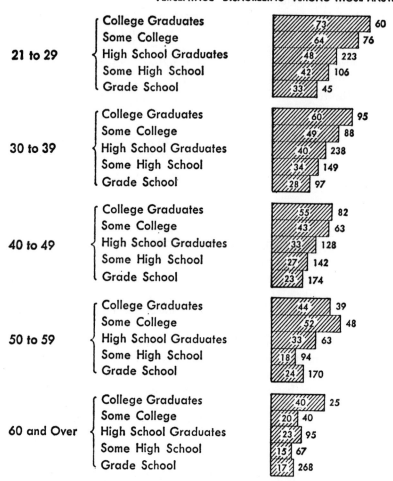

Figure 5-3. The older generation and the less educated are more likely to be "rigid categorizers." Data are for the "more interested" only. Also excluded are about 3 per cent who did not express an opinion on this question. Numbers at right of bars give size of samples.

in not letting children talk back to parents are less likely to be tolerant on our scale of tolerance toward selected types of nonconformists.

Likewise, we get a relationship between strict conformity in child-training and intolerance toward the kind of adult nonconformity we are studying (Table 5-3).

Clearly, there are psychological elements in common between these attitudes toward child-training and our scale of tolerance.

Table 5-2. Attitudes toward Child-Rearing

	PERCENTAGE DISTRIBUTION OF SCORES ON SCALE OF TOLERANCE*				NUMBER OF CASES
	Less Tolerant	In Between	More Tolerant	Total	
"Disagreed"	7	38	55	100	979
"Agreed" (authoritarian answer)	19	56	25	100	1,717

* Excluding 3 per cent who did not answer.

Now, as before, let us see how age and education are related to these attitudes toward child-training. Figure 5-4 tells the story. In the case of both authoritarian and conformist attitudes, the pattern of response by age and education is remarkably similar to Figure 5-2. Within every age group the tendency exists, though somewhat less consistent among the oldest than among the youngest, for the less educated to approve authoritarian and more conformist child-rearing practices. Also within educational groups, particularly among the better educated, the older tend more to be authoritarian and conformist than the younger.

Just as education tends to introduce shadings of categorization between true and false, strong and weak, etc., so, presumably, it tends to encourage respect for dissenting points of view. In school, people are taught about great dissenters of history, including the founding fathers of this nation. The farther pupils go up the educational ladder, the more likely they are to learn to respect the right of people to be different from themselves, *even if* and *especially when* they disapprove of such people. This ought to be reflected in attitudes toward child-rearing. To allow a child to differ with his parents and to develop his own individuality—as long as this tendency does not lead to antisocial behavior or delinquency—is apparently much more common in better educated families than in others, in spite of the fact that the words "talk back" used in our question may to some people imply defiance rather than mere difference of opinion.

But let us not overlook another fact shown in Figures 5-3 and 5-4. That is the tendency for older people, especially among the better educated, to have more rigidly authoritarian or conformist attitudes toward child-training than younger people *at the same educational level*. Is this a mere function of aging, of hardening of the arteries? It could be, but it seems highly unlikely in the light of what we know about *changing cultural patterns* in the last thirty years. The people of fifty and over, at any educational level, were more

Table 5-3. Child-Rearing and Conformity

	PERCENTAGE DISTRIBUTION OF SCORES ON SCALE OF TOLERANCE*				NUMBER OF CASES
	Less Tolerant	In Between	More Tolerant	Total	
"Disagreed"	8	41	51	100	1,142
"Agreed" (conformist answer)	19	55	26	100	1,484

* Excluding 5 per cent who had no opinion.

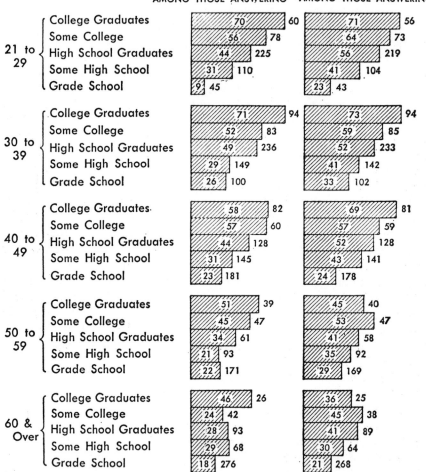

Figure 5-4. *Older generation and less educated are less likely to oppose authoritarian and conformist child-rearing practices. Numbers at right give size of samples.*

likely themselves to have grown up in authoritarian families than the people in their twenties and thirties. "Life with Father" is as antique as the gaslight. Moreover, the climate of formal education is different today from what it was a generation ago. Corporal punishment has almost disappeared from the schools. Progressive education, even though its more extreme forms of permissiveness may be rare, has penetrated to some degree into every little red schoolhouse. The older forms of drill and discipline have been replaced by efforts to motivate the child to develop his own enthusiasms and incentives to learn, and some people, including some educators, think the pendulum may have swung too far. Be that as it may, what we see in Figures 5-3 and 5-4—especially the latter—may be the effect, above all others, of a changing *climate* of education in both school and family.

If this is true, we need to be very cautious about guessing that when the man or woman, at a given educational level, who is thirty today becomes sixty, he or she may be less tolerant than now.

Table 5-4. Tolerance and Optimism

	PERCENTAGE DISTRIBUTION OF SCORES ON SCALE OF TOLERANCE				NUMBER OF CASES
	Less Tolerant	In Between	More Tolerant	Total	
"My life will be better" (optimists)	9	42	49	100	1,717
All others	18	53	29	100	1,046

Optimism as a Psychological Variable. What we have just said may lead some to conclude that *mere aging by itself* is not an important consideration at all. Before leaping to that conclusion, we need to look closely at another variable. In Chapter 3 of *Communism, Conformity, and Civil Liberties,* we noted that the very first question asked in the interview was: *On the whole, do you think life will be better for you or worse, in the next few years than it is now?* We observed that, in spite of many anxieties, the largest proportion of which had to do with financial, health, and other matters that were personal or familial, the majority of the cross-section seemed to be optimistic about their personal future.

Now there is substantial psychological theory which would predict a relationship between optimism about personal affairs and tolerance toward nonconformists. Optimism is not a perfect index of lack of anxiety. Some optimists may be very anxious people who are whistling in the dark. But the idea is that the individual who is very troubled, for whatever reason, needs to blame someone aside from himself for his troubles. (We discussed this same mechanism in Chapter 3 of *Communism, Conformity, and Civil Liberties,* but in the much more specific context of anxieties about war.) It may be a quite unconscious process. The dark forces of Communism, some of whose followers can be suspected of operating in disguise as loyal Americans, are one of the obvious targets for blame, directly for the world's troubles and indirectly, if sometimes unconsciously, for one's personal troubles. It is consistent with such a theory, though not necessarily proof of it, that we find optimists more likely to be tolerant of nonconformists on our scale (Table 5-4) than are other people. (Those who predicted that

life for themselves would be better in the next few years than it is now constituted 63 per cent of the interested cross section with whom we are dealing.
We call them "optimists." Those who said life would be worse constituted
11 per cent; those who said life would be worse, 21 per cent; and those who said "don't
know," 5 per cent. We lump all these together, not as pessimists, but as less
hopeful, on the whole, than the "optimists.")

The relationship is significant, in spite of the imperfections of optimism
as an index and also in spite of a further psychological expectation, namely,
that some people will be both optimists and relatively free of anxiety primarily because they have found a comfortable scapegoat to blame for their
troubles. Such a sequential relationship, if it occurs, could be delineated only
by a much more penetrating examination than the interview on which this
study is based.

Now optimism is a variable that we should expect to have some relation
both to education and age, as it does indeed, according to Figure 5-5 and
with a pattern on the whole very much like the patterns of the preceding
diagrams.

The education variable could have some direct relationship to optimism-
pessimism because, presumably, education should equip a person to handle
better the fear of the uncertain and unknown. But, with even more plausibility and less subtlety, we can simply point out that the more educated a
person is, *on the average*, the more income he is likely to have and the
better and probably more secure is his future. He therefore has greater cause
for personal optimism on economic grounds alone.

But what about optimism and age within a given educational group?
First, let it be noted again that Figure 5-5 shows a quite regularly declining
proportion of optimism with age at each educational level, with the exception
of the grade school people, who are relatively low at all age groups. For
example, for college graduates the figures by age are 87, 90, 74, 64, and
35 per cent. One can plumb some psychological depths on the subject of
age and optimism, but there are also plausible expanations on the surface.
Obviously, a person of eighty can hardly be as hopeful about his future in
the next few years as a man of thirty. The older one gets, the more physical
infirmities he or she acquires and the more worries about security. Physical
and social factors that are inevitable accompaniments of aging would tend
to combine in the production of increased personal anxiety, which would
tend to produce increased pessimism, which in turn would tend to produce
increased intolerance, at least in some people. Here, then, we have a factor
which should operate to make the person of sixty, say, somewhat less likely
to be tolerant than he himself was at thirty.

This analysis has been based solely on the three-fifths of the national
cross section which we have labeled as "more interested" in the internal
Communist threat and the methods of dealing with it. This subgroup is a
strategic one to study because it includes most, though not all, of the people

QUESTION: On the whole, do you think it will be better for you or worse, in the next few years than it is now?

PERCENTAGE ANSWERING "BETTER" AMONG ALL RESPONDENTS

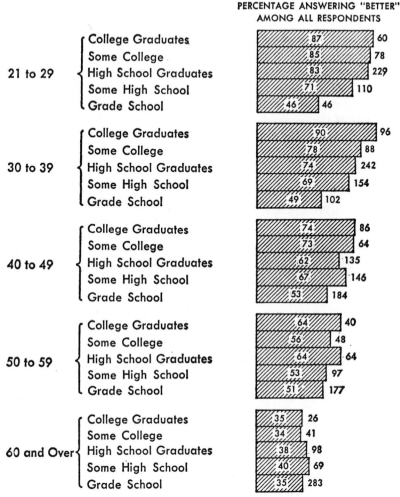

Figure 5-5. *The older generation and the less educated are less likely to be optimists. Data are for "more interested" only. Numbers at right give size of samples.*

who can be expected to translate opinions into action. A separate analysis has been made of the "less interested" segment of our cross section, duplicating in most respects what we have presented in this chapter for the "more interested." The data hardly need be reported here, because without any important exceptions they show the same patterns that have been exhibited in this chapter. The only exceptions are occasionally among the better educated people who happen to be among the "less interested." They are so few in number, however, that no conclusions about them can be safely drawn. Most of the above analysis also has been run in duplicate for the American Institute of Public Opinion and National Opinion Research Center surveys separately. The number of cases in some of the boxes gets too small for confident analysis, but it can be reported that the broad conclusions reached in this chapter, especially as based on Figures 5-1 to 5-5, would be identical if either survey had been used alone.

Throughout this chapter, attention has been focused on the "more interested" block of the national cross section, but not on our special sample of arbitrarily selected community leaders. These leaders, it must be remembered, are not part of the national cross section. We shall conclude the chapter with a brief analysis of the community leaders when differentiated by age and education.

THE YOUNGER AND BETTER EDUCATED COMMUNITY LEADERS ARE THE MOST LIKELY TO TOLERATE NONCONFORMITY

Study of the community leaders adds confirmation to what was reported above. As we learned in Chapter 2 of *Communism, Conformity, and Civil Liberties,* the leaders, on the average, were much more likely than others to be tolerant toward nonconformists.

Table 5-5. Tolerance, Education, and Age

	Percentage Scoring "More Tolerant" on Scale	Number of Cases
College graduates	79	673
All others	51	827
Under 50	70	864
50 and over	59	634

We now can report that among the community leaders the most tolerant were found among the relatively younger and better educated. Since the leaders tend to be well educated and middle-aged, we shall analyze them by two age groups, under fifty and fifty and over, and by two educational groups, college graduates and others. Findings for all leaders combined are shown in Table 5-5.

It will be remembered from Chapter 2 of *Communism, Conformity, and Civil Liberties* that fourteen types of community leaders appear in this special sample. Among these fourteen, there were enough cases in each of the two educational categories—college and noncollege—to permit twelve comparisons by education. (Presidents of bar associations were all college graduates except one; only five of the presidents of labor union locals were college graduates.) In all twelve comparisons, without exception, the college graduates were more tolerant than the noncollege graduates. Enough cases were available to make thirteen comparisons by age (only four of the presidents of the Parent-Teachers' Association were fifty years old or over). In twelve of the comparisons, those under fifty were more likely to be tolerant on our scale than those fifty and over. In one case (chairmen of the school board), the younger and older chairmen were tied in percentage among the more tolerant.

As might be expected, the community leaders were less likely than the cross section to fall into the classes which we called "rigid categorizers" or "endorsers of authoritarian or conformist attitudes toward child-rearing." Nevertheless, many of the leaders did fall into each of these classes, and those who did tended to be less tolerant of nonconformists on our scale than those who did not. The one exception to the picture which we have seen in the cross section was with respect to the "optimism" variable. Four out of five of the leaders said that they thought life would be better for them in the next few years than it is now, as compared with three out of five in our cross section of "interested" people. But so few of the remainder of the leaders said life would be worse (most saying it would be "about the same") that there is no difference on our tolerance scale between those who said "better" and all others.

All in all, we may find in the special sample of leaders the same general patterns, with minor exceptions, that we found in the cross section. Clearly, the younger generation of leadership tends to be more tolerant than the older generation which it will gradually be replacing.

6

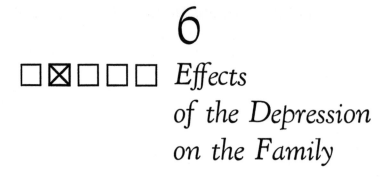 *Effects of the Depression on the Family*

Here are two excerpts from a programmatic study on the family published in 1937 as one of a series of monographs issued by the Social Science Research Council to blueprint needed research on social aspects of the depression. The author was executive secretary of the project as a whole, which resulted in some excellent monographs but which did not generate the expected amount of subsequent research, mainly because war came, concern about the depression dwindled, and much potential data were irretrievably lost.

The first paper, a brief excerpt from the introduction to the monograph on the family, by the present author and his colleague, Paul F. Lazarsfeld, may be of some interest because of its effort to classify the kinds of general problems to which research, initiated only after the worst of the depression was over, might direct itself.

The second excerpt illustrates, with several numerical examples, the possibility of doing research on the possible impact of the depression on marriage as an institution. Other sections of the monograph deal with the effects of the depression on the total marriage rate as a whole and on other aspects of family life. The reader will note efforts to operationalize such concepts as that of "impulsive" marriages and to relate them either to already existing census data or to unpublished data that might be reanalyzed.

It must be remembered that the idea of sampling surveys of the general population, such as constitute almost a staple of social research today, had hardly come over the horizon at this period of time. Consequently, official data of necessity had to be the major source of data. Today the relative ease with which one can conduct a national survey may be tempting students of social science to overlook the riches that await imaginative analysis of published or unpublished data that already have been collected as part of some official record. Often one finds students rushing off to study some inadequate little sample of a few hundred cases that they collect themselves, when they might have done a far superior study by utilizing the mammoth compendiums, often unpublished, that repose in official archives.

A. *Some Preliminary Considerations*

Theoretically, one might conceive of two general types of situations in which depressions and marriage and the family might be interrelated. In statistical terminology, they may be described as follows:

1. *Corresponding cyclical fluctuations with no alteration of the secular trend.* An example is the relationship between the marriage rate and the business cycle. Scores of studies in the past hundred years, covering many of the countries of western Europe as well as the United States, have shown that when business is good, the marriage rate is high, and when business is bad, the marriage rate is low.

2. *Corresponding cyclical fluctuations, with an alteration of the secular trend.* For purposes of correlational analysis, the cyclical fluctuations are dissected from the trend and treated as independent of it. The justification is that the trend is known often to be a product of a multitude of slowly changing factors, such as increasing mechanization, urbanization, communication, education, and secularization. Nevertheless, it is theoretically possible for a depression, by accelerating or decelerating some major components of the secular trend, to produce some alteration in the slope of the trend. No clear-cut example is at hand, demonstrating such an effect on the family over a considerable period of time. Yet such depression effects, not amenable to precise quantification, may be the most significant of all. If one could plot a curve showing over many decades the proportion of the family budget that went to the care of aged parents, there doubtless would be positive cyclical fluctuations corresponding to periods of depression. The social security legis-

"Statement of Purpose," from Chapter 1, pp. 3-6, *Research Memorandum on the Family in the Depression*, Bulletin 29, by Samuel A. Stouffer and Paul F. Lazarsfeld, New York: Social Science Research Council, 1937.

lation growing out of the depression of the 1930's may alter this trend in the future and may reduce the magnitude of the cyclical fluctuations in the social series in the depressions of the future. From the scientific standpoint, this type of depression influence differs from the cyclical type in that its occurrence ordinarily is not predictable in advance. One could have predicted the decline in the marriage rate in the depression; one could not have predicted the passage of the Social Security Act.

Studies of the relationship between depressions and social institutions such as marriage and the family take on additional significance for sociology if we look at a depression as a specimen of the more general concept "crisis situation." In any great mass crisis, such as drought, pestilence, flood, or general unemployment, there is an increase in the functions of government and a substitution of collective action for individual and familial action. Relief funds, for example, supplement or replace the earnings of the breadwinner or the income of the family enterprise such as the farm; and protective functions, such as the care of the sick, tend to be transferred from the family to the community or state. From still another point of view, the depression as a specimen of "crisis situation" invites sociological study. It may be that in the efforts to adjust to the shock of depression, or to war, or other dramatic crisis situations, *change* itself becomes temporarily a habit, and in such a period of fluidity of attitudes and habits, the most rapid strides are taken to overcome lags of long standing between technological developments and social institutions. Thus, while social security legislation might have been attained in the course of time, its arrival was no doubt speeded up by the depression of the 1930's.

The student of marriage and the family can start with three rather well-established facts:

1. Fewer families are begun by marriage during a depression.
2. Fewer families are augmented by births during a depression.
3. Fewer families are broken by divorce during a depression.

These three findings were well established before the depression of the 1930's, and there is ample evidence that the events of recent years correspond to what past findings would have led one to expect.

If, however, the student seeks to go much beyond these three gross relationships, he will find data for past depressions largely or wholly lacking.

Time after time he will be forced to deal with only one cycle, namely, that beginning its downswing in the winter of 1929–1930, reaching low points in the autumn of 1932 and early spring of 1933, and irregularly climbing since. Any study which is limited to this period is necessarily less satisfactory than a study that compares relationships through several cycles of depression and prosperity. Indeed, the findings often will have to be regarded as tentative or suggestive, rather than conclusive, in so far as they attempt to attribute a change in marriage or the family to the depression. Yet the accumulation of hypotheses, illustrated by the happenings in the 1930's, may enrich sociological theory and provide a useful basis for research in future cycles of depression and prosperity. Such research must begin some time. It would have been desirable if it could have started a century earlier— or, at the least, with the depression of the 1890's. Lacking past bases, we can hope to extract, before it is too late, some facts from the depression of the 1930's that can be handed on as a legacy to the research workers of the future.

There are, of course, some problems that may be considered answerable if only one depression is considered. The factors operating to reduce the birth rate are so subtly associated with general trends in the so-called "urbanization of attitudes" and "secularization of life" that one obviously needs several cycles before one can feel confident in attributing a *given amount* of decline in births to a depression. Yet when one limits the inquiry to asking whether a depression *tends* to reduce or increase the birth rate, one may conceivably use data from a single depression to make a prediction likely to be verified in all depressions reasonably comparable in character. This is made possible by considering separately the forces operating to increase or decrease the birth rate and asking how the depression tends to affect each of these forces. Thus, the economic pressures on those families to whom children would be a luxury consumption good might be expected to increase and therefore to encourage the use of contraception. Moreover, social attitudes in opposition to contraception might be expected to weaken in the face of the apparent oversupply of population with millions unemployed and in the face of the necessity of public support of child-bearing in relief families. On the other hand, the security and medical care provided by relief may have encouraged child-bearing in the relief population, while among the general population the expense of contraceptives may have deterred their use. If these factors each could be examined and if it could be found reasonable that the effect of the first two should be much greater than the effect of the last two, one would be on safer ground in interpreting the depression decline in the birth rate as "due to" depression, even though adequate data were available for only one depression period.

B. Effects on Marriage as an Institution

Two important tendencies among others have been noted in American marriage during the past generation. Both tendencies represent a break with older traditions. One tendency might be described as the tendency to view

"Marriage and the Sex Mores," from Chapter 6, pp. 153-176, *Research Memorandum on the Family in the Depression*, Bulletin 29, by Samuel A. Stouffer and Paul F. Lazarsfeld. New York: Social Science Research Council, 1937.

marriage mainly as a device to legalize sexual intercourse, carrying few obligations and no necessary expectation of permanence of union or of children to carry on the family name. For want of a better word, these may be called "impulsive" marriages. The other tendency is for an increase in marriages which cross religious, nationality, and socio-economic class lines. These are called "mixed" marriages. The two tendencies are similar in many ways, and an increase in "mixed" marriages may be produced by many of the same factors that produce an increase in "impulsive" marriages in general. The social implications of "mixed" marriages, particularly as they are indexes not only of changing attitudes toward marriage, but also, more widely, of assimilation and of the breakdown of stratification, are such, however, that it seems wise to treat the two tendencies more or less separately.

In addition to these two tendencies, there is another important factor, concerning which, however, American data permit no assumption as to the longtime tendency. This is the factor of pregnancy before marriage. As will be discussed subsequently, data for Australia show that the number of marriages in which the bride was pregnant declined much less during the depression than the number of marriages that did not result in the birth of children within seven months of marriage. In Australia at least one-fifth of all marriages involve pregnant brides. A study by one of the writers of Wisconsin cities, reported for the first time in Table 6-6, suggests that the proportion is far from negligible in the United States. No consideration of the effects of the depression on the institution of marriage would be complete unless some account were taken of the possible effects of the depression on "forced" marriages.

The subjects of "impulsive" marriages, "mixed" marriages, and "forced" marriages will be taken up in order, keeping in mind, of course, that the categories are not mutually exclusive.

"IMPULSIVE" MARRIAGES

The passage of legislation in a large number of states prior to the depression to make hasty or impulsive marriages more difficult may be regarded as an effort to arrest a growing trend away from marriage undertaken with more traditional attitudes.[1] What happened in the depression?

Let us assume, for a moment, that we were able to classify marriages along a continuum with the most "impulsive" at the left. Let us assume that we found that the percentage of marriages to the left of a fixed point on this scale increased steadily during the twenty years up to 1929, but decreased sharply during the depression and remained lower upon recovery from the

1. Vernier, Chester G. *American Family Laws.* Stanford: Stanford University Press. 1931. Vol. I Pp. 54-58, 199-203; and Hall, Fred S. "Marriage and the Law." *Annals of the American Academy of Political and Social Science.* 159:110-15. January 1932. See also U.S. Bureau of the Census. *Marriage and Divorce.* 1922 to 1932 annually.

depression than in predepression years. We might then be justified in an inference that the effect of the depression was to arrest the tendency toward "impulsive" marriages, although even here we would need to show that the arrest was not produced as a cumulative effect of the legislation passed in predepression years.

Let us assume, on the other hand, that the percentage of marriages to the left of a fixed point on our scale actually increased during the depression at a faster rate than previously and that this increase continued upon recovery. We might then be justified in assuming that the tendency of the depression was to restrain those couples to whom marriage would be a solemn obligation and to encourage light and impulsive undertaking of the marriage vows among a greater proportion of the young people.

Theoretically, in which of these two directions would one expect the depression to exert its influence?

One argument might proceed somewhat as follows: The depression presumably weakened the respect for custom and tradition with respect to economic matters; therefore, it might be inferred that this weakening carried over to other aspects of life. Old Puritan ideals, such as the ideal of thrift, were subjected to repeated shocks. The depression presumably weakened the authority of parents, particularly of parents who were themselves casualties of the economic disaster. In so far as the depression increased mobility, it may have torn an increasing number of young people loose from parental ties. The net effect, consequently, would be to increase the proportion of marriages made without parental knowledge or consent and to increase the proportion of marriages entered into without a religious or moral obligation to live together "until death do us part" or to produce children. In further support of this position, it might be suggested that in so far as the depression accelerated the spread of knowledge of contraception among the unmarried, it tended to increase marriages undertaken without the expectation of producing children. Finally, it might be argued that the asssurance of relief care, as the depression proceeded, tended to remove the restraint which lack of funds for support might have had on "impulsive" marriages.

A counter argument might proceed somewhat as follows: Much of the same reasoning that would lead one to think that the weakening of custom and tradition due to the depression should increase the proportion of "impulsive" marriages might also be invoked to show that the result should be a decrease. Why, indeed, it may be asked, should couples whose principal object in marriage was the legalization of sexual intercourse bother about those legalities, once the older conceptions of marriage had been altered? Would not the effect of the depression be to increase casual and extra-legal unions rather than marriages with lightly assumed obligations? As for the authority of such parents as were themselves casualties of the depression, the effects of this decline in prestige may have been more than compensated by an increased obligation on the part of the older children to provide for the parents at the cost of not marrying. As for increasing mobility, there is, first, a doubt as to whether mobility increased during the depression, and second, a possibility that the tendency of such mobility as existed was more strongly in the direction of young unmarried people returning to parental protection than in the direction of such people leaving home. Finally, it may be argued that the advent of relief and subsequent "loss of morale" may have induced many permanent unions to be started on the basis of relief financing.

The writers are quite confident that case studies could be made that would supply examples of and insight into all the tendencies hypothecated in either argument, yet would leave unanswered the question as to whether the one set of forces was more potent than the other. The problem may be too complex to permit an adequate separation of all of the pushes toward and pulls against "impulsive" marriage. Moreover, it is quite obvious that even if we were sure (as we are not) of the general tendency of the depression to weaken conventions, we can not infer from this general tendency what would be the effect on marriages during the depression and recovery as compared with former years, and for such data we must turn to sources for a statistical study.

Unfortunately, the term "impulsive" is quite inadequate. By such a marriage is here meant one into which couples enter for the legalization of their sexual companionship, more or less hastily, in contrast to one in which serious thought is given to solemnity of the vows or to the obligation to produce children and to carry on the family name. Such a description, essentially psychological, is unworkable statistically. Some indexes must be sought with the hope that they may have some relationship to the intangibles.

No single index would seem adequate. Only if all, or most, of several indexes showed a strong tendency in the same direction, would there be a basis for an inference that the shift during the depression was toward, or away from, "impulsive" marriages. Among such indexes might be the following:

1. Marriage in a community other than residence of the bride and groom, especially in "Gretna Greens."

2. Marriage by a magistrate rather than a clergyman.

3. Divorce or separation within five years of marriage, especially if no children had been born.

These indexes would seem to have more validity if used in connection with younger couples, say, those among whom the bridegrooms were twenty-one or under, than in connection with older couples. The reader doubtless can cite from his own acquaintance numerous examples of couples whose attitude toward marriage at the time of marriage was in keeping with the older conventions yet who would be classified under 1, 2, or 3. Further exploration of the meaning of these indexes is needed. More studies like the work of Burgess and Cottrell (who find a close relationship between 1 and 2 and an unsatisfactory marital adjustment) are desirable.[2] The relationship between divorce and these indexes could be studied directly by an examination of the divorce records on file in a number of states. One such study, made in Wisconsin in 1932 by Young and Dedrick,[3] shows that the probability of a divorce was much greater if Wisconsin residents married in adjoining states and also that the period elapsing between divorce and remarriage was much less for such marriages. Ogburn,[4] using correlation analysis, finds for American cities in 1920 a significant correlation between early marriage and divorce, a correlation which persists after such factors as nativity and the percentage engaged in manufacturing are held constant. One must note, however, that what we are seeking are indexes of attitudes with which couples enter marriage, and the fact that a given marriage ended in divorce is not necessarily an indication of a frivolous attitude toward marriage at the inception. The indexes at best can do little more than provide a basis for inference as to the *direction* of the shift in attitudes in the depression.

One especially serious fault of these indexes is the possible tendency of "forced" marriages, in which the bride is pregnant, to be included in disproportionately large numbers among nonresident and magistrate marriages.

Let us consider research that might be done involving the indexes mentioned.

1. *Did marriage in a community other than the residence of the bride and bridegroom tend to increase during the depression, and was this increase maintained upon recovery?*

Published data provide an answer to this question for only one state, Massachusetts, as far as the writers know, although unpublished tabulations might be available for upstate New York, where published figures by communities refer to place of bride's residence only and not to place of marriage, and for a number of other states. The Massachusetts data are summarized in Table 6-1.

It will be seen that there was a steady straight-line trend of increase in the proportion of marriages in the left-hand column prior to the depression and that between 1930 and 1933 the trend continued upward unabated. It must be remembered that the industrial depression hit Massachusetts textile centers earlier than other parts of the country. In 1934–1935, with the upswing of the business cycle, there was some evidence of a reversal of the trend. It is quite clear that the Massachusetts evidence is in favor rather than against

2. Burgess, E. W. and Cottrell, L. S. "The Prediction of Adjustment in Marriage." *American Sociological Review.* 1:737-51. October 1936. The findings reported above appear in unpublished manuscript tables, quoted here by permission.

3. Young, Kimball and Dedrick, C. L. "Variation in the Duration of Marriages Which End in Divorce, with Special Reference to State of Wisconsin." *Journal of the American Statistical Association.* 27:160-67. June 1932.

4. Groves, E. R. and Ogburn, W. F., *American Marriage and Family Relationships.* New York: Henry Holt & Co., 1928. Pp. 374-78.

Table 6-1. Percentage Distribution of Marriages According to Whether Performed in Town or City of Which Nuptial Parties Were Residents: Massachusetts, 1919-1935*

Year	Groom and Bride Nonresidents	Bride Nonresident	Groom Nonresident	Groom and Bride Residents	Total
1919	12.1	5.2	23.0	59.7	100
1920	12.0	5.4	23.5	59.2	100
1921	13.7	5.3	24.0	57.1	100
1922	13.5	5.3	23.2	58.1	100
1923	13.5	5.5	22.8	58.2	100
1924	14.2	5.8	23.4	56.7	100
1925	14.5	5.9	24.1	55.4	100
1926	14.8	6.3	24.4	54.6	100
1927	15.7	5.8	24.8	53.7	100
1928	17.2	6.1	25.1	51.6	100
1929	16.8	6.4	25.4	51.4	100
1930	17.7	6.2	26.0	50.1	100
1931	18.4	6.3	26.0	49.3	100
1932	19.5	6.3	25.4	48.7	100
1933	19.0	6.1	24.4	50.4	100
1934	18.0	5.9	24.4	51.7	100
1935	18.1	5.7	24.2	52.0	100

* Annual Report on the Vital Statistics of Massachusetts, Mass. Pub. Doc. No. 1.

an affirmative answer to the first part of our question and tends to be in favor of a negative answer to the second part. This suggests that, if the depression continued the trend toward nonresident marriages within Massachusetts, the depression also may have generated a reaction which showed up during the recovery period. As far as the writers know, there were no statutory changes in Massachusetts or neighboring states sufficient to affect the marriage rate appreciably during the past decade, although this possibility should be checked carefully by anyone carrying forward a study in more detail.

It would be illuminating to break down the Massachusetts series, or a sample of it, by age of bride and bridegroom, previous marital condition, and whether or not married by a magistrate. This breakdown would require, of course, a study of the original marriage certificates. A similar study could be made in any state in the union, though most conveniently in those states which file applications for marriage licenses or copies of these applications at their state capitals.

Another approach to the problem would be to study the incidence of marrying before the depression, during the depression, and during recovery, in countries which have a reputation as "Gretna Greens." Some of these "Gretna Greens," such as Elkton, Maryland, Crown Point, Indiana, and Waukegan, Illinois, are nationally famous for the number of nonresident marriages, often of the "runaway" type.[5]

The student must be careful to remember that "Gretna Greens" usually

5. See U.S. Bureau of the Census, *Marriage and Divorce*, 1924. P. 13.

are located near state borders and that the number of marriages will fluctuate according to changes in state laws. For example, several hundred Wisconsin couples were married annually in Winona, Minnesota, following the passage of the so-called "eugenics" law in Wisconsin. In 1931 Minnesota established a five-day waiting period between the license and marriage, and by 1932 the total number of marriages in Winona was less than half the number prior to 1931. On the other hand, changes in local practice will alter the marriage rate in a "Gretna Green," even though the laws in the states involved are unchanged. The decline in marriages between 1934 and 1935 in Lake County, Illinois, doubtless may be explained by such a change in practice.

It would be desirable to summarize changes in marriage legislation and judicial interpretation in the depression period. From correspondence with the attorney generals in forty-three states, the writers believe that changes in marriage laws were probably no more numerous in the depression than in the four or five years preceding. Colorado, Idaho, Iowa, Minnesota, Ohio, and Wyoming established a five-day waiting period in 1931, Oregon a three-day waiting period in 1933, and Montana and Pennsylvania a three-day waiting period in 1935. The waiting period was repealed or amended, however, in Colorado, Idaho, Iowa, Montana, North Carolina, and Wyoming.

2. *Did the proportion of marriages performed by magistrates tend to increase at a faster rate during the depression than the proportion of marriages performed by clergymen, and was this increase maintained upon recovery?*

If it were found that the proportion of magistrate marriages took a jump during the depression, one should hesitate before assuming that this necessarily meant a widespread secularization of attitudes toward marriage. The fee paid to magistrates is usually somewhat less than the fee paid to clergymen. Nevertheless, it seems reasonable to assume that some tendency toward secularization of attitudes toward marriage would be indicated. (One state, Kentucky, which did not permit civil marriages previously, amended its law in 1932 in order to permit them.) Some case studies would be helpful in giving some insight into the changed meaning, if any, of marriages by magistrates during the depression.

As far as the writers know, no data pertaining to this point are tabulated in any state. In at least fifteen states,[6] the title of the officiator, whether clergyman or magistrate, appears on the marriage license or application in a space provided for the title, and it would be a very simple matter to make a hand count of the licenses on file. It would be even more desirable to use a sampling procedure (if funds did not permit a more detailed study) and compare religious and civil marriages over a time period, with respect to age of the couple, previous marital condition, residence or nonresidence, and perhaps other breakdowns. This could best be done if the data were coded and punched on cards.

6. Alabama, California, Connecticut, Delaware, Florida, Kansas, Massachusetts, Michigan, Mississippi, New Hampshire, New Jersey, New York, Rhode Island, South Dakota, and Vermont.

A possible clue as to what might be found in the United States is suggested by the trend in the percentage that civil marriages are of all marriages in Australia. (See Table 6-2.) The depression hit Australia in 1928

Table 6-2. Civil Marriages as a Percentage of All Marriages: Australia, 1921-1934*

Year	Percentage	Year	Percentage
1921	4.4	1928	7.1
1922	4.7	1929	7.6
1923	5.1	1930	9.2
1924	5.7	1931	10.0
1925	5.7	1932	9.7
1926	6.1	1933	8.9
1927	6.6	1934	8.3

* Commonwealth Bureau of Census and Statistics, *Australian Demography*, 1934 and previous years.

and reached its depth in 1931–1932, business improving slowly but definitely since. It will be seen that there was an upward trend in civil marriage and that this upward trend was given a boost by the depression, but that upon recovery there was a recession.

3. *Did the proportion of depression marriages ending in separation or divorce within five years increase at a faster rate during the depression than prior to the depression, and was this increase maintained during the recovery period? Especially, was there an exceptional increase in childless marriages ending in divorce?*

These questions can be studied at the present time only as they relate to marriages in the beginning of the depression. Later they can be studied with respect to all depression marriages. It would be especially valuable if these questions were studied with 1 and 2 as background factors in the tabulations. It is hardly necessary to point out the care which must be taken in interpretation, lest an increase in early divorces among those married later in the depression as compared with the divorces among those married earlier in the depression be attributed to a more frivolous attitude toward marriage. The conditions facilitating divorce must themselves be carefully examined.[7]

"MIXED" MARRIAGES

For an analysis of the social implications of this question, the reader is referred to Donald Young, *Research Memorandum on Minority Peoples in the Depression*, in this series.[8]

At least three types of mixed marriage may be distinguished for purposes of statistical study:

7. Stouffer, Samuel A. and Lazarsfeld, Paul F. *Research Memorandum on the Family in the Depression.* New York: Social Science Research Council, 1937. Bulletin 29. Chapter III.

8. Studies in the Social Aspects of the Depression. New York: Social Science Research Council.

1. Marriages in which one party was of one religious faith, the other of a different faith.

2. Marriages in which one party belonged to one foreign nationality group, the other party belonged to a different foreign nationality group or was of older American stock.

3. Marriages in which one party belonged to one socio-economic stratum, the other to a different stratum.

1. *Did intermarriage between religious groups increase at a faster rate during the depression than prior to the depression, and was this increase maintained during the recovery period?*

This question has implications not only with respect to the breaking away from family and nationality traditions, but also with respect to the effects of the depression on religion.

For purposes of illustrating the general problem, we shall confine the discussion to Catholic–non-Catholic intermarriage. Mixed marriages involving Catholics are of two types: those which are performed by the church and those which are not. Strictly speaking, the latter do not involve Catholics, since the Catholic spouse automatically deprives himself of affiliation with the church.

Each Catholic parish in most dioceses reports annually to its diocesan office the number of marriages performed by the church in the parish. In some dioceses these are divided into two groups—marriages in which both parties are Catholics and marriages in which one party is not a Catholic. For a few of the dioceses, the numbers of Catholic and mixed marriages are reported in the *Official Catholic Directory*.[9] Figures for only four dioceses are available in the yearbooks for a sufficient period of time to give any indication of the trend. The ratios of mixed to Catholic marriages in these four small and very unrepresentative dioceses, namely, Des Moines, Iowa, Fargo, North Dakota, Lafayette, Louisiana, and Omaha, Nebraska, show a fairly consistent picture of a steady rise until the beginning of the recovery period and then a sudden spurt upward. The unweighted averages of the four ratios are as follows:

1927	22.0
1928	22.8
1929	24.3
1930	23.8
1931	25.0
1932	26.4
1933	28.7
1934	32.1
1935	32.6

This is very fragmentary evidence, and points to the desirability of compiling further data from unpublished diocesan records. Marriage records as pub-

9. *Official Catholic Yearbook.* New York: P. J. Kenedy & Sons. 1936 and earlier years.

lished in the *Official Catholic Directory* must be used with much caution, since the writers have noticed a good many obvious inaccuracies and have found some evidence of the use of estimates instead of actual figures. By going directly to diocesan offices, however, one should be able to get reasonably accurate figures.

It is probably impossible to secure accurate data on the number of Catholics who give up their religious affiliation by marrying outside of the church. Some inferences might be drawn from a study of resident marriages performed during Lent in a Catholic community, since Catholic marriages are few in number during Lent. If there were some reason to believe that the number of eligible Catholics remained constant over a period of years or increased or decreased at a fixed rate, one might infer from a large increase in marriages during Lent in depression years that the depression encouraged nonchurch marriages. A special caution that must be observed arises from the fact that some couples are married by a magistrate and later are remarried by a priest. It might also be possible to form some index of the marriage of Catholics outside the church by a study of the names on marriage licenses. Where one of the parties has an obvious Italian, Polish, or French Canadian name, it is highly possible that this person is or was a Catholic. The number of all Catholics who were married by magistrates can then be expressed as a percentage of all Catholics who became married in each year in the community being studied.

Some clue as to what might be found in America is provided by Canadian marriage statistics, which report religion of bride correlated with religion of groom. These figures suggest that the proportion of mixed marriages increased steadily between 1921 and the onset of the depression. During the depression the proportion of mixed marriages continued to increase, until 1934, when recovery was well under way. The figures, as computed by the writers from Canadian annual reports, appear in Table 6-3.

One interesting suggestion that comes from this table is the possibility that the depression may tend to widen the gap between male and female "out-marriages." The theory might be advanced that a Catholic woman, in a period when she sees her chances of marrying lessen, is under stronger pressure than a man to marry outside of her religious fold. Prior to the depression the difference between male and female percentages was not higher than 3.4 in any one year; during the depression it rose to 4.5.

2. *Did intermarriage among different nationality groups increase at a faster rate during the depression than prior to the depression, and was this increase maintained during the recovery period?*

Intermarriage of members of different nationality groups is reported for only one area, namely, upstate New York. Unless, as is the case in New York but is not the case in most states, the certificate carries data on country of birth of the parents of the bride and groom, it would be difficult to make direct tabulations from an original study of the marriage certificates. (A num-

Table 6-3. Marriages between Catholics and Non-Catholics, by Catholic Grooms and Brides, as Percentage of Total Catholic Grooms and Brides: Canada and Divisions, 1921-1935*

	PERCENTAGE OF CATHOLIC GROOMS MARRYING NON-CATHOLIC BRIDES					PERCENTAGE OF CATHOLIC BRIDES MARRYING NON-CATHOLIC GROOMS				
YEAR	Canada (Excluding Quebec)	Quebec	Ontario	Maritime Provinces	Western Provinces	Canada (Excluding Quebec)	Quebec	Ontario	Maritime Provinces	Western Provinces
1921	14.5	...	14.1	7.6	20.8	16.3	...	14.4	10.0	24.0
1922	14.9	...	14.5	8.4	20.1	16.3	...	14.3	11.0	22.8
1923	14.5	...	14.1	7.8	20.0	17.2	...	15.3	11.2	24.5
1924	14.6	...	12.9	8.3	21.8	17.3	...	15.3	10.4	25.2
1925	14.2	...	12.7	7.1	21.4	17.2	...	14.1	10.4	26.6
1926	15.1	1.1	14.1	7.4	21.6	17.6	1.8	15.4	10.1	25.6
1927	15.3	1.2	13.9	7.6	22.7	18.7	1.8	16.2	11.1	27.3
1928	16.4	1.4	15.3	9.3	22.1	19.4	2.0	17.3	12.7	26.2
1929	16.6	1.4	14.7	9.5	23.5	19.6	2.2	17.7	12.5	26.7
1930	16.9	1.6	16.1	8.0	23.6	20.7	2.6	19.5	11.8	28.1
1931	17.7	1.6	16.9	9.8	23.5	21.6	2.6	20.6	13.4	27.9
1932	17.7	1.7	17.1	8.3	23.9	22.2	2.8	20.7	13.2	26.3
1933	18.3	1.7	17.1	8.7	26.2	21.9	2.7	20.5	11.7	30.2
1934	17.5	1.7	17.4	7.4	24.6	21.2	2.5	21.2	11.0	28.1
1935	16.9	1.6	16.4	7.2	26.7	20.3	2.3	20.2	11.8	29.1

* Dominion Bureau of Statistics, *Vital Statistics,* 1921 and following years. Data for 1935 were supplied in advance of publication by courtesy of the Dominion Statistician.

ber of states do ask this data.[10]) Even in the case of New York state, there are difficulties with respect to most nationalities. One cannot determine directly, for example, whether a girl with Irish-born parents who marries a man with native-born parents actually is marrying a man of Irish descent. The case of Jews is, of course, complicated by the additional fact that Jews whose fathers were born in Poland cannot be directly distinguished from Poles whose fathers were not Jewish but were born in Poland. One solution of the difficulty would be to base the study of the original certificates on the names of the contracting parties, not on the nativity data alone. There are difficulties, especially with Jewish names, but errors involved in the interpretation of descent by the use of names are likely to be small.[11] More experimental research on the validity of inferring descent from names would, however, be desirable.

Perhaps the least ambiguous nationality group of relatively large size reported in the upstate New York published tables is Italian. Since 1928, the

10. New Hampshire, Rhode Island, California, New York (exclusive of New York City), Vermont, Oregon, Delaware.

11. For example, correlating some index of the impact of the depression on each city, such as decline in postal receipts, telephones, new cars registered, or percentage of families on relief, with the increase or decrease in the percentage married, holding various factors constant. Partial correlation is applied to marriage data most extensively in Groves and Ogburn, *op. cit.*

first year for which data were obtained by nativity of parents of bride and groom, the trend among natives with Italian fathers is indicated in Table 6-4.

This table is introduced not so much because of the intrinsic information it gives as because it illustrates some of the difficulties of making interpretations. First, we need a longer series, in order to be more nearly sure whether changes during the depression represented continuations or reversals of a longer trend. Second, we should hesitate about attributing a small change in a single year to nonchance fluctuations. Since the percentages are based on only two to four thousand cases annually, a shift in one year must be 2 or 3 per cent to be outside the range presumably attributable to chance. Third, we need some conception of the shifting proportions of the various groupings in the general population; for example, the category "native of native parentage" includes in the general population an increasing number of Italian descent.

Subject to these and other cautions, two or three interesting questions are raised from the tables. During the depression did the girls tend in greater proportions to marry natives whose parents were born in some foreign country other than Italy? With the decline in numbers of eligible Italian born males, did the girls tend to marry native males with Italian fathers in sufficient

Table 6-4. Percentage Distribution of Marriages of Italian Grooms and of Italian Brides, by Nativity of Spouse: Upstate New York, 1928-1934*

NATIVE-BORN BRIDES WITH ITALIAN FATHERS, ACCORDING TO NATIVITY OF THEIR GROOMS

YEAR	Groom Born in Italy	Groom Native; Father Italian	Groom Native; Father Native	Groom Native; Father Foreign But Not Italian	Groom Born in Foreign Country But Not Italy	Total
1928	40	39	10	7	4	100
1929	36	43	11	6	4	100
1930	33	48	11	4	4	100
1931	28	49	12	7	4	100
1932	25	49	12	10	4	100
1933	20	52	14	10	4	100
1934	18	55	17	7	3	100

NATIVE-BORN GROOMS WITH ITALIAN FATHERS, ACCORDING TO NATIVITY OF THEIR BRIDES

YEAR	Bride Born in Italy	Bride Native; Father Italian	Bride Native; Father Native	Bride Native; Father Foreign But Not Italian	Bride Born in Foreign Country But Not Italy	Total
1928	9	51	19	17	4	100
1929	8	53	20	16	3	100
1930	10	54	21	11	4	100
1931	7	55	20	15	3	100
1932	7	53	20	16	4	100
1933	6	55	20	17	2	100
1934	5	51	20	21	3	100

* New York State Department of Health, *Annual Reports.*

proportions to compensate? Finally, the patterns of change in the upper and lower halves of the table differ in several interesting respects, particularly, the first three columns. Especially interesting is the suggestion that women may have been encouraged by the depression to make "out-group" marriages more than men.

Another eventual source for study of intermarriage in the depression will be the 1940 Census of population, if a special tabulation can be made of the punch cards, for a sample region or regions, giving nationality of husband and wife by duration of marriage. For purposes of comparison a special tabulation should be made from the original census schedules for 1930 and 1920. The cost, however, might be prohibitive, and the results might be too ambiguous to justify the effort. The most economical source for a statistical study, everything considered, probably would be the original marriage certificates, using names as a supplementary index of nationality, as previously discussed.

3. *Did the proportion of marriages between members of two socio-economic classes tend to increase faster during the depression than formerly, and was this increase maintained upon recovery?*

We have practically no information on intermarriage between members of two socio-economic classes at any period. Yet the implications of this information for a study of social stratification in the United States are obvious. It is generally thought that a man is more likely to marry a woman below his status than is a woman to marry a man below her status. The depression may be thought to have altered these probabilities, since a woman who sees her chances of marrying somebody in her own class lessened may have an additional incentive to accept a proposal from a man with lower socio-economic status than her own.

While no data have been published, this problem can be studied directly by a tabulation of available materials in two states, Rhode Island and New Hampshire. In these states the applicant for a marriage license must report the occupation of the father of bride and groom. Not all the reports will be accurate, of course, but it should be possible to classify the occupations into very broad socio-economic groups, along the line of Edwards' classification,[12] though perhaps not making such fine distinctions. An analysis of the table showing socio-economic class of bride's father by socio-economic class of groom's father could be made for a period of years. These might be simple hand tabulations, though punching and machine sorting would facilitate the work, especially if further breakdowns by age or other factors should be desired.

Although New Hampshire and Rhode Island are apparently the only

12. Edwards, Alba M. "A Social-Economic Grouping of the Gainful Workers of the United States." *Journal of the American Statistical Association*, No. 184. 28:377-387. December 1933.

states collecting direct information on occupation of parents of bride and groom, at least twelve other states obtain the names of the parents.[13] Most of these also obtain the maiden name of the mother. For brides and grooms whose parents reside in large cities, it would be quite feasible to check these names against the entries in the city directory, which usually reports occupation with sufficient accuracy for classification in broad categories. If the mother's given name is known, this facilitates the identification, since many directories report a wife's name in parenthesis. The address of bride or groom also would aid in facilitating identification of parents in the directories. Numerous cautions would need to be observed, particularly in making interpretations, if a large number of names must be omitted through failure to make identifications.[14] In such an analysis the assumption would be made that cyclical fluctuations by socio-economic classes are fluctuations in the frequency of marrying, not in the base population of the classes, which would be assumed not to fluctuate in cycles. This assumption probably would be true for broad socio-economic groupings though not necessarily for specific occupations.

Australian marriages are classified by occupation and industry of the bridegroom in *Australian Demography*. The Australian data could be studied directly by a statistical analysis of the tables. A preliminary analysis by the writers indicates, for selected occupational groups in which the classification seemed to be reasonably comparable, that the 1930–1932 deficit in marriages was relatively greatest among workers in the building trades, light industries, and finance, was somewhat less in the group called "professions," and was slight in agriculture.

"FORCED" MARRIAGES

In this context the word "forced" is used to indicate the fact that the couple became the parents of a child within less than seven months after marriage; it does not necessarily imply that the marriage took place because of parental pressure. The couple, indeed, may have been engaged before conception took place. Almost nothing is known about the normal proportion of marriages in the United States in which conception occurs before marriage, nor is there any information available on the extent to which such marriages are "hurried up" by parental pressure against the bridegroom's will. Theoretically, one would expect that the diffusion of contraception gradually would tend to reduce the number of such marriages; yet it is quite possible that the increasing sex freedom before marriage (thought to prevail, though never proved) might encourage risk-taking among sufficient numbers of

13. Alabama, California, Connecticut, Iowa, Massachusetts, Michigan, Mississippi, New Jersey, New York, Vermont, Virginia, and Wisconsin.
14. Stouffer, S. A. "Trends in the Fertility of Catholics and Non-Catholics," *American Journal of Sociology*. 41:151. September 1935. (See also chapter 8 of this volume.)

young people to offset the increasing immunity provided by wider knowledge of contraception.

The general subject of the effects of the depression on the sex mores is discussed subsequently. . . .[15] If, as is possible, the decline in the depression in economic opportunities to support a wife and family was associated with an increase in sex relationships among the unmarried, the depression may have stimulated the development of habit patterns which could have a considerable lasting influence on the institution of marriage. Young couples may have been encouraged to live together without the sanction of matrimony, not marrying unless their association resulted in pregnancy. Thus, there may have been thousands of unofficial "trial marriages." The influence of these possible depression practices on the generation reaching marriageable age during the recovery period may have been such as to encourage further experimentation with this practice.

There are at least three reasons why the ratio of "forced" marriages to all marriages might possibly be expected to increase during the depression.

1. These social, economic, and racial classes in which pregnant brides are most frequent might also include a larger proportion of the people described earlier,[16] as those least likely to be deterred from marrying.

2. Lack of funds may reduce the number of abortions.

3. If the pregnancy becomes known to a relief agency, arrangements may be forthcoming to finance with relief funds the marriage and confinement.

Australia reports births by duration of marriage of the mother, thus making it possible to observe whether the proportion of marriages followed by births within seven months of marriage increased or decreased during the depression (Table 6-5).

The Australian depression, beginning in 1928, reached its low point in 1931, with improvement since. The "forced" marriages declined slightly in absolute numbers during the depression, but the decline was negligible as compared with the decline in other marriages. In the recovery years, 1933 and 1934, the "nonforced" marriages increased sharply, while "forced" marriages

Table 6-5. Percentage of Marriages Followed by Births within Seven Months of Marriage: Australia, 1921-1934*

Year	Percentage	Year	Percentage
1921	22.2	1928	23.5
1922	21.6	1929	23.3
1923	21.0	1930	25.7
1924	20.8	1931	27.6
1925	20.9	1932	24.3
1926	21.4	1933	23.6
1927	22.0	1934	20.8

* Commonwealth Bureau of Census and Statistics, *Australian Demography,* 1934 and previous years.

15. Stouffer and Lazarsfeld, *op. cit.,* pp. 176 ff.
16. Stouffer and Lazarsfeld, *ibid.,* pp. 140-153.

increased only slightly. The ratio of illegitimate births to all first births remained practically constant between 1921 and 1933, dropping, however, in 1933 and 1934.

It is possible that American figures would not indicate as large a proportion of marriages resulting in births within seven months as do the Australian statistics. Statistics for a large city or a state could be obtained by questionnaires as a byproduct of a checkup on the accuracy and completeness of marriage and birth registration. One of the writers sent out questionnaires to check the completeness of birth registration in Wisconsin cities and received replies from 97 per cent of the people who could be located by the postal service.[17] (This required an original letter and four followup letters.) These questionnaires did not ask the date of marriage, since the mailing list had been secured from marriage certificates, but it seems unlikely that this information would be withheld if requested confidentially from an official government agency for the purpose of checking the accuracy and completeness of the official marriage records. From the study referred to above, a special tabulation made for the present monograph shows facts for the year 1930 (Table 6-6).

These figures are 97 per cent complete, as of all couples married in 1930 who could be reached by the postal service and who resided together at least

Table 6-6. Number and Percentage of Marriages in 1930 Resulting in Births within Seven Months, by Occupation of Bridegrooms, and Age and Religion of Brides: Wisconsin Cities of 20,000 and Over

	WHITE COLLAR			SKILLED			SEMI-SKILLED AND UNSKILLED		
	Number of Marriages	Number of Births Within 7 Months	Per Cent of Marriages Resulting in Births	Number of Marriages	Number of Births Within 7 Months	Per Cent of Marriages Resulting in Births	Number of Marriages	Number of Births Within 7 Months	Per Cent of Marriages Resulting in Births
MILWAUKEE AND SUBURBS									
Bride under 21 at marriage									
Catholic	65	12	18.5	141	37	26.2	183	45	24.6
Non-Catholic	173	29	16.8	200	40	20.0	277	60	21.7
Bride 21 to 25 at marriage									
Catholic	151	10	6.6	151	14	9.3	122	14	11.5
Non-Catholic	292	11	3.8	200	22	11.0	218	29	13.3
OTHER CITIES OVER 20,000									
Bride under 21 at marriage									
Catholic	38	3	7.9	57	12	21.1	105	36	34.3
Non-Catholic	112	24	21.4	114	24	21.1	267	95	35.6
Bride 21 to 25 at marriage									
Catholic	88	8	9.1	64	8	12.5	65	10	15.4
Non-Catholic	202	16	7.9	108	16	14.8	173	36	20.8

17. Stouffer, S. A., *ibid.* P. 163.

one year, subject to the limitation that the bridegroom was a resident of a Wisconsin city of 20,000 or over at the time of marriage and that the marriage took place in some Wisconsin city of that size or larger or in any one of ten selected counties bordering Wisconsin. A serious error might be made, however, if a generalization should be extended to cover not only these couples but also such parties as could not be located by the postal service. Those who could be reached by the postal service represented about 70 per cent of those on the original list. Since a disproportionate share of those unlocated may have separated without bearing children, the percentages shown above may be a little too high.[18]

These data are reported not because they throw any light on the depression, but because they illustrate a procedure that may be used anywhere to get a time series extending through the depression period, especially if a more general mailing list is used and the questionnaire requests confidential information as to date and place of marriage.

18. Among all Catholics to whom letters were sent, Table 6-6 includes 78 per cent; among non-Catholics, 63 per cent. The most serious bias, that due to failure to answer mail received, is practically eliminated. Almost all of the "missing" cases were families which the post office could not locate in 1934. Let us make an extreme assumption—namely, that among the "missing" families the percentage of marriages resulting in birth within seven months of marriage was only half as great as among those "found." This would reduce the two highest percentages in Table 6-6 (Other Cities, Semi-skilled and Unskilled) from 34.3 per cent for Catholics to 30 per cent, and from 35.6 per cent for non-Catholics to 29 per cent. It is a simple matter for the reader to make similar calculations for other groups.

7

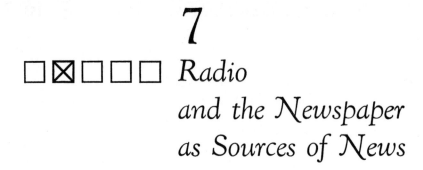 *Radio*
and the Newspaper
as Sources of News

Here are excerpts from two studies made by the author in the field of communications. This research, done before the age of television, sets up a series of propositions as to the relative advantages of radio and the newspaper, respectively, as a source of news, and uses national survey data to test these propositions.

The second paper examines the influence of radio news broadcasting on the function of the newspaper, again setting up some propositions and seeking to test them by an examination of data on actual newspaper circulation. Over and beyond the intrinsic interest that some of the ideas may have for students of communication, the way in which propositions are made operational, such that they can be tested with available data, may be of some interest.

The author was invited by Paul F. Lazarsfeld to make these studies, which appear with the appropriate credit in his volume, *Radio and the Printed Page*.

A. *Preference for the Radio or for the Newspaper as a News Source*

A PRELIMINARY SPECULATION

Let us first draw up a hypothetical list of the advantages of the radio over the newspaper as a source of news. From the factors influencing reading and listening that have been elaborated in Chapter 4 of *Radio and the Printed Page*, we may select the following:

Advantages of Radio	*Advantages of the Newspaper*
Delivers the news first.	Delivers news more fully (at least, the routine news).
Can be heard without cost, once the overhead for the radio and current is paid.	Caters to interest of minority groups, such as those who read the financial pages or society page, without losing larger audience.
Can be heard while one is doing other work.	Does not require attention at some specified hour.
Can be heard with a minimum of mental effort.	Permits selection by the reader and skipping of uninteresting news.
In special events, can give sense of intimate participation through sound effects and voices of personalities.	Permits the reader to set his own pace and to reread where he does not understand.
	Presents news pictures.

To which classes of people are the specific advantages of the two media likely to be of marked importance?

The radio's advantage in delivering the news first is likely to vary directly with the elapsed time between the radio program and the delivery of the daily paper containing no later news. Hence, we should expect this advantage to be more pronounced in rural regions than in urban, more pronounced in sparsely populated areas such as the Mountain States than in states on the north Atlantic seaboard. The differential might be of importance to city people, too. Psychologically the significance of the differential probably is that much of the newspaper news, having been anticipated by the radio, no longer relieves suspense. A radio news listener turns to a sports page not to find out how the baseball games came out but, if at all, to read details and "dope." That the "dope" can be readable and even exciting is evident particularly in the sports pages of an afternoon paper, which long before the advent of radio was forced to reckon with the fact that the morning paper took the cream of the announcements of triumphs and defeats. The tech-

Radio and the Printed Page by Paul F. Lazarsfeld, pp. 214-221. New York: Duell, Sloan and Pearce, 1940.

nique of the afternoon sports section is to provide gossip and to build up news suspense. Perhaps we have here a clue to a change in psychological function which the radio will tend to force upon the newspapers generally.

Two of the radio's advantages, that news listening involves no appreciable cost (once the radio is paid for) and that the radio news can be heard without appreciable mental effort, would possibly vary inversely in importance with the economic and educational status of the listeners. It should be found again that radio as a source of news is preferred more as we follow the cultural scale downward in the group under investigation.

Those who should appreciate most the radio's advantage of being heard without interfering with other work are the housewives, especially those who have no maids and do their own housework. At one time or another, however, this advantage also may be appreciated by other members of the family. It is an advantage, for example, that may be considered of value to drivers of automobiles equipped with radios.

The newspaper's advantage in delivering the routine news more fully would presumably vary directly with the interest in news, and we have already seen on pages 145–151 of Chapter 3 of *Radio and the Printed Page* that there is evidence to support this assumption.[1]

The newspaper's advantage in serving specialized interests of minorities among its readers without alienating the general audience—for example, with the stock-market quotations and the financial page, the society page with its personal accounts of routine social events, and the sports page—is difficult to evaluate in terms of the class of people to whom this specialization is most important. Certainly the radio is handicapped by being forced to find a least common multiple of interest.

The newspaper's advantage of not requiring attention at specified hours would probably be appreciated more by urban dwellers, whose habits are irregular, than by others. If one is out for the evening, one may miss the radio programs entirely, but the newspaper can lie about for later reading if one is not prepared to read it at the moment of its arrival.

The advantage of the newspaper in permitting the reader to skip uninteresting news, to select what he wants, and to set his own pace is possibly of relatively small importance, since the radio news summary is usually brief. Moreover, if the news in uninteresting, one can tune out the program or simply ignore it, though only at the risk of missing something interesting to come. It is somewhat risky to guess what type of people would find the

---

1. Presumably the newspaper's advantage of being more detailed in its news reports varies with the degree of suspense to be found in the news situation. If there are big events afoot, such as a Presidential election, war, or major kidnaping, the radio does not at once eliminate suspense, and the newspaper, though its actual news breaks may be for many people several hours behind the radio, carries interpretations and speculations that serve to heighten the suspense and intensify the excitement. The more exciting and suspended the event, the more likely it is that the newspaper and the radio will be complementary and actually stimulating. In times of crisis, . . . both radio and newspaper increase their audience.

newspaper an advantage on this score. Presumably it is the persons who are bored by news that scan the headlines and concentrate on other than news sections of the paper. On the other hand, the fact that the newspaper permits a reader to set his own pace might conceivably be of some advantage to two relatively small but different groups of people. One kind would be those who though interested in news may not be able to follow radio's swift verbal presentation adequately—a group likely to be on a low economic and educational level. The other kind would be those who are critically minded and wish to study what is reported about a news event, even though they are quite competent to follow the oral reports—a group likely to have a high economic and educational level.

The newspaper's advantage in presenting news pictures would doubtless be appreciated by all classes of the population.

We should expect in general, then, that for routine news coverage radio's advantages would be most appreciated by people in the lower economic levels, by women, and by people in rural areas and that consequently these persons would tend to prefer radio as a source of news. Conversely, the newspaper's advantages would appeal most to those with higher economic status, to men, and to urbanites, and they would be likely to prefer the newspaper.

MEDIUM PREFERENCES OF VARIOUS POPULATION GROUPS

To test these speculations regarding medium preference, data from several sources can be offered. First we shall present material from a representative sample of 5,528 persons in the northern states from coast to coast:[2] it was collected in April, 1939, and analyzed by the Office of Radio Research. This

Table 7-1. Sex, Economic Level, and Locality as Affecting Preference for Radio as Source of National and Foreign News*

SIZE OF LOCALITY AND ECONOMIC STATUS	PER CENT PREFERRING RADIO		NUMBER PREFERRING RADIO	
	Males	Females	Males	Females
POPULATION OF 100,000 AND OVER				
High	30.5	37.7	167	89
Medium	45.7	51.9	484	264
Low	49.3	46.5	371	170
POPULATION OF 2,500 TO 100,000				
High	30.3	56.1	188	57
Medium	43.6	58.9	456	236
Low	56.6	65.4	251	159
FARMS AND TOWNS UNDER 2,500				
High	44.7	58.0	132	50
Medium	53.2	58.6	549	319
Low	56.9	69.7	239	122

* Radio owners only. Percentages are computed on the basis of those who express a definite preference only.

2. States excluded (because of inadequacy of the data) are Alabama, Arkansas, Florida, Georgia, Kentucky, Louisiana, Mississippi, North Carolina, Oklahoma, South Carolina, Tennessee, Texas, and Virginia.

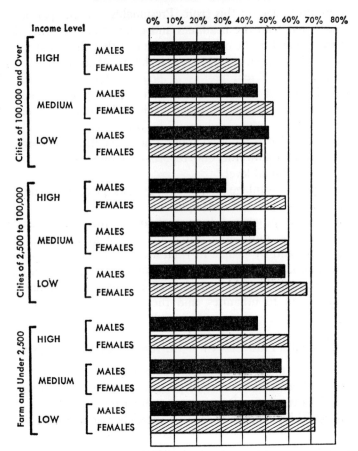

Figure 7-1. *Proportion among those with a preference who prefer the radio to the newspaper for their national and foreign news.*

is by far the most comprehensive sample of its kind that has been available up to the present time. It is based on face-to-face interviews of persons classified by the methods used in the polls of the American Institute of Public Opinion.

Table 7-1 gives for eighteen different groups of people the proportion of those who prefer the radio to the newspaper as a source of foreign and national news.[3] Figure 7-1 is a corresponding graphical presentation. In terms of group differences, the results are very clear-cut: (1) preference for radio over print increases with decreasing economic status; (2) women exhibit

3. The figures represent the percentage of all regular news consumers who (1) answered that they prefer the radio when asked, "Do you prefer to get your national and foreign news over the radio or in a daily newspaper?" or who, (2) while they were regular radio news listeners, said they did not read the daily newspaper regularly. The small number who indicated "no preference" are excluded from this table.

a stronger preference for radio than do men; (3) preference for radio is greater among rural people than among people in metropolitan centers (cities with a population of over 100,000). The speculative results outlined above are, then, plainly corroborated.

The chart is set up in such a form as to permit study of each of the three distinctions separately. In each population group, for instance, and on practically every economic level, the percentage of women preferring radio is larger than the percentage of men. It can be seen, on the other hand, that the increase of radio preference with decreasing economic level holds true for practically all residential groups and for both sexes.

The reader may wish to dwell a few moments on the details of these figures. He will see, for instance, that men of low economic status equal or even surpass the radio preference of women of high economic status. Obviously economic differences are more decisive than sex differences. Similarly, rural men have a higher radio preference than metropolitan women, so that the residential differences, too, are more important than sex differences. Economic and residential differences seem, by and large, to be about equally decisive. If we follow all three distinctions in the direction in which they tend to increase radio preference, we find more than twice as much preference for radio among rural women on a low income level as among metropolitan men on a high income level (69.7 against 30.5 per cent). An interpretation of these figures is practically identical with the general analysis attempted on preceding pages.[4]

B. Effects of Radio upon Newspaper Circulation

THE CHANGING FUNCTION OF THE NEWSPAPER

If the increased popularity of radio is not detrimental to newspaper reading, then newspapers, too, should show rising circulation in times of crisis. To test this assumption, a newspaper was studied for the duration of the Czechoslovakian crisis in the fall of 1938, during which the personal interviews just reported were taken. Figure 7-2 shows the daily circulations of the *Chicago Daily News*, an afternoon paper, from August 1 to October 1, 1938, the circulations being expressed as percentages of the circulations on the corresponding days of the week in 1937. The curve shows a sharp and

Radio and the Printed Page by Paul F. Lazarsfeld, pp. 263-272. New York: Duell, Sloan and Pearce, 1940.

4. The single exception to the general trend (among metropolitan people of low cultural level) is not statistically significant. Yet, if in a larger sample a significant discrepancy occurred—that is, if metropolitan females of low cultural level had less preference for the radio than males—a suggestion might be advanced that metropolitan women of low economic status include many foreigners who cannot understand spoken English as well as do male members of their families and therefore are likely to prefer a newspaper in their native tongue.

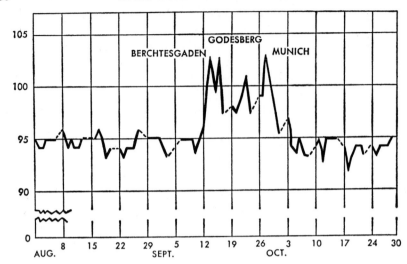

Figure 7-2. How a newspaper's circulation grew in a European crisis. Ratio of the circulation of the Chicago Daily News *in autumn, 1958, to corresponding days in 1937.*

quite well-sustained increase in circulation, with peaks corresponding to Berchtesgaden, Godesberg, and Munich, respectively.

Even if research should finally prove that people don't read less news, or that they read even more, because they get news over the air, news broadcasts still might have a profound effect upon newspapers. Two possibilities come to mind at once: radio might affect the editorial content of newspapers, and it might impair them economically by cutting in on their advertising revenues.

Up to the advent of radio, the newspaper had two functions: reporting what happened, and interpreting the importance of the event. Since radio is the quicker in reporting events, the newspaper is likely to lose its role as a carrier of scoops. When we open the paper we probably know already, from the radio, the major events. But what we don't yet know is how they happened, what all the parties concerned say about them, and what they probably meant. So far radio does not yet compete with the newspaper in documentation or interpretation—not to mention pictorial evidence. One quite conceivable development in the newspaper is a progressive shift from the reporting to the elaborating function of news service.

A number of interesting investigations of this possible change could be undertaken. How, for instance, have headlines already changed? Do they, more and more, feature details of events rather than the occurrence itself? And what about election returns? They are a great occasion for the radio, and the tendency of the broadcasts to reduce the circulation of election-night daily newspaper extras is well known. An interesting question is whether the night's broadcast increases public interest in election news published in the *next* day's paper—particularly, the next afternoon's paper. The suspense in general may be relieved by the night's broadcast, but the radio whets the appetite for more details in the newspaper.

An illustration of such a possible study of election events in their consequences on radio and the press is provided by an analysis of circulation figures of the *Chicago Daily News,* an afternoon paper, during several election periods. The data, appearing in Figure 7-2, show that this newspaper gradually lost most of the excess circulation produced by election-night extras, but held or increased its excess circulation on the day following each election. This is true with Presidential elections, off-year elections, and city mayoralty elections. Here, then, is inferential evidence of the changing function of the newspaper.

THE LONG-TERM TREND IN NEWSPAPER CIRCULATION

The most tempting way to study the effect of radio on newspaper circulation would be to analyze the existing circulation figures, but three major difficulties make an interpretation very hazardous:

1. If newspaper reading increases or decreases, radio will be only one of several causes. The growing importance of foreign affairs, the breakdown of rural isolation, and other factors will have to be kept steadily in mind.

2. Radio can affect newspaper reading in various ways. News broadcasts might make the news content of the paper more or less interesting. But listening to any kind of program could occupy the time formerly available for newspaper reading, and all sorts of stimulations coming over the radio (for instance, dance orchestras broadcasting from night clubs) might change the entire pattern of the public's leisure-time activities. Again, radio touches the destinies of newspapers by competing for a place in businessmen's advertising budgets.

3. Newspaper reading is not synonymous with news reading. The remarkable development in the picture form of news reporting might have an influence upon newspaper circulation that would spuriously be attributed to radio if it were overlooked.

Apart from these general factors there is a special reason that inferences about radio's long-time effects are dangerous when derived from general newspaper-circulation data. Circulation figures relate to the total number of papers sold, not the total number of families taking newspapers. Many families may take two or three papers. If many of these families, because of the radio, reduced the number of papers taken, the papers' circulations might drop, even if the radio encouraged a large number of non-newspaper-reading families to take newspapers for the first time. The newspaper figures might in this case show a loss; at the same time there would be an increase of news reading among the public.

It is likely that the radio first invaded families able to take a daily newspaper. By the time of the 1930 census, radio ownership varied from 12 per cent of the families in the East South Central states to 55 per cent in New England. By 1938, according to the estimates by the Joint Committee on Radio Research, radio ownership had risen to 60 per cent in the East South Central states, to 92 per cent in the Middle Atlantic and New England states, and to 95 per cent on the Pacific coast. By this time practically all the regular newspaper subscribers undoubtedly had radios. The growth in radio ownership since 1930 probably represents an accretion, year by year, of successive groups who even before they possessed radios were less ardent newspaper readers than the groups preceding them in radio ownership. The effect of the radio on newspaper circulation among these people would be particularly important to study, but there would be no way of interpreting the trends to indicate whether there was an increase or decrease in newspaper reading after these people obtained radios. As indicated before, any increase of reading in this group might cancel a decrease in the circulation of extra papers among the earlier radio owners and stauncher newspaper readers; or the reverse might be true.

If, however, a rather special hypothesis can be set up, general newspaper-circulation figures cautiously handled may be of some interest. Here are three such hypotheses and the actual findings concerning them:

1. *Expectation.* If, as studies previously discussed seem to show, the radio's advantages to rural listeners were greater relatively than its advantages to urban listeners, then one would expect the circulation for newspapers to increase more or to decline less (say, between 1929 and 1937) in the immediate trade area of the city than in the outlying territory.

FINDINGS[5] (limited to cities of 15,000 and over, all of whose papers were Audit Bureau of Circulations (ABC) papers in both 1929 and 1937): Table 7-2 divides 181 cities into two groups, one of increasing and the other of decreasing aggregate newspaper circulation. About half of the cities with

Table 7-2. Changes of Newspaper Circulations in Central and Outlying Areas of 181 Cities

	NUMBER OF CITIES FOR WHICH CIRCULATION CHANGED MORE IN:	
	Local and Suburban Area	Outlying Area
Cities with *increasing* aggregate circulation	60	60
Cities with *declining* aggregate circulation	10	51

5. An individual study of each city was made at the office of the Audit Bureau of Circulations in Chicago. All cities which changed the boundaries of their retail trading zone in the time period considered were omitted, as also were cities with one or more non-ABC papers. *Editor and Publisher* tables on this must be disregarded entirely because so many cities altered the boundaries of their zones and *Editor and Publisher* ignores this change. The reader should know that these and the following findings required more than a month of statistical work, which was carried through by Professor Stouffer and his assistant.

an increasing circulation showed greater increases in the rural areas than in local and suburban areas. Those factors that make for an increase (for example, improved service) seem, then, unrelated to special circulation areas. The decrease of circulation, however, is much more likely to take place in outlying areas. Five-sixths of the cities that lost newspaper circulation lost more heavily in outlying areas, where the time advantage of radio is likely to be more effective. A special tabulation (not reproduced here) showed that the same relationship holds true also if the circulation figures are analyzed separately for the eastern, western, and southern parts of the country.

2. *Expectations.* Since radio news, as we have seen in Chapter 5 of *Radio and the Printed Page,* tends to favor national news at the expense of local affairs, the local newspaper might hold up more successfully because it still performs a function that radio has not taken over.

FINDINGS (all daily circulation, ABC and other, pooled for each city): Table 7-3 shows that for three regions alike, conforming to expectation, newspaper circulations in the smaller cities held up better. Only about half of the big cities' newspapers increased their circulations between 1929 and 1937, while more than two-thirds of the small-town papers showed such an increase.

Table 7-3. Per Cent of Cities of Different Size Showing an Increase in Daily Newspaper Circulation in Different Areas (1929 to 1937)*

	REGION		
SIZE OF CITY	East	West	South
100,000 and over	50	45	65
25,000 to 100,000	59	56	78
15,000 to 25,000	68	68	84

* This table, compiled from data in *Editor and Publisher,* includes newspapers that are not members of the Audit Bureau of Circulations. The publisher's estimates of circulation in such cases are not always dependable, but failure to include such newspapers results in a much more serious bias. For classification by city size, 1930 census figures are used.

3. *Expectation.* The afternoon papers probably get the major news breaks—especially on foreign and national political news and in the central and western time zones—but may not have so much time as the morning paper for the preparation of detailed interpretive materials. Since the newspaper's news-break value, in comparison with its feature value, is reduced by radio, the morning paper should be benefited at least in the local areas.

FINDINGS: (1) The percentage of morning circulation in the total morning and evening circulation has increased on an almost straight-line trend ever since World War I. The pattern is about the same since 1930 and before. (2) In a sample of cities for which data were available by special analysis at the Audit Bureau of Circulations between 1929 and 1937, the morning papers in twenty-five out of forty-five cities (56 per cent) held up better than the evening papers in local and suburban circulation. This is perhaps the fairest comparison of morning and evening papers, since the evening papers necessarily have a different and shorter radius of distribution from the center of a city. These findings seem to conform with the expectation that morning papers may suffer relatively less damage from the radio than evening papers. However, the results are not decisively corroborative, and further studies are called for.

General circulation figures, then, give certain leads if they are studied under special conditions. The analysis attempts to create a kind of semi-experimental situation by dividing areas according to the differential role radio is likely to play. The trends selected in the preceding samples can be summarized as follows:

The newspaper fared better in urban as compared with rural areas; this phenomenon could be due to the time advantage that radio has outside the centers of distribution of print. The newspaper fared better in small than in large cities; this might be because the radio does not compete in the presentation of routine personal news items of local interest. The morning newspaper did somewhat better than the evening paper, and this might be because the morning paper is frequently "analytical" and therefore less subject to radio's competition than the afternoon paper, which is more dependent upon its straight news content at least in regard to current daily events.

8

□ ☒ □ □ □ *Trends*
in the Fertility
of Catholics
and Non-Catholics

This study, one of the earliest in the author's career, belongs more in the category of historical investigation than in the category of hypothesis testing. It is one of the earliest inquiries made in the United States comparing trends in fertility among Catholics and non-Catholics and is somewhat unique in its approach, since the main part of the study consisted of tracing the fertility of a large sample of married couples, starting with the official record of their marriage license and the religion of the officiating clergyman. Since these data represented only the residents of selected cities in one state, the author attempted to generalize further by using the indirect methods of partial correlation on census data of other large American cities.

When a pioneering study like this, made a quarter of a century ago, is compared with the kind of analyses of differentials of fertility by religion in the recent publication, *Family Planning, Sterility, and Population Growth,* by Freedman, Whelpton, and Campbell, one has some measure of the progress that has been possible in social science by the

"Trends in the Fertility of Catholics and Non-Catholics," *American Journal of Sociology,* 41 (September, 1935), pp. 143-166. Copyright 1935 by the University of Chicago.

introduction of sampling survey methods. By interviewing a representative cross section of American women, based upon a probability sample, the authors were able to analyze not only religious differentials in fertility, but to investigate directly both attitudes toward child-bearing and the actual frequency of use of contraception.

A rather unique opportunity has arisen, in connection with a more general investigation in the field of vital statistics, to secure an extensive body of data on differential fertility with respect to Catholics and non-Catholics.[1]

The research here reported has traced the fertility of 40,766 Wisconsin urban families, married between 1919 and 1930, from the time of their marriage to December 31, 1933. Of these families, 14,426, or 35 per cent, were married by Catholic priests. No families were included if the husband was over thirty at marriage or if the wife was over twenty-five at marriage.

When the families are broadly classified by occupation of the husband and standardized fertility rates are computed in such a manner as to make equal, throughout the period covered, the proportion of Catholics and non-Catholics in each age and occupational class, it is found that the fertility rates of Catholic families have declined more rapidly, both in amount and percentage, than the fertility rates of non-Catholic families.

For example, among residents of Wisconsin cities of over 20,000 (except Milwaukee and suburbs) who were married in 1919 and 1920 by a Catholic priest, the average standardized number of confinements during the calendar year of marriage and the $6\frac{1}{2}$ years following was 207.6 per 100, as compared with 172.5 per 100 families not married by a priest and therefore non-Catholics—a Catholic excess of 20 per cent. Among families married in 1925 and 1926, the corresponding Catholic rate was down to 180.6, as compared with a non-Catholic rate of 154.2—a Catholic excess of 17 per cent. Another way of describing the differential is to say that the Catholic rate declined 14 per cent while the non-Catholic rate declined 11 per cent.

The same general tendency, although more striking, existed among residents of Milwaukee and suburbs. Among those married in 1919 and 1920, the Catholic fertility was 201.4 and the non-Catholic fertility was 155.2—a Catholic excess of 30 per cent. Among those married in 1925 and 1926, the

1. The present report is a revision of a paper read at Section K, American Association for the Advancement of Science, Minneapolis, June 25, 1935. The larger investigation of which this study is a part was carried on at the University of Wisconsin and the Wisconsin State Board of Health, September, 1933, to May, 1935. It was financed by a grant from the Research Committee of the Graduate School of the University of Wisconsin, supplemented extensively by CWA and student FERA funds. Special acknowledgment is due L. W. Hutchcroft, chief statistician of the Wisconsin State Board of Health. Acknowledgment is due also to Professor Kimball Young and Miss Alice V. King, University of Wisconsin; Dr. T. F. Murphy, Bureau of the Census; Dr. C. A. Harper, Wisconsin State Board of Health; Dr. Alfred Briggs, Wisconsin Emergency Relief Administration; the Madison Chamber of Commerce; the Wright Directory Company, Milwaukee; and Miss Mae Bergfors, Miss Marion Hoffman, and T. C. Robarge.

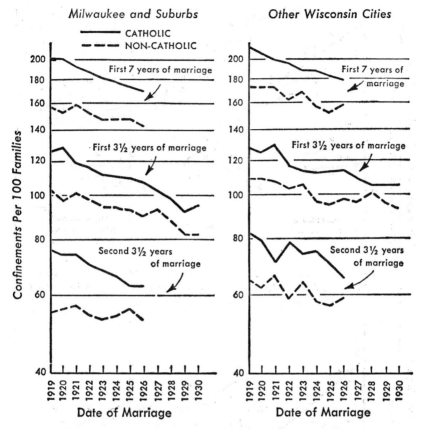

Figure 8-1. *Trends in confinements per 100 families, by religion, residence, and interval after marriage. Standardized to equalize and hold constant, throughout the time period, the proportion of Catholics and non-Catholics in each age group, by occupation (semilogarithmic scale).*

Catholic fertility was 171.4 and the non-Catholic fertility was 145.3—a Catholic excess of 18 per cent. Otherwise expressed, the Catholic fertility rate declined 15 per cent, while the non-Catholic rate declined only 6 per cent.

A brief study of the series plotted in Figure 8-1 is sufficient to confirm the fact that these trends were progressive through the time period studied, in spite of fluctuations which may be attributable in large part to chance. When the data are subdivided and resubdivided in various ways, many interesting details as to Catholic and non-Catholic fertility by occupational classes and by linguistic groups come to light. Figures 8-2 and 8-3 show that in twenty-three of twenty-four groups by age, occupation, residence, and interval after marriage the Catholic fertility declined and that in twenty-one of the subclasses the Catholic fertility declined faster, on the average, than the non-Catholic fertility. Figure 8-4 shows that the Catholic decline took place in every linguistic group in every occupational class.

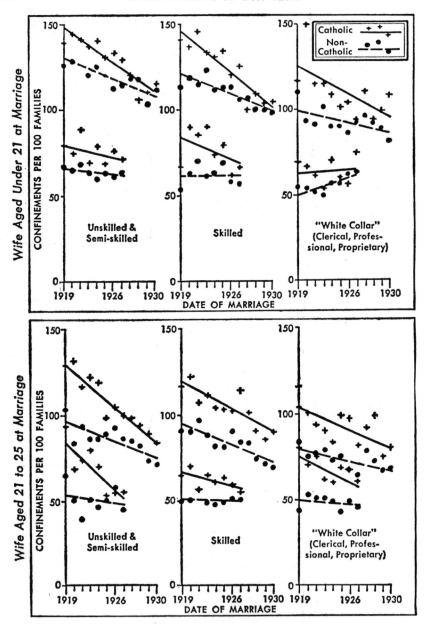

Figure 8-2. *Milwaukee and suburbs—trends in confinements per 100 families, by religion, age, occupation, and interval after marriage. Longer series represent first 3½ years of marriage; shorter series, second 3½ years.*

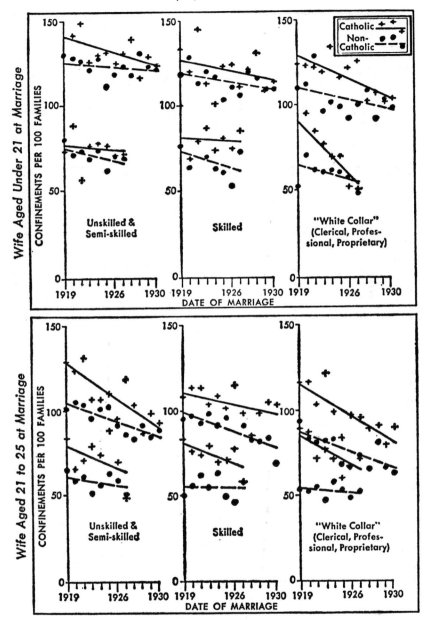

Figure 8-3. *Wisconsin cities other than Milwaukee—trends in confinements per 100 families, by religion, age, occupation, and interval after marriage. Longer series represent first 3½ years of marriage; shorter series, second 3½ years.*

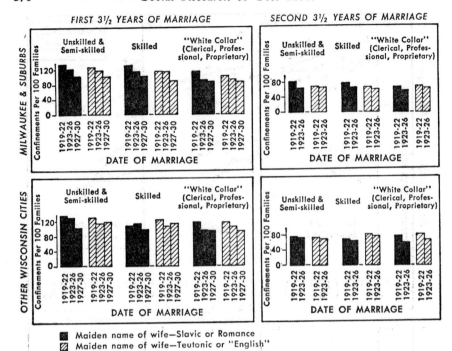

Figure 8-4. *Catholics only—trends in confinements per 100 families according to linguistic group of wife's maiden name, by occupation, residence, and interval after marriage. Rates standardized for age of wife.*

The effect of this analysis of trends within subclasses would be to strengthen a hypothesis that the Wisconsin evidence for a more rapid decline among Catholics than among other people (in comparable age groups) is sufficiently general to apply to many other American cities. That such a hypothesis may be correct is further suggested, though not proved, by a partial correlation analysis using several series of published census figures for American cities as a whole. This study, reported at the conclusion of the present paper, suggests that the cities with a larger percentage of Catholics tended to decline in fertility at a relatively faster rate between 1920 and 1930 than the cities with a small percentage of Catholics, the tendency remaining after several factors are "held constant."

The families used in the investigation represent, the writer believes, a substantially complete reporting of families living in 1934 in Milwaukee or suburbs or other Wisconsin cities, subject to the following restrictions:

1. They were married between 1919 and 1930, inclusive, in Milwaukee and its suburbs of Shorewood, Wauwatosa, and West Allis; in all other Wisconsin cities of over 20,000 or their suburbs;[2] and in Waukegan, Rockford,

2. These cities are Appleton, Beloit, Eau Claire, Fond du Lac, Green Bay, Janesville, Kenosha, La Crosse, Madison, Manitowoc, Oshkosh, Racine, Sheboygan, Superior, and Wausau.

Freeport, Woodstock, and Belvidere, Illinois; Winona and Duluth, Minnesota; and Menominee, Michigan.

2. It was the first marriage of both parties.

3. The bridegroom was thirty years old or under at marriage and the bride was twenty-five years old or under.

4. The bridegroom at marriage was a resident of Milwaukee or suburbs or some other Wisconsin city of over 20,000.

5. The address of the family could be located in a recent city directory and reached by the postal service. While two-fifths of the families married since 1919 could not be found (see note 6 for further discussion), questionnaires were sent out and returned by about 97 per cent of those actually located by the postal service—an unusually high percentage.

In summary, 40,766 families in the group studied, as compared with the general urban population, represent a restricted age range, which covers, it is true, the most fertile years; they are a group perhaps more definitely urbanized than the general urban population, which, of course, includes also families in which the bridegroom lived on a farm or in a small town at time of marriage and families married on farms or in small towns where presumably the bride resided; they are a somewhat less mobile group than the general population, since they comprise only those still known to be living in a Wisconsin city of 20,000, though not necessarily the city of residence of the bridegroom; and, finally, it is a selection including first marriages only and a larger-than-average proportion of those whose marriages have not been dissolved by divorce or death in the early years of marriage. Many of these necessary restrictions greatly strengthen the validity of conclusions that may be drawn concerning a group with the characteristics specified. But each restriction imposes a caution against too easy wider generalization. While some broader inferences may properly be drawn, the Wisconsin findings per se apply strictly only to the group as delimited above.

The following steps were taken in compiling the data:

1. For each couple, the names and ages of the bridegroom and bride and the occupation of the bridegroom at time of marriage were copied on an individual card. The religion of the officiating clergyman or the fact that the officiator was a magistrate was coded directly on the card at the same time, from an indexed file of officiators' names compiled especially for this study. If a name did not appear in the file, it was copied on the card and investigated subsequently to determine whether or not it was that of a Catholic priest. In less than 2 per cent of the cases, the officiator's status could not be determined, and these cards were excluded from the study.

2. The latest city directory for the city of residence of the bridegroom was consulted to determine whether or not the couple was still residing in that city. The fact that the maiden name of the wife is recorded in parenthesis in the directory following the name of the husband made identification easy, except in a very few cases. If the name was not found in the latest directory, a similar search was made through the two previous direc-

tories if the volumes were published biennially and through the three previous annual Milwaukee directories. Sometimes the name of the wife only was found, in which case her latest available address was copied and a special notation made. The search was not confined to the directory for city of residence of the husband at marriage, but was extended, where necessary, to all other directories for the cities studied.

3. An additional search was made in a directory published, as nearly as possible, four years after the date of marriage. From this directory the husband's occupation was again recorded. It was this occupational entry that was used eventually as the basis for classification of the families into three broad occupational groups, namely, professional, proprietary, and clerical. It was possible to check these data subsequently against occupation of father as reported on birth certificates, and the agreement was excellent.

4. Since the research reported in the present paper is only part of a larger project, it should be explained that one of the major parts of the larger project was a check on the completeness of birth registration in Wisconsin cities. In connection with this check, the Bureau of the Census granted the use of its franking privilege for obtaining information from families as to names and dates of birth of their children, living and dead. Letters written on United States Department of Commerce stationery and approved by the Bureau of the Census were sent to all addresses on the cards, pledging the parents that if their child's name was not properly registered, they would be notified. The response was excellent, upward of 97 per cent of those who could be reached by the post office responding either to the first letter or to one of a series of follow-up letters. In keeping with the pledge given, every child's name was looked up in the records of the Wisconsin State Board of Health. The check on the completeness of registration was directly in charge of L. W. Hutchcroft, chief statistician for vital statistics, who is reporting the results in a separate publication. There seems little reason to doubt that the families made a practically complete report. If they had no children, they were requested to return the blank with the notation "no children." A check on the returns to repeated requests does not seem to indicate any appreciable bias, because those with no children might be more likely to be better represented in the 3 per cent not reporting than in the 97 per cent who replied. The questionnaire returned by the family also indicated the date of death of husband or wife, if either were deceased, and the approximate date of separation, if there had been a separation or divorce.

5. When the information from the questionnaires had been transferred to the original cards, a history was available on the fertility of each family by year of marriage, age of wife, husband's occupation, and religion of the officiating clergyman. Names and ages of husband and wife on the questionnaires were carefully checked against the names on the cards to eliminate cases in which the clerks had used too much imagination in matching the names in the directories.

DISCUSSION OF WISCONSIN FINDINGS

By considering the fertility in the year of marriage and the three calendar years following, it was possible to secure one time series covering marriages between 1919 and 1930, inclusive. On the average, the year of marriage and the three calendar years following represented about 3½ years of marriage, for Catholics and non-Catholics alike. This interval is referred to, for brevity, as *"the first 3½ years of marriage."* By considering the fertility in the fourth, fifth, sixth, and seventh calendar years following marriage, it was possible to secure a second time series covering the eight years from 1919 to 1926, inclusive. Only the first six months of the seventh calendar year were included, thus giving a duration of 3½ years. This interval is referred to as *"the second 3½ years of marriage."* The two intervals combined, comprising the calendar year of marriage and the 6½ years following, are referred to as *"the first seven years of marriage."* Confinement rates were used instead of live-birth rates, twins counting as one confinement; stillbirths the same as live births. If live-birth rates had been used, however, there would have been no material alteration of results.

Table 8-1 and Figure 8-1 summarize the major findings of the Wisconsin study. Only those marriages are included, from 1919 through 1926, in which husband and wife were still living together at the conclusion of the first seven years of marriage. From 1927 on, only those marriages are included in which husband and wife were still living together on January 1, 1934.[3] Standardized confinement rates were computed by applying the specific rates from Tables 8-2 and 8-3 to the calculated number of families within each broad age and occupational group, by religion and year of marriage, which would have appeared if the average proportion of Catholics and non-Catholics in each age and occupational group had been (*a*) alike, (*b*) equal to the average proportion throughout the period studied, and (*c*) constant throughout the period. Not only did the Catholics, both in Milwaukee and suburbs and the other cities, decline in fertility at a somewhat faster rate than the non-Catholics during the first seven years of marriage, but also this differential in decline appeared in the first 3½ years of marriage as well as in the second 3½ years. There is no trace of a decline in fertility among the non-Catholic group in Milwaukee in the second 3½ years of marriage, while the non-Catholic group in the other cities declined only slightly.

Tables 8-2, 8-3, and 8-4 and Figures 8-2 and 8-3 exhibit the same data for each of the three broad occupational groups, by age of wife, residence, and interval after marriage. Since the average number of confinements per 100 families married in a given year and falling within a given occupational and

3. No appreciable progressive bias seems to be introduced. On several series between 1919 and 1926 the same assumptions were made, for checking purposes, as between 1927 and 1930, without producing noticeable changes from the results secured with the foregoing assumptions.

Table 8-1. Trends in Confinements per 100 Families, by Religion, Residence, and Interval after Marriage

DATE OF MAR-RIAGE	NUMBER OF FAMILIES		FIRST 3½ YEARS OF MARRIAGE		SECOND 3½ YEARS OF MARRIAGE		FIRST 7 YEARS OF MARRIAGE	
	Catholic	Non-Catholic	Catholic	Non-Catholic	Catholic	Non-Catholic	Catholic	Non-Catholic
MILWAUKEE AND SUBURBS								
1919	621	988	126	103	76	55	202	158
1920	710	1,143	128	97	74	56	201	153
1921	646	1,006	118	102	74	57	192	159
1922	733	1,125	116	98	70	54	186	152
1923	784	1,304	112	94	68	53	180	147
1924	724	1,251	111	94	66	54	177	148
1925	759	1,268	110	93	63	56	173	148
1926	783	1,359	107	90	63	53	170	143
1927	824	1,336	103	93	..	..	...	...
1928	855	1,370	99	88	..	..	...	...
1929	1,080	1,617	92	82	..	..	...	...
1930	810	1,324	95	82	..	..	...	...
OTHER WISCONSIN CITIES								
1919	331	770	128	109	83	65	212	174
1920	458	878	125	109	80	62	205	172
1921	396	769	129	107	71	66	199	173
1922	411	834	116	103	79	59	195	162
1923	416	904	113	105	74	64	187	169
1924	428	936	112	97	75	58	187	156
1925	394	967	113	95	70	57	182	152
1926	423	965	114	98	65	59	179	157
1927	469	1,023	109	96	..	..	...	...
1928	463	1,114	105	101	..	..	...	...
1929	498	1,164	105	96	..	..	...	...
1930	410	925	105	93	..	..	...	...

Standardized to equalize and hold constant, throughout the time period, the proportion of Catholics and non-Catholics in each age group by occupation.

religious group is necessarily small, wide annual fluctuations are possible through chance alone. Straight-line trends were put through each series by least squares,[4] facilitating a visual comparison and also making possible a test of the significance of the difference between any two rates of decrease or any groups of rates.

Let us consider the twelve Catholic and non-Catholic comparisons of fertility in the first 3½ years of marriage. These twelve comparisons are independent of one another, being based on different sets of families. A first approximation to testing the significance is to add appropriate terms of the binomial $(\frac{1}{2}+\frac{1}{2})^{12}$.

4. In order to get an accurate estimate of the residual variance, the lines were fitted, not by minimizing the sums of the squares of the deviations of the annual means, but rather by minimizing the sums of the squares of the deviations of the number of confinements in each family.

Table 8-2. Milwaukee and Suburbs—Trends in Confinements per 100 Families, by Religion, Age, Occupation, and Interval after Marriage

DATE OF MAR- RIAGE	NUMBER OF FAMILIES		PERCENTAGE OF FAMILIES WHERE WIFE WAS UNDER 21 AT MARRIAGE		CONFINEMENT RATES							
					Wife Under 21 at Marriage				Wife 21–25 at Marriage			
					FIRST 3½ YEARS OF MARRIAGE		SECOND 3½ YEARS OF MARRIAGE		FIRST 3½ YEARS OF MARRIAGE		SECOND 3½ YEARS OF MARRIAGE	
	Cath- olic	Non- Cath- olic	Cath- olic	Non- Cath- olic	Cath- olic	Non- Cath- olic	Cath- olic	Non- Cath- olic	Cath- olic	Non- Cath- olic	Cath- olic	Non- Cath- olic
UNSKILLED AND SEMI-SKILLED												
1919	184	241	47	53	139	126	79	67	129	104	93	65
1920	264	298	48	55	144	128	75	65	132	84	69	51
1921	207	247	43	56	141	142	88	68	117	94	73	40
1922	244	287	50	50	137	120	69	64	122	86	80	51
1923	276	357	52	58	140	125	78	60	119	86	70	47
1924	253	406	58	59	131	120	68	63	99	89	53	51
1925	280	341	42	52	133	113	76	61	105	93	55	58
1926	267	411	57	60	129	115	72	64	100	86	55	45
1927	271	399	55	60	120	118	..	..	99	85	..	..
1928	325	421	50	58	106	118	..	..	94	82	..	..
1929	438	613	49	53	110	104	..	..	89	74	..	..
1930	302	476	60	55	115	111	..	..	84	72	..	..
SKILLED												
1919	274	411	39	44	141	113	67	53	116	91	65	50
1920	263	433	44	40	137	119	90	63	122	90	70	51
1921	242	356	39	40	146	115	85	70	107	97	57	57
1922	288	437	40	42	133	123	90	61	111	88	65	49
1923	274	461	42	47	131	112	73	63	104	82	61	48
1924	294	442	41	46	134	113	79	69	103	81	63	49
1925	294	475	45	42	120	113	62	58	102	90	59	51
1926	305	481	41	45	125	106	67	57	113	84	55	51
1927	316	425	44	48	100	107	..	..	101	83	..	..
1928	279	423	44	49	109	100	..	..	90	74	..	..
1929	332	472	43	48	103	100	..	..	85	71	..	..
1930	292	393	48	50	104	98	..	..	89	69	..	..
WHITE COLLAR												
1919	163	336	22	29	117	110	69	55	116	84	80	44
1920	183	412	28	30	150	93	67	54	101	75	70	53
1921	197	403	24	31	115	91	62	52	93	77	75	51
1922	201	401	30	31	115	102	54	50	90	79	62	51
1923	234	486	26	31	108	90	70	57	83	73	60	49
1924	177	403	27	33	102	90	60	57	98	75	68	43
1925	185	452	30	33	104	87	57	62	97	67	67	49
1926	211	467	30	34	94	93	75	64	82	64	60	45
1927	237	512	30	36	111	97	..	..	92	78	..	..
1928	251	526	28	34	98	92	..	..	98	72	..	..
1929	310	532	31	31	99	89	..	..	74	66	..	..
1930	216	455	30	37	108	82	..	..	79	67	..	..

In all twelve cases, the Catholic fertility rates declined. The likelihood that this was due to chance can be called $(\frac{1}{2})^{12}$, or one chance in 4,096.

In eleven of the twelve cases, the Catholic fertility declined faster than

Table 8-3. Wisconsin Cities Other than Milwaukee—Trends in Confinements per 100 Families, by Religion, Age, Occupation, and Interval after Marriage

DATE OF MAR-RIAGE	NUMBER OF FAMILIES		PERCENTAGE OF FAMILIES WHERE WIFE WAS UNDER 21 AT MARRIAGE		CONFINEMENT RATES							
					Wife Under 21 at Marriage				Wife 21–25 at Marriage			
					FIRST 3½ YEARS OF MARRIAGE		SECOND 3½ YEARS OF MARRIAGE		FIRST 3½ YEARS OF MARRIAGE		SECOND 3½ YEARS OF MARRIAGE	
	Cath-olic	Non-Cath-olic	Cath-olic	Non-Cath-olic	Cath-olic	Non-Cath-olic	Cath-olic	Non-Cath-olic	Cath-olic	Non-Cath-olic	Cath-olic	Non-Cath-olic
UNSKILLED AND SEMI-SKILLED												
1919	108	302	41	53	150	130	73	80	128	101	83	65
1920	179	352	47	53	142	128	88	71	124	105	66	59
1921	144	326	47	59	149	126	57	73	132	104	71	61
1922	154	353	57	59	126	121	77	69	107	96	79	52
1923	179	404	51	58	130	128	78	74	107	102	74	57
1924	184	414	60	60	132	111	77	62	111	103	88	63
1925	175	418	55	56	125	119	71	70	96	92	70	59
1926	183	471	48	57	131	123	72	69	118	86	48	51
1927	202	465	56	62	139	118	...	..	104	84	..	..
1928	190	536	53	60	117	131	...	..	87	92	..	..
1929	223	552	53	58	129	123	...	..	99	85	..	..
1930	162	414	62	60	123	121	...	..	93	89	..	..
SKILLED												
1919	122	252	34	37	133	118	100	76	108	95	83	50
1920	149	265	48	40	120	129	69	64	113	97	76	56
1921	128	234	45	48	145	113	79	80	113	93	74	62
1922	131	251	46	49	113	120	87	70	104	99	79	55
1923	124	277	43	49	102	117	74	64	108	91	70	64
1924	115	278	50	51	123	104	82	61	102	96	72	50
1925	110	298	46	50	124	111	75	53	115	78	78	46
1926	121	268	45	49	111	106	85	73	99	91	58	58
1927	142	273	44	50	121	120	...	..	85	83	..	..
1928	136	277	48	49	131	116	...	..	99	82	..	..
1929	138	322	44	53	108	109	...	..	105	84	..	..
1930	124	207	46	52	114	110	...	..	103	69	..	..
WHITE COLLAR												
1919	101	216	25	23	124	110	76	52	116	93	89	54
1920	130	261	30	31	123	112	95	70	116	83	87	53
1921	124	209	26	31	122	129	84	62	103	81	72	55
1922	126	230	34	36	119	96	77	60	122	82	77	47
1923	113	223	31	38	134	102	69	61	99	83	72	58
1924	129	244	35	40	116	99	69	60	83	68	60	53
1925	109	251	21	40	122	92	52	57	97	67	67	49
1926	119	226	30	39	125	100	50	48	95	73	72	52
1927	125	285	38	41	102	108	...	..	88	65	..	..
1928	137	301	41	36	107	91	...	..	90	81	..	..
1929	137	290	33	40	102	103	...	..	79	67	..	..
1930	124	304	30	35	103	98	...	..	89	63	..	..

Table 8-4. Summary of Average Confinement Rates, Average Annual Increases or Decreases, Number of Families, and Weights, by Religion, Occupation, Residence, and Interval after Marriage

	WIFE UNDER 21 AT MARRIAGE				WIFE 21–25 AT MARRIAGE			
	FIRST 3½ YEARS OF MARRIAGE		SECOND 3½ YEARS OF MARRIAGE		FIRST 3½ YEARS OF MARRIAGE		SECOND 3½ YEARS OF MARRIAGE	
	Catholic	Non-Catholic	Catholic	Non-Catholic	Catholic	Non-Catholic	Catholic	Non-Catholic
AVERAGE CONFINEMENT RATES								
Milwaukee, etc.								
Unskilled, etc.	126.4	118.1	74.8	63.6	105.9	84.4	67.6	51.1
Skilled	122.1	109.5	75.9	61.5	103.6	83.6	61.8	50.7
White collar	108.3	92.5	64.2	56.6	90.8	72.5	66.3	48.3
Other cities								
Unskilled, etc.	131.2	123.0	74.7	70.4	108.7	94.2	71.1	58.0
Skilled	120.3	114.0	80.5	66.6	104.2	88.7	74.0	55.0
White collar	115.1	102.2	72.3	58.9	98.0	75.5	74.4	52.4
AVERAGE ANNUAL INCREASE (+) OR DECREASE (−) IN CONFINEMENT RATE*								
Milwaukee, etc.								
Unskilled, etc.	−3.43	−2.12	−1.06	−0.65	−4.25	−1.96	−4.58	−0.83
Skilled	−4.10	−1.92	−2.23	0.00	−2.70	−2.04	−1.38	−0.23
White collar	−2.67	−1.12	+0.39	+1.71	−2.35	−1.17	−2.56	−0.53
Other cities								
Unskilled, etc.	−1.74	−0.32	−0.69	−1.23	−3.44	−1.88	−2.25	−0.87
Skilled	−1.07	−0.92	−0.36	−1.72	−1.19	−1.95	−2.12	−0.14
White collar	−2.33	−1.35	−5.62	−1.48	−3.11	−2.00	−3.06	−0.38
NUMBER OF FAMILIES								
Milwaukee, etc.								
Unskilled, etc.	1,688	2,510	982	1,440	1,623	1,987	993	1,148
Skilled	1,473	2,348	925	1,516	1,980	2,861	1,309	1,980
White collar	722	1,762	422	1,061	1,843	3,623	1,129	2,299
Other cities								
Unskilled, etc.	1,102	2,905	669	1,729	981	2,102	637	1,311
Skilled	691	1,546	446	995	849	1,656	554	1,128
White collar	463	1,101	278	652	1,011	1,939	673	1,208
WEIGHTS†								
Milwaukee, etc.								
Unskilled, etc.	0511	0356	2018	1357	0520	0426	1988	1706
Skilled	0572	0370	2027	1248	0432	0306	1438	0949
White collar	1213	0504	4761	1862	0455	0239	1754	0849
Other cities								
Unskilled, etc.	0841	0312	3231	1139	0890	0412	2941	1239
Skilled	1222	0592	4494	2039	0943	0510	3380	1619
White collar	1878	0826	7537	3154	0822	0402	2865	1546

* $b = \Sigma xy/\Sigma x^2$, the slope of a straight line plotted in Figures 8–2 and 8–3.

† Weight $= 1/\Sigma x^2$, used in caclulating chance error of b or difference between two b's. To the reported digits o $1/\Sigma x^2$ one must prefix 0.000. For example, the values of $1/\Sigma x^2$ in the upper left-hand corner are 0.0000511, 0.0000572' and 0.0001213, respectively. For use of these weights, see note 5.

the non-Catholic fertility, as measured by the comparative magnitude of b, the straight-line slope. The likelihood that this is due to chance can be called $(\frac{1}{2})^{12} + 12(\frac{1}{2})^{12}$, or 13 chances in 4,096.

If we consider the twelve comparisons of fertility in the second $3\frac{1}{2}$ years of marriage, we find:

In eleven of the twelve cases the Catholic fertility rates declined, the likelihood that this is due to chance being 13 in 4,096.

Among the eleven cases in which the fertility rates declined, the Catholic decline was the greater in nine. In the case in which the Catholic rate increased, the non-Catholic rate increased even more. The difference between Catholic and non-Catholic slopes is negative, therefore, in ten cases out of twelve. The likelihood that this is due to chance can be called $(\frac{1}{2})^{12} + 12(\frac{1}{2})^{12} + \frac{1}{2}(12.11)(\frac{1}{2})^{12}$, or 79 in 4,096.[5]

Table 8-4 exhibits some other interesting findings:

In all instances, the average non-Catholic confinement rates were highest in the unskilled labor group, next highest in the skilled labor group, and lowest in the white-collar group. The Catholic confinement rates followed this pattern exactly in the first $3\frac{1}{2}$ years of marriage but not in the second $3\frac{1}{2}$ years of marriage.

5. These are very crude tests, but they are sufficiently decisive to make more delicate tests unnecessary in demonstrating the significance of the general results. To test the significance of differences between the rates of decline in any two subgroups, the reader may use the formula

$$t = (b_1 - b_2)/\sigma \text{ difference}$$

where

$$\sigma \text{ difference} = \sigma_0 \ (1/\Sigma x_1^2 + 1/\Sigma x_2^2)^{\frac{1}{2}}$$

For comparisons pertaining to the first $3\frac{1}{2}$ years of marriage, take $\sigma_0 = 76.44$; second $3\frac{1}{2}$ years of marriage, $\sigma_0 = 67.70$. These values of σ_0 were estimated by summing the squared residuals from the regression lines in all subgroups and dividing by the number of families less twice the number of subgroups. The symbol b is the slope of the straight line and is reported in Table 8-4, along with the value of $1/\Sigma x^2$. To illustrate: test the significance of the difference between rates of decline in the first $3\frac{1}{2}$ years of marriage among Catholic and non-Catholic skilled workers, respectively, whose wives were twenty-one to twenty-five at marriage. From Table 8-4, $b_1 = -2.70$, $b_2 = -2.04$, $1/\Sigma x_1^2 = 0.0000432$, $1/\Sigma x_2^2 = 0.0000306$, whence

$$t = \frac{-2.70 - (-2.04)}{76.44(0.0000738)^{\frac{1}{2}}} = -1.0$$

a normal deviate which we interpret as not significant.

The test may be applied to any comparisons of pairs of slopes in Table 8-4, except to a comparison between the decline in the first and second $3\frac{1}{2}$ years of marriage, respectively, which is based on the same group of families. In comparing any two annual averages in Tables 8-2 and 8-3, or general averages in Tables 8-4 and 8-5, the usual formulas for the standard error of a difference between two means applies. Take $\sigma = \sigma_0$, as above. In testing any individual b in Table 8-4, write $t = (b - B)/\sigma_0 \ (1/\Sigma x^2)^{\frac{1}{2}}$, where B is hypothetical, as for example, 0.

Table 8-5. Catholics Only—Trends in Confinements per 100 Families According to Linguistic Group of Wife's Maiden Name, by Occupation, Residence, and Interval after Marriage

DATE OF MARRIAGE	NUMBER OF FAMILIES		CONFINEMENT RATE			
			FIRST 3½ YEARS OF MARRIAGE		SECOND 3½ YEARS OF MARRIAGE	
	Slavic and Romance	Teutonic and "English"	Slavic and Romance	Teutonic and "English"	Slavic and Romance	Teutonic and "English"
MILWAUKEE AND SUBURBS						
Unskilled and semi-skilled						
1919–22	641	258	136	126	81	69
1923–26	688	388	122	117	65	66
1927–30	824	512	102	102	..	..
Skilled						
1919–22	621	446	132	115	77	67
1923–26	642	525	116	115	66	61
1927–30	658	561	103	90	..	..
White collar						
1919–22	298	446	114	101	68	69
1923–26	286	521	93	92	57	65
1927–30	358	656	89	88	..	..
OTHER WISCONSIN CITIES						
Unskilled and semi-skilled						
1919–22	197	388	135	130	77	73
1923–26	261	460	129	113	74	70
1927–30	261	516	102	118	..	..
Skilled						
1919–22	155	375	108	122	69	84
1923–26	156	314	113	107	65	78
1927–30	173	367	97	112	..	..
White collar						
1919–22	118	363	118	117	79	83
1923–26	103	367	95	104	60	68
1927–30	140	383	94	91	..	..

Rates standardized for age of wife.

In all instances, the average non-Catholic confinement rates among families in which the wife was under twenty-one at marriage were higher (in most cases, very much higher) than among families in which the wife was twenty-one to twenty-five at marriage. The Catholic confinement rates followed the same pattern, exactly in the first 3½ years of marriage, and in four out of six cases in the second 3½ years. (The trend toward earlier marriage has been quite marked among Catholics and non-Catholics alike—see columns 3 and 4 of Tables 8-2 and 8-3.)

In all instances, the average non-Catholic confinement rates among Milwaukee families were lower than those among families living in other Wisconsin cities. The Catholic confinement rates followed the same pattern, exactly in the first 3½ years of marriage, and in four out of six cases in the second 3½ years.

These three sets of uniformities would strengthen an assumption that the causes and mechanisms, whatever they may be, of differential fertility among Wisconsin urban Catholics, must have much in common with the causes and mechanisms of differential fertility among non-Catholics.

In order to secure a more detailed understanding of the decline in Catholic fertility by occupational groups, an effort was made to subdivide each subgroup once more on the basis of some kind of index of nationality. Except for those born abroad (a very small minority), no direct data on nationality were available. It was decided, therefore, to attempt a classification of Catholic families into very broad groups on the basis of their names. The maiden name of the wife was used as a basis for classification, partly on the ground that she would be less likely to anglicize it before her marriage than would a husband his name. It was possible, with relative ease and rather surprising apparent accuracy, to code the families in four broad linguistic groups, namely, Slavic and other eastern European, Romance, Teutonic, and "English." The Slavic and other eastern European names were predominantly Polish, especially in Milwaukee. The Romance names were predominantly Italian in Milwaukee and about evenly divided between Italian and French (presumably, French Canadian) in the other cities. The Teutonic names were predominantly German, with a small number of Flemish and Dutch. The so-called "English" names were names common to American stock of Irish and English extraction.

An inspection of the detailed tables of fertility by linguistic groups within each Catholic occupational class revealed a rather surprising uniformity of trend, although there were many aberrations attributable to chance because of the very small numbers in some subgroups. Since the Slavic and Romance groups tended to behave more or less alike, they were combined for purposes of summary and graphic presentation into one group; likewise, the Teutonic and so-called "English" groups were combined into one. Standardized rates were computed to control the factor of age. The results are exhibited in Table 8-5 and Figure 8-4. While there are certain curious differences of detail, some of which may be due to chance, the evidence is unmistakable that a decline in fertility during the whole period considered was common to both linguistic groups, in all occupational classes, in both Milwaukee and suburbs and the other cities, in both the first $3\frac{1}{2}$ years and the second $3\frac{1}{2}$ years of marriage. While there is some evidence that the decline in fertility set in somewhat earlier among the Teutonic-English families than among the Slavic-Romance families, it is clear that the latter have been cutting their fertility to about the same point as their fellow-Catholics.

It is not within the scope of the present study to investigate the mechanisms by which this decline in the fertility rate was brought about. It cannot be proved from these data that contraception actually was used, although scattered evidence from birth-control clinics in Wisconsin, as in other American cities, has indicated a desire on the part of some professed

Catholics for birth-control information. However, if contraception (including *coitus interruptus*) was not used extensively, the only other explanation would be an increase in continence, since age has been for all practical purposes a constant throughout the period, since no biological change could account for such a sharp decline in fertility, and since the Ogino-Knaus "rhythm" method of birth control, which has ecclesiastical approbation, appeared too late to have an appreciable influence during the time period covered by this study.

The cautious student, in reaching his own conclusions about the possibilities of generalizing to other urban areas from the present study, should review at this point the description on pages 166 and 171 of the limiting characteristics of the group of 40,766 urban families studied.[6]

EVIDENCE FROM OTHER AMERICAN CITIES

As a very tentative approach to a wider generalization, extending to urban areas in other states, the writer has investigated the relation between the percentage of Catholics and the decline in fertility by indirect correlation

6. In general, there is slight a priori reason for expecting that conclusions would have been reversed if the group had been more inclusive. The largest single unknown is the differential fertility among the families who could not be located in a city directory or reached by the postal service.

The percentage of Catholics who were "lost" decreased from 35 among those married in 1919–1921 to 24 among those married in 1928–1930. If we assume that the fertility of those who were "lost" was somewhat less than average, because of death, separation, etc., our results might possibly be slightly biased in the direction of showing too great a decrease for Catholics. No reasonable hypothesis as to the fertility of these "unknowns" would correct the reported figures sufficiently to remove the evidence for a definite downward trend in fertility, as any reader can check for himself by simple calculation. For example: suppose a given confinement rate based on a 65 per cent early sample is 100 and one based on a 76 per cent late sample is 90. Suppose that there was no decline whatever in the confinement rate of the missing cases, a quite improbable event. Let their constant confinement rate be 90. Then the adjusted early rate would be $(.065 \times 100) + (.035 \times 90)$ $= 96.5$, while the later rate of 90 would remain as before. If, however, the "unknowns" should include an increasingly large number of families who have separated and if these families have relatively few children, the figures reported in this study actually may be a slight understatement of the decline in a more inclusive population.

Similarly, the reported decline in non-Catholic rate may be slightly biased, because the percentage of "lost" families varies from 45 per cent among those married in 1919–1921 to 39 per cent among those married in 1928–1930. Since a sample check on these families in the records of the State Board of Health showed a good many of them to have been divorced and to have had fewer than the average number of children, we may conclude that the non-Catholic confinement rates as reported are somewhat higher throughout the entire period than in a more inclusive population and that perhaps the progressive decrease has been slightly greater than reported. There are many possible offsetting factors, however, and in no case would a reasonable hypothesis about these "unknowns" reverse the general conclusions that the Catholic fertility has fallen faster than the non-Catholic fertility.

It should be kept in mind throughout that the figures as reported represent a 97 per

procedure. The direct methods used in the Wisconsin study are too costly and laborious for extensive application. Unfortunately, published census data are none too satisfactory. From the *Census of Religious Bodies* of 1926, the reported number of Catholics was obtained, and the percentage of Catholics in 1926 in each American city over 25,000 in both 1920 and 1930 was computed by dividing the reported number of Catholics by the 1926 population as estimated by linear interpolation. Since all members of a Catholic family are counted as church members, the percentage of Catholics in the total population is probably a better figure to use than the percentage of Catholics among church members of all denominations, some of whom do not count young children as church members. There are doubtless considerable discrepancies, owing to the fact that the Catholic parishes are not necessarily contiguous with city boundaries. Fertility figures are equally unsatisfactory. Birth rates as reported annually by the Bureau of the Census must be rejected on two grounds, first, that until 1935 births have not been allocated to place of residence of the mother, and, second, that there are large differentials in the completeness of birth reporting. It was finally decided to use the ratio of children under five to 100 married women twenty to forty-four years old. Children under one year are not completely enumerated in the census, but there may be little reason to assume wide differentials in under-enumeration from city to city or between 1920 and 1930. The correlation was then sought between x_1 the percentage of Catholics in 1926, and x_2, the ratio between the 1930 and 1920 fertility, where the 1930 and 1920 fertility was measured in terms of the ratio of children under five to married women twenty to forty-four years old.

The cities were divided into three groups: (1) cities of 100,000 and over in 1930; (2) cities of 25,000–100,000 lying within the metropolitan area (as defined by the 1930 census) of cities of 100,000 or over; and (3) other cities of 25,000–100,000. Cities in the South Atlantic, East South Central, and West South Central states and Utah were excluded.

The correlation tables showed that in every group of cities, as the percentage of Catholics increased from city to city, the ratio of 1930 fertility to 1920 fertility decreased. The correlation coefficients, shown in Table 8-6, are not high, but all are in the direction which would be expected if the trends in Wisconsin cities were general throughout at least the northern and western cities of the United States. There may have been an exception in some New England mill cities, especially those heavily populated by French Canadians, Portuguese, and Italians.

Among the married women twenty to forty-four years old the proportion of older, and presumably less fertile, women increased between 1920 and 1930. This increase apparently was associated with the percentage of Catho-

---

cent complete enumeration of those couples married in the indicated cities who could be reached by the postal service. For the "universe" as thus defined no material correction is therefore necessary.

Table 8-6. Correlations between Percentage of Catholics in Northern and Western United States Cities and Ratio of 1930 Fertility to 1920 Fertility, Holding Various Factors Constant

	74 Cities of Over 100,000	56 Cities of 25,000– 100,000 Within Metropolitan Areas	96 Cities of 25,000– 100,000 Outside Metropolitan Areas
r_{12}	−0.31	−0.34	−0.44
$r_{12.3}$	−0.18	−0.09	−0.31
$r_{12.4}$	−0.39	−0.39	−0.48
$r_{12.5}$	−0.21	−0.32	−0.39
$r_{12.34}$	−0.26	−0.25	−0.36
$r_{12.35}$	−0.06	−0.08	−0.29
$r_{12.345}$	−0.16	−0.29	−0.35

x_1 = percentage of Catholics in 1926 estimated population

x_2 = ratio between (a) the number of children under five per 1,000 married women twenty to forty-four in 1930 and (b) the number of children under five per 1,000 married women twenty to forty-four in 1920

x_3 = ratio between (a) the percentage aged thirty-five to forty-four among the married women twenty to forty-four in 1930 and (b) the percentage aged thirty-five to forty-four among the married women twenty to forty-four in 1920

x_4 = percentage of families living in owned or rented homes with an equivalent rental of less than $30 per month

x_5 = ratio between the percentages of foreign-born whites in 1930 and 1920

lics in such a way as to account for part of the apparent correlation. All the correlations between x_1 and x_2 are somewhat reduced when x_3, the ratio between the percentages of married women twenty to forty-four who were thirty-five to forty-four in 1930 and 1920, respectively, is "partialed out." Another factor, x_4, the percentage of families in 1930 living in rented or owned dwellings with an equivalent rental of less than 30 dollars per month, is so associated with the other variables that when it also is "held constant" the correlations between x_1 and x_2 tend to rise. This index presumably reflects not only general economic level, but also, to some extent, exposure to metropolitan influence, in so far as this factor is not controlled by the original subdivision of cities into three groups. Introduction of still another factor (whose presence in such an analysis is perhaps debatable, since it may "partial out" too much of the variability properly attributable to Catholic church membership), namely, x_5, the percentage of increase or decrease in the percentage of foreign-born whites between 1920 and 1930, again reduces the correlation somewhat, except in the suburban cities of 25,000–100,000. The final partial correlations are −0.16 for the seventy-four cities of over 100,000, −0.29 for the fifty-six smaller suburban cities, and −0.35 for the ninety-six other smaller cities.[7] Of these three, only the last is clearly significant, taken by itself, though the second is almost too large to have been expected by chance alone. The correlations are all in the same direction, however; and the weighted average of z, which corresponds to $r_{12.345} = −0.28$, is four times its standard error and therefore is not attributable to chance.[8]

7. An inspection of the scatter diagrams for the cities of 100,000 and over showed that four New England cities—Fall River, New Bedford, Lowell, and Providence—diverged widely from the rest of the group. Omission of these cities would have raised $r_{12.34}$ from − 0.26 to − 0.31 and $r_{12.345}$ from − 0.16 to − 0.21.

8. The term z is the transformation of r, based on the method in R. A. Fisher, *Statistical Methods for Research Workers* (fourth ed.), sec. 35.

Too much weight must not be given to these correlation findings in generalizing from the Wisconsin study. But such evidence as they suggest is at least in the direction of strengthening, rather than weakening, the hypothesis that, on the average, the Catholic fertility has been dropping faster, both absolutely and relatively, than the non-Catholic fertility in the northern and western cities of the United States.

As a final caution, it should be re-emphasized that this report deals only with the larger urban populations. It is quite possible, indeed probable, that different trends prevail in smaller cities and rural areas.

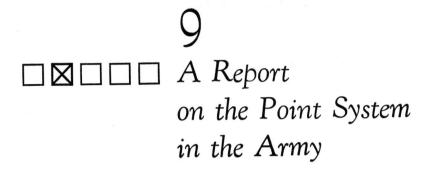

9

☐ ☒ ☐ ☐ ☐ *A Report*
on the Point System
in the Army

The author has chosen to include in this compilation just one example of a type of research report designed to give an executive succinct information requested to guide an administrative decision. Much of the original work of the Research Branch was, of course, of this type. The author, like other social scientists similarly trained, has either supervised or consulted on numerous action studies in civilian life, either for private corporations or foundations, for governmental organizations, or for his university.

The present example is a report sent, via the Special Planning Division of the War Department, to General Marshall shortly before V-J Day, the time of the surrender of Japan. The point system for discharge of soldiers, proposed by the Research Branch on the basis of surveys made during the preceding year on soldiers' attitudes, had been adopted by the War Department and applied immediately after the surrender of Germany. But there were strong pressures from some important generals to change the system after V-J Day, especially to reduce or eliminate points for combat credit, in order to retain as long as possible the best trained men and give priority in discharge to those with less experience. From one military-efficiency point of view, this demand was not unreasonable. But what about morale implications? General Marshall personally ordered a quick study, which was made in a two-week period on samples all over the world. Results in each theater were cabled to Washington, where data were consolidated and forwarded in the following report within one week of the completion of the field work.

The report, as will be seen, did uncover a good deal of dissatisfaction about measuring combat credit by the number of combat stars (one for each campaign). Supplemental credit for awards such as the combat infantryman's badge was indicated as possibly desirable. On the other hand, the probable bad morale effects of *lowering* combat credit were made clearly evident. General Marshall's final decision was to leave the point system unchanged.

Opinions of Soldiers throughout the World about a Post-V-J-Day Point System

This report, made at the request of the Special Planning Division, War Department Special Staff, records the opinions of a world-wide cross section of enlisted men with respect to a post-V-J-Day point system. The survey was made in the two-week period ending July 24, 1945. Results are based on the opinions of men with less than 85 points, since it is assumed that most men with 85 points or more will have been released by V-J-Day and plans for post-V-J-Day release would not be relevant to them.

SUMMARY

On the whole, men favor the present point system by a decisive majority, as has been previously reported.[1] Looking ahead to the period after the defeat of Japan, the majority want the point system retained in general outline and vote *against* discharging special categories of troops outside the point system if it would delay discharges under the point system. While the men want the point system retained, there are some changes that would be desired by substantial numbers and probably be acceptable to the majority.

Weights for Present Factors. More men vote to keep the weights unchanged after V-J-Day for any given factor now in the score card than vote to raise or lower the weights. There is, however, sufficient demand for an increase in overseas credit to justify giving serious consideration to raising

"Opinions of Soldiers throughout the World about a Post-V-J-Day Point System," from Chapter 11, pp. 540-546, *The American Soldier: Combat and Its Aftermath*, Vol II, by Stouffer, Suchman, DeVinney, Star, and Williams. Princeton: Princeton University Press, 1949.

1. Report B-159, *World-wide Attitudes toward Further Service and Redeployment.*

it. There is considerable support for raising overseas, combat, and longevity credit relative to parenthood credit. The men are almost unanimous against lowering credit after V-J-Day for overseas, combat, and longevity.

Method of Determining Combat Credit. While combat men are dissatisfied with the method of awarding campaign stars, the evidence shows that they would strongly resent eliminating campaign stars from combat credit. A special study in ETO shows that there would be general approval of giving points for the Combat Infantryman's Badge—men who are not entitled to this badge voting for the idea as well as those who wear the badge.

Parenthood and Dependency. Although more men would revise parenthood credit downward than upward, the majority would go along with a

Table 9-1. Detailed Findings: Opinions about Changing Weights for the Present Four Factors (World-wide Cross Section)

	Would Not Change Points	No Opinion	PERCENTAGES Would Raise Points	Would Lower Points	Total
Overseas credit	46%	15%	35%	4%	100%
Combat credit	60	16	20	4	100
Longevity credit	60	19	19	2	100
Parenthood credit	48	16	15	21	100

plan to give credit for every child instead of just the first three. Even more would favor giving points for dependents other than children. There is less support for the idea of giving additional points for wives, about half of those with opinions approving and half disapproving.

Credit for Age. The majority favor giving credit for age. The optimum credit would appear to be about one point per year beginning at age eighteen.

Discharge of Various Categories Outside the Point System. There would be general opposition to discharging various categories of men outside the point system—unless it did not very much delay other men getting out under the point system. There would be somewhat less opposition to blanket discharges of men who have been in the Army a long time or men over thirty-five than to discharges of fathers, men not physically qualified for overseas duty, or men who have been in the Army too short a time to complete their training. Substitution after V-J-Day of the "first in, first out" plan for the point system is voted down, by nearly two to one, among those with opinions. A third of the men are so strongly opposed to the "first in, first out" idea that they say they would be "burned up about it."

Detailed statistics documenting these findings are presented in Table 9-1.

Since only a minority vote to raise or lower the points for any one factor after V-J-Day, these data would support the proposition to leave the present weights unchanged after V-J-Day. If, however, any change in weights is contemplated, the data give some important indications of what changes might conceivably be acceptable and what would not.

If only one weight were to be changed, an increase in the *overseas credit* would probably be the most acceptable. A further cross tabulation of the above data shows, for example, that 43 per cent of those with opinions believe that twelve months overseas should have more weight than one child, while only 10 per cent believe that one child should have more weight than twelve months overseas. The rest are content with the present relative weights of the two factors. Three-fifths of those who would raise overseas credit would raise it to two points per month.

Any cut in combat credit or longevity credit would be directly contrary to the overwhelming opinion of the men.

A minority (21 per cent) favors the outright cutting of credit for parenthood. As can be shown by detailed cross tabulations, an even larger proportion would favor readjusting points so that overseas, combat, and longevity credit would have a higher ratio to parenthood credit than is the case now. This could be accomplished, of course, either by raising overseas, combat, and longevity credit or by lowering parenthood credit. It is unlikely, however, that parenthood credit could be cut now without severe psychological hazard.

Method of Determining Combat Credit. As previous reports have shown,[2] there is much disaffection among combat men overseas over the use of campaign stars for calculating combat credit.[3] This must *not*, however, be interpreted as forecasting a willingness to dispense with credit for campaign stars after V-J-Day. To the contrary, as the table previously reported shows, only 4 per cent of the men in the world-wide cross section would *lower* the present credit for campaign stars and decorations. Even among troops in the United States who are not entitled to campaign stars only 7 per cent would lower the credit.

In other words, there is practically unanimity on not lowering combat credit. A special study (made only in ETO) shows that only 17 per cent of a representative cross section of men in the European theater would oppose *adding* credit for the Combat Infantryman's Badge. The opposition among field force combat veterans is 9 per cent, field force noncombat veterans 18 per cent, air force men 19 per cent, and comzone men 26 per cent. This is

2. Report B-159, *World-wide Attitudes toward Further Service and Redeployment.*

3. For example, a special study in ETO shows that a cross section of men interviewed in July, 1945, would like to see higher credit given to some classes of troops with campaign stars than to other troops with campaign stars. Entitled to the *highest* credit, in the men's opinion, would be rifle and heavy weapons companies, tank and tank destroyer companies, combat engineer units, and aid men and other combat medics. *Next* would come recon platoons, air force combat crews, field artillery batteries, cannon companies, and chemical mortar outfits. *Last* would come medics in field hospitals, regimental headquarters troops, division headquarters troops, division quartermaster troops, and, at the bottom, army and corps headquarters troops. But only a small minority would deny combat credit to units facing the least hazard. Sixty per cent of the men in the ETO cross section said they wanted time in combat counted in the point score *in addition* to credit for campaign stars and decorations. Only 3 per cent would reduce credit for campaign stars and decorations.

Table 9-2

Question: "Below are several plans which could be used after V-J-Day for giving points for combat. If you had to choose, which one of these plans would you rather have used?"	First Choice, Per Cent
A. The present plan of giving points for campaign stars and decorations	40
B. Points would be given for campaign stars, but not for decorations	5
C. Points would be given for the Purple Heart and for decorations which were given for outstanding bravery in action, but not for other decorations or for campaign stars	4
D. Points would be given for time in combat, but not for campaign stars or decorations	36
E. I don't care which of these plans is used	15
Total	100

about as high a consensus as will be obtained in the Army for any proposal and strongly supports the wisdom of considering the inclusion of the Combat Infantryman's Badge in the point system. Some numerically small groups who have been exposed to enemy fire might still be dissatisfied, but it should reduce to a minimum the present large volume of protests from the men who have done the main fighting on the ground.

Another special study made on August 7, 1945, of a battalion of Category II Infantry veterans just shipped to the United States shows that very few of them would react favorably to a plan that would give points for the Purple Heart and for decorations that were given for outstanding bravery in action but that would not give points for other decorations or campaign stars.

Table 9-2 shows that several times as many men favored the present plan as favored Plan C. The men also were asked to indicate their second choice. If those who voted for Plan D, which is popular but impracticable, are redistributed according to their second choices, it will be seen (Table 9-3) that the present method of computing campaign stars is still decisively preferred to Plans B or C by this sample of infantry veterans.[4]

The present method of figuring combat credit is clearly defective, and even with the addition of the Combat Infantryman's Badge (and, possibly, similar badges for medical aid men and the like), complaints must be expected. But the world-wide data, plus the supplementary small-sample information just reported, show that such complaints would be insignificant as

Table 9-3. First Choice of Men Who Preferred A, B, C, and E, Plus the Second Choices of the Men Who Preferred Plan D

Prefer:	Per Cent
A. The present plan of giving points and campaign stars for decorations	63
B. Points would be given for campaign stars but not for decorations	10
C. Points would be given for the Purple Heart and for decorations which were given for outstanding bravery in action, but not for other decorations or for campaign stars	11
D. I don't care which of these plans is used	16
Total	100

4. Quite similar figures are obtained from samples of Class II Air Force and Service Force troops just shipped to the United States, with even greater preference for the present system.

compared with the morale damage which can be predicted if credit for campaign stars and decorations were to be lowered or eliminated.

Parenthood and Dependency. As has been shown, there is considerable resentment against the high points for parenthood credit. A majority would favor giving points for dependents other than wife or children, and a smaller majority would favor giving points for every child, instead of just the first three (Table 9-4). Attitudes toward giving points for being married, even without children, are quite evenly divided, with those opposed being quite strong in their opposition (data based on world-wide cross section).

Table 9-4

Question: "How would you feel about giving points after V-J-Day for . . .?"	Dependents Other Than Wife or Children, Per Cent	Every Child Instead of Only the First Three, Per Cent	Being Married, Even If There Are No Children, Per Cent
A fine idea—I would favor it very much	40	39	30
A pretty good idea	23	16	16
I wouldn't care one way or the other	14	13	14
Not such a good idea	15	18	19
A poor idea—I would be burned up about it	8	14	21
Total	100	100	100

Overseas men are much stronger in their opposition to proposals that points be given for additional children or wives than are men in the United States who have not been overseas.

Credit for Age. Relatively few men are opposed to adding age to the point system after V-J-Day (Table 9-5).

Table 9-5

Question: "How would you feel about giving points after V-J-Day for age?"	World-wide Cross Section, Per Cent
A fine idea—I would favor it very much	44
A pretty good idea	20
I wouldn't care one way or the other	12
Not such a good idea	15
A poor idea—I would be burned up about it	9
Total	100

The proper point credit for age, if it is to conform with men's opinions, would apparently be to give one point per year of age. This is tested indirectly by such questions as given in Table 9-6.

Table 9-6

Question: "Here are two men, both are married, both have never served overseas. Which of them should get out of the Army first after V-J-Day?"	World-wide Cross Section, Per Cent
Martin, who is 25 years old, in the Army 4 years	47
Clark, who is 35 years old, in the Army 3 years	53
Total	100

Since the vote splits approximately fifty-fifty, this would indicate that ten years of age and one year in the Army are approximately equated. If the overwhelming majority had voted for letting Martin out first, this would have meant that the men thought a year in the Army should count *more* than ten years of age. The opposite would be true if the vote had been for Clark. Similar paired comparisons showed that a two-to-one majority rated a year overseas or two campaigns as worth more than ten years of age, while a majority voted to give less credit for a child than for ten years of age. This, of course, reflects inconsistency in the point system, which in the judgment of the men now underrates overseas and combat credit as compared with parenthood credit. Such discrepancies would tend to become reconciled if overseas credit is raised and combat credit either is raised or is extended by including the Combat Infantryman's Badge.

Only 12 per cent would start age credit at age thirty-five. The largest proportion favored starting at age eighteen:

	Per Cent
Favor starting at 18	41
Favor starting at 25	15
Favor starting at 30	10
Favor starting at 35	12
Don't care	22
Total	100

Discharge of Various Categories Outside the Point System. In general, the great majority of the men either would oppose the discharge of special categories of men outside the point system or favor it *only* if it did not very much delay other men getting out under the point system. Relatively more approval is given to letting out men with long service or men over thirty-five than to other categories (Table 9-7).

When soldiers throughout the world were asked directly what they would

Table 9-7

PERCENTAGE DISTRIBUTION IN WORLD-WIDE CROSS SECTION

PLAN TO RELEASE AFTER V-J-DAY OUTSIDE THE POINT SYSTEM ALL MEN WHO ...	Would Favor It Even If It Delayed Other Men Getting Out under the Point System	Would Favor It Only If It Did Not Very Much Delay Other Men Getting Out under the Point System	Would Not Favor It at All	No Opinion	Total
Have been in the Army four or five years or longer	32	48	19	1	100
Are over 35 years of age	22	53	24	1	100
Are fathers	17	41	41	1	100
Are not physically qualified for overseas duty	15	41	43	1	100
Have been in the Army too short a time to complete their training	3	17	79	1	100

think of substituting for the point system the "first in, first out" plan—letting men out of the Army in the same order as they came in—the men with opinions voted against it by nearly two to one. It should be noted that 32 per cent checked the extreme category: "A poor idea—I would be burned up about it."

	World-wide Cross Section, Per Cent
A fine idea—I would favor it very much	20
A pretty good idea	13
I wouldn't care one way or the other	7
Not such a good idea	28
A poor idea—I would be burned up about it	32
Total	**100**

HOW THIS STUDY WAS MADE

For this study, five large representative cross sections of enlisted men were surveyed, anonymously, in the last two weeks of July, 1945. The samples comprise representative cross sections of soldiers in (1) the European Theater of Operations, (2) Pacific Ocean Areas, including the Marianas and Okinawa, (3) India-Burma, (4) overseas returnees in the United States, and (5) men without overseas service. These data permit an accurate report for each of the areas covered, and with proper weighting and some allowance for error in filling in gaps for commands not fully covered, also permits an estimate of opinion on a world-wide basis which is reliable with an error probably not exceeding 5 per cent.

10

□ ☒ □ □ □ *Attitudes*
as Related to
Subsequent Behavior

All research on attitudes and values is haunted by the possibility that verbal expressions by respondents may bear no relation to the subsequent behavior of these people. Attempts to relate attitudes and subsequent behavior have been most numerous and perhaps most successful where the behavioral criterion is voting in an election for a candidate as planned or carrying out an intention to purchase a particular consumer product.

The two papers included below are examples of research in the Army taken from *The American Soldier*. While the underlying research in these papers may seem quite simple and straightforward, these are good examples of problems which contain numerous headaches for the empirical researcher. Many of the difficulties and pitfalls that had to be circumvented will be fairly obvious to the experienced researcher, but their nature and magnitude may not be readily appreciated by some who are willing to take for granted that relationships between attitudes and behavior either necessarily exist or do not.

The first paper deals with attitudes as related to subsequent behavior in combat, the second with attitudes as related to subsequent promotion.

A. *Attitudes before Combat and Behavior in Combat*

The chapters in *The American Soldier,* Vol. II, contain a body of facts unique in the annals of war. Opinions of combat troops, both ground and air, have been ascertained and analyzed quantitatively. Thus, it is possible to compare, with confidence in the representativeness of the responses, the feelings of men of varying degrees of experience or responsibility as they faced their combat jobs.

Before proceeding to a description of the attitudes of combat troops, it is desirable to discuss frankly, with such evidence as is at hand, the following question: "Suppose that many combat soldiers did have unfavorable attitudes. What of it? They fought, didn't they?" This chapter provides data which document the point that attitudes did mean something in terms of combat performance.

It was not until November, 1943, that the Research Branch was enabled to make a detailed study of troops with combat experience, except for scattered interviews with wounded combat veterans in hospitals. At that time a survey was made of the combat veterans in ten rifle companies of the First Division, just arrived in England after successful campaigns in North Africa and Sicily. The study showed that these veterans, while exhibiting a rather fierce pride in their outfit, were more embittered than perhaps any other soldiers who had been studied by the Research Branch. The majority felt that they had done their share as compared with other soldiers—a few of them repeating a *mot* current in the division. "The Army consists of the First Division and eight million replacements." Only a handful expressed any zeal for further combat, and a special tabulation showed that men who had been decorated for gallantry with the DSC or Silver Star were just as bitter as the rest.

The Research Branch report on the First Division was read by the Chief of Staff of the Army and sent by him to members of the General Staff for

By Samuel A. Stouffer, Arthur A. Lumsdaine, and Marion Harper Lumsdaine. Section I and part of Section III of Chapter 1 were written by Stouffer, based on his analysis of attitude data whose collection in Europe was initiated by Robert B. Wallace and of casualty data whose statistical treatment in Washington was organized by A. J. Jaffe, following a preliminary study made in Europe under the direction of Robin M. Williams, Jr. Section II is based on a research study carried out in Europe under the direction of Arthur A. Lumsdaine, who shared responsibility for the analysis and presentation with Marion Harper Lumsdaine, who also wrote part of Section III. The study in Section II made use of data on recruits collected under the direction of William W. McPeak in the United States, and in the European follow-up the technique for obtaining combat performance ratings was developed jointly by Arthur A. Lumsdaine and Irving L. Janis.

"Attitudes before Combat and Behavior in Combat," from Chapter 1, pp. 3-30, *The American Soldier: Combat and Its Aftermath,* Vol. II, by Stouffer, Suchman, DeVinney, Star, and Williams. Princeton: Princeton University Press, 1949.

comment. A number of constructive suggestions for improving the situation for the combat soldier were brought forward, as well as admonitions from some quarters that the "gripes" of combat soldiers should not be taken too seriously.

The Chief of Staff felt that the value of the First Division study would be enhanced if comparable data were available for other combat divisions, and therefore he ordered such studies made. He personally selected three divisions in the Pacific for survey—the Seventh, Twenty-fifth, and Forty-third. Thus began a series of surveys of combat troops that provides the basic data for *The American Soldier*, Volume II. The first large-scale study of opinions of combat flying personnel was made in the spring of 1944 at the request of the commander of the Eighth Air Force.

A persistent question mark remained: How do we know that the men's verbal reports have any relation to their subsequent performance in combat? It can be argued, forcefully, that griping is an outlet that helps make the hard life of a combat man a little more tolerable; therefore, griping is a healthy, positive sign. An alternative position would be that, while a certain amount of griping is healthy, too much is indicative of an unhealthy psychological atmosphere.

Chapter 1 of *The American Soldier* is a contribution toward the elucidation of this problem, in that it shows that attitudes toward combat are related to subsequent behavior in combat. The chapter is in three sections. Section I compares attitudes prior to D-Day of men in the 108 rifle companies and in thirty-four of the thirty-six heavy weapons companies in four divisions with the nonbattle casualty rates of these same companies in Normandy in June and July, 1944. In this study 12,295 men participated. In Section II, Chapter 1, Volume II, of *The American Soldier*, the attitudes of individual soldiers in a sample of infantrymen are compared with ratings of the battle performance of these same individuals in Europe made a year later. Section III of Chapter 1 serves as a methodological appendix to Sections I and II, giving the technical reader further details of how these studies were made.

SECTION I.   COMPANY ATTITUDES AND NONBATTLE CASUALTY RATES
IN COMBAT

Design of the Study. This report compares attitudes toward combat by companies before D-Day with nonbattle casualty rates of the same companies after D-Day, based on the First, Fourth, Ninth, and Twenty-ninth Divisions.[1]

Three related attitudes are analyzed: willingness for combat, confidence in combat stamina, and confidence in combat skill.

---

1. Attitude data throughout this section are from S-128, January, 1944 (First and Ninth Divisions) and S-129, April, 1944 (Fourth and Twenty-ninth Divisions).

The score on willingness for combat is based on answers to two questions with different check lists:

Which of the following best tells how you feel about getting into an actual battle zone?

Which of the following best describes your own feeling about getting into combat against the Germans?

The score on confidence in combat stamina is based on answers to three questions:

Do you feel that you are in tough enough physical condition for going into combat?

If and when you get into combat how well do you think you will stand up under battle conditions?

Do you think you are in good physical condition?

The score on confidence in combat skill is based on answers to three questions:

Do you feel that you are now trained and ready for combat or do you need more training?

If you were given a group of men and told to take charge of them all by yourself on a mission under enemy fire, how well do you think you would do?

Do you think that you have been given enough training and experience so that you could do a good job in taking charge of a group of men on your own in combat?

A detailed analysis of how the scores were derived from the check lists of answers to these items is presented in Section III of Chapter 1, Volume II, of *The American Soldier*. Each individual analyzed in a given company received a score on these three attitudes, and a company average was then computed on each attitude. The average sample per company was eighty-seven, with considerable variation in sample size.

Statistics on nonbattle casualty rates by companies in Normandy in June and July, 1944, are used as a criterion with which to compare the company averages on the pre-D-Day attitude variables. Nonbattle casualty rates indicate the number of combat men who became ineffective for reasons other than wounds or other battle injuries. They are by no means to be regarded as complete and infallible indexes of combat efficiency, let alone combat performance. But no other reliable measure was available. In one division that saw heavy and continuous fighting in Normandy, an intensive effort was made by the ETO staff of the Research Branch to find the best possible criteria. Opinions of staff officers and field commanders on individual company performance were sought but were not serviceable as criteria because of wide disagreement. How does one compare a company with a brilliant performance in one action and a later undistinguished record with a company that did its job day after day faithfully amid heavy casualties but was never conspicuous?

Decorations for gallantry were studied and discarded as criteria because of command variation in the awards. AWOL's were simply too few in the Normandy campaign to provide useful indexes at the company level. Psychiatric casualties varied with the command, possibly not so much in relation to incidence of psychiatric breakdowns as to the degree of indulgence on the part of the command and the local medical personnel. In one division the division psychiatrist informed the research team that, although the psychiatric rate was twice as high in one regiment as in another, the difference was in his opinion entirely attributable to differences in policy in the two regiments with respect to labeling or not labeling nonbattle casualties as "exhaustion" cases.

After a laborious study, the research team arrived at the conclusion that the only index, at the company level, that could be defended as both reliable and meaningful would be the nonbattle casualty rate.[2] Certainly, if A Company loses a *third* of its men during a campaign as nonbattle casualties while B Company loses only a *tenth* of its men in this way, the latter company is the more effective company—everything else equal. Moreover, an unknown but possibly large percentage of the nonbattle casualties in Normandy may have been psychiatric or psychosomatic cases. This was summer, there were no serious epidemics, trench foot was not yet a problem, there was no malaria. Some units may have had much more serious exposure to risk of illness than others, but if we concentrate our analysis on *a comparison of companies within the same regiment*, variability in physical environment should tend to even out over a two-month period.

One factor responsible for variability in nonbattle casualty rates of companies can be partly controlled, namely, the incidence of battle casualties. If a company loses half of its original strength in the first week, there will be fewer survivors exposed to risk of nonbattle casualties than if it has only a few battle casualties initially.

Compensating, however, is the possibility that the shock of a heavy initial loss may be more productive of psychosomatic disorders among the survivors than would a smaller initial toll. Correlations, exhibited later in this report, indicate that the nonbattle casualty rate tended to be higher in those companies with the greater number of man-days of exposure to risk. Consequently, the index used expresses the nonbattle casualties in a company during the eight weeks beginning June 6, 1944, as a *ratio* ($\times$ 100) of the average number of men available for duty per day throughout the period, thus:

$$\text{Nonbattle casualty rate} = 100 \times \frac{\text{number of nonbattle casualties}}{\text{average number of men available per day}}$$

2. This index, like one based explicitly on psychiatric casualties, is subject to some differences in command practice—but very much less so than would be an index based solely on "exhaustion" cases.

Since we are interested in relating the attitudes of men in companies studied prior to D-Day to nonbattle casualty rates of the same companies after D-Day, it is desirable to base the nonbattle casualty rates on only those men who *originally landed in Normandy with a given company*. Battle and nonbattle casualties in eight weeks among the original personnel were very high, as is shown in Table 10-1.

In order to compute casualty rates by companies based on the original men who landed in Normandy, it was necessary to go back to the original morning reports of the companies. This analysis was carried out by the Research

Table 10-1. Casualties among Soldiers Originally Entering Normandy with Their Units during Eight Weeks Beginning June 6, 1944*

	RIFLE COMPANIES		HEAVY WEAPONS COMPANIES	
	Officers	Enlisted Men	Officers	Enlisted Men
Strength on June 6	779	21,557	308	6,156
Strength on July 31	204	8,708	138	3,786
Percentage July 31 strength of original strength	26.2	40.4	44.8	61.5
Battle casualties	535	12,846	160	2,277
Battle casualties as a percentage of original strength	68.7	59.6	51.9	37.0
Nonbattle casualties	82	2,928	27	746
Nonbattle casualties as a percentage of original strength	10.5	13.6	8.8	12.1

* First, Fourth, Ninth, and Twenty-ninth Divisions. Replacements received after D-Day are excluded from this table. Nonbattle casualties here represent the category "sick, nonbattle casualty" only. Nonbattle injuries, AWOL's, and transfers to other units also were causes of separation. Successive casualties to the same individual are counted as separate casualties. The strength on July 31 is the original strength minus all separations plus all returns to duty. Hence, the percentages in a given column do not add to 100.

Branch in Washington, working from photostats of all the morning reports of the letter companies in the Infantry regiments of four divisions. It was a detailed and laborious accounting operation. The steps in the process are outlined later in this report. Suffice it to say here that the morning reports proved quite adequate for the task. The accounting procedures set up enabled errors made in filling out the reports under field conditions to be largely detected and reconciled, and the rates here used may be taken as accurate with an average error of not over 1 or 2 per cent.

We have, then, two sets of indexes: on the one hand, average attitude scores by company on willingness for combat, confidence in combat stamina, and confidence in combat skill, based on surveys made before D-Day; and, on the other hand, nonbattle casualty rates in the eight weeks beginning June 6, 1944, among the men who landed in Normandy with these same companies.

Company Attitudes and Company Nonbattle Casualty Rates. The units surveyed included two veteran divisions, the First and the Ninth, and two nonveteran divisions, the Fourth and the Twenty-ninth—all of whom were destined to play a conspicuous role in Normandy. Unfortunately for the purposes of the present analysis, a long time elapsed between the time of the attitude surveys and the Normandy landing. This was especially the case in the veteran divisions, which were surveyed late in January, 1944—over five months before D-Day. The nonveteran divisions were surveyed in April, 1944—a little less than two months before D-Day. After the time of the survey, the veteran divisions received substantial replacements who were trained with their units and who made the invasion with them. A small sample study, not large enough for basing company comparisons, was made in the Ninth Division in April, and this serves as something of a bridge for interpreting changes between January and April.

Between the periods of the attitude surveys and D-Day there were, then, substantial changes in the personnel of companies, especially in the veteran divisions, and some changes in officer leadership. After D-Day there were very great changes in leadership. As Table 10-1 has shown, battle casualties among company officers were high, and hence the turnover in leadership was high. The 108 rifle companies in the study retained, at the end of the eight weeks following June 6, only 26.2 per cent of their original company officers, while the heavy weapons companies retained 44.8 per cent. In addition to casualties, the rifle companies lost 10.5 per cent of their officers by transfer and the heavy weapons companies 14.9 per cent. Many of the casualties had returned to duty before the eight-week period was up.

Because of the changes between the time of the attitude surveys and D-Day and because of the variability of conditions in Normandy and the turnover in officer leadership, one would not expect a high correlation between company attitudes at the time of the survey and nonbattle casualty rates in Normandy. Under these conditions a significant association, even if not high, between initial attitudes and subsequent combat behavior should be all the more convincing a demonstration of the fact that (a) attitudes as here studied are not mere casual and idle verbal expressions, (b) attitudes persist through time, and (c) they relate to other behavior which is important. The reader must remember that the present comparison is of *units*, not of individuals. The individuals in the attitude studies were queried anonymously and an equating of individual responses with subsequent individual combat behavior was not possible in this study. The problem can be stated as follows:

If the average score in A Company on willingness for combat was higher (that is, better) than the average score in B Company, did A Company tend to have a *lower* nonbattle casualty rate in the eight weeks beginning June 6, 1944, than B Company? Similarly with average scores on confidence in combat stamina and confidence in combat skill. If the attitude scores reflect merely "healthy" negative attitudes toward combat, there should be no significant correlation. If better attitude scores tend to be predictive of lower nonbattle casualty rates and if worse attitude scores tend to be predictive of higher nonbattle casualty rates, then the correlations should tend to be negative. Here, of course, a correlation coefficient with a negative

Table 10-2. Rifle Companies—Correlation Coefficients of Pre-D-Day Attitude Scores and Nonbattle Casualty Rates in Normandy

	NONBATTLE CASUALTY RATES CORRELATED WITH SCORES ON		
	Willingness for Combat	Confidence in Combat Stamina	Confidence in Combat Skill
VETERAN DIVISIONS			
First Division			
16th Regiment	+0.01	−0.56	−0.01
18th Regiment	−0.70	−0.14	−0.12
26th Regiment	−0.25	−0.41	−0.32
Average	−0.31	−0.37	−0.15
Ninth Division			
39th Regiment	−0.25	−0.45	−0.26
47th Regiment	−0.72	−0.28	−0.05
60th Regiment	−0.60	−0.66	−0.13
Average	−0.52	−0.46	−0.15
NONVETERAN DIVISIONS			
Fourth Division			
8th Regiment	−0.30	−0.19	+0.04
12th Regiment	−0.32	−0.34	−0.40
22nd Regiment	−0.25	−0.46	−0.32
Average	−0.29	−0.33	−0.23
Thirty-ninth Division			
115th Regiment	+0.16	−0.19	−0.72
116th Regiment	−0.32	−0.54	−0.35
175th Regiment	−0.43	−0.16	−0.51
Average	−0.20	−0.30	−0.53
Average veteran regiments	−0.42	−0.42	−0.15
Average nonveteran regiments	−0.24	−0.31	−0.38
Average all regiments	−0.33	−0.37	−0.27

Each correlation is based on nine companies.

sign means a *positive* predictive relationship between "good" attitudes and the index of efficiency furnished by the nonbattle casualty rate. Thus, a negative correlation means that the better the attitudes, the "better" (i.e., lower) the nonbattle casualty rate.

Let us look first at the rifle companies, which should be studied separately from the heavy weapons companies because the combat conditions and battle casualties of rifle companies are much more severe than those of other infantry units.

Table 10-2 shows, among rifle companies, that the correlation coefficients of attitude scores and nonbattle casualty rates, though low, *tend to be negative.*

In ten out of twelve regiments, the scores by companies within the regiments on willingness for combat tend to be negatively correlated with the nonbattle casualty rates. This means that in ten out of the twelve regiments, those companies with the *worst* attitudes *tended* to have the *highest* nonbattle casualty rates, and vice versa. If positive or negative correlations were equally probable, the likelihood of getting by chance as many as ten negative correlations in a sample of twelve would be 79 in 4,096, or less than 2 per cent. The average correlation coefficient for the twelve regiments was −0.33. This does not mean, of course, that bad attitudes necessarily "caused" bad performance. Both might be reflections of other variables, such as actual physical condition. We are here focusing on the fact that attitudes tended to *predict* subsequent performance.

In all twelve regiments negative correlations indicate that the lower the average scores on confidence in combat stamina, the more likely the company would be to have a high nonbattle casualty rate. The average correlation is −0.37.

Table 10-3. Heavy Weapons Companies—Correlation Coefficients of Pre-D-Day Attitude Scores and Nonbattle Casualty Rates in Normandy

	NONBATTLE CASUALTY RATES CORRELATED WITH SCORES ON		
DIVISION	Willingness for Combat	Confidence in Combat Stamina	Confidence in Combat Skill
First	−0.82	−0.53	−0.55
Ninth	−0.11	−0.21	−0.74
Fourth	−0.07	−0.55	−0.81
Twenty-ninth	−0.64	−0.07	+0.18
Average	−0.41	−0.34	−0.48

Within each division the attitude scores and casualty rates of the three heavy weapons companies in each regiment are recorded as deviations from the regimental average for the three companies. Each correlation in the First and Fourth Divisions is based on nine companies; in the Ninth and Twenty-ninth on eight, since data were not available for two companies.

In eleven of the twelve regiments the correlations are also negative between scores on confidence in combat skill and nonbattle casualty rates, with the average correlation being −0.27.

Table 10-2 is based on rifle companies. When we study separately the heavy weapons companies in the same regiments, we find that the correlations among heavy weapons companies are also negative (Table 10-3). Since there are only three heavy weapons companies per regiment, the correlation coefficients are based on the division rather than the regiment, after expressing each company's attitude score and casualty rate as a deviation from its regimental mean. Two weapons companies, one in the Ninth Division and one in the Twenty-ninth Division, were unavailable for the attitude survey; hence, the total number of weapons companies involved is only thirty-four instead of thirty-six. The average correlation of nonbattle casualty rates with scores on willingness for combat was −0.41, with scores on confidence in combat stamina −0.34, and with scores on confidence in combat skill −0.48.

While the correlations among either rifle or heavy weapons companies are not high, their consistency in sign establishes beyond reasonable doubt the fact of a tendency for companies with the worse attitudes to have the higher nonbattle casualty rates, and vice versa.

The basic data from which Tables 10-2 and 10-3 are drawn are shown in Tables 10 and 11 in Section III of Chapter 1, Volume II, of *The American Soldier*.

In view of the fact that combat conditions and command practices affecting nonbattle casualty rates differed widely from one regiment to another even within a given division, it seemed unlikely a priori that a relationship between attitude averages for entire regiments and nonbattle casualty rates would be particularly meaningful. Actually, when a regimental attitude score is expressed as a deviation from the division mean and such deviations for the twelve regiments are correlated with corresponding deviations in nonbattle casualty rates, the correlation, just as in the case of companies within regiments, turns out to be negative. All the correlations are low, except possibly that between willingness for combat and nonbattle casualty rate, which is −0.59, when each regimental score is the average of rifle companies only. The corresponding correlation when confidence in combat stamina is used as the sorting variable is −0.28, and when confidence in combat skill is used, −0.13. For regimental averages using heavy weapons companies only, the correlations are −0.03 with willingness for combat, −0.19 with confidence in combat stamina, and −0.20 with confidence in combat skill. In view of the fact that no further replication was possible and in view of the numerous a priori uncertainties about the meaning of the nonbattle casualty index for regimental comparisons, these data should not be cited as providing evidence either for or against the validity of attitude scores for regimental comparisons. A comparative test for whole divisions is even more hazardous—not only because of the conditions affecting the nonbattle casualty rates but also because two of the divisions in the present study were surveyed three months before the other two divisions.[3]

A further question is now in order. Granted that the consistency of the correlations between precombat attitudes and nonbattle casualty rates by companies indicates the tendency toward an association, how much difference does it make? There is a distinction between what may be called statistical significance and what may be called practical significance. Let us now look at the data from the latter point of view.[4]

---

3. Because the First and Ninth Divisions were surveyed in January and the Fourth and Twenty-ninth in April (the latter with somewhat different forms of questions) no direct comparison of the mean attitude scores of the veteran and nonveteran divisions is possible. Somewhat more defensible would be a comparison, on the one hand, of the mean attitude scores of the First Division with those of the Ninth, and a comparison, on the other hand, of the mean attitude scores of the Fourth Division with those of the Twenty-ninth. We see at once that the picture is mixed. The mean scores of the First Division were somewhat higher than the Ninth on willingness for combat and confidence in combat stamina, but somewhat lower than the Ninth on confidence in combat skill. The mean scores of the Fourth Division were somewhat lower than the Twenty-ninth on willingness for combat and confidence in combat stamina, but somewhat higher on confidence in combat skill. What about comparative nonbattle casualty rates? The average rate in the Ninth Division, 30, was higher than in the First, 21. The average rate in the Twenty-ninth Division, 24, was higher than in the Fourth, 19. But the conditions faced by the various divisions were so different that the nonbattle casualty rate, while very meaningful for comparing companies within the same regiment, may no longer have much significance. For example, two

Suppose that a regimental commander before D-Day had known the score of his nine rifle companies on willingness for combat. How much actual difference would he have had a right to expect between the average nonbattle casualty rates of his three rifle companies with the best attitude scores as compared with the three companies with the worst scores? Let us illustrate by the Eighth Regiment of the Fourth Division, where the correlation between nonbattle casualty rates and scores on willingness for combat was shown in Table 10-2 to be −0.30. From Table 10 in Section III of Chapter 1, Volume II, of *The American Soldier*, we can see that the three companies with highest scores on willingness for combat are A, B, and I, with nonbattle casualty rates of 18, 8, and 20, respectively. The medium three companies are C, G, and L, with nonbattle casualty rates of 16, 24, and 31. The lowest three are E, F, and K, with rates of 17, 34, and 33. Averaging the nonbattle casualty rates for each group of three companies, we have

	Average Nonbattle Casualty Rate
A, B, I	15.3
C, G, L	23.7
E, F, K	28.0

In this regiment, the companies with the highest scores on willingness for combat had a substantially lower average nonbattle casualty rate than companies with medium or low scores.

If we repeat this process for all twelve regiments and pool the results, we have the picture shown in Figure 10-1, which also exhibits the results of comparable tabulations based on grouping companies within a regiment according to scores on confidence in combat stamina and, finally, on confidence in combat skill. Among the three rifle companies in each of the

---

regiments of the First Division, the Sixteenth and Eighteenth, took severe punishment at Omaha Beach, but the division as a whole was largely engaged in a holding operation until the final break-through in late July and sustained relatively light casualties after the landing attack. The battle casualties in the Ninth Division were much higher than in the First Division and were sustained throughout June and July, although the division did not disembark in Normandy until a week after D-Day. Both the Fourth and Twenty-ninth Divisions had very heavy battle casualties throughout the Normandy campaign. Both participated in the landings, during which the 115th Regiment of the Twenty-ninth Division took more severe punishment than other regiments in these two divisions.

For official accounts of action, see "Omaha Beachhead" (1946) and "St.-Lô" (1947), two monographs in the *American Forces in Action* series published by the Historical Section of the War Department.

4. In any analysis of relationships, one can focus on the measure of correlation or on some measure of regression. The latter can be practically unimportant even if a correlation is rather high or can be practically important even if the correlation is rather low.

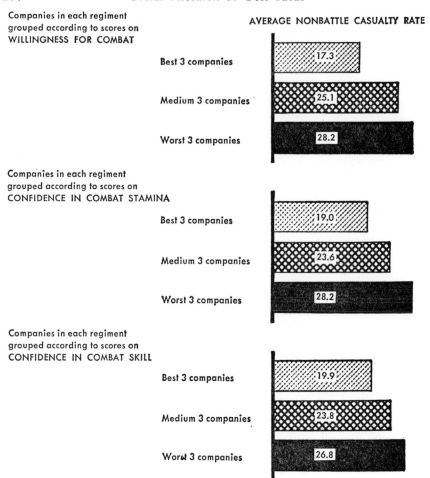

Each bar represents 36 companies.

Figure 10-1. Rifle companies in four divisions—average nonbattle casualty rates in Normandy as related to pre-D-Day attitude score.

twelve regiments with worst pre-D-Day scores on willingness for combat, the average nonbattle casualty rate in Normandy was 28.2, which is 1.62 times the average nonbattle casualty rate of the three companies in each regiment with best scores on this attitude. Corresponding ratios are 1.47 when confidence in combat stamina is the sorting variable and 1.35 when confidence in combat skill is the sorting variable.

From the standpoint, then, of practical as well as merely statistical significance, the relationship would seem to be important. In advance of D-Day, attitudes could have been known which would have sorted out companies destined to have an average nonbattle casualty rate 35 to 62 *per cent* greater than that of another group of companies.[5]

While there was variation from regiment to regiment in the ratio of the average nonbattle casualty rate in the three companies with worst attitude scores to that of the three companies with best scores, it is important to note that the ratio was greater than unity in almost every case, as is shown by Table 10-4.

Table 10-4. Rifle Companies—Average Nonbattle Casualty Rate of Three Companies with Worst Attitudes in Their Regiments Expressed as a Ratio of Average Rate of Three Companies with Best Attitudes, by Regiments

	Companies Grouped by Scores on Willingness for Combat	Companies Grouped by Scores on Confidence in Combat Stamina	Companies Grouped by Scores on Confidence in Combat Skill
First Division			
16th Regiment	1.09	1.59	1.00
18th Regiment	1.65	1.04	0.95
26th Regiment	1.19	1.48	1.43
Ninth Division			
39th Regiment	1.39	2.00	1.25
47th Regiment	1.54	1.13	1.45
60th Regiment	2.00	1.58	1.52
Fourth Division			
8th Regiment	1.82	1.17	1.12
12th Regiment	1.24	1.09	1.53
22nd Regiment	1.46	2.06	1.46
Twenty-ninth Division			
115th Regiment	0.92	1.23	1.55
116th Regiment	2.09	2.17	2.08
175th Regiment	2.32	1.59	1.73
All regiments	1.62	1.47	1.35

The foregoing discussion applies to rifle companies only. But much the same picture is obtained from an analysis of the heavy weapons companies. Since there are only three such companies to a regiment, the best company in each regiment on a given attitude variable was selected and an average nonbattle casualty rate computed for the best from all twelve regiments. The same was done with the worst company on a given attitude variable and for the "middle" company, except that no "middle" companies are available for two regiments, in each of which one of the heavy weapons companies was unavailable for study. The pattern, shown in Figure 10-2, is quite similar to that in Figure 10-1, though the average nonbattle casualty rates are all considerably lower in heavy weapons companies than in rifle companies. Table 10-5 examines for consistency the ratios of nonbattle casualty

5. Of course, a regimental or higher commander should know enough about his companies so that he too should be able to sort them out on a basis better than chance alone, without this statistical information. How well in these divisions the command could have done this is not known.

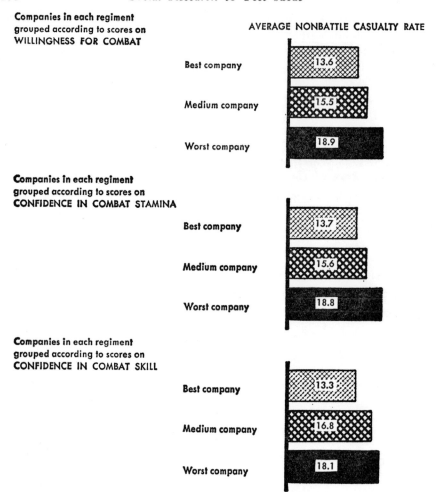

Companies in each regiment
grouped according to scores on
WILLINGNESS FOR COMBAT

AVERAGE NONBATTLE CASUALTY RATE

Best company — 13.6

Medium company — 15.5

Worst company — 18.9

Companies in each regiment
grouped according to scores on
CONFIDENCE IN COMBAT STAMINA

Best company — 13.7

Medium company — 15.6

Worst company — 18.8

Companies in each regiment
grouped according to scores on
CONFIDENCE IN COMBAT SKILL

Best company — 13.3

Medium company — 16.8

Worst company — 18.1

Top and bottom bars in each group are based
on 12 companies. Middle bar is based on 10
companies, as 2 companies were unavailable
for survey.

Figure 10-2. Heavy weapons companies in four divisions—average nonbattle casualty rates as related to pre-D-Day attitude scores.

incidence among the companies with the worst attitude scores in their respective regiments to the nonbattle casualty incidence of companies with the best attitudes. In each of the four divisions, on all three attitudes, the ratio *exceeds unity*, although there is considerable variation from division to division.

As was the case with rifle companies, so also with respect to heavy weapons companies it is evident that the nonbattle casualty rate in Normandy tended to be substantially higher among companies with relatively unfavorable pre-D-Day attitudes than among companies with relatively good attitudes.

There is still another practical way in which we may look at the correlations between attitudes and nonbattle casualties: As before, let us suppose that we knew in advance of a campaign the scores of the nine rifle companies in a regiment on willingness for combat. Let us pick the three best companies on this attitude and ask: "How often would I guess exactly right in predicting that a given company among the three with highest attitude scores would turn out to be among the three with lowest nonbattle casualties?"

By chance alone, one would guess exactly right a third of the time. Actually, as Figure 10-3 shows, one would have guessed exactly right, in the present study, twenty-two out of thirty-six times. That is, among the three rifle companies with best attitudes in each of twelve regiments, twenty-two out

Table 10-5. Heavy Weapons Companies—Average Nonbattle Casualty Rate of Companies with Worst Attitudes in Their Regiments Expressed as Ratio of Average Rate of Companies with Best Attitudes, by Divisions

	Companies Grouped by Scores on Willingness for Combat	Companies Grouped by Scores on Confidence in Combat Stamina	Companies Grouped by Scores on Confidence in Combat Skill
First Division	1.50	1.12	1.02
Ninth Division	1.32	1.55	1.65
Fourth Division	1.48	1.75	2.10
Twenty-ninth Division	1.22	1.22	1.14
All divisions	1.39	1.36	1.36

of thirty-six turned out to be among the bottom three—and therefore best—in their regiments in nonbattle casualty rates in Normandy. Of the fourteen errors, six were extreme. That is, six out of the thirty-six companies best in attitudes actually turned up among the worst in nonbattle casualty rates.

If we look in Figure 10-3 at the thirty-six companies with the *worst* scores on willingness for combat, we see that seventeen of the thirty-six were among those making the worst record on nonbattle casualties and that there are only three extreme discrepancies. That is, among the thirty-six rifle companies with the worst scores on willingness for combat, only three of these companies were among the thirty-six in the Normandy campaign with the lowest nonbattle casualty rates.

The picture is about the same, though perhaps not quite so good, when we use as sorting variables confidence in combat stamina or confidence in combat skill (Figure 10-3).[6] The same tendency seen in rifle companies is present also, though somewhat less strikingly, among heavy weapons companies.

Confidence in the stability of these relationships is strengthened by the fact that the pattern is quite consistent within each of the four divisions.

6. The three variables are intercorrelated and the results of taking all three into account simultaneously would be only a little better than the results in treating each variable individually.

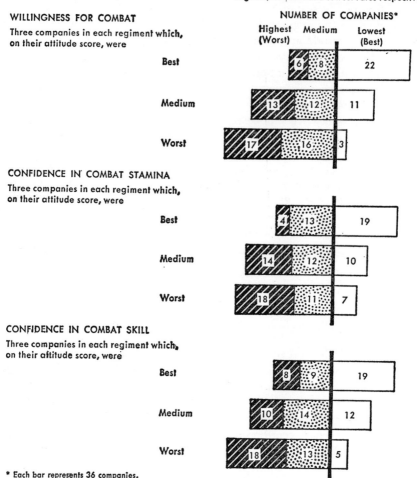

NONBATTLE CASUALTY RATES
Three companies in each regiment with
highest, medium and lowest rates respectively

WILLINGNESS FOR COMBAT

Three companies in each regiment which,
on their attitude score, were

NUMBER OF COMPANIES*

Highest   Medium   Lowest
(Worst)   (Best)

Best   6   8   22

Medium   13 12   11

Worst   17 16   3

CONFIDENCE IN COMBAT STAMINA

Three companies in each regiment which,
on their attitude score, were

Best   4   13   19

Medium   14 12   10

Worst   18 11   7

CONFIDENCE IN COMBAT SKILL

Three companies in each regiment which,
on their attitude score, were

Best   8   9   19

Medium   10 14   12

Worst   18 13   5

* Each bar represents 36 companies.

Figure 10-3. Relationship between rank of rifle companies within a regiment in attitudes and in nonbattle casualty rates (four divisions).

We have now reviewed the general evidence, which shows a low but consistent and statistically significant correlation between attitudes toward combat of companies before D-Day and the nonbattle casualty rates in these companies during the Normandy campaign. We have seen also that the correlation is of practical importance, since, depending on the attitude sorting variable used, companies with the worst attitudes tended to have from 30 per cent to 60 per cent higher nonbattle casualty rates (basing figures on all four divisions) than companies with the best attitudes. Finally, we have seen how few *extreme* errors would have been made in predicting in advance of the campaign how companies with given attitudes would show up relatively in nonbattle casualty rates. A further interesting problem merits some attention, namely, comparisons between predictions based on the attitudes of veterans and those based on the attitudes of nonveterans.

Attitudes of Veterans and Nonveterans. It will be remembered that two of the four divisions, the First and the Ninth, were veteran divisions. Before coming to England to prepare for the Normandy invasion, both divisions had seen action in North Africa and Sicily. The Fourth and Twenty-ninth Divisions were to have their baptism by fire in France.

Unfortunately, a direct comparison of the average attitude scores of the two veteran divisions and two nonveteran divisions is complicated by the fact that the First and Ninth were surveyed in late January, 1944, while the Fourth and Twenty-ninth were not surveyed until April. There may have been changes in the average level of attitudes between January and April. Moreover, the form of the check list used on the questions on willingness for combat was different in April.

It happened, however, that a small sample resurvey of the Ninth Division was made in April, 1944. The sample was not large enough for company-by-company comparisons, since the average number of cases per company was only thirty-three and many companies were represented in the sample by only a handful of men. The same questionnaire was used as in the Fourth and Twenty-ninth Divisions. The First Division was not resurveyed in April.

If we combine the rifle companies in each regiment of the Ninth Division in three groups of three companies each, according to nonbattle casualty rates in the eight weeks beginning June 6, we can compare the average attitude scores in January and April and also can break these scores down for veterans and nonveterans separately. It must be remembered that the Ninth Division (and the First Division as well), while veteran outfits, received a substantial number of replacements without combat experience who were integrated into the units during the months prior to the Normandy landing. Since these nonveterans were part of the cohort who made the invasion, they have been included in all of the nonbattle casualty rate computations along with veterans in the same outfits. They need, however, to be distinguished sharply from replacements received *after* the Normandy landing. It will be remembered that replacements of the latter type were carefully excluded from the computation of nonbattle casualty rates and, of course, were not represented in the attitude surveys.

Figure 10-4, comparing attitudes of veterans and nonveterans in rifle companies in the Ninth Division in January and April, brings out some quite interesting facts. In *both* surveys, the companies with the best record on nonbattle casualty rates (that is, the lowest rates) tended to have the best attitude scores (that is, the highest scores). This was true among nonveterans

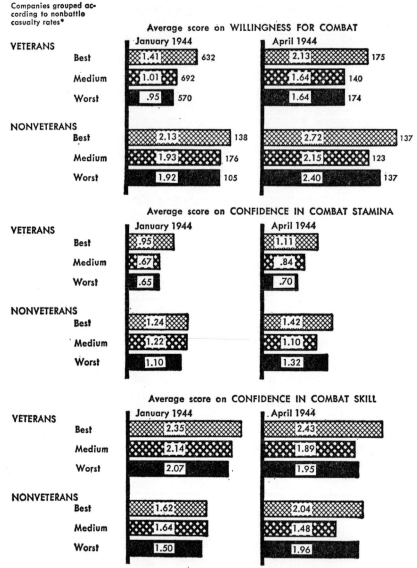

Companies grouped according to nonbattle casualty rates*

Average score on WILLINGNESS FOR COMBAT

January 1944 | April 1944

VETERANS
Best — 1.41 / 632 | 2.13 / 175
Medium — 1.01 / 692 | 1.64 / 140
Worst — .95 / 570 | 1.64 / 174

NONVETERANS
Best — 2.13 / 138 | 2.72 / 137
Medium — 1.93 / 176 | 2.15 / 123
Worst — 1.92 / 105 | 2.40 / 137

Average score on CONFIDENCE IN COMBAT STAMINA

January 1944 | April 1944

VETERANS
Best — .95 | 1.11
Medium — .67 | .84
Worst — .65 | .70

NONVETERANS
Best — 1.24 | 1.42
Medium — 1.22 | 1.10
Worst — 1.10 | 1.32

Average score on CONFIDENCE IN COMBAT SKILL

January 1944 | April 1944

VETERANS
Best — 2.35 | 2.43
Medium — 2.14 | 1.89
Worst — 2.07 | 1.95

NONVETERANS
Best — 1.62 | 2.04
Medium — 1.64 | 1.48
Worst — 1.50 | 1.96

* Companies grouped as "best," for example, are the three companies in each regiment with the lowest nonbattle casualty rates.

Figure 10-4. Comparison of veterans and nonveterans in Ninth Division rifle companies grouped according to nonbattle casualty rates in Normandy (January and April, 1944).

as well as veterans, although the relationship may have been somewhat sharper among veterans. Between January and April many replacements were received, and the attitudes of the replacements in April do not seem to be as closely related to subsequent unit nonbattle casualty rates as the attitudes of veterans in both January and April.[7] What is most interesting to observe, however, is the fact that *nonveterans had consistently better attitude scores on willingness for combat and confidence in combat stamina than veterans.* On the other hand, *veterans tended to have better attitude scores on confidence in combat skill than nonveterans.* This same relationship is seen in the First Division in January, although no replication for April is available.

Figure 10-5 provides a further interesting summary of attitudes in the rifle companies of the Ninth Division in April, 1944. Here we compare the average attitude scores (the higher scores being more favorable) of veteran noncoms and veteran and nonveteran privates.[8] Clearly, the relative favorableness of the various subgroups depends on the attitude studied. On willingness for combat and confidence in combat stamina, the nonveteran privates make showings as good as or better than the veteran noncoms and definitely better than the veteran privates. But on confidence in combat skill, as almost surely would be expected if the measures used are valid indexes, the highest scores are made by the veteran noncoms and the lowest scores are made by the nonveteran privates, although the veteran privates make scores almost as low.

Further light is thrown on the differences in attitude patterns if we go back to the original scores and examine cross tabulations. Table 10-6 shows, as would be expected both from the nature of the variables and as an artifact of the check lists used in deriving the scales, that there is quite a high correlation between the scales on confidence in combat stamina and confidence in combat skill. The correlations between each of these scores and willingness for combat are equally high. But let us focus our attention, not on the size of the correlations, but rather on the *difference in pattern* of relationship as between veteran noncoms at one extreme and nonveteran privates at the other. (The categories in the original 5 × 5 tables are arbitrarily grouped in Table 10-6 so that, for all groups combined, the number of cases falling above and below the principal diagonal are about equal.)

7. It is possible that, as Figure 10-4 suggests, the average attitude scores of veterans improved between January and April. For all three groups of companies there was a slight improvement in scores on confidence in combat stamina, but in two of the three groups of companies there was a deterioration in scores on confidence in combat skill. On the other hand, there was a large and, at first glance, impressive improvement among veterans in scores on willingness for combat. However, as has been mentioned in the text, there was a change in the check list in the April survey from the check list used in January on the two questions involved in the willingness for combat score. The change would not seem to be important enough to account for so large a shift, but question wording is tricky business, and it is well not to make too much of the data in Figure 10-4 as representing a real improvement in veterans' attitudes.

8. The fact that all the bars for, say, confidence in combat skill, are longer than all the corresponding bars for, say, confidence in combat stamina, has, of course, no necessary significance. The absolute length of bars is an artifact of the way the scores were derived, and only *relative* comparisons can be made. This caution applies to both Figure 10-4 and Figure 10-5.

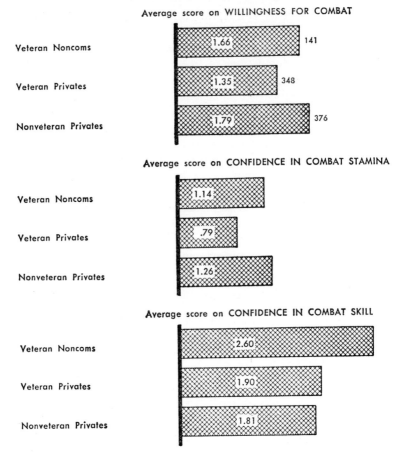

Figure 10-5. Ninth Division rifle companies—comparison of attitudes of veteran noncoms and of veteran and nonveteran privates, April, 1944.

Among veteran noncoms, in Table 10-6, the cases on the principal diagonal are nineteen, fifteen, thirty-five. Fourteen cases lie above the diagonal—noncoms who may be thought of as having *relatively* higher (that is, better) scores on confidence in stamina than on confidence in skill. A total of fifty-eight cases lie below the diagonal—noncoms who may be thought of as having *relatively* higher scores on confidence in skill than in stamina. Thus, of the seventy-two cases lying off the diagonal, only fourteen, or 19 per cent, are of the former type. Making corresponding computations for veteran privates and nonveteran privates, we can summarize the cases which lie off diagonal for the three groups in Table 10-7. These significant differences are, of course, just what would be expected *if the attitude variables have some specific meaning in addition to representing, as they doubtless also do, a general attitude toward combat.*

Table 10-6. Ninth Division—Correlations between Scores on Confidence in Combat Skill and Confidence in Combat Stamina, April, 1944

SCORE ON CONFIDENCE IN COMBAT STAMINA	SCORE ON CONFIDENCE IN COMBAT SKILL			Total
	0, 1	2	3, 4	
Veteran Noncoms				
2, 3, 4	2	7	35	44
1	5	15	36	56
0	19	11	11	41
Total	26	33	82	141
Veteran Privates				
2, 3, 4	9	12	48	69
1	34	29	43	106
0	100	37	27	173
Total	152	78	118	348
Nonveteran Privates				
2, 3, 4	19	41	71	131
1	61	51	24	136
0	82	14	13	109
Total	162	106	108	376

In summary, then, we have seen from Figure 10-5 that on two of the variables—willingness for combat and confidence in combat stamina—the nonveteran privates had better attitudes than the veteran privates, and as good or better attitudes than the veteran noncoms. On the third variable, confidence in combat skill, the veterans had better attitudes than the nonveterans. In other words, the complaint pattern is different for veterans and nonveterans. But does this difference in complaint patterns imply a difference between veterans and nonveterans in eventual nonbattle casualties? Since all three attitudes have been shown earlier to have a correlation, on a company basis, with nonbattle casualty rates, there is no necessary basis for inference, on an a priori basis, that veterans would differ widely from nonveterans in nonbattle casualty rates. Empirical data are required.

It would be ideal if we were in a position to compute separate nonbattle casualty rates for these three groups, all of whom were represented in the initial quota of troops landing in Normandy. The labor cost in obtaining and processing the necessary data was prohibitive at the time. However, at least a clue is obtained from a careful study of just one regiment—the Thirty-ninth Regiment of the Ninth Division. Payroll rosters of rifle companies of this Regiment were obtained for sample months throughout the year prior to the

Table 10-7

	Above the Diagonal (Stamina Scores Relatively Higher than Skill Scores)	Below the Diagonal (Skill Scores Relatively Higher than Stamina Scores)	Total	Percentage with Stamina Scores Relatively Higher than Skill Scores
Veteran noncoms	14	58	72	19
Veteran privates	55	107	162	34
Nonveteran privates	121	51	172	70

Normandy invasion. Separate cards were made out for each individual, on the basis of each payroll, recording name, serial number, and rank. By collating these cards, it was possible to classify all of the men in the companies as of the invasion date as to whether or not they had belonged to the regiment during either the North African or Sicilian campaigns or both. Then the cards were checked against the morning reports for the eight weeks beginning June 6, and if an individual was recorded in a morning report as a battle or nonbattle casualty, the fact was entered on his card. From this clerical operation it was possible to construct Table 10-8, which shows that there was only a small difference—not statistically significant—between nonbattle casualty rates of the three subgroups, as measured by the ratio of nonbattle casualties to initial strength. A better measure would have been the ratio of nonbattle casualties

Table 10-8. Ninth Division, Thirty-ninth Regiment—Casualties in Rifle Companies in Eight Weeks Beginning June 6, 1944

	Initial Strength	Battle Casualties as a Percentage of Initial Strength	Nonbattle Casualties as a Percentage of Initial Strength
Veteran noncoms	361	46.5	14.1
Veteran privates	704	45.6	17.4
Nonveteran privates	532	48.1	16.7

to the average daily strength—the measure used in the larger study—but this was not computed because of the large additional amount of labor which it would have required. It is not likely, however, that the more appropriate ratio would have changed the general picture presented by Table 10-7. Under the circumstances, while the nonbattle casualty rate of veteran noncoms is lower than that of veteran or nonveteran privates for the regiment, the data cannot be regarded as definitely indicating what to expect in other regiments with similar experiences. It would be desirable if further tabulations of other regiments could eventually be made.

The data from the special tabulation for the Thirty-ninth Regiment throw some further light on company differences. Figure 10-6 shows that in rifle companies in which veterans tended to have relatively low nonbattle casualty rates, the rates for nonveterans in the company tended to be low also. In companies in which veterans had high nonbattle casualty rates, the rates for nonveterans tended to be high also. The correlation coefficient is +0.80. These data suggest that factors—either in the combat situation or in the initial psychological atmosphere or in both—which differentiate companies from one another are more significantly related to nonbattle casualty rates than factors which differentiate veterans from nonveterans.

The foregoing analysis may have a bearing on the interpretation which must be placed on soldiers' complaints as analyzed in later chapters of Volume II of *The American Soldier*. When "old beat-up Joe" complained and said he was in no shape for further fighting, this did not necessarily mean that he was more likely to become a nonbattle casualty than a non-

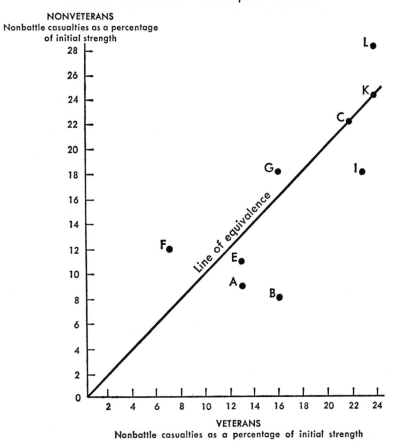

Figure 10-6. Ninth Division, Thirty-ninth Regiment, rifle companies—correlation between nonbattle casualty rates of veterans and nonveterans who constituted initial strength at be-ginning of invasion, by companies.

veteran in the same outfit. Very striking data shown in Chapter 5, Volume II, of *The American Soldier*, Chart III and Table 12, tend to show that the old veteran was not by any means considered by platoon leaders to be the most efficient soldier in the platoon, after several months' exposure to combat. On the other hand, when a nonveteran complained that he needed a lot more training before he would be up to fighting, this did not necessarily mean that he would acquire escape from battle by the sick route when he got there. Both responses without doubt often served as rationalizations for not wanting to do a dirty job—and it is quite understandable that the veteran should tend to use the "physical condition" excuse, while the nonveteran, as we have seen, tended more to use the "need more training" rationalization. With respect to the direct questions on willingness for combat, it is quite probable that neither veterans nor nonveterans were enthusiastic about combat. All the evidence studied in later chapters of Volume II of *The American Soldier* points to lack of enthusiasm. But the fact that the veteran had been through battle may have given him a feeling of earned permission to say more frankly what he thought than the nonveteran felt he could admit, even anonymously. This may account, in some degree, for the difference in scores on expressed willingness for combat as between veterans and nonveterans.

At the same time, the evidence reviewed in this section shows, with little room for doubt, that *companies* in which *more than the average* number of men had low scores on willingness for combat, confidence in combat stamina, or confidence in combat skill, were conspicuous among those units with high nonbattle casualty rates. The correlations are consistent and, taken as a whole, statistically significant, and the difference in nonbattle casualty rates between companies with the best and worst attitudes are certainly large enough to be considered important. Furthermore, the relationships hold up in the companies of both experienced and inexperienced divisions.

Therefore, we have one answer to the question with which this chapter opened, "Suppose that many combat soldiers did have unfavorable attitudes. What of it? They fought, didn't they?" The answer is, "Yes, they fought," but companies with more than their share of such men tended to have higher nonbattle casualty rates in Normandy than other companies—in other words, had fewer combat effectives on the battle line than companies with better initial attitudes.

In Section III, Chapter 1, Volume II, of *The American Soldier*, we review the derivation of the attitude scores used and the procedure for computing the nonbattle casualty rates.

The foregoing analysis has represented a comparison of average attitude scores, *by companies*, before D-Day with nonbattle casualty rates in those companies after D-Day. This was a study of unit behavior, not of individual behavior, because the questionnaires were administered anonymously and did not contain enough identifying data about the individual to permit a comparison of the individual's attitude and his subsequent combat record. . . . Section II, Chapter 1, Volume II, of *The American Soldier* deals with a somewhat smaller study—as compared with that in Section I—relating the attitudes of a sample of infantry recruits to their *individual* combat performance in Europe over a year later. The study represents the only available data directly relating attitudes to the combat performance of individual men.[9]

9. A more elaborately designed study to accomplish this same purpose was undertaken near the close of the war, in cooperation with the commanding general of a B-29 wing in the late stages of training in the United States. Detailed attitude questionnaires were filled out on an anonymous basis by all personnel, officer and enlisted. From the background information on the questionnaire it was possible, by checking against official records, to identify every questionnaire. Faith was kept with the respondents, in that this information was in the sole custody of the Research Branch in Washington and not accessible to anyone in Army Air Forces. At the same time, in cooperation with the office of the Air Surgeon, a special record form was designed and printed to enter all needed data on mis-

B. *Attitudes Reflecting Adjustment to the Army as Related to Subsequent Promotion of the Respondents— A Case Study*

To illustrate directly the way in which attitudes from the four areas of adjustment became associated with advancement in the Army, we need data which will relate such attitudes to *subsequent* advancement. This will be done in the present section, based on three samples of men whose attitudes were surveyed when they were relatively new recruits, whose questionnaires, though filled out anonymously, afterwards were identified, and whose careers were followed for a few months after the survey.[10]

Sample A comprises 378 privates whose attitudes were surveyed in September, 1943. Their attained rank as of January 1, 1944, was ascertained, and a fifth were found to have become privates first-class (Pfc.'s), which is the first rung up the promotion ladder. Four-fifths were still privates on January 1.

Sample B comprises 376 privates whose attitudes were surveyed in November, 1943, and some of whom by March, 1944, had become noncoms (mostly corporals).

Sample C comprised 102 men who, when surveyed in November, 1943, had already attained the grade of Pfc. The majority of them had become noncoms by March, 1944. The great difference in promotion rates between Samples B and C illustrates the great importance that seniority in rank, once established, exercised in subsequent promotion.

All these men were relatively new recruits, having entered the Army during the summer of 1943. In these samples, owing to the operations of Selective Service at the time these men entered the Army, 90 per cent of the men twenty-five years of age or over were married, while 82 per cent of the men

---

"How Personal Adjustment Varied in the Army," from Chapter 4, pp. 147-152, *The American Soldier: Adjustment during Army Life*, Vol. I, by Stouffer, Suchman, De-Vinney, Star, and Williams. Princeton: Princeton University Press, 1949.

---

sions performed, washouts, casualties, illness, etc., for each crew member. A special research officer was assigned to wing headquarters to keep these records. Plans were approved for periodic resurveys of the attitudes in the wing after each fifteen missions or so. However, the wing arrived in the Pacific only a few days before the capitulation of Japan, and the projected study became a casualty of the peace. No study was made in Air Forces comparable to the investigation in infantry described in the present chapter. However, the chapters in Volume II of *The American Soldier* on attitudes in the Air Forces have an advantage for purposes of interpretation over chapters on Ground Forces, since attitudes of crew members usually can be studied in relation to the specific number of missions flown.

10. The three samples of attitude data were obtained in an Infantry division in the fall of 1943.

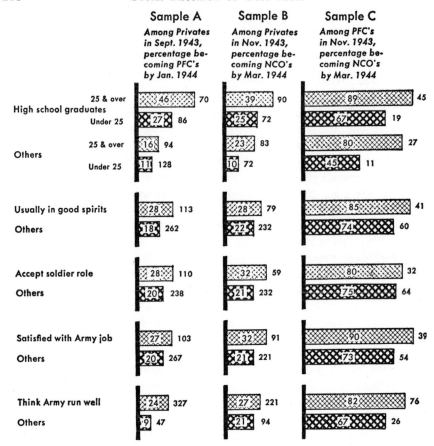

Figure 10-7. *Proportions promoted, as related to education and age and to attitudes, holding education and age constant. Data from S-60 and S-70, September and November, 1943. Numbers at the end of each bar indicate the observed number of cases on which percentages are based, except in the case of the standardized percentages by categories of attitude items, where "adjusted totals" are presented. (See the explanation in footnote 2, page 117, of* The American Soldier, *Vol. I.) These equivalent totals are somewhat smaller than the observed totals.*

under twenty-five years of age were unmarried. Hence, it is not practical here to analyze marital condition separately from age. When tabulations are presented by age, it must be remembered that age here reflects marital condition also.

Let us now look at Figure 10-7. The top sets of bars show the relationship of education by age to promotion. The sets of bars below show the relationship to promotion of attitude items—good spirits, soldier–war worker, job satisfaction, and how well is the Army run—holding both age and education constant.

Let us look first at Sample A. The chance of moving from private in

September to Pfc. in January was associated with both education and age. Of the high school graduates twenty-five and over, 46 per cent were promoted to Pfc. by January; of those under twenty-five, only 27 per cent. Of the non-high school graduates twenty-five and over, 16 per cent were Pfc's by January; of those under twenty-five, only 11 per cent. The same type of pattern is seen in Sample B. The high school graduates and the older men had the best chance of moving from private in November, 1943, to noncommissioned officer by March, 1944. The number of cases in Sample C is much too small for satisfactory reporting, but here, again, we see that among the older men, as among the younger men, the high school graduates had a better chance than others to move from Pfc. in November to NCO in March, while among both high school graduates and others, the men twenty-five and over had a better chance of promotion than the younger men.

We see then, just as we see in Chart I of Section II in Chapter 4, Volume I, of *The American Soldier*, that promotion depended, at least in part, on factors associated with education and age. Education, of course, is associated with AGCT scores and Mechanical Aptitude scores, as well as with other factors such as attitudes. Age played an important role. As has been mentioned, this division contained two rather distinctly different products of the draft—older married men who had been passed by in the first rounds of Selective Service and youngsters who had only recently become eligible for the draft. It apparently was thought better to have older men leading younger men than the reverse.

The chances of promotion, then, were related to factors associated with education and age. But *attitudes* are among the factors associated with education and age. How were the chances of promotion related to these *attitudes?*

Let us illustrate with an example. Take the area of personal commitment, using the question, "If it were up to you to choose, do you think you could do more for your country as a soldier or as a worker in a war job?" Consider only Sample A. The percentages in the four education-age groups who said in September that they could do more for their country as soldiers than as war workers were as follows:

H.S. graduates 25 and over	28	(70)
H.S. graduates under 25	52	(86)
Others 25 and over	17	(94)
Others under 25	38	(128)

Here we see the same type of relationship between personal commitment and education and age which we have encountered on an Army-wide basis earlier. . . . The *better educated,* who as a class had the better chance for subsequent promotion, and the *younger men,* who as a class had a worse chance than older men for subsequent promotion, were more likely to express acceptance of the soldier role.

Now let us break the sample down further and form Table 10-9. The number of cases in some of the subgroups becomes very thin, but we see in this table two facts. One, that within each educational and age class the men with the better attitude in September had a somewhat better chance for subsequent promotion. In other words, *independent of age and education*, attitude contributed in some degree to subsequent promotion. Two, that *independent of attitude*, the high school graduates and the older men had the better chance for promotion.

The same direction of tendency appears in Samples B and C, although the number of cases in the latter is much too small for reliable analysis.

Also, we see in other attitude areas how attitudes are involved in the relationship between education and age and chances of promotion. In the case

Table 10-9

	PERCENTAGES PROMOTED AMONG THOSE WHO	
	Accepted the Soldier Role	Did Not Accept the Soldier Role
H.S. graduates 25 and over	55 (20)	42 (50)
H.S. graduates under 25	29 (45)	24 (41)
Others 25 and over	25 (16)	14 (78)
Others under 25	14 (49)	8 (79)
Weighted average*	28 (110)	20 (238)

* The weights used were 70, 86, 94, and 128, respectively.

of personal *esprit*, the better educated were more favorable in their prepromotion attitudes, while there was no consistent age difference. In the case of satisfaction with status and job and with criticism or approval of the Army, the better educated tended to be *less* favorable than the less educated, while again age differences were inconsistent.[11] But in all three cases, when the data are broken down as in the personal commitment example cited above, the men *within* a given subgroup by age and education who had the better attitudes also had the better chances of subsequent promotion.

In other words, good attitudes seemed to *pay*.[12] This conclusion is summarized by the bars in the lower part of Figure 10-7, where the percentages

11. The inconsistency of the age differences may reflect the confounding of age and marital condition. While the Army-wide data cited in Section I, chapter 4, Volume I., of *The American Soldier*, showed the older men in the Army, generally, to be more favorable in these two attitude areas than younger men, the Army-wide data at the same time showed no consistent differences among married men, holding age constant.

12. It must be made clear that the attitude questionnaires were filled out anonymously and were not seen by anybody in authority in the division. Therefore, the surveys themselves could have exerted no direct influence on promotions. It is true that the research team from Washington identified the questionnaires by matching background information like data of birth, date of enlistment, and state of residence with corresponding information on the Form 20 personnel cards. This was necessary in order to trace the future promotions of the men. But this information was retained by the Research Branch and by agreement not made available to the division command.

promoted as related to attitudes are graphed. These are standardized percentages, that is, weighted averages like the 28 per cent and 20 per cent shown in our illustrative example for the soldier–war worker question. The reader will find these two percentages graphed in Figure 10-7 for Sample A opposite the category "Accept soldier role" and "Others."

The data for some additional items are presented in Table 10-10. These

Table 10-10. Proportions Promoted, as Related to Attitudes, Holding Education and Age Constant by Standardization

	Sample A: Among Privates in Sept., 1943, Percentage Becoming Pfc.'s by Jan., 1944	Sample B: Among Privates in Nov., 1943, Percentage Becoming NCO's by Mar., 1944	Sample C: Among Pfc.'s in Nov., 1943, Percentage Becoming NCO's by Mar., 1944
Think fair to be drafted	24 (242)	27 (186)	81 (76)
Others	19 (122)	20 (166)	63 (30)
In good physical condition	24 (114)	40 (80)	80 (50)
Others	18 (231)	20 (210)	77 (42)
Seldom worry about combat injury	21 (236)	29 (201)	80 (78)
Others	24 (140)	16 (110)	75 (24)
Expect to do O.K. in battle	25 (270)	32 (189)	81 (74)
Others	15 (103)	15 (127)	70 (26)
Think Army's control not too strict	29 (216)	28 (143)	81 (54)
Others	12 (159)	22 (168)	74 (48)
Think AWOL serious	28 (237)	28 (182)	79 (79)
Others	14 (128)	20 (126)	79 (17)
Think officers interested in EM	26 (193)	29 (178)	80 (55)
Others	16 (182)	19 (135)	73 (44)

Data from same sources as Figure 10-7. Numbers in parentheses are "equivalent totals" as used in Figure 10-7.

data reinforce the evidence from Figure 10-7 of the consistency with which, in Samples A, B, and C, the men who expressed the more favorable attitudes tended also to have the better chances for subsequent promotion—education and age held constant.[13]

13. Because of this consistency, the differences in promotion rates as between men sorted by initial attitudes are significant at the 5 per cent level. This is true for the four attitude items shown in Figure 10-7, and it is also true for the supplementary items shown in Table 10-10, with one exception—the item on worry about battle injury, where the difference is significant for Sample B, but because of a reversal in Sample A, the final test falls short of indicating significance at the 5 per cent level.

The test of significance used on these items was as follows: first, for a given item and a particular sample the value of $x = (p_1 - p_2)/\sigma p_1 - p_2$ was calculated using $p_o q_o (1/n_1 + 1/n_2)$ as a convenient estimate of the variance, where p_o was the percentage promoted in the entire sample. Since there were three independent samples and since it was desired to take account of the sign of $(p_1 - p_2)$, the three values of x were summed and divided by $\sqrt{3}$, the standard error of their sum. The values of n shown in Figure 10-7 and Table 10-10 for comparisons on the attitude items and used in computing tests of significance are "equivalent numbers" computed by the method described earlier. . . .

We have just looked closely at certain facts that might, at first glance, have seemed paradoxical. The fact that the better educated, even though generally more critical of the Army than other men, tended to get ahead faster than other men takes on a different meaning when we see that among the better educated taken alone, those with the better attitudes toward the Army got ahead faster, and similarly among the less educated taken alone. Likewise, the fact that the older married men, though tending to be deficient as compared with younger unmarried men in wholehearted personal commitment, tended to get ahead faster is seen in somewhat different light when we observe that among older married men taken alone those with higher personal commitment were preferred for subsequent promotion, and similarly for younger unmarried men taken alone.

In the case both of education and of age or marital condition, other factors than attitudes surely played important parts in selection for advancement, as we have seen.

11

□ ☒ □ □ □ *Four Programmatic Essays*

In selecting papers for the present compilation, I have given first priority to studies that exhibit actual empirical research in a variety of areas on a variety of problems of interest to social scientists. It may be of some interest to conclude Part I of this volume with four essays which are more of a programmatic character, although the first of them, on a study of social mobility, does report some illustrative substantive data.

After collaborating several years with two colleagues, Professor Talcott Parsons and Dr. Florence Kluckhohn, in a graduate research seminar in social mobility, out of which the present paper arose, I have been interested in the development of a diagnostic instrument which can be used by counselors in the public schools. Some years have gone into the improvement of this device, one form of which is designed for junior high schools and one for senior high schools. This inventory, which is called *Your Educational Plans*, is published by Science Research Associates. It is designed as a timesaver for the overworked counseling systems, obtaining from individual students quite a wealth of information as to attitudes and expectations, organized in sociological categories which have seemed to be significant and summarized in compact form, with the aid of modern data-processing equipment, to give the counselor the initial clues helpful to him in clinical, personal interviews with children or their parents.

The second paper, *Quantitative Methods in the Study of Race Relations*, is an unpublished essay read at the dedication of Park Hall at Fisk University in 1955. I have maintained a continuing interest in race relations ever since my association with the research project which led to Myrdal's *An American Dilemma*. In about a hundred quite compact pages on the Negro soldier, *The American Soldier* brings together a variety of research studies carried out under my general direction during the war. Although many of the individual inquiries left much to be desired, these studies have been cited perhaps as frequently as any product of the Research Branch.

With respect to the study of race relations, this paper makes one point, among others, that I would especially like to underline because of its applicability to research strategy in general. This has to do with the tactical research advantages of studying communities in transition— for example, as they move from segregated to integrated school systems. More and more, I am convinced that social scientists can magnify the significance of their efforts if they deliberately seek out situations for study in which a crisis has occurred, or at least a rapid change. A good recent example of this kind of study, using some of the explicit concepts of reference group theory illustrated earlier in this volume, is Pettigrew's and Campbell's study of the ministers in Little Rock, *Christians in Racial Crisis*.

The third paper in this group is a little piece entitled *Sociological Factors Favoring Innovations*, which appeared in Clark, editor, *Consumer Behavior: Research on Consumer Reactions* in 1958. While somewhat whimsical in style, this essay represents some rather serious reflection, not only about social change, but also about the more general problem of levels of explanation in sociology.

The final paper in this series, *Sociological Theory and Public Opinion Research*, was presented at the Third World Congress of Sociology in Amsterdam in 1956. The paper is intended as an effort to perform a marriage between some sociological theory and research tactics and to adumbrate certain interests that have most recently been in the forefront of my research activity, particularly having to do with community leadership and the organization of opinion. This happily is a subject of increasing concern to American scholars, both in political science and sociology.

A. The Study of Social Mobility: Some Strategic Considerations

Of all the ladders by which social mobility is achieved in America today, the most important is probably that of education. Perhaps there always will be a considerable number like so many of our nineteenth-century tycoons who were able to achieve great worldly success with meager schooling, or some who can jump a rung or two on the ladder of a fortuitous marriage. But research is hardly needed to demonstrate that the occupations characteristic of the middle as well as the higher social ranks of our populations are increasingly demanding formal education. This is seen increasingly for example, in business, where the larger corporations are recruiting their future management mainly from the ranks of college graduates and where automation, in both factory and office, is creating demands for unprecedented numbers of engineers.

Hence, the pressures on our colleges are likely to become intolerable within a decade unless there is great expansion, particularly among the public universities and colleges, especially junior colleges.

In spite of the unprecedented surge of youth for higher education, there are still great inequalities in our population in demand for college.

As obviously should be the case, the high school students of today who are planning college tend to come from the higher bracket of intelligence scores. But the word "tends" implies no more than a moderate association between average ambition and potential ability. For our colleges and universities are crowded with thousands of students, usually children of white-collar parents, who lack the ability to succeed in college unless standards are low. At the same time there are thousands of others with high potential abilities, usually children of working class or farm parents, who stop their formal education at high school or earlier.

How large a proportion this latter group is among all those with ability depends on where we draw the line with respect to ability. About three years ago, Dale Wolfle, reviewing a variety of nation-wide studies, estimated the proportion missing out on college as about half of those in the top quartile of intelligence.

A good deal is known about who these people are. They tend to be rural more than urban, within metropolitan cities they tend to be children of working class parents more than of white-collar parents, and they tend to be girls more often than boys.

It is easy to sum it all up by saying that the basic variable is income. It costs more for a rural boy or girl to go off to college than for a city boy or

"The Study of Social Mobility: Some Strategic Considerations," an unpublished paper read at the American Sociological Society meeting, September, 1956.

girl, who can, if necessary, live at home, commute to a reasonably good college, and perhaps have a part-time or even full-time job on the side. Also, the proportionate drain on the income of urban white-collar families for college education of their children is obviously less, on the average, than that on urban working class families—whose average income is smaller and whose families are larger. Moreover, when a family cannot afford a college education for all its children, the family is likely to give priority to the boys, since college seems more of a necessity vocationally to boys than to girls, however useful college may be to girls in helping them make a "good" marriage.

If the answers were as simple as this, there would be little need for sociological study. But the answers are not that simple. Over a period of several years two of my colleagues, Professor Talcott Parsons and Dr. Florence Kluckhohn, and myself have conducted a graduate research seminar and, aided by a grant from the Russell Sage Foundation, have explored various ramifications of this problem. We have studied several thousand high school children in industrial and residential suburbs of metropolitan Boston and followed them up to note whether or not they went to college. We and our students have administered questionnaires and analyzed school records and have conducted informal interviews in some depth with samples of students and their fathers and mothers.

That, even among bright working class children, family income is not the only or possibly even the most important factor in decision for college is evident. Many of these children who are poorest financially go to college; many of the relatively better off do not. We believe that the differences that may be significant in motivating the child to higher education are found not so much in ability to pay as in differences in value orientations of the parents and in techniques of implementing those orientations.

With respect to values, the evidence is not so much of antipathy for college on the part of parents—in our samples this seems quite rare. Neither can it probably be called apathy or indifference. Rather, there seems to be a lack of serious belief that college would be a possibility—"in the cards"— for their own child, even though he is bright and even though other bright children at the same economic level do go to college. And, as we shall see, when parents do wake up to the possibility of college for their child, it may be too late. The child may already have irrevocable habits and attitudes that do not lend themselves to good school performance, even if he has the potential ability.

With respect to implementation, parents can have values conducive to motivating their children to the kind of school performance that makes college both possible and attractive, yet lack skill in manipulating the appropriate rewards and punishments. Such skill is particularly necessary in neighborhoods where there are high alternative rewards available to the child, especially to the boy, in play groups and gangs of his age-mates. Parental failure at motivation and discipline can be especially conspicuous when there is homework to be done in the evening, in competition with movies, hotrods, or other youthful attractions. Parents of middle-class children also may exhibit various degrees of ineptness, but their problem with respect to motivation is much simpler, since the whole ethos of a middle-class neighborhood conspires to help the child internalize the sanctions necessary for adequate school performance.

These considerations set the stage for a discussion of the strategy of future research. If the boys and girls of potential high ability are to have the opportunity to realize their birthright, the schools must be able to work with parents, at an early age, to help the parents realize (a) that college is a possibility and (b) that adequate school performance in the elementary school, junior high school, and senior high school is a prerequisite. More than that, parents must be helpful not only in acquiring this cognitive understanding but also in learning how best to implement it in their own training of the child. But, to achieve these ends, we need to know much more than we do at the present time about the entire educational cycle—from first to twelfth grade—and to know how the perils differ at different ages of the child. On this subject, there is very little sociological and psychological literature.

Let me illustrate the problem—or rather frame the problem without explaining anything—with some data that we collected in the spring of 1957 from one senior high school in an industrial suburb of Boston. All the students filled out questionnaires about intentions of going to college, and these we matched up by school records of intelligence (the California mental test) and school marks.

Table 11-1 shows the usual picture, namely, that college intentions are associated with intelligence scores, economic status, and sex, each variable being independently important. Actually, rather few of the white-collar families in this community probably would be classified above lower middle class on a Warner scale, since fathers' occupations tended to be those of clerical workers or small tradesmen; otherwise, white-collar college intentions would be higher. We have no data on income, but believe that while the average white-collar income may be higher than the average working class income, the two frequency distributions, if available, would overlap greatly, with the income of many workers' families exceeding that of families which we have labeled white collar. Data are shown in Table 11-1 only for the upper four deciles of intelligence scores.

The number of cases is small, but not too small to reveal some further interesting and significant facts. In Table 11-1 look at the left-hand column of percentages—"Not in the College Preparatory Course." If previous studies where we actually traced high school graduates to colleges are a guide, rarely will these boys and girls not in the college preparatory course ever enroll in college. About a tenth were expressing college plans, and a very few may eventually go—for example, an exceptional athlete. But we will not be much

Table 11-1. How College Plans of Students in a Massachusetts High School Vary by I.Q., Social Status, and Sex

	PERCENTAGE DISTRIBUTION			TOTAL	N
	NOT IN COLLEGE PREPARATORY COURSE	IN COLLEGE PREPARATORY COURSE			
		Not Planning College	Planning College		
TWO HIGHEST I.Q. DECILES					
White-collar fathers					
Boys	9	21	70	100	34
Girls	22	24	54	100	41
Working class fathers					
Boys	19	39	42	100	41
Girls	42	16	42	100	33
NEXT TWO HIGHEST I.Q. DECILES					
White-collar fathers					
Boys	25	37	38	100	24
Girls	41	18	41	100	22
Working class fathers					
Boys	47	28	25	100	32
Girls	75	12	13	100	42

in error if we assume that those not in college preparatory are not on the college ladder.

Choice of high school curriculum is made in this and many, if not most, urban high schools at the end of eighth grade. Some who elect the college preparatory course at this time transfer later to a commercial, general, or trade course, usually as the result of poor marks; but it is extremely rare for a student to switch to college preparatory after beginning in another curriculum. Hence, for those who at the end of eighth grade have chosen not to go to college preparatory, there has been something approaching an irrevocable decision.

Table 11-1 illustrates the fact that bright girls are much more likely than bright boys to drop off the college ladder at the end of eighth grade by not entering the college preparatory course. This apparently is in response to the obvious vocational attractions of the commercial course, preparing a girl for office work. Boys, on the other hand, tend to be more likely than girls to enter the college preparatory course and still not have serious college plans.

Next, let us look at Table 11-2, which shows how well or poorly these same boys and girls were doing in school at two periods—in first and second grades and in seventh and eighth grades. Marks of all students in these two periods were converted into numbers. A mark is here arbitrarily called "high," for simplicity, if it is in the upper 40 per cent of the class and called "low" if it is not.

Consider the left columns, those whose grades were low at both periods. The working class children are more likely to be in this category than the

Table 11-2. How Primary and Junior High School Marks of Students in a Massachusetts High School Vary by I.Q., Social Status, and Sex

	PERCENTAGE DISTRIBUTION				TOTAL	N
	First and Second Grade Marks Low, Junior H.S. Marks Low (− −)	First and Second Grade Marks Low, Junior H.S. Marks High (− +)	First and Second Grade Marks High, Junior H.S. Marks Low (+ −)	First and Second Grade Marks High, Junior H.S. Marks High (+ +)		
TWO HIGHEST I.Q. DECILES						
White-collar fathers						
Boys	18	18	3	61	100	34
Girls	4	19	7	70	100	41
Working class fathers						
Boys	34	15	16	35	100	41
Girls	18	15	12	55	100	33
NEXT TWO HIGHEST I.Q. DECILES						
White-collar fathers						
Boys	29	12	38	21	100	24
Girls	15	. .	35	50	100	22
Working class fathers						
Boys	41	18	13	28	100	32
Girls	24	24	18	34	100	42

Table 11-3. How Primary and Junior High School Marks are Related to Plans for College, by I.Q., Social Status, and Sex

	PERCENTAGE DISTRIBUTION										GRAND TOTAL
	NOT IN COLLEGE PREPARATORY OR, IF SO, NOT PLANNING COLLEGE					IN COLLEGE PREPARATORY AND PLANNING COLLEGE					
	P J − −	P J − +	P J + −	P J + +	Total	P J − −	P J − +	P J + −	P J + +	Total	
TWO HIGHEST I.Q. DECILES											
White-collar fathers											
Boys	9	12	. .	9	30	9	6	3	52	70	100
Girls	2	12	5	27	46	2	7	2	43	54	100
Working class fathers											
Boys	24	. .	14	20	58	10	15	2	15	42	100
Girls	15	9	6	28	58	3	6	6	27	42	100
NEXT TWO HIGHEST I.Q. DECILES											
White-collar fathers											
Boys	12	4	38	8	62	17	8	. .	13	38	100
Girls	10	. .	30	19	59	5	. .	5	31	41	100
Working class fathers											
Boys	38	12	13	12	75	3	6	. .	16	25	100
Girls	22	22	16	27	87	2	2	2	7	13	100

white-collar children and boys much more likely than girls. As would be expected, those highest in intelligence are least likely to be found here— but note that 34 per cent of the brightest working class boys made relatively low marks both in primary and in junior high school.

Finally, in Table 11-3 we can get some hint of the relationships to college intentions of primary and junior high school performance. It is, no doubt, a significant correlation in most groups, but it is by no means a simple picture. The brightest white-collar boys and girls who are planning college have pretty consistent records of high grades, as do most other categories of girls. But the brightest working class boys and both classes of boys in the I.Q. group next below have a pretty mixed record.

The left half of Table 11-3 is especially interesting because here we can get at least some clues as to when those who are not college oriented fell off the ladder. For example, take the 58 per cent of brightest working class boys who are not planning college. They break down into 24 per cent whose grades were low in primary and junior high school, 14 per cent who made a good start but slipped in junior high school, and 20 per cent whose grades were good both times.

Because of the small sample size, these particular percentages are quite unreliable, of course, but they can serve as an illustrative framework for the strategical considerations that I think are of central importance, namely, that our sociological studies must go back to the early years and follow the entire school career.

Eventually, we may find some social or psychological syndromes which differentiate bright children who fall off the ladder at different points in time. We have hints in Table 11-3 that the picture for girls is different from that for boys. Girls are likely to make good early marks but not elect the college course. Boys are less likely than girls to make good early marks, in spite of the fact that more of them will eventually go to college. Among the bright boys who fall by the wayside, there are several types—for example, those who never got a good start, those who got a good start and slipped in junior high school, those who lost interest in schoolwork some time in senior high school, and finally those who did good schoolwork throughout but considered high school as terminal.

The research problem, as I see it, is to delineate such types clearly and search for the factors which may be most characteristic in the family background and family attitudes, in the peer group and its attitudes, and in other attributes of the child's organizational environment or reference system. It now seems quite unlikely that any great monolithic theory will be very helpful. We need *limited* theories that generate operational hypotheses appropriate to each of the types of children we are studying.

Now as to the data collection. Small statistical studies of the kind I illustrated today are of very limited value. Why? Because you cannot subdivide the data into enough boxes. Suppose you had as many as 1,000 bright boys of working class families who got off to a poor start and 1,000 bright boys who got off to a good start but slipped. You want to compare their parents as to income, possibly type of work, education of father and mother, and possibly ethnic origin. You want to compare attitudes of parents toward school and, possibly, methods of discipline. You want to know something about how these two groups differ in family composition—number of siblings, order of birth. Is the middle child disadvantaged? To test such a question, the number of siblings must be held constant. You want to know something about the neighborhood. You want to know who the child's best friends are, about his peer groups, if any, etc., etc. Well, you will find it extremely difficult to isolate and evaluate such factors with anything less than an extremely large sample. Our suggested 1,000 of each would not be nearly enough. Large masses of data can be obtained, but they will cost a good deal of money.

At the same time intensive clinical studies need to be encouraged, because they may be productive of hypotheses, even if not proof. To illustrate, Dr. John Spiegel and Dr. Florence Kluckhohn have come up with a singularly interesting set of observations and hypotheses with respect to what they call "informal role allocation" in the family. If parents ascribe certain expectations even to an infant—for example, "he's our clown," "he's our scholar"— these ascriptions, it is suspected, can become almost ineradicable personality orientations.

Finally, there is no better ready-at-hand sociological laboratory for experimental tests of hypotheses than our public schools. For example, it may turn out that with many families the problem of not pushing their boy or girl to college is largely cognitive—they simply do not know or believe that college is a realistic possibility. Suppose in N schools a systematic planned program were carried out just to show parents of bright children only college is feasible. In N matched schools nothing different is done from what is done already. Many such designs can be dreamed up, for use not only in high school but in the elementary grades.

There is no single royal road to knowledge about the problems we are discussing, any more than there is a single soverign remedy for all diseases. Sociology must face up honestly and courageously to the fact that, as in the study of disease, proof is costly and that assertions as to proof that do not stand up have not earned their right to a respected niche in the canon of science.

B. Quantitative Methods in the Study of Race Relations

As one of the students of Robert E. Park, I appreciate the opportunity to be present on this historic occasion.

I have been asked to make some comments on the future use of quantitative methods in the study of race relations.

The research methods that Park trusted most were those of the trained

"Quantitative Methods in the Study of Race Relations," an unpublished paper read at the Park Hall Dedication Program, Fisk University, March 31, 1955.

newspaper man. He did not have an allergy for quantitative methods as such—witness the extensive use of statistics in the pioneering studies in human ecology—but he objected to sociologists who would count and correlate the trivial, ignoring the important issues. In the field of race relations, few people have had more acute sociological insights—as is evidenced in the collected papers assembled under the leadership of Charles S. Johnson and published under the title of *Race and Culture*. But one will look in vain in this volume either for the use of quantitative data or for explicit suggestions for their use.

I believe—and shall spell out in some detail—that quantitative studies will play an ever-increasing role in studies of race relations in the United States. But if so, it will be because the admonitions of Park have been heeded, that we do not narrowly equate the scientific with the measurable and that we do not waste our shining statistical tools on issues which are strategically insignificant.

The situation is well illustrated by the remarkable research opportunities that are opened up by the efforts to adjust to the Supreme Court decision on integration. In community after community, it will be possible to make before-during-after case studies on the process of change. The work of Ashmore, Williams and others shows what can be done at just the level at which Park liked to have his students work. It is fashionable today to say that a descriptive study of a community in change is using anthropological research methods. Whether we call them anthropological, or as Park would not have been ashamed to say, journalistic, is immaterial. In some instances explicit inquiry with questionnaires and scales and tests of significance may be possible and desirable. But if we let pass an unparalleled opportunity to observe systematically the forces of social change in the next few years in American communities because of a misplaced devotion to precision, we shall do sociology the greatest of disservice.

One of my valued experiences was the opportunity to associate with Gunnar Myrdal and his able staff in the research that led to *An American Dilemma*. Yet I have regretted that the acclaim which greeted Myrdal's brilliant analysis of the ideological forces in the changing situation with respect to the Negro has tended to deflect attention to other forces, described in *An American Dilemma*, that are of equal or greater importance. In particular, let me refer to the consequences of the great migration to the North.

I see those consequences as threefold:

1. By the concentration of millions of votes in the populous states of New York, New Jersey, Pennsylvania, Ohio, Michigan, Illinois, Indiana, and Missouri—with California soon to be added to this list—Negroes have come to achieve potentially irresistible political power. I say potentially because they have yet to use this power to even a fraction of its possibility. Even if there had never been an ideological change anywhere, the sheer, naked power of the Northern Negro vote could have a compelling force, since the

Negro vote, if it is not the docile captive of any one political party, can tip the balance in any election.

2. The Negro in the North, in spite of all the handicaps of overcrowding in housing and in schools, is getting a chance through education to demonstrate more dramatically and effectively than ever to the whole country the fact that color not only should be, but is, irrelevant to achievement.

3. The combination of these two factors, namely, (1) naked political power, which guarantees that local FEPC and other regulations will not be a complete farce, and (2) the visible, demonstrable talents of the educated Negro, emerge as a social force with a sledge-hammer effect on values as old as slavery.

It is well to talk, as Myrdal does, of the uneasy conscience of those who are forced to try to reconcile their faith in the Bill of Rights with the fact that the Negro, newly revealed to be a full-fledged human being, also is entitled to these rights. This uneasy conscience, at least as it abides in the intellectuals, certainly softens the resistance to the powerful social forces mobilized as a consequence of the northward migrations. I believe, however, that the most crucial factor in the causal sequence is not the contributions of psychology and anthropology to shaping one horn of the dilemma by proving that the Negro was a human being, with no need to take second place to anybody, but rather the mounting pressure provided by the Negro himself, armed with political power and education.

Now, this story of the consequences of the Northern migration has not been adequately told. In telling part of the story, statistics are essential, and fortunately three important classes of Census or other official statistics are available. First, we need to trace the growth of Negro populations in the North. Second, we need to study in detail the voting statistics. There can be no doubt, for example, that without almost a unanimous Negro vote in 1948 Truman would have been defeated in an electoral landslide. In any fairly close state election in any of the large Northern states, the Negro vote is enough to tip the balance. How this vote has been used since 1930 needs to be studied more carefully than has been done by specialists in political science. Certain critical areas—like Philadelphia, Chicago, Detroit, St. Louis—need to be analyzed in great detail from actual election statistics. Third, we need to know how the educational and occupational level of the Negro is rising, decade by decade. These facts are embedded in Census reports. But they have received wholly inadequate analysis, in view of the fact that they probably testify to one of the greatest social revolutions of our time.

Such statistics alone have little meaning, as Park would have been among the first to point out, unless seen in the context of their significance as indexes of crucial social changes. Case studies of communities are needed. Why, for example, cannot Negroes get everything they want, by way of political action, in most of our Northern metropolitan areas, if they utilize their power to elect or defeat? I don't know the answer, but here is a challenge to a new generation of social scientists to find out, and descriptive studies, whether or not they use statistics, are needed.

Prejudice against Negroes is, of course, only a special case of prejudice in general. At quite another level of analysis than I have been discussing thus far, we need to deploy all available resources of sociology, anthropology, and psychology to understand better the nature of prejudice.

It is my fear that psychologists may have led us astray—particularly when they suggest that prejudice is a matter of individual pathology. I suspect, though I know we cannot prove it, that the correct answer may be quite different.

Most people are conformists. Whatever the norms are in their communities, they will tend to conform to these norms. It takes as much courage for a Mississippian to take a liberal attitude on the race issue as it would for me, a Northern college professor, to come out against racial integration in the schools. Neither the Mississippian who goes along with the official Mississippi position against the Supreme Court decision nor the New England college professor who hopes for rapid integration deserves to be castigated as warped personalities, because they conform to the norms of those associates whose sanctions are most salient to them. Indeed, the suggestion which some psychological studies of prejudice offer, that so-called prejudiced people are necessarily sick personalities who need treatment, is to fly in the face of much that we know about social structure and cultural values.

This is an area in which we need much more searching investigation and in which quantitative methods have an important place.

Two kinds of studies are needed in volume: (1) surveys of attitudes and (2) experimental studies.

With respect to surveys of attitudes, we have come quite a way in the improvement of our tools of research since the early days of Park at Chicago, or even since Myrdal. We have learned a good deal about sampling, about interviewer bias, about systematic nondirective as well as direct questioning, about scale construction, and about tests of significance. We are beginning to learn something about projective techniques. Let me speak very briefly on each of these points.

In the case of sampling, we now know how to draw and carry out a probability sample that approximates closely the ideal of giving each individual in a designated population an equal chance of being caught. Such samples are very expensive, and there will always be some bias of nonresponse. But as experience accumulates, over scores of surveys, both theory and practice improve. Some kinds of problems remain to be solved. For example, if we want to draw a probability sample in the South and want to use white interviewers to interview whites and Negro interviewers to interview Negroes, we are in serious trouble. For it is a costly business to determine in advance which address in the sample is that of a white family and which is that of a Negro family, except in solidly segregated areas.

Studies of the effect of interviewing have made it repeatedly clear that, on issues touching race problems, many Negro respondents do not tell white interviewers the same thing they tell Negro interviewers. It is the fashion to say that only the latter get at the truth. But what Negroes say to whites also can constitute important data, particularly when contrasted with what they say to members of their own race. It is possible that this very discrepancy may serve, in some instances, as a key to understanding social pressures.

With respect to asking questions, we are training interviewers more effectively in nondirective techniques. This is particularly important if we are to get a better understanding of the depth or salience of attitudes. In a recent study that I directed on the subject of attitudes toward the internal Communist threat and toward the civil rights of nonconformists, we used the first twenty minutes or so of the interview to probe into worries, concerns, and anxieties in general without a single direct and specific suggestion. If a respondent said, "I am worried about my son," the interviewer was supposed to keep the conversation going by saying something like, "You are worried about your son?" We think that by these methods we are able to place the concerns which we were specifically studying in a more accurate general setting than if we had fired a barrage of direct questions.

I cannot take time here to elaborate on the progress made in a single decade on the subject of scaling. Historically, it is of interest to note that the cumulative scaling technique associated with the name of Guttman is a refinement of the idea introduced by Bogardus in his famous scale of social distance. Guttman's theory of principal components and Lazarsfeld's theory of latent structures are exciting intellectual events that are important, not just methodologically as measuring devices, but substantively in formulating conceptual schemes as to the nature of attitudes. On the practical operations side, we are learning how to construct scales with remarkable internal consistency, especially with what has been called the H-technique. A scale of tolerance for nonconformists, for example, used in our recent nation-wide study, has a reproducibility above 0.95, even for people with only a grade school education. Given many such batteries, each tapping different aspects of the subject of conformity or prejudice, we should eventually be able to use factor analysis for isolating more sharply principal dimensions of a broad domain of attitudes and values. New electronic computing machines make possible carrying through elaborate factor analyses in a matter of days instead of months. We are just at the threshold of exploitation of the possibilities thus opened.

There are important advances in statistical theory that facilitate analysis. To mention only one point out of many—we are learning how to use simple-order statistics to provide quick and satisfactory tests of significance in a small fraction of the time required by more conventional approaches.

Finally, we are beginning to learn how to use projective tests that employ indirect means to break through a respondent's mechanisms of defense. I say beginning—because the very large literature to date is still highly controversial and is cluttered with unproved claims. One approach which has promise is the third-person approach or something akin to it. Getzels asked an entire dormitory of Northern college girls how they would feel about having a Negro as a roommate. The official mores being liberal, most girls said that they personally would have no objections whatever. But when the girls were asked how their friends in the same dormitory would feel, many tended to think their friends wouldn't like the idea! Hovland and Sherif reworked data of the kind once reported by Hinckley and others to the effect that white and Negro judges who were asked to sort Thurstone-type statements on attitudes toward Negroes agreed in their judgments of the scale position of statements. They found that this was not true among judges with extreme attitudes. Disagreements were so considerable and so consistent as to suggest that judges' ratings actually might serve as a valuable instrument for indirectly probing the judges' own personal attitudes. Projective tests involving nonverbal stimuli, like ink blots or T.A.T. pictures, possess inherent complexities of statistical validation, but recent work like that of McClelland on a need-achievement test is especially promising.

Armed with the new tools now being forged and tested, we should be able to learn far more in future surveys than in the past about the extent to which attitudes on race relations merely reflect the measurable local social norms or represent deviations associated with differing degrees of anxiety, rigidity, and the like in the personality structure. As of today, I am inclined to bet on the proposition that most such attitudes represent the playing out of expected social roles more than they represent idiosyncratic personality aberrations. But when the cake of custom breaks down—as it is likely to do in the years ahead as a result of the great social forces mentioned earlier in this paper—there may be more and more people in serious role conflicts, with the result that personality idiosyncrasies may become increasingly important as determiners of attitude

I have discussed the use of quantitative tools in attitude surveys. Now a final and brief word as to the use of quantitative tools in experimental studies.

Time does not permit a review of the progress of experimentation in the field of attitudes involved in race relations. For an excellent up-to-date summary, we have Gordon W. Allport's book on *The Nature of Prejudice* and Gardner Lindzey's *Handbook on Social Psychology*.

If we are to isolate the crucial variables and measure their effects, the only sure way is through the controlled experiment. Any other methods, however useful, end with plausibility rather than proof of an "if, then" proposition. Three out of several broad lines of experimentation are especially promising:

One, in the general area of communication, seeks to test various propositions as to the conditions making for attitude change. The work of Hovland and associates in the Research Branch of the Army Information and Education Division during World War II, and since at Yale, is a model of this kind of effort. And they are not studying trivial problems.

Two, in the general area of cognition and perception, attempt is being made to sort out some basic principles by which we perceive and classify the objects in our environment. At first glance, the kind of experiments which Bruner and his associates are doing at Harvard may seem far removed from the subject of race relations. But they may come eventually to have a direct bearing on some of the most crucial variables in interpersonal relationships.

Three, in the broad area of experimental studies of small groups—at Michigan, Minnesota, Harvard, and an increasing number of centers—we are beginning to learn a great deal about the mechanisms by which a group limits and controls expressions by its members. Through role-playing and the use of stooges, it is possible to test hypotheses of wide significance. Lindzey's experiments on the displacement of aggression on a scapegoat are an example.

In each of these types of experimental areas and in many others, the design is such that a measurable outcome can be secured. Quantitative measuring devices and statistical evaluation of level of significance provide the acid tests.

Laboratory experiments permit controls not present in "natural" experiments, but obviously have various kinds of limitations because of artificiality of imposed conditions. Our enthusiasm for laboratory controls should not deter us from less definitive research on "natural" situations. Hence, I come back to a point mentioned at the beginning of this paper. The next few years bid fair to provide a wonderful opportunity to study communities in transition, as they move from segregated to integrated school systems. As I suggested, it is to be hoped that such studies will not be mere mechanical measurements of before-and-after opinions but will involve qualitative descriptions of the whole process of social change. But it is to be hoped that here and there will arise an opportunity to combine the best in quantitative survey analysis with the best in qualitative observation, and such studies may be among the most important we can make. With some rigor in design, by comparing different communities and different outcomes, we may even be able to produce a reasonable facsimile of a controlled experiment. Of all the studies in *The American Soldier,* there is none in which some of us take more pride than the "quickie" we were able to do on the attitudes of white soldiers toward Negro troops fighting in the same companies with them. Because we caught these attitudes in the very midst of a situation of change and action, we were able to get sharp findings which never would have been possible in a static cross-section survey of attitudes.

And now I close. I have sought to suggest a few ways in which quantitative methods can help in the future. Analysis of census data and election statistics, of attitude surveys, experimental studies, and observations made at specific points of change all can help us to a better sociological and psychological theory of race relations. And they also can help, just as I would like to think our Army study did, to a better appreciation by the public of the wisdom of Robert E. Park, when he said, in his essay *Behind our Masks*, "Whenever representatives of different races meet and discover in one another—beneath the differences of races—sentiments, tastes, interests, and human qualities generally that they can understand and respect, racial barriers are undermined and eventually broken down."

C. *Sociological Factors Favoring Innovations*

Sometimes it seems as if there are almost as many theories of social change as there are sociologists writing about it. Some of these writers, wedded to a particular theory, are quite dogmatic. The monolithic cause of change through the ages is found convincingly to reside in ideology, or in geography, or in psychology, or in technology, or in some other single "ography" or "ology."

To take one of these positions and argue it with force is rather satisfying and can win applause for subtle and profound thinking. To take an eclectric position is to invite doubts and confusion, and whatever clarity is achieved is likely to be equated with superficiality.

Since I intend to be eclectic, it may help if I begin with a parable. Let us call it the parable of the dead duck. The story is simple. A duck was shot dead by a hunter at daybreak in a Michigan marsh. Now the problem. What was the cause of the duck's demise?

Well, there is a physiological explanation. The duck died because of a hemorrhage, which left the heart no blood to pump. And there is a psychological explanation. The duck died because the hunter was the kind of person he was—if he had had different frustrations in his youth, he might not have become a bird-killer. We might take quite a psychoanalytic dive on this one, but let's skip it. And there is an ideological explanation. If the culture of Michigan were like that of some parts of India, the killing of a duck—or of any other animal, for that matter—would be reprehensible. And there is a geographical explanation. Note that our duck died in a marsh. No hunter probably would have been waiting for him on top of a hill. Finally, consider a technological explanation, the gun that killed him, a product of centuries of technical progress in the manufacture of lethal hardware.

Now the point of this parable is, first, that every one of these explanations of the cause of the duck's death is correct. And, of course, many additional explanations could be dreamed up. Second, the explanations are at different

"Sociological Factors Favoring Innovations," From Chapter 7, pp. 52-60, *Consumer Behavior, Research on Consumer Reactions,* edited by Lincoln H. Clark, New York: Harper & Brothers, 1958.

levels. The next time you witness a big argument in a bull session, just notice whether or not the argument is kept going by mixing up levels. Jones insists Smith's explanation is wrong, but Smith may be talking along a track at one level, while Jones wants to restrict the discussion to his own level, which he claims is the only one.

All this has especially appropriate relevance to a discussion of factors in social change, in particular, of factors favoring innovation. I shall try, at least, to keep various levels of explanation differentiated. And I shall limit my remarks to factors favoring innovation in America.

Let us start with a complex of factors at the ideological level.

There is no doubt that the American cultural heritage with its Puritan ethic has provided, since our nation was founded, a climate of ideas favorable to innovation. My colleague, Dr. Florence Kluckhohn, has summarized comparative studies of cultures all over the world, by grouping the big guiding ideas of these cultures into a limited number of types of what she calls basic orientations.

To illustrate: Every culture has its own orientation toward time. Some look backward toward the past, like the classical Chinese. Some live mainly in the present, without either much tradition or systematic planning, like many Spanish Americans. It has always been typical of American culture that the basic orientation is predominantly future. Even if a family has not achieved too much in its own lifetime, there is hope that the children will achieve more, and each successive generation sees to it that its youngsters, on the average, get more education than the elders.

Somewhat akin to the time orientation is the basic idea as to responsibility and authority. In some cultures, which Dr. Kluckhohn calls lineal, deference is to ancestors and the elders; in some, deference is mainly to the group or the community; in others, as in America, the emphasis is mainly on the individual. Extreme deference to ancestors or extreme deference to community opinion is in many cultures a major factor in resistance to social change.

One other orientation may be noted. It has to do with the kind of life activity that is most valued. In some cultures, including our own, it is work, achievement, getting things done. In some other cultures, the way leisure is used is more respected than the way work is done. Except in the Old South, there has been little of the country squire tradition in America. The fact that a man is more respected in America for his success in business than for his taste in the selection of fine wines has been deplored by some of our European friends. But it is the cultures that rate production higher than consumption which seem to be the innovators. One possible exception may be noted here, however. In so far as innovations depend on basic science, there is something about the system of orientations that argues against American eminence. Pure science as such has no concern for the practical. We have respected an Edison more highly than a Gibbs—indeed, how many of us ever heard of

Gibbs? Until recently, America was as far behind Europe in pure science as it was, and still is, in music or painting.

These basic orientations—eyes on the future, individualism, and respect for the practical doer, along with other basic attitudes we might enumerate—all are factors favoring innovations in a culture. These orientations have not changed much throughout American history. De Tocqueville would not have to revise very much today what he said more than a century ago in his famous account of American ways of thinking and acting. True, there are some persons who fear that our orientation toward individualism is weakening, with an increasing pressure to conform, not to past ideas, but to the current ideas in one's community. There is an alarming intolerance of nonconformity, as was shown in a nationwide study I published . . . in my book *Communism, Conformity, and Civil Liberties*. But also most encouraging was the finding that local community leaders, as well as the better educated and the younger generation, were more tolerant of nonconformists than were the rank and file, the lesser educated, and the older people, respectively.

There are some writers who would account for American hospitality for innovations solely in terms of ideology. But let us remember the parable of the duck and look at some other levels of explanation.

There is our geography, for example. The Indians did not accomplish much with it, but it has been wonderfully adapted to a people endowed with the cultural orientations just described. The climate, the soil, the minerals, and above all the vastness of the area provide the greatest economic base on earth. For generations the frontier beckoned migrants. This sheer movement in space is a most important factor with respect to innovations. People who live generation after generation in the same village are likely to be extremely hostile to new ideas or new ways of doing things. Particularly important is the tendency of newly married couples to live in communities different from their parents, with freedom to live as they please without the clammy hands of an older generation forever on their necks. The old geographical frontier is gone, but the richness and variety of American resources is such that mobility is as great today as ever in our history.

But geography by itself does little more than provide a favorable setting for a people whose ideology is receptive to innovations. We must consider the tools with which such people work. This brings us to the subject of technology and social change, and there are some who would explain all or most changes in the western world as a direct consequence of changes in technology.

Certainly, human nature is not much different today from what it was in the days of Homer. Geographic changes have been relatively slight since the last Ice Age. What has changed most has been technology. Inventions breed inventions and create new desires. They also create new problems and require further inventions in the social or political field to solve these problems. Look at the automobile, for example, and the revolution it has wrought in two short generations. Indeed, it is tempting to brush aside all other variables and deal with social change solely in terms of changes in technology.

Such a temptation gets us into trouble. Take such a great event as the mass migration of the Negroes to the North that got into full swing during World War I. This can be attributed to technological change, but a simpler level of explanation would be in terms of the unprecedented convergence of two catastrophic events. At the same time that the boll weevil was destroying cotton in much of the old Black Belt, a labor vacuum was created in war-swollen Northern industries by the stoppage of European immigration. Northward into that vacuum poured the Negroes, their old precarious living already made more precarious by what was happening to cotton. The plausibility of this level of explanation makes us wary of attributing all important changes to changes in technology.

Nevertheless, the influence of inventions and changes in technology is so vast, so direct, and often so immediate that such changes deserve a central place in our discussion.

There is a good deal of writing on the sociology of invention, notably by Professor W. F. Ogburn and Dr. S. C. Gilfillan of the University of Chicago. I can do no more here than to allude briefly to certain aspects that relate to conditions making for slow or rapid innovations.

We start with the fact that almost all inventions are not completely new discoveries, like a hitherto uncharted island appearing before Captain Cook, but are rearrangements, and often rather slight rearrangements at that, of previously existing inventions. This fact is extremely important to keep in mind, for it means that the number of such inventions tends to increase at a geometric rate, just as the inherent tendency of organisms is to reproduce at a geometric rate. At any given point in time, the probability of a new invention tends to be directly proportional to the size of the technological base— that is, to the number of inventions already existing. Consequently, the pessimists who from time to time have pontificated as to the slowing down of the inventive processes have always been proved wrong.

It is with much confidence that we can say, if everything else is equal, inventions will increase at a geometric rate. But everything else is never quite equal, and the inventive process, though resembling the reproductive process in its inherent tendency to a geometric rate of increase, can be speeded up or slowed down in many ways.

For example, there is usually a long period of time elapsing between the first working model of an invention and its practical or commercial success. Enormous amounts of capital may be required for the development. The tremendous growth of research and development departments in almost all American industries today, with the resources to deploy whole teams of scientists and engineers on a promising lead, is sure to cut down the average time lag.

Sometimes an invention remains undeveloped for long periods because of lag in development of some critical component. For example, it is said that the jet engine would have appeared much earlier than it did, except for the inability of metallurgists to come up with alloys capable of withstanding unprecedented heat. However, as technological progress moves along all fronts, the probability is vastly increased that a new development, depending simultaneously on several of these fronts, will become speedily feasible.

One of the most ancient of proverbs says that necessity is the mother of invention. Like most proverbs this is at least a half truth, but necessity is a rather complex idea. Necessity can be very evanescent indeed. I remember when I was a boy, in a small town in Iowa, a local inventor came up with a triumphant gadget for cutting the river ice with a power saw attached to a Fordson tractor. He soon had a thriving business selling his outfits to ice houses all over the Middle West, aided by the effective slogan, "Keep the horse manure off the ice." Unhappily, just as need was widely appreciated for his machine, ice plants everywhere collapsed, owing to the coming of the electric refrigerator, and our local inventor went broke.

Necessity, moreover, can be created where it never before existed. Never in the history of mankind has there been such a success in creating a mass demand for gadgets and shifting them from the luxury to the necessity class as is the achievement of American advertising and marketing. Today we are just in the infancy of a new era in mass communication, stimulated by the miraculous selling power of television, and in the future even more than in the past the old proverb is likely to be paralleled by the adage that invention is the mother of necessity.

In the interest of a balanced presentation, much that I have had to say is obvious, though I hope not to the point of boredom. To continue in the same vein, very briefly, we cannot, of course, overlook the fact that innovations that are costly will not succeed where there is no purchasing power. The South has needed summer air conditioners almost as much as the North has needed winter furnaces, but, until the purchasing power developed, air conditioners, however economically produced and skillfully marketed, could not be sold in quantities. Purchasing power is one of the most important, even if it is perhaps the most obvious, of all the factors entering into our equation as to innovations. I shall not elaborate further except to point out that, in the last analysis, purchasing power depends primarily on man-hour productivity, which in turn depends on technology and organizational know-how. Included in the organizational know-how is not only that of management, but also that of labor. In the long run, technological improvements in efficiency increase both total production and production per man-hour, but the short-run effects on a local labor force can be decidedly adverse. One of the hardest lessons our society is learning is how to compensate the temporary losers because of technological innovations so that they will not be motivated to resist innovations that have a long-run benefit to all society.

This, of course, is only a special case of a more general problem, the solution to which is perhaps the best test of a democracy's strength—namely, the ability to achieve long-run general goals when their attainment damages short-run local interests. Happily, in the field of industrial production, our more enlightened labor leaders and management are showing ever-increasing appreciation of the fact that productivity is the key to purchasing power and are cooperating increasingly to facilitate a productivity rise through greater automation.

At this point, let us now retrace our main ideas and see how they add up with respect to the outlook for innovations, at least in the near future.

We have considered four main groups of factors related to social change, namely, ideological, geographical, and technological factors, together with purchasing power based on productivity.

The ideological factors change very slowly; consequently, it is unlikely that any change in these in the near future will affect innovations. The only danger spot I see is in the area of individualism. It would be very unfortunate if the country became increasingly intolerant of strange or bizarre ideas. But there are grounds for optimism, as I indicated. The younger generation is more tolerant of new ideas than its elders, so are community leaders generally, and so are the better educated—with high school education and above. And education is in the process of a vast and unprecedented extension.

Likewise, the geographical factors are for all practical purposes a constant. We have seen how geography fitted so neatly the basic American ideologies to encourage technological development. There is no reason to anticipate a change. True, as we pointed out, the geographical frontier is gone, but there is no sign that mobility is decreasing—on the contrary, there is every reason to expect it to increase. And mobility, like education, breaks the cake of custom and encourages hospitality to ideas and things that are new and different.

By contrast, with the relatively static character of the ideological and geographic factors, we can expect the developments in technology to be highly dynamic. The crucial point to keep in mind here is the inherent geometric rate of growth of inventions, each of which is usually a rearrangement of two or more older inventions or clusters of inventions. It is increasingly less likely as time goes on that progress in one technical area will come to a standstill because another technical area is unworked—our science and engineering, fed by enormous investments by private industry as well as by the government and academic institutions, is growing fantastically along a long solid front. At the same time, the average time lag between first working models and final products is undoubtedly shortening. Moreover, the techniques and facilities for selling new products to a mass public are improving all the time—the latest shot in the arm being the potential opened up by television.

Any student of the theory of inventions and technological change could hardly help being bullish, given these considerations, about a continuation and, indeed, an acceleration of the trend of innovations.

Actually, it is only when we look at the fourth and last of our four main sets of factors that we come up with a serious question mark. This refers to productivity and purchasing power. Since increased productivity and purchasing power are themselves so largely a product of inventiveness in technology and management, we ought to be in the clear here too. But not quite. If an atomic war came, all bets would be off. And even though some of our economist friends think they know how to prevent a major depression through wise use of government spending and controls, one can never be absolutely sure that a big dip in national purchasing power is impossible, even if rather unlikely.

However, barring war and depression, it does look as though the means to purchase, as well as the will to purchase the innovations that our technology is prepared to deliver, will continue to go up as man-hour productivity in agriculture and industry goes up.

We have been trying today to look at the big picture and not just one segment of it. It might have been more intellectually exciting to pick out one level of explanation—say, at the level of ideology, and explore it intensively with psychological and anthropological subtleties, and perhaps a discreet cry of alarm. But when, as in our parable of the duck, we look at not one but several levels of explanation, we are confronted with evidence that most, if not all, of the social forces seem to be conspiring in one direction.

D. *Sociological Theory and Public Opinion Research*

The invention of the techniques used in public opinion polls has presented to the sociologist a challenge that is mighty in its potentialities. This challenge as yet has been taken up by few scholars as compared with the numbers who can be expected to do so in the next few years.

There are several reasons for this lag. One is the fact that so many of our best sociological theorists are unacquainted with the technical intricacies of empirical research using the tools of the public opinion analyst. Another is the fact that public opinion polls, being quite costly even when relatively small samples are used, are usually undertaken to serve a practical rather than a theoretical purpose. For example, they tend either to be simple, brief, popular summaries of current mass opinion for publication in newspapers or more elaborate surveys to aid industrial firms with their marketing and personnel problems. The former are too sketchy to have much interest for the sociological theorist; the latter are often confidential and therefore un-

"Sociological Theory and Public Opinion Research," *Transactions of the Third World Congress of Sociology*, 8 (August, 1956), pp. 306-312.

available. A third reason for the lag in sociological analysis of public opinion surveys is the fact that most such surveys have been concerned with mass opinion, without differentiation among sentiments of, say, influentials and noninfluentials. Only if the respondents are differentiated in relevant ways can we hope to use these techniques for analyzing the sociologically important aspects of the structure of public opinion and the processes of opinion change.

For the purpose of the present discussion, it is of some importance to distinguish between the interests of psychological and sociological theorists, respectively. The difference is, of course, largely one of emphasis, and each may use the others' theoretical concepts in addition to his own.

The psychologists tend to see an individual's opinions as an expression of his personal needs. If he is worried or frustrated, he will tend to project these anxieties upon objects in his environment in such a way as to reduce these anxieties. This process colors perception of a given object or situation, so that two people do not see the same thing. Tendencies to act, as well as rationalizations of such tendencies, will reflect the way the environment, as perceived, impinges on personal needs.

The research problem for the psychologist is to use verbal reports or nonverbal acts of the individual as a basis for constructing an inference as to needs which are blocked, satisfied, or sublimated by varieties of acts or potential acts.

On the other hand, the sociologist, though also concerned with the individual, is primarily interested in an analysis of those forces which tend to lead groups or blocs of individuals to hold the same opinion or to take the same action, even if their specific individual needs are extremely varied. The sociologist seeks to utilize data from public opinion polls in the spirit of Durkheim, who, of course, was obliged to use much less direct data for most of his inferences.

A concept most fruitful to the sociologists is that of "reference group," or "reference category." Many of the beliefs, attitudes, opinions, or indeed actions of an individual are not likely to deviate very far from the norms of the group that is most likely to exercise sanctions over his conduct. Therefore, one of the first research problems of the sociologist in analyzing public opinion is to identify the relevant group or class memberships of an individual.

All this is pretty obvious, but how to do it in any concrete research situation is not obvious. There are two main reasons. First, all of us are members of many groups or categories, and, especially if we live in modern urban societies, we are members of groups that sometimes have conflicting norms or values. Second, with respect to most, if not all, issues about which opinions are held, the norms or values of any one of these groups are not likely to be clear-cut and rigid, but are more likely to permit a certain amount of deviation—sometimes a very large amount.

Let us consider each of these problems in a little more detail.

First, how do we determine which reference groups or categories are likely to be most relevant in a given situation? For example, social class, or religious affiliation, or political party, or immediate friendship group, or even broad categorical classifications like sex or age brackets? Perhaps the most common procedure is to make sure that these memberships are recorded on a questionnaire along with the opinion and then to determine a posteriori by cross tabulation which particular blocs agree internally on a given issue and differ most widely, on the average, from other blocs. Such analysis is usually crudely empirical and quite devoid of theory, except for common-sense hunches. Thus, we may find that 60 per cent of the Catholics hold Opinion X as compared with only 20 per cent of the Protestants. Further cross tabulation may refine this. For example, we may discover that 80 per cent of Catholic women and only 40 per cent of Catholic men hold Opinion X. But, useful as such information may be, it is still quite superficial, as compared with what we would like to know about the structure of opinion.

Since a person may belong to a multiplicity of groups with sometimes conflicting norms, we would like to know the relative weight of the pressures that impinge upon him, when these norms conflict. A person might have in his work group many fellow workers and close acquaintances who are quite irreligious and leftist in their political and economic views. On the other hand, his immediate kinfolk may be strongly religious and not at all leftist. Which set of group norms will be more decisive for him?

It is not too hard to theorize about such conflicts. For example, unless one particular solution has been deeply internalized, a person probably will be most likely to speak or act in such a way as to incur the minimum of disapproval. If the potential sanctions of one group are heavy and of the other group light, he will tend to avoid the heavy sanctions.

The moment, however, that we translate such ideas into operational research, the complexity and difficulty of the problem begin to manifest themselves. What do we mean by "heavy" or "light" sanctions? And must we not introduce a further concept, namely, the estimated probability of an expression of opinion or an action being found out by each of our two groups? For example, a particular action might incur only moderate disapproval from Group A, which, however, would be almost certain to find out about it. On the other hand, it might incur extremely strong disapproval from Group B, but, by contrast Group B might have a low probability of finding out about it. We would like to know how an individual perceives each of these alternatives. The direct research procedure would be simply to ask him, in an interview or on a questionnaire. This can be done, though it requires very skillful research design. But, unhappily for us as researchers, our respondent may not be able to verbalize the dilemma situation. Much of what goes on may be below the threshold of consciousness and not involve a rational calculation which can be described. Yet the ultimate behavior may involve an intuitive weighing of risks which has quite the same effect. Our only research recourse may be to ascertain this indirectly, inferring it from statements he makes more generally about the two conflicting groups in a variety of situations.

But even if we can determine which reference groups or categories are relevant to an individual in a given situation, we are faced by further difficulties in making an indirect inference as to the effect of possible sanctions. These difficulties lead to a consideration of the second point raised earlier, namely, that the norms of values of any group are not likely to be clear-cut or rigid, but are likely to permit a certain amount of deviation. How do we find out about this permissible range of deviation?

Researchwise, we are limited in our alternatives. With small groups we can observe overt nonverbal behavior, as the anthropologist does in a primitive village or as the sociologist or psychologist does in studying groups at work or under laboratory observation. But, much of the time, we must depend on verbal statements made by an adequate sample of group members. Moreover, if, as is both practically and theoretically highly important, we need to distinguish ideal norms from actual norms, our only recourse is to verbal reports.

There can be more than one level of idealization of norms. For example, there may be a "norm in the sky" to which no one actually conforms, although lip service may be paid to it, as in the case of the Christian ideal of turning the other cheek. There may be a lower level of norm that is upheld as a practical working ideal but that is more often honored by the breach than by the observance. And then there may be a behavioral level of norm, representing more or less the modal expected behavior. This is likely, as was suggested, to be accompanied by a considerable range of permissiveness—that is, punishment for nonconformity "depends on the circumstances." There are good theoretical grounds for expecting this range ordinarily to be much greater in the case of informal conduct among friends or relatives than in the case of formal conduct of a contractual character.

Whatever the level, we are likely to need to resort to verbal reports to ascertain the range of permissible deviation and the varying severity of sanctions.

In the past few years there has been an increasing amount of research seeking either to learn directly how individuals solve conflicts of values or indirectly by inference from a knowledge of the value systems of the reference groups involved. But we still need much more research experience before we are able to lay down good rules either for determining which reference groups are relevant to an individual in a given situation or for evaluating the ideal or actual norms of a given group, taking into account their ranges of variability.

We have dealt, however, with only one aspect, albeit an important one, in the mapping of the structure of opinion in a given situation. Let us now consider a further aspect, arising from the different roles members of a group play within that group. We are interested, particularly, in opinion initiation and leadership because it becomes so crucial in understanding the relation-ship between opinion and action.

On this subject there has been a good deal of sociological thinking and some quite promising research. But the empirical studies are still not suffi-ciently numerous to tell us how useful varieties of typological classifications of leadership, as proposed theoretically, are likely to be.

For example, a distinction which seems useful is that between the "inno-vator" and the "influential." The innovator, being the first by whom the new is tried, may be considered something of a crackpot by his fellows. Whereas, the influential may be slow to pick up new ideas or adopt new practices, but once he does, his prestige is powerful in getting others to follow suit. We know so little, however, about the various kinds of persons or roles which may be associated with these two types that generalizations are very dangerous. There is some reason to guess that the primary effect of mass communications, such as magazines, newspapers, radio, and television, is to change or solidify the opinions of each of these types of leaders and that the rank and file of people are much less influenced by the mass communica-tions and much more influenced by word of mouth communication within their work groups or friendship groups. But there may be considerable varia-tion in this pattern depending on the type of issue, and theory without research is not likely to be very fruitful.

Only recently have public opinion polls made a special effort to seek out potential innovators or influentials. Some of the best work in this area has been in the field of market research, where manufacturers are interested in the adoption of new products, new brands, or new models. There is, how-ever, some reason to believe that processes by which political ideas are propagated and nourished may bear only a slight resemblance to the processes by which consumers are influenced to purchase products.

Attitudes of voters and attitudes of consumers probably have one important aspect in common, however. That is the extent of apathy or indifference on the part of the great mass of people. At election time in a democracy the newspapers and politicians create the illusion of great popular excitement. This excitement may not be wholly an illusion, but the interpretation of the excitement as representing deep personal involvement on the part of the mass of the public almost surely is. Careful efforts to measure involvement or intensity of sentiment usually show how shallow it is. Rather, it resembles for many people the spectator interest surrounding a national or regional sports event. Similarly, the apathy or indifference of the average person with respect to differences between brands of consumer products is also dis-couraging to those concerned with advertising. Loyalty to a brand most of the time may represent nothing more than convenience buying. One may use the same toothpaste for years, not at all because he is enthusiastic over it, but simply because it is too much bother to experiment with other brands.

Popular reports of public opinion polls all too frequently go astray in overestimating the meaningfulness of an issue to an individual respondent. There are now some quite sophisticated research techniques for evaluating the depth of feeling with which an opinion is held and the degree of involvement. But they are still used very sparingly because of time and cost in any particular survey.

The fact that in many situations it may be the opinions of only a small handful of persons that are deeply rooted can lead easily to the assumption that in such situations mass opinion is irrelevant. Indeed, this assumption may often be true with respect to a specific issue—especially one which is too technical for the average person to understand or too remote from his daily life. What he says to an interviewer may have little or no predictive value as related to anything he might in the future say or do about it. Numerous examples might be cited from polling experience. But it does not follow that the underlying latent directions of his general attitude are irrelevant. If he is strongly prejudiced against capitalism, for example, it is important to know about this prejudice even if a particular complicated issue involving capitalism is one about which he really has no genuine opinion.

These observations suggest the need for a better theoretical analysis of the relationship of innovators, influentials, and the masses in various types of situations at various levels of attitudes—also of the impact of media like the press and television. It is quite unlikely that such a theoretical analysis will be done successfully at a professor's desk. What is most needed now is some rather limited middle-range theories which can be operationally tested with data from actual public opinion polls designed with the theories in mind. Incidentally, it is not impossible that the best work of this kind in the next few years will be in the marketing research field, because industry, in seeking to influence the consumer, has such a large stake in getting information that delineates opinion structure accurately and is willing to pay the heavy costs of such research.

Now may I sum up. The sociological theorist is concerned with the structure of public opinion and how it changes. He has little interest in mere marginal figures as to how many people in a sample say they favor this or that kind of proposition. His interest, rather, is with the way opinions of individuals are related to groups or categories to which these individuals belong. He would like to be able to generalize about the conditions that lead reference groups of certain kinds to be more influential than reference groups of other kinds. He is interested in the norms of such reference groups and the sanctions by which these norms are enforced. The ascertainment of these norms is a theoretical and empirical problem of no little difficulty. But they can be ascertained. Moreover, the sociological theorist is interested in attitudes as held by those with different roles within a group and how mass media impinge on these people. Especially important are the leaders and, again, the classification of crucial types of leadership roles—the "innovator" or the "influential," for example—is one of challenging difficulty. It becomes all the more important when we recognize the lack of personal involvement of the masses of people in most specific issues, whether political or economic.

This brief paper has centered on the interests of the sociological theorist and has not taken into account the variables which are of major concern to the psychologist. The latter are of obvious importance, and no comprehensive theory of public opinion can afford to neglect them. But it is the duty of the sociologist, *qua* sociologist, to proceed as far as he can on a sociological level. If he gives up too quickly, and drops to the psychological level, he may fail to account for variables that, if understood, would explain most of the variance in many situations involving public opinion.

The public opinion polling technique—like the electron microscope—is one of those inventions that magnifies our vision. It opens up new vistas, permitting the empirical test of theoretical propositions that can be rigorously formulated with operational definitions of each variable. Sociology much needs a corps of young investigators trained in sociological theory *and also* in research design involving questionnaire-making and statistical analyses. From their labors can emerge not a mere body of speculations, not a mere mass of undigested statistical tables, but a sociological science of public opinion.

Part Two

12

□ ☒ □ □ □ *Notes*
on the Case Study
and the Unique Case

This paper is a minor piece that was written as the consequence of discussions with some of the coauthors of *The Prediction of Personal Adjustment,* a monograph sponsored in 1941 by the Social Science Research Council. It is an effort to set down rather systematically and rigorously what in effect goes on when the analyst of a single clinical case makes a prediction about this individual's behavior. A particularly cogent subsequent treatment of this problem is found in Meehl, *Clinical versus Statistical Prediction; a Theoretical Analysis and a Review of the Evidence.*

Although mainly identified with quantitative studies, I have long been interested in the uses of qualitative case material and, indeed, wrote my doctor's thesis on this subject. In many studies I have used qualitative data extensively—for example, in the survey reported in *Communism, Conformity, and Civil Liberties* (1955) there was more interviewing time devoted to free, unstructured responses than in almost any nation-wide survey that up to this time had been administered to a national probability sample.

"Notes on the Case-Study and the Unique Case," from pp. 240-249, *The Prediction of Personal Adjustment,* Bulletin 48, edited by Paul Horst. New York: Social Science Research Council, 1941. Also Samuel A. Stouffer, "Notes on the Case-Study and the Unique Case," *Sociometry,* Volume 4, November, 1941, pp. 349-357. J. L. Moreno, Editor.

A perennial controversy in the social and psychological sciences is that between advocates of statistics and advocates of the case study method. Although nobody disputes the importance of the case study as a procedure for getting new ideas, some statisticians unfortunately fail to recognize adequately the importance of the case study as a procedure for making direct predictions about the behavior of an individual. This lack of recognition may be due partly to the fact that those who have undergone a rigorous discipline in quantitative methods develop a bias against the loose and sometimes pretentious vocabulary so often used by exponents of the case study, as well as against the tendency of some of these exponents to lay claims to certainty of prediction that are unsupported by either logic or empirical evidence. The same charge of making extravagant claims is laid at the door of the statisticians by experts in the use of the case method.

Perhaps we can get to the heart of the difficulty if we examine the concept of the unique case. The case study procedure makes a prediction, it is said, by "analyzing the unique dynamic configuration of traits within the individual."

WHAT IS A CONFIGURATION?

Suppose that we want to predict success in some activity for a given individual named Smith. For simplicity, let us assume that we can rate Smith as of two separate time periods, with respect to three behavior items, each of which is described in four mutually exclusive categories, qualitative or quantitative, as follows:

	Time t	*Time t'*
Trait *a*	$a_1 a_2 a_3 a_4$	$a_1' a_2' a_3' a_4'$
Trait *b*	$b_1 b_2 b_3 b_4$	$b_1' b_2' b_3' b_4'$
Trait *c*	$c_1 c_2 c_3 c_4$	$c_1' c_2' c_3' c_4'$

Let the underlined symbols indicate the ratings for Smith. They tell us that at time t his trait configuration was $a_2 b_1 c_4$; at time t' it was $a_3' b_1' c_3'$.

Although $a_2 b_1 c_4$ are reported as of a single time interval t, the pattern actually may represent sequences within that time interval, e.g., $a_2 b_1$ may be followed by c_4. Similarly, within the time interval t', $a_1' b_1'$ may be followed by c_3'. The notation here is intended to be quite general. For example, $a_2 b_1$ may represent Smith's report that b_1 is an "effect" of a_2 or may represent the investigator's inference that b_1 is an "effect" of a_2. It must be remembered that such a report or recorded inference, even if subject to error, may be a datum that can be treated either by the statistician or the case-history investigator just like any other item for predicting Smith's successs in an activity. An excellent discussion of this point, with many practical suggestions for research, appears in a manuscript by Paul F. Lazarsfeld . . . entitled "The Art of Asking Why."[1]

Consider a single cross section in time, for example, time t. The number of possible *static configurations* of the kind $a_2b_1c_4$ is $4^3 = 64$. If ten traits were to be considered simultaneously, the number of configurations would be $4^{10} = 1,048,576$.

Next, consider an individual's rating on a single trait in the two time periods as constituting a *simple dynamic configuration*. Smith's simple dynamic configuration with respect to trait a would be a_2a_3'. The number of possible simple dynamic configurations with respect to any specified trait is $4^2 = 16$.

Finally, let us consider Smith's ratings on all three traits in both time periods as constituting a single complex dynamic configuration. Smith's *complex dynamic configuration* is $a_2a_3'b_3b_1'c_4c_3'$. Such a configuration might be illustrated by the fragment of a case history. Before Smith was married, he got into fast company (a_2) and drank heavily (b_1) and, perhaps because of drink, had great difficulty holding a job (c_4). Since marriage he has given up the fast company (a_3') although he still drinks too much (b_1'), and, consequently perhaps, has been having some, though less, difficulty in holding his job (c_3'). The number of possible complex dynamic configurations of this type $(4^3)^2 = 64^2 = 4,096$. If there were ten traits, the number of possible complex dynamic configurations would be $(4^{10})^2 = (1,048,576)^2 = 1,099,511,627,776$.

With such an astronomically large number of different complex dynamic configurations possible from a relatively small number of trait categories and with only two time periods, it is evident how easy it is to make classifications that put every individual in the world in a different configuration. (This is the general principle, of course, by which a small number of traits are used, in configurational analysis, to identify an individual from his fingerprints.)

Now, our problem is, knowing Smith's pattern a_2a_3', b_1b_1', c_4c_3', etc., how can we predict his success or failure in a given activity?

It will be instructive to compare and contrast the approaches by the statistician and case-study investigator, respectively, to this problem. Consider, first, the statistician.

HOW THE STATISTICIAN PREDICTS

If the number of possible configurations is small and the sample of individuals is very large, such that numerous individuals are characterized by a common configuration, the statistician's task is simple. All he needs to do is

1. Paul F. Lazarsfeld, "The Art of Asking Why, Three Principles Underlying the Formulation of Questionnaires," in Katz, Daniel, *et al.*, eds., *Public Opinion and Propaganda*, Part 5, Chapter 11, p. 675.

to observe the proportion of successes among those characterized by each given configuration and to make a direct actuarial prediction. For example, for trait a there are only sixteen possible simple dynamic configurations involving one subcategory in each of the two time periods. Let us assume that out of 100 individuals with a_2a_3', 80 succeed in a given activity and 20 fail. Then the best actuarial prediction that can be made for Smith on the basis of trait a alone is that he will succeed. The statistician would expect to be correct about 80 per cent of the time on such predictions and wrong about 20 per cent of the time, the exact percentage of correct predictions being subject to sampling error.

Direct applications of this method breaks down, however, when the number of possible configurations becomes so large that no sample is large enough to provide an experience table. Thus, even a very large sample may not yield a single example of an individual who is characterized by a particular complex dynamic configuration, out of a possible 4,096, such as $a_2a_3'b_1b_1'c_4c_3'$. Hence, when confronted with Smith, who is characterized by this pattern, the statistician ordinarily is helpless unless he can recombine various configurations in such a way as to get a small number of groups in which a sufficient number of individuals will fall.

There are a great many methods by which the statistician can make these recombinations. Only a few examples will be mentioned.

One method might be to make a direct typological reduction. Thus, he might reduce the number of configurations by cutting each trait to two categories:

	Time t	Time t'
Trait a	A_1A_2	$A_1'A_2'$
Trait b	B_1B_2	$B_1'B_2'$
Trait c	C_1C_2	$C_1'C_2'$

This yields the investigator only sixty-four types of complex dynamic configurations with which to work. Or he might simplify still further by treating B_1C_1 and B_2C_1 as members of the same class $(BC)_1$ and B_1C_2 and B_2C_2 as members of another class $(BC)_2$ in time t and by using similar groupings for time t'. Then he gets

	Time t		Time t'	
Trait a	A_1	A_2	A_1'	A_2'
	$(BC)_1$	$(BC)_2$	$(BC)_1'$	$(BC)_2'$

or only sixteen types of complex dynamic configurations. It will be noted that the relationship of the type A_1A_1' $(BC)_1$ $(BC)_1'$ has precisely the same general structure as the relationship from which it was derived, except for a sacrifice of detail. With only sixteen types, the statistician is able to observe enough individuals in each type to acquire data for direct actuarial prediction. Much information about Smith was lost in order to make this prediction possible. A factor analysis of some sort might provide a method of typological reduction with a minimum loss of information.

A different procedure, relatively new to most statisticians, is the use of the discriminant function, by which a frequency distribution of prediction scores is worked out for the successful individuals in the trial sample and another frequency distribution of prediction scores is worked out for the unsuccessful individuals. The method would assign weights to the sub-categories of traits at each time period in such a way as to maximize the difference between the means of the two frequency distributions. By referring to these two distributions, the likelihood that a person who possesses a given prediction score will be successful can be determined. If Smith has that score, an actuarial forecast can be made for him on the basis of the sample experience.

Much more common is the statistical procedure of assigning arbitrary or item-analysis weights to each subcategory and computing by simple addition a prediction score for each individual in the trial sample. All individuals whose prediction scores fall in the same class interval are treated alike, regard-less of the different configurations that they may possess. (The time factor might be handled in various ways, for example, by treating the direction of change in each item as a separate item with its own set of weights.) If 75 out of 100 whose prediction scores fall in the same class interval succeeded, and if Smith's prediction score falls into that class interval, the usual actuarial prediction can be made. This is the method used in parole prediction.

These statistical procedures have in common the operation involving a sacrifice of information about the individual configurations. This sacrifice is made in order to obtain broad enough classes to assure an adequate number of cases from the trial sample in each class. It is an artifact to treat thousands of different configurations as belonging to a single class, supposedly homoge-neous. If the classes are too broad and too heterogeneous, the statistician will make many bad guesses.

HOW THE CASE-STUDY INVESTIGATOR PREDICTS

Let us turn now to the case-study investigator who is confronted with a dynamic configuration $a_2a_3'b_1b_1'c_4c_3'$ for Smith. Like the statistician, he may possess no experience about the success and failure of others in this one out of thousands of possible configurations.

He may, and frequently actually does, operate much as the statistician operates, by making typological reduction, or by mentally assigning informal predictive weights on various traits separately, which weights he combines in some informal way. If he lacks the numerical information from the trial sample that the statistician requires, he makes up for the lack by assuming some value out of his general experience. The outcome is an actuarial prediction, of necessity less accurate on the average than would have been possible if numerical experience tables were available.

While this description perhaps characterizes fairly well certain of the operations performed by the case-study investigator, it is far from adequate. Statisticians who criticize the case method because of pretentious claims made for its accuracy are likely to be thinking of such a description or are overlooking another operation that is also frequently performed.

The additional operation is one that the case-study investigator can perform because of the extreme flexibility available to him as contrasted with the rigidity of the statistical framework. This flexibility enables the case-study investigator to economize by seeking out a limited number of traits that seem important for Smith and by analyzing them intensively while ignoring other traits. True, the statistician can and does ignore traits. (One way he does it is to give the traits zero values for Smith.) But the case-study investigator can do what the statistician cannot do, namely, concentrate on an intensive, detailed, free-flowing analysis of the configuration of the limited number of traits *that he thinks are important in Smith.* Moreover, he is not bound by any prior list of traits but can add others freely. Thus, he might decide to ignore traits b and b' and c and c' entirely for Smith, but consider d and d'. Or he might get a detailed developmental history of Smith, introducing observations on additional time periods, represented by a'' and d'' in time t'' and by a''' and d''' in time t'''. Thus, Smith's complex dynamic configuration may be represented by his behavior over several time intervals. In the first time interval the contribution to the configuration may be $a_2 d_1$, in the second $a_3' d_2'$, in the third $a_3'' d_2''$, and in the fourth $a_3''' d_3'''$.

The investigator must now predict Smith's success. If he is familiar with other configurations somewhat like Smith's and knows how they turned out, he will apply this knowledge to Smith. Such a prediction is, of course, not only implicitly actuarial but is likely to be subject to gross error. If the investigator is not familiar with any other configurations remotely resembling Smith's, he probably is as helpless as the statistician in the same situation, unless—note the reservation—unless the time series on Smith alone is of a very special kind. Specifically, the sequence of observations on Smith *must contain information on Smith's success at one or more points of time in activities resembling that for which a prediction is to be made.* Thus, if at time t, when Smith's behavior pattern or trait pattern was $a_2 d_1$, he was a success in an activity similar to that being predicted, and if at time t', when his pattern was $a_3' d_2'$, he also was a success—in fact, if he always seemed to be a success—there ordinarily would be considerable confidence that he would succeed again. It should be carefully noted, however, that, even in this favorable circumstance, prediction can not be made with complete certainty, for the following reasons:

1. The assumption that the new situation is analogous is subject to various kinds of error.

2. The assumption (often not explicit, but necessarily present) that it is the general rule that people who succeed in past situations will continue to succeed does not refer to an invariable sociological law, because none has been demonstrated. It refers rather to a hypothesis, which, if carefully studied, would be found to have exceptions—hence, to be a "law" of an actuarial character.

If the second point above be questioned, and there may be some who would question it, one can make the point clearer, perhaps, by another example. Suppose, when Smith had configuration a_1d_1 at time t, that he failed in an activity, as also when he had the configuration $a_3'd_2'$ at time t'. But suppose he was successful at t'' and t'''. The prediction may now be that he will succeed, on the implied, if not specified, assumption that people who are improving will succeed in the future. The language of common sense is full of such usages, sometimes making an explicit recognition of the general relationship, as when we say, "I think he'll grow out of those bad habits as he gets older; folks usually do."

One reason that some case-study investigators have difficulty recognizing the point that a projection of an intra-individual trend implies a reference to a general relationship is that they sometimes phrase their forecast in more complicated language than that used above. For example, they do not say simply, "Smith is improving; therefore, he will succeed," but they say, "Smith has been improving, and he now is characterized by a behavior pattern $a_3'''d_3'''$, which makes for success, as compared with his earlier behavior pattern a_2d_1, which made for failure." But how does the investigator *know* that "$a_3'''d_3'''$ makes for success" and that "a_2d_1 makes for failure"? He cannot know, unless he has had experience with persons whose configuration was similar to $a_3'''d_3'''$ and to a_2d_1. If he is using that experience, he is making an explicit actuarial reference, and without adequate data if these configurations are rare.

Even when the prediction for Smith is made solely on his individual time sequence, the ultimate test is a statistical one and can be made empirically. The test is not for Smith as an individual but as a random member of a class of individuals concerning whom the investigator makes predictions with about the same feeling of confidence. If the investigator has felt about the same confidence in fifty previous cases as in Smith's case and has been correct forty times, the best actuarial forecast is that he is correct about Smith, but, of course, Smith may become one of his mistakes, and this cannot be known in advance.

Let us summarize the operation on Smith of the case-study investigator. Many times his operations are the same as those of the statistician—for example, he may use typological reduction, or he may relate certain traits of Smith to his past experience with other cases. Unlike the statistician, he is free to concentrate intensively on variates or configurations he thinks important in Smith and to explore, at will, especially taking advantage of cues from repetitions or sequences in Smith's success and failure experience over time. If Smith's dynamic configuration cannot be compared in whole or in part with that of other individuals whose success or failure is known, the investigator must obtain this special kind of time sequence—record of success and failure—or he is helpless. Even if the investigator secures this unique time sequence of success and failure of Smith, the ultimate forecast depends in part on the correctness of whatever general theory is implicit in the projection of the trend.

CONCLUDING REMARKS

Although the trend is to replace many case-study operations by quantitative techniques easy to administer, especially when prediction must be made quickly for a large number of individuals, the case study is likely to continue to be a useful—often indispensable—supplement to the work of the statistician, even in situations where the value of the statistician's methods is most obvious. If the case method were not effective, life insurance companies hardly would use it as they do in supplementing their actuarial tables by a medical examination of the applicant in order to narrow their risks. Its great virtue in direct prediction is its flexibility, permitting an intensive study of the configuration of selected factors in a time setting.

No detailed comments are needed about the important contribution of the case-study procedure as a fruitful source of new ideas, which can be eventually set up as hypotheses for explicit statistical checking. Few statisticians, if any, will dispute that function of the case study. In conclusion, however, at least one point should be made to indicate how one of the principal present advantages of the case method could also be better utilized by the statistician. The case method, as has been emphasized, often relies heavily on information about an individual's record of success or failure in situations analogous to that about which a prediction is to be made. There is no reason, of course, why such a record should not be an explicit entry as one of the predictive items in a formal statistical analysis. Sometimes it is. In parole studies, past record of recidivism becomes one of the most powerful predictive items. The case study has no monopoly on the use of such time trends, and still greater use of such information, together with that of typologies which are dynamic in that they indicate sequences or connections in time, should improve statistical prediction.

The statistician and the case-study investigator can make mutual gains if they will quit quarreling with each other and begin borrowing from each other.

13

□ ☒ □ □ □ *Some Ideas and Tools to Help in Correlation Analysis*

Early in his career the author contributed quite a number of methodological papers having to do with correlation and sampling. Some of these were essays dealing with the applications of new techniques to sociology and social psychology, and some were proposals of new methods and new measures. Out of these three brief examples are presented in this chapter, all having to do with correlation. The first is an introduction of a new measure of combined partial correlation that is a rather simple device and easy to compute and that seems to satisfy a certain need not otherwise met.

The second paper in this chapter is an essay on the application of correlation to sociology that, like the preceding paper, was published in the *Journal of the American Statistical Association.* At the time this essay was written, partial and multiple correlations were even more in vogue in sociology than today. Most quantitative studies relied upon census tabulations, which meant that variables in which one was interested often could not be apprehended directly. For example, Ogburn, in analyzing factors in the 1928 presidential campaign, used data on the percentage of Catholics in the county and on the percentage of people voting for prohibition in a county as correlated with the vote for Al Smith, in order to ascertain the impact of Catholicism and wetness, respectively, on Smith's vote. This was before the day of sample surveys. We now would approach this question much more directly by finding out how individual Catholics, for example, do vote and perhaps by supplementary questions probing more deeply into why. Whenever the number of cases collected permits the direct subdivision of groups such that several variables can be dealt with simultaneously, we often now can make a more incisive analysis than is possible with ordinary quantitative correlation procedures.

However, the new electronic computers are making it possible to do multivariate analyses with numerous variables so cheaply that a great increase in interest in partial and multiple correlation may be in the making. It is for this reason that the paper, "Reliability Coefficients in a Correlation Matrix," which was published in *Psychometrika*, is included. This paper contains the mathematical outlines of a method well adapted to the new computers that would enable one, by making various estimates of the relative unreliability of the different variables involved, to estimate the effect of this unreliability on all kinds of derived measures, such as partial regression coefficients or partial correlation coefficients.

A. A Coefficient of "Combined Partial Correlation" with an Example from Sociological Data

Occasionally, there is need for a measure of correlation that seeks to show the combined relation between a dependent variable and two or more independent variables, after one or more other independent variables are "held constant" by partial correlation. For example, if one is studying juvenile delinquency in a city's census tracts, one may wish not only to appraise the relationship between juvenile delinquency and the percentage of native whites, holding various economic indexes "constant," but, in addition, may wish to appraise the combined relation between juvenile delinquency and *all* these economic indexes, holding percentage of native whites "constant." It may be that one has two or three series of indexes of economic conditions in the tracts, such as median rental, unemployment, or dependency rates.

While the procedure doubtless has been used frequently before, especially when the variable to be "partialed out" is the trend of a time series, and while there can be nothing new about the concept mathematically, the writer

"A Coefficient of 'Combined Partial Correlation' with an Example from Sociological Data," *Journal of the American Statistical Association*, 29 (March, 1934), pp. 70-71.

has not seen it explicitly recorded that the measure of what is here called "combined partial correlation" is obtainable directly by a simple extension of the usual correlation theory.[1]

The problem is simply that of finding the multiple correlation between one dependent variable and $s - 1$ independent variables when $n - s$ variables are held "constant."

Consider $v_1, v_2, \ldots, v_i, \ldots, v_s$, each of which is a corresponding deviation from a different regression plane, such as $X_i = f(X_{s+1}, X_{s+2}, \ldots, X_n)$. Then, as is evident from the usual correlation theory, the squared multiple correlation coefficient of these residuals may be written

$$R^2_{(v_1)\ (v_2\ \cdots\ v_s)} = 1 - (1 - r^2_{v_1 v_2})(1 - r^2_{(v_1 v_2)\ (v_2)}) \cdots (1 - r^2_{(v_1 v_s)\ (v_2\ \cdots\ v_{s-1})})$$

If the plane $X_i = f(X_{s+1}, X_{s+2}, \ldots, X_n)$ is of the type

$$X_i = b_0 + b_1 X_{s+1} + b_2 X_{s+2} + \cdots + b_{n-s} X_n$$

we have
$$r^2_{v_1 v_2} = r^2_{(12)\ (s+1,\ s+2,\ \cdots\ n)}$$
$$r^2_{(v_1 v_s)\ (v_2)} = r^2_{(13)\ (2,\ s+1,\ s+2,\ \cdots\ n)}$$

$$\cdot \quad \cdot \quad \cdot \quad \cdot \quad \cdot \quad \cdot \quad \cdot \quad \cdot \quad \cdot \quad \cdot \quad \cdot \quad \cdot$$

$$r^2_{(v_1 v_s)\ (v_2\ \cdots\ v_{s-1})} = r^2_{(1s)\ (23\ \cdots\ s-1,\ s+1,\ \cdots\ n)}$$

Hence $R^2_{(v_1)\ (v_2\ \cdots\ v_s)}$, may be written

$$R^2_{1(23\ \cdots\ s)\ (s+1,\ s+2,\ \cdots\ n)}$$
$$= 1 - (1 - r^2_{(12)\ (s+1,\ s+2,\ \cdots\ n)}) \cdots (1 - r^2_{(1s)\ (23\ \cdots\ s-1,\ s+1,\ \cdots\ n)})$$

The order of the subscripts in the factors of the right-hand side may be altered to provide a numerical check.

If there are only four variables,

$$R^2_{1 \cdot 23 \cdot 4} = 1 - (1 - r^2_{12 \cdot 4})(1 - r^2_{13 \cdot 24})$$

may be written as

$$\frac{r^2_{12 \cdot 4} + r^2_{13 \cdot 4} - 2r_{12 \cdot 4} r_{13 \cdot 4} r_{23 \cdot 4}}{1 - r^2_{23 \cdot 4}}$$

AN EXAMPLE

From 184 census tracts in Cleveland, Ohio, where $X_1 = $ log juvenile delinquency rate, $X_2 = $ log unemployment rate, $X_3 = $ log dependency rate, and

1. Mordecai Ezekiel has treated what at first sight may be thought to be an analogous problem. He seeks the relationship between $(X_1 - b_{12, 34}X_2)$ and X_3 and X_4, thus obtaining the correlation between one variable and two others, after eliminating from the *dependent* variable that part of its variation imputed (by the analysis) to a *single one* of the independent variables. For the formula and discussion see Ezekiel, *Methods of Correlation Analysis*, p. 185, and for the derivation see *ibid.*, appendix, pp. 383-384. Upon examination it will be observed that the aim, approach, and results are quite different from those submitted in the present paper.

X_4 = percentage of native whites, we have $r_{12 \cdot 4} = +0.5396$ and $r_{13 \cdot 24} = +0.4489$, whence $R_{1 \cdot 23 \cdot 4}$, the combined partial correlation between delinquency and the indexes of economic conditions in the tracts, "holding constant" percentage of native whites, is 0.58. The point of interest may be the comparison between $R_{1 \cdot 23 \cdot 4}$ and $r_{14 \cdot 23}$, the latter being almost zero (-0.04, although r_{14} was -0.51).[2]

Another type of situation in which the above formulas may be particularly useful arises when there are, let us say, three variables and there is some good reason to believe that X_1 and X_3 are parabolic functions of X_2. Any power of X_2 may, as is well known, be treated as an additional independent variable, which we may call X_4. Hence, the combined partial correlation between X_1 and the first and second powers of X_2, holding X_3 "constant," may be found directly from

$$R^2_{1 \cdot 24 \cdot 3} = 1 - (1 - r^2_{12 \cdot 3})(1 - r^2_{14 \cdot 23})$$

The estimate of the sampling variance of $R^2_{1(23 \ldots s)(s+1, s+2, \ldots, n)}$ possibly would be about the same as that of $R^2_{1(23 \ldots s)}$ after making allowance for the degrees of freedom involved in removing the variables held "constant." It would be valuable to investigate this sampling distribution, if it has not already been studied.

B. Problems in the Application of Correlation to Sociology

Sociologists are gradually discovering that there is rather little place for simple correlation between two variables in their field. As Frank A. Ross said, in a searching paper read at Cincinnati in 1933, a sociological problem seldom involves a simple relationship between A and B, but usually involves a relationship between A, B, C, D, and other factors.[3] When this lesson is learned, the first forward step toward a sound statistical analysis has been taken. The second step involves the consideration of how to separate the effects of the several factors involved in the problem. In discussing this second step, we shall not hesitate to say things that may be painfully obvious to the expert statistician or to use nontechnical language, now and then, at the expense of the nicest mathematical precision.

"Problems in the Application of Correlation to Sociology," *Journal of the American Statistical Association*, 29 (March, 1934), supplement, pp. 52-58.

2. The writer is indebted to Henry D. Sheldon, Jr., now of the Population Division, Bureau of the Census, Washington, D.C., for the data from which this illustration is constructed. The data $R_{1 \cdot 23 \cdot 1}$ and $r_{14 \cdot 23}$ may be compared in the same way as any two partial correlations (except for algebraic sign). Perhaps $R^2_{1 \cdot 23 \cdot 4}$ and $r^2_{14 \cdot 23}$ or $1 - \sqrt{1 - R^2_{1 \cdot 23 \cdot 4}}$ and $1 - \sqrt{1 - r^2_{14 \cdot 23}}$ provide better comparisons.

3. Frank A. Ross, "The Use of Statistical Data and Techniques in Sociology," Chapter XV in L. L. Bernard (ed.), *The Fields and Methods of Sociology*.

In general, there are three methods of separating the effects of several factors. First, the *direct* method of classification into subgroups, which always is preferable if the data are sufficient and for which are available tests of significance, such as provided by R. A. Fisher's analysis of variance if the dependent factor is on a quantitative scale or by the chi-square test or kindred methods if the dependent factor is expressed in the form of attributes. Second, the *indirect* method of partial correlation. Third, a combination of the direct and indirect methods.

When any of these three procedures is followed in sociology, one often finds that the apparent influence of a single factor is rather small. This usually means that a finding is subject to too large a chance fluctuation to be regarded as more than a mere tendency. Nevertheless, a mere tendency may be important. For example, W. F. Ogburn discovered by partial correlation a slight tendency—very slight, but too large to be reasonably attributed to chance—for the birth rate to be lower in American cities where there was more early marriage than in cities where there was less early marriage, suggesting that the knowledge of birth control encouraged early marriage.[4] Sociologists need not be discouraged because relationships are generally not high, but we must remember that this fact requires even more caution than is necessary in fields of research where knowledge of one or more factors yields rather complete understanding of the dependent variable. Let us enumerate briefly a few problems.

1. *The measures or indexes used in a study may be of varying reliability or validity.* By reliability is meant: Does the index measure something consistently? By validity is meant: Granted that the index measures something consistently, is it really describing what we think it is describing? W. F. Ogburn and Nell Talbot made an interesting statistical analysis of the 1928 presidential election.[5] They sought the net relationships between Smith's vote in certain counties and indexes of wetness, Catholicism, urbanization, and other factors. Now the value of the partial correlation between the index of wetness of a county and Smith's vote depends not only on the accuracy of the index of wetness but also on the accuracy of the other indexes. If the factor of wetness is unreliably measured and the factor of Catholicism is reliably measured, the partial correlation found between Smith's vote and wetness ordinarily would be too low, and the partial correlation found between Smith's vote and Catholicism would be too high. Granted, however, that the indexes are measuring something reliably, ultimate interpretation depends on what meaning is given to the indexes, that is, on their validity. The index of Catholicism taken was the percentage of Catholics in the county. Since the partial correlation was positive, it appeared that an

4. E. R. Groves and W. F. Ogburn, *American Marriage and Family Relationships*, Chapter XVI.

5. W. F. Ogburn and Nell S. Talbot, "A Measurement of the Factors in the Presidential Election of 1928," *Social Forces*, VIII, 175-83.

increase in the percentage of Catholics from county to county, other factors being equal, was associated with an increase in the percentage of votes received by Smith from county to county. But is a large percentage of Catholics in a county an index of pro-Catholic sentiment and a small percentage of Catholics an index of anti-Catholic sentiment? Is it not quite possible, at least in the northern states, that there is as strong anti-Catholic sentiment in some counties in which Catholics and non-Catholics are in equal numbers and in conscious competition, as in some other countries which have few Catholics? The danger lies in the necessity for succinct summary—a reader, if not an author, is apt to read too much into the figures.

Another aspect of the problem just discussed is the varying reliability or validity of a particular index in different segments of a single study. Henry D. Sheldon, Jr., in a study of juvenile delinquency in Cleveland . . .[6] found that unemployment was a useful index of economic conditions in certain census tracts of the city but was quite unsatisfactory in other tracts, while other single economic indexes, such as median rental, percentage of dwellings renting for a given figure or less, dependency, or home ownership, were equally spotted in the generality of their applicability.

Still another situation is interesting—that in which a variable is inaccurately measured, but in which the error may be considered constant. Sanford Winston studied the relationship between illiteracy and several other social factors.[7] Now, if it is true that the number of illiterates omitted bore a constant proportion to the number enumerated, the correlation coefficients will be unaltered by the error. But this is not true with the regression equation. Winston projected his regression plane to estimate under what conditions illiteracy might be expected to reach zero. Such a projection is a brave tour de force under any circumstances, but the fact, if true, that the size of the error in reporting illiteracy is in constant proportion to the number enumerated would likely alter his conclusion. On the other hand, if, as is more likely, the number of illiterates omitted is not in constant proportion to the number enumerated, the partial correlation coefficients themselves are subject to error—in this case, they are possibly too low.

2. *Usually, sociological studies fall considerably short of explaining all the variation in the factor for which we are trying to account.* This would not introduce serious difficulties if we could assume that the unmeasured factors were not associated with the independent variables that we have measured. Usually, we cannot assume this. Ogburn and Talbot, in studying Smith's vote, were, of course, unable to measure the importance of Hoover's promise to abolish poverty and put a chicken in every pot. It is quite possible that the relative importance of wetness as an issue might have been considerably altered in their final results if an index of the effect of the prosperity issue could have been devised. Another example: In studying juvenile delinquency,

6. See also the example given in this chapter on pages 263-264.
7. Sanford Winston, *Illiteracy in the United States.*

by finding the relationship between various factors and delinquency in census tracts, it is almost impossible to measure the role of what Thrasher calls "interstitial areas," near railroad yards, coal dumps, etc., where boys' gangs are thought to thrive. If it were possible to measure the "interstitiality" of an area, we might considerably lower the partial correlation between delinquency and the percentage of foreign-born and Negroes, since these "interstitial" areas are thought to have a considerable percentage of foreign-born and Negroes.

If we cannot get measures of missing factors, what is the way out? The writer sees no way out at present, except watchful caution in interpreting results. But suppose we can get measures of several additional factors? We are likely to find ourselves with a problem requiring the correlation of a half a dozen factors, and it is an open question whether the resulting complication is not too much for us. Some studies in rural sociology and economics have used as high as fourteen or fifteen variables. One is inclined to suspect that this is verging toward absurdity. Are our minds big enough to grasp the significance of so many intricate interrelations?

3. *Partial correlation is likely to "partial out" elements in such a way as to remove much of the commonly understood meaning from a particular index.* In the study of Smith's vote, what is the meaning of an index of urbanization (i.e., percentage of people in a county who live in cities) when indexes of wetness, Catholicism, foreign-born, etc., are "held constant?" Ogburn and Talbot's study found a slight negative relationship in this case; that is, the larger the percentage urban in a county, the smaller Smith's share in the vote, other factors constant. At first glance, this seems incredible, since one of the issues in the campaign was supposed to be Main Street versus the Sidewalks of New York. But the correlation simply means that if all counties had the same indexes of wetness, Catholicism, foreign-born, etc., Smith would have received slightly less support in the counties with a comparatively large urban population than in counties with a comparatively small urban population. It does not mean that "urbanization," as the term is commonly understood, and Smith's vote were negatively associated. The term "urbanization" as commonly understood involved something more than the mere proportion of people in a county living in a city; it involves a complex of sociological and psychological factors, including some of the very elements which are partialed out by indexes of wetness, Catholicism, and foreign-born. In other words, the simple correlation between Smith's vote and percentage urban actually may show the relationship between Smith's vote and so-called urbanization more adequately than does the partial correlation. The partial correlation may have been valid, but it is easy for the reader to read "urbanization" into these findings, in spite of the authors' cautions.

A special problem arises when it is desired to use two measures of the same factor in a partial correlation analysis. Suppose that one has available two indexes of economic status in census tracts of a city, neither of which is ideal, but some combination of which is better than the use of either index to the exclusion of the other. If one measures the relationship between juvenile delinquency, let us say, and one index of economic status, holding "constant" the percentage of foreign-born and Negroes and the other economic index, such a partial correlation is practically devoid of meaning. A procedure is needed for measuring the combined correlation between juvenile delinquency and the two economic indexes, holding percentage of foreign-born and Negro constant. The writer has proposed a simple device that, it is hoped, may help to accomplish this result.[8]

4. *Even if the indexes are reliable and valid throughout the range of the data, a rectilinear correlation system may obscure important variations in relationship in different regions of the data.* Suppose that we divide the census tracts of a city into four groups, according to the percentage of home ownership. We may find that within Groups I and II a partial correlation between juvenile delinquency and the percentage of foreign-born and Negroes is high, holding the other factors constant, while within Groups III and IV the partial correlation may be low. This difference may be very important; yet it would be averaged out if all the data were analyzed in a single correlation scheme. Indeed, one suspects that a difference of this kind is likely to be the rule rather than the exception in sociological studies. The reason for this suspicion is that so many sociological scatter diagrams are nonlinear. The nonlinearity frequently may be handled conveniently by using logarithms, but often a more illuminating attack is to break the data into subgroups and analyze each subgroup separately by a partial correlation scheme if the data are sufficiently numerous, as they usually are not.

5. *Lastly, there is as yet no agreement on how to evaluate the so-called "relative importance" of two factors in their net association with the dependent variable.* It is largely a matter of defining "relative importance." Perhaps, as a matter of common sense, we are interested in relative importance in somewhat the same way as is the grain speculator, who is considering wheat futures and wants to know whether to give more weight to a drought in Kansas in one month than in another month. Unfortunately, among the various correlational procedures for evaluating relative importance, there is none that has a simple meaning readily communicable to the lay reader if defined with mathematical exactness. We can speak precisely and not be understood by our general audience, or we can speak inexactly, with the result that another sociologist can make a different set of conclusions based on apparently the same assumptions.

Suppose that the partial correlation between juvenile delinquency and percentage of foreign-born and Negroes is 0.20, while that between juvenile

8. "A Coefficient of Combined Partial Correlation with an Example from Sociological Data," *Journal of the American Statistical Association*, March, 1934. (See also Section A of this chapter.)

delinquency and economic status is 0.40. Now we are really interested in accounting for the variability in delinquency—that is, we want to know why some areas have so many juvenile delinquents and why some have so few. If we could account for all of the net variability in juvenile delinquency by our knowledge of foreign-born and Negroes, holding economic status "constant," our partial correlation would be unity. However, we can account for only a part of the net variability this way. The question is: What proportion can we account for, and how does this compare with the proportion that we can account for by our knowledge of economic status, holding foreign-born and Negroes constant?

We can make a variety of answers, depending, first, on how we choose to measure the variability. If we measure the variability by the variance, the average squared deviations from the mean, the square of a partial correlation coefficient has been interpreted as telling what proportion of the net variance in juvenile delinquency is accounted for by one factor, holding another factor constant. By comparing the squares of the two partial correlation coefficients, 0.20 and 0.40, we say that their relative importance is as 0.04 to 0.16 and that one factor is four times as important as the other. But we have based this conclusion on the arbitrary choice of the variance as the measure of variability. It is perhaps just as reasonable to use, instead, the standard deviation. However, if we use the standard deviation as a basis, we have at least two choices.

1. If r^2 is the proportion of the net variance of Y associated with X, then there is some justification for saying that r is the proportion of the net standard deviation of Y associated with X. We now compare 0.20 and 0.40 and have one factor only twice as important as the other.

2. If r^2 is the proportion of the net variance of Y associated with X, then $1 - r^2$ is the proportion *not* associated with X. It follows that $(1 - r^2)^{\frac{1}{2}}$ is the proportion of the net standard deviation of Y not associated with X. Now note: If $(1 - r^2)^{\frac{1}{2}}$ is the proportion of the net standard deviation of Y which is not associated with X, the proportion which is associated with X must be $1 - (1 - r^2)^{\frac{1}{2}}$. If we adopt this as our measure of importance, we find that one factor is now 4.1 times as important as another.

A modification of these approaches is to compute the value β^2, which is the square of the partial regression coefficient when all the variables are expressed in standard deviation units. β^2 is taken as the measure of the so-called importance of the factor considered, and a comparison of the two values of β^2 provides a measure of relative importance. Instead of using β^2, however, there is some justification for preferring a value based on the product $\beta \times r$, where r is the simple correlation coefficient between the dependent variable and independent variable considered. We shall get a different numerical result, depending on the procedure used.

Still another approach to an evaluation of the relative importance of two factors is by considering not variability, but simply slope itself. The comparison may be of two values of b, the partial regression coefficient, if the units are strictly comparable, or else of the two values of β, the transformed b.

The point of our foregoing illustrations is that the interpretation that we make as to the relative importance of two factors depends entirely on which of these seven methods (there are still others) we select for measuring the importance. Some statisticians prefer one device, some prefer another; and the writer knows at least one mathematical statistician who believes that all the attempts to compare the relative importance of two factors are fallacious. Perhaps, indeed, the problem itself is a false lead. The writer knows nothing about chemistry, but doubts whether a chemist would see any point to the question: Which is more important in forming water—oxygen or hydrogen? The fact that there are two parts hydrogen to one part oxygen hardly can mean that hydrogen is twice as important. Yet, somehow, one still has the feeling that the wheat speculator in weighing the relative importance of drought in two different months, or the sociologist, in trying to discover whether a raising of economic status is ultimately more important than a reduction of foreign-born in coping with juvenile delinquency, is asking a legitimate question.

Many other important problems might be raised. Particularly, the writer would like to call attention to difficulties in evaluating the sampling errors when correlation data used are areas contiguous in space or points successive in time. Nothing has been said as to the variety of results obtained depending on the size of area when the study has a geographical base. Nor has anything been said here about the treatment of qualitative factors.

This discussion has emphasized difficulties in the application of partial correlation in sociology and necessarily has skimped consideration of the positive values of the method. Indeed, there is yet to be demonstrated an adequate substitute when data are limited. To older and wiser heads some of the apparent difficulties discussed may not be difficulties at all. We who are less experienced statisticians will earnestly appreciate the guidance that can be given in helping us to make the practical application of partial correlation in sociology as logically and esthetically satisfying as the beautiful mathematical concept itself.

C. Reliability Coefficients in a Correlation Matrix

Given s fallible tests $t_1\ t_2, \cdots, t_s$, to express the conventional correlation determinant

$$\Delta = \begin{vmatrix} 1 & r_{t_1 t_2} & \cdots & r_{t_1 t_s} \\ r_{t_1 t_2} & 1 & \cdots & r_{t_2 t_s} \\ \cdot & \cdot & \cdot & \cdot \\ r_{t_1 t_s} & r_{t_2 t_s} & \cdots & 1 \end{vmatrix} \tag{1}$$

"Reliability Coefficients in a Correlation Matrix," *Psychometrika*, 1 (June, 1936), pp. 17-20.

in terms of the intercorrelations between parallel forms comprising each test t_i. Write

$$t_1 = z_{1_1} + z_{1_2} + \cdots + z_{1_k} + \cdots + z_{1_{m_1}}$$
$$t_2 = z_{2_1} + z_{2_2} + \cdots + z_{2_k} + \cdots + z_{2_{m_2}}$$
$$\cdot \quad \vdots \quad \cdot \quad \cdot \quad \cdot \quad \cdot \quad \cdot \quad \cdot \quad \cdot \quad \cdot \quad \cdot \quad \cdot$$
$$t_i = z_{i_1} + z_{i_2} + \cdots + z_{i_k} + \cdots + z_{i_{m_i}}$$
$$\cdot \quad \cdot \quad \cdot \quad \cdot \quad \cdot \quad \cdot \quad \cdot \quad \cdot \quad \cdot \quad \cdot \quad \cdot \quad \cdot$$
$$t_s = z_{s_1} + z_{s_2} + \cdots + z_{s_k} + \cdots + z_{s_{m_s}}$$

where each z_{i_k} is one of m_i parallel forms comprising test t_i and is expressed in standard measure, that is,

$$z_{i_k} = (X_{i_k} - \bar{X}_{i_k})/\sigma_{i_k}$$

in which X_{i_k} is a raw score and $\bar{X}_{i_k}$ and σ_{i_k} are the mean and standard deviation, respectively, of the raw scores. Since

$$\sigma^2{}_{z_{i_k}} = 1, \quad \sigma^2{}_{t_i} = m_i + 2(r_{i_1 i_2} + r_{i_1 i_3} \cdots + r_{i_{m_i-1} i_{m_i}})$$
$$= m_i[1 + (m_i - 1)\bar{r}_{ii}]$$

where

$$\bar{r}_{ii} = 2(r_{i_1 i_2} + r_{i_1 i_3} + \cdots + r_{i_{m_i-1} i_{m_i}})/m_i(m_i - 1)$$

is the average of the $m \, (m-1)/2$ reliability coefficients.

Write $r_{t_i t_j} = \Sigma \, t_i t_j / n \, \sigma_{t_i} \, \sigma_{t_j}$, where n is the number of individuals taking the tests. Since $\Sigma \, z_{i_k} z_{j_k}/n = r_{i_k j_k}$,

$$\Sigma \, t_i t_j/n = r_{i_1 j_1} + r_{i_1 j_2} + \cdots + r_{i_i j_{m_j}} + \cdots + r_{i_{m_i} j_1} + r_{i_{m_i} j_2} + \cdots + r_{i_{m_i} j_{m_j}}$$
$$= m_i m_j \bar{r}_{ij}$$

where $\bar{r}_{ij}$ is the average of the $m_i m_j$ intercorrelations. We then have [9]

$$r_{t_i t_j} = \frac{m_i m_j \bar{r}_{ij}}{\{m_i m_j[1 + (m_i - 1)\bar{r}_{ii}] [1 + (m_j - 1)\bar{r}_{jj}]\}^{\frac{1}{2}}}$$

$$= \frac{\bar{r}_{ij}}{\left\{\left[\dfrac{1 + (m_i - 1)\bar{r}_{ii}}{m_i}\right]\left[\dfrac{1 + (m_j - 1)\bar{r}_{jj}}{m_j}\right]\right\}^{\frac{1}{2}}}$$

$$= \frac{\bar{r}_{ij}}{(d_{ii} d_{jj})^{\frac{1}{2}}} \tag{2}$$

where $d_{ii} = [1 + (m_i - 1)\bar{r}_{ii}]/m_i$

9. Equation 2 is identical, though it is expressed in different notations, to Equation 147 in Truman L. Kelley, *Statistical Method*, page 197. It is assumed that each parallel form comprised in t has unit weight. If the m_i forms are assigned varying weights w_k ($k = 1, 2, \ldots, m_i$), Kelley's Equation 149, page 198, may be used.

Substituting Equation 2 in Equation 1, we have

$$\Delta = \begin{vmatrix} 1 & \dfrac{\bar{r}_{12}}{(d_{11}\,d_{22})^{\frac{1}{2}}} & \cdots & \dfrac{\bar{r}_{1s}}{(d_{11}\,d_{ss})^{\frac{1}{2}}} \\ \dfrac{\bar{r}_{12}}{(d_{11}\,d_{22})^{\frac{1}{2}}} & 1 & \cdots & \dfrac{\bar{r}_{2s}}{(d_{22}\,d_{ss})^{\frac{1}{2}}} \\ \cdot & \cdot & \cdots & \cdot \\ \dfrac{\bar{r}_{1s}}{(d_{11}\,d_{ss})^{\frac{1}{2}}} & \dfrac{\bar{r}_{2s}}{(d_{22}\,d_{ss})^{\frac{1}{2}}} & \cdots & 1 \end{vmatrix} \tag{3}$$

$\Delta = \Delta'/d_{11}\,d_{22}\,\cdots\,d_{ss}$,

where

$$\Delta' = \begin{vmatrix} d_{11} & \bar{r}_{12} & \cdots & \bar{r}_{1s} \\ \bar{r}_{12} & d_{22} & \cdots & \bar{r}_{2s} \\ \cdot & \cdot & \cdots & \cdot \\ \bar{r}_{1s} & \bar{r}_{2s} & \cdots & d_{ss} \end{vmatrix} \tag{4}$$

while any $(s-1)$-rowed minor of Δ,

$$\Delta_{ij} = \frac{(d_{ii}\,d_{jj})^{\frac{1}{2}}}{d_{11}\,d_{22}\,\cdots\,d_{ss}}\,\Delta'_{ij}$$

where Δ'_{ij} is the corresponding minor of Δ'.

As all values $r_{ii} \to 1$ and as all values $r_{ij} \to r_{i_k j_k}$, the correlation between any two parallel forms in t_i and t_j, Equations 3 and 4 approach the form

$$\Delta = \begin{vmatrix} 1 & r_{12} & \cdots & r_{1s} \\ r_{12} & 1 & \cdots & r_{2s} \\ \cdot & \cdot & \cdots & \cdot \\ r_{1s} & r_{2s} & \cdots & 1 \end{vmatrix}$$

As m_i, the number of parallel forms of the ith test, $m_i \to \infty$ (so that $1/m \to 0$),

$$d_{ii} = \left[\frac{1}{m_i} + \left(1 - \frac{1}{m_i}\right)\bar{r}_{ii}\right] \to \bar{r}_{ii}$$

whence from Equation 2

$$r_{t_i t_j} \to \frac{\bar{r}_{ij}}{(\bar{r}_{ii}\,\bar{r}_{jj})^{\frac{1}{2}}}$$

a form of the correlation between measures of the ith and jth tests "corrected for attenuation," permitting us to write, from Equation 4

$$\Delta = \Delta''/\bar{r}_{11}\,\bar{r}_{22}\,\cdots\,\bar{r}_{ss} \tag{5}$$

where

$$\Delta'' = \begin{vmatrix} \bar{r}_{11} & \bar{r}_{12} & \cdots & \bar{r}_{1s} \\ \bar{r}_{12} & \bar{r}_{22} & \cdots & \bar{r}_{2s} \\ \cdot & \cdot & \cdots & \cdot \\ \bar{r}_{1s} & \bar{r}_{2s} & \cdots & \bar{r}_{ss} \end{vmatrix}$$

It is thought that these relationships may help to make explicit some of the assumptions implicit in the use of test measures in correlation analysis, as well as to provide a practical technique for estimating the probable effects on final correlation results of improving a part or all of the tests by including additional parallel forms.[10]

Examples of Derived Measures When s = 3. From Equation 4, when $s = 3$, we have

$$r_{t_1 t_2 \cdot t_3} = \frac{\Delta_{12}}{(\Delta_{22}\,\Delta_{11})^{\frac{1}{2}}} = \frac{\Delta'_{12}}{(\Delta'_{22}\,\Delta'_{11})^{\frac{1}{2}}} = \frac{\bar{r}_{12}\,d_{33} - \bar{r}_{13}\,\bar{r}_{23}}{[(d_{11}\,d_{22} - \bar{r}^2_{13})\,(d_{22}\,d_{33} - \bar{r}^2_{23})]^{\frac{1}{2}}} \tag{6}$$

$$\beta_{t_1 t_2 \cdot t_3} = \frac{\Delta_{12}}{\Delta_{11}} = \frac{\Delta'_{12}}{\Delta'_{11}}\left(\frac{d_{22}}{d_{11}}\right)^{\frac{1}{2}} = \frac{\bar{r}_{12}\,d_{33} - \bar{r}_{13}\,\bar{r}_{23}}{d_{22}\,d_{33} - \bar{r}^2_{23}}\left(\frac{d_{22}}{d_{11}}\right)^{\frac{1}{2}} \tag{7}$$

$$R^2_{t_1 \cdot t_2 t_3} = 1 - \frac{\Delta}{\Delta_{11}} = 1 - \frac{\Delta'}{\Delta'_{11}\,d_{11}} = \frac{\bar{r}^2_{12}\,d_{33} + \bar{r}^2_{13}\,d_{22} - 2\bar{r}_{13}\,\bar{r}_{13}\,\bar{r}_{23}}{d_{11}\,(d_{22}\,d_{23} - \bar{r}^2_{23})} \tag{8}$$

Equations such as these may prove valuable not only in cases where d_{ii} and $\bar{r}_{ij}$ are known, but also in cases where it is desired to insert various guessed values of d_{ii} and $\bar{r}_{ij}$. As m_1, m_2, and m_3, the number of parallel forms, approach ∞, $d_{ii} \to \bar{r}_{ii}$, from Equation 5, permitting us to rewrite Equation 6, for example, as

$$r_{t_1 t_2 \cdot t_3} = \frac{\bar{r}_{12}\,\bar{r}_{33} - \bar{r}_{13}\,\bar{r}_{23}}{[(\bar{r}_{11}\,\bar{r}_{33} - \bar{r}^2_{13})\,(\bar{r}_{22}\,\bar{r}_{33} - \bar{r}^2_{23})]^{\frac{1}{2}}} \tag{9}$$

a useful form provided that we feel reasonably safe in our estimates of $\bar{r}_{ii}$ and $\bar{r}_{ij}$.

10. This paper presents a further generalization of results obtained by setting each $t_i = s_i + s'_i$, as reported by the writer in "Evaluating the Effect of Inadequately Measured Variables in Partial Correlation Analysis," *Journal of the American Statistical Association,* June, 1936. Applications given in this paper make use of sociological and economic data, though it would be very easy to find examples in the psychological field.

14

□ ⊠ □ □ □ *The H-Scale*

Among the various technical ideas that the author has had a hand in developing, few seem to have been used more widely than that which is called the H-technique, a simple and practical method for greatly improving cumulative scales. The book *Measurement and Prediction* had introduced two quite different approaches to measurement, one the Guttman scalogram approach and the other the Lazarsfeld latent-structure approach. Practical difficulties in achieving desired levels of accuracy led in the following years to a good deal of frustration. The H-technique, which is really quite a simple-minded idea, seems to remove some of the most serious practical disabilities in achieving a Guttman scale that has high reproducibility and reliability. It will be seen in the theoretical illustration how useful the Lazarsfeld latent-structure method proved to be in showing why the H-technique could be expected to render the service it does.

A Technique for Improving Cumulative Scales

This paper introduces a simple new procedure for obtaining a cumulative-type scale which should have properties of high reproducibility, high test-retest reliability, and high stability from sample to sample in rank order of

"A Technique for Improving Cumulative Scales," by Samuel A. Stouffer, Edgar F. Borgatta, David G. Hays, and Andrew F. Henry, *Public Opinion Quarterly*, 16 (Summer, 1952), pp. 273-291.

This research, carried out at the Harvard Laboratory of Social Relations, was supported in part by the United States Air Force under Contract AF33 (038)-12782 monitored by

cutting points. Moreover, none of these properties need be obtained at the cost of restricting the scale to content of too narrowly limited specificity or to questions with too uniform a format. We shall call the new procedure the H-technique.

Actually, the H-technique produces a Guttman scale or a Lazarsfeld latent-distance scale with one important modification. Instead of using only one item to determine a given cutting point on the scale, as in the conventional procedure, the H-scale uses two or more items.

The basic idea of the cumulative scale is that all items have a structure such that a person who answers "Yes" to any item to which p proportion of respondents answers "Yes" will tend to answer "Yes" to all other items to which larger than p proportion of the respondents answer "Yes."[1] In the case of a perfect Guttman m-item scale, respondents can be ordered without error into $m + 1$ classes. Each item serves to define the limits of one class or rank group.

In practice, however, perfect Guttman scales are not likely to occur. There will be errors in response to any particular item. Hence, some of the respondents will fall into nonscale types—that is, they will say "No" to one or more items that are more frequently approved than an item to which they say "Yes." How many errors are permissible before the hypothesis of scalability of a set of items is rejected is an arbitrary matter. Guttman sets a minimum standard of 90 per cent "reproducibility"—that is, at least nine times out of ten, on the average, if we know a respondent's rank, we should be correct in specifying his response to any particular item. There are further requirements: (a) that the errors thus made with respect to any single item must not exceed the number of correct calls of either positive or negative response, whichever are fewer and (b) that the errors be at random, such that not too many individual respondents have identical scale patterns. Hundreds of scales have been constructed which approximate these minimum standards, but sometimes these standards have been attained under less than happy circumstances.

Most commonly, perhaps, the errors have been held down by keeping the number of items few—say four or five—and the fraction used in the scale of all the information initially available may be very small. A questionnaire may contain a dozen items, each allowing as many as four or five possible

---

the Human Resources Research Institute. Permission is granted for reproduction, translation, publication, and disposal in whole and in part by or for the United States Government.

1. For general orientation in cumulative scales, see Samuel A. Stouffer, *et al.*, *Measurement and Prediction*, Princeton University Press, 1950. Chapter 1 by Stouffer gives an overview of the problems; Chapters 2 to 9 by Louis Guttman and Edward A. Suchman deal with Guttman scale theory; Chapters 10 and 11 by Paul F. Lazarsfeld deal with the theory of latent structures.

categories of response. Item analysis may show that most or all of these items are correlated with the total score, yet it may be possible to use only a few of these items in a single scale. Furthermore, scales ordinarily use only dichotomous responses; trichotomies have been used, but the necessary conditions are rarely met. Hence, information is lost in two ways—through elimination of items and consolidation of responses.

If out of a dozen or so initial questions only four or five form a scale, there is, as Guttman and others have warned, great risk of overcapitalization on chance unless the scale is thoroughly replicated. Even more serious, perhaps, is the possibility that the four or five items hold together merely because they have something highly specific in common—either in phrasing of content or in format—and lack the generality of meaning which the author has been seeking. This is one of the more serious charges directed at conventional Guttman scaling.

These considerations have led to an insistence on the desirability of requiring at least ten or a dozen items to hang together in an initial scale—even if, once scalability is established, a smaller number of items, perhaps only four or five, may be selected for practical eventual use in applying the scale.

But a ten- or twelve-item cumulative-type scale is easier to talk about than to accomplish. As we increase the number of items and, as almost always happens, are confronted with pairs of triplets of items with about the same frequency of favorable response, we almost invariably increase the number of nonscale types. With a four-item scale that has a reproducibility of 0.90, as many as 40 per cent of the respondents may be nonscale types. With a ten-item scale that has a reproducibility of 0.90, it is possible for nearly 90 per cent of the respondents to be nonscale types—that is, to have an error on at least one item. Thus, we have the somewhat paradoxical situation that increasing the number of items may strengthen our confidence in the scalability of an area under consideration and in the generality of the dimension that the scale is defining, at the same time that it creates more nonscale types and thus introduces more ambiguity in ordering respondents. And the closer some of the original items are to each other in frequency, the less likely that the rank order of items will remain invariant from sample to sample.

Consider two items with 50 per cent and 55 per cent favorable, respectively. Suppose the fourfold table from the items looks as follows:

		ITEM 2		
		Unfavorable	Favorable	
	Favorable	5	45	50
ITEM 1				
	Unfavorable	40	10	50
		45	55	100

There are only five apparent errors (in the upper left-hand corner). But, unless we have a very large sample, we can by no means be confident that in replications Item 2 will continue to have a larger favorable frequency than will Item 1.[2] Consequently, scale patterns classified as correct in one sample would be classified as incorrect in another.

The obvious remedy, namely, to use a very large initial sample in determining the scale types, is not always feasible and is no panacea. It is quite possible that a particular item will have a special significance for some segment of the population not adequately covered in the initial sample and hence will have a larger or smaller frequency through such a nonchance factor. Hence, reversals are not at all unlikely, even if the items are spaced relatively far apart.

Only by spacing the cutting points of our scale quite widely can we guard against reversals. This limits us to a four- or five-item scale. It may indeed be that a small number of rank groups is sufficient for the practical task of this particular scale in ordering individuals. If so, is there some way by which we can utilize more of the available information and can build greater precision into the cutting points than is usually feasible if each cutting point depends on the responses to one item alone?

This is the task of the H-technique. Instead of using one item to determine a given cutting point, we use two, three, or even more. In effect, what we are doing is to convert the responses to two or more observed items into a response to a "new" item, which we call a *contrived* item.

Suppose that the following three observed items have approximately the same frequencies of "Yes, often" responses:

1. Do you have sick headaches? Yes, often; Yes, sometimes; No.
2. Do you have trouble sleeping? Yes, often; Yes, sometimes; No.
3. Do you have backaches? Yes, often; Yes, sometimes; No.

Now, provided further, that each of these items at the cutting point used satisfies the condition of correlating with a provisional scale based on all observed items, we combine the responses to the three into a new contrived item.

There are at least two ways of scoring this new contrived item. If an odd number of items is used, such as three as in the present example, an individual can be arbitrarily scored as positive if he answers "Yes, often" to the majority of questions. Or, the number of simultaneous "Yes, often" responses to the three items can be recorded and the "best" cutting point of the contrived item determined, in conjunction with other contrived items, by the conventional Guttman procedures.

Here we have treated "Yes, often" as a positive response and others as negative. We might, however, have treated "Yes, sometimes" as a positive

2. This is easily seen, for example, by testing a null hypothesis as to the differences between the frequencies favorable in the two items. We have $x^2 = (10 - 5 - 1)^2/15 = 1.1$, with one degree of freedom.

response also and could proceed exactly as above if the three items had about the same positive frequency by this definition and if at this cutting point there was a satisfactory correlation with a provisional scale.

Actually, it might be that the "Yes, often" response to one item had about the same frequency as the "Yes, often" plus the "Yes, sometimes" responses to the other items. Then these three items, in spite of different cutting points, could be converted into a contrived item.

Furthermore, Item 1, cut at "Very often," might be used with Items 2 and 3, and at the same time Item 1, cut at "Very often" plus "Sometimes," might be used over again with two other items. Thus, different response categories of the same item may contribute to more than one contrived item. This tends to maximize the information obtainable from a single set of observed items each of which has multiple response categories.

A THEORETICAL ILLUSTRATION OF THE ADVANTAGES
OF THE H-TECHNIQUE

The perfect Guttman scale is a limiting case of the Lazarsfeld latent-distance model that postulates that respondents are ordered into latent classes. The Lazarsfeld model makes it possible to compute the probability that a particular response pattern to individual questions will be given by a member of a given latent class. (In the perfect Guttman case these probabilities are either unity or zero.)

Let us now examine a special case of five latent classes equally populated. Let us assume that we have four observed items and that a favorable response to a given item has a probability of occurrence from members of a given latent class according to the schedule that follows:

| | ITEM | | | |
Latent class	1	2	3	4
I	0.9	0.9	0.9	0.9
II	0.1	0.9	0.9	0.9
III	0.1	0.1	0.9	0.9
IV	0.1	0.1	0.1	0.9
V	0.1	0.1	0.1	0.1

For example, the probability that Item 3 will be endorsed by a member of Latent Class III is 0.9; the probability that it will be endorsed by a member of Latent Class IV is 0.1.

Consider now a particular response pattern to the four items simultaneously: Item 1+, Item 2−, Item 3+, and Item 4+. The probability that this response pattern $+ - + +$ would be produced by a member of Latent Class I is $0.9 \times 0.1 \times 0.9 \times 0.9 = 0.0729$. The probability that it would be produced by a member of Latent Class II is $0.1 \times 0.1 \times 0.9 \times 0.9 = 0.0081$.

Or take response pattern $- - + +$. The probability that it would be pro-

Table 14-1. Probability That Response Patterns Will Be Given by Members of the Classes, and Recruitment

RESPONSE PATTERNS	LATENT CLASS					SUM	PROPORTION OF ALL CASES WITHIN A SPECIFIED RESPONSE PATTERN (SUM ÷ 5)
	I	II	III	IV	V		
++++	0.6561	0.0729	0.0081	0.0009	0.0001	0.7381	0.14762
+++−	0.0729	0.0081	0.0009	0.0001	0.0009	0.0829	0.01658
++−+	0.0729	0.0081	0.0009	0.0081	0.0009	0.0909	0.01818
+−++	0.0729	0.0081	0.0729	0.0081	0.0009	0.1629	0.03258
−+++	0.0729	0.6561	0.0729	0.0081	0.0009	0.8109	0.16218
−++−	0.0081	0.0729	0.0081	0.0009	0.0081	0.0981	0.01962
−+−+	0.0081	0.0729	0.0081	0.0729	0.0081	0.1701	0.03402
−−++	0.0081	0.0729	0.6561	0.0729	0.0081	0.8181	0.16362
−−−+	0.0009	0.0081	0.0729	0.6561	0.0729	0.8109	0.16218
−−+−	0.0009	0.0081	0.0729	0.0081	0.0729	0.1629	0.03258
+−−+	0.0081	0.0009	0.0081	0.0729	0.0081	0.0981	0.01962
−−−−	0.0001	0.0009	0.0081	0.0729	0.6561	0.7381	0.14762
−+−−	0.0009	0.0081	0.0009	0.0081	0.0729	0.0909	0.01818
+−−−	0.0009	0.0001	0.0009	0.0081	0.0729	0.0829	0.01658
++−−	0.0081	0.0009	0.0001	0.0009	0.0081	0.0181	0.00362
+−+−	0.0081	0.0009	0.0081	0.0009	0.0081	0.0261	0.00522
Σ	1.0000	1.0000	1.0000	1.0000	1.0000	5.0000	1.00000

duced by a member of Latent Class III is $0.9 \times 0.9 \times 0.9 \times 0.9 = 0.6561$, while the probability that it would be produced by a member of Latent Class I is $0.1 \times 0.1 \times 0.9 \times 0.9 = 0.0081$.

There are sixteen response patterns in all, and the probability that each will be given by a member of a given latent class is shown in Table 14-1. The following observations may be made from Table 14-1:

1. The theoretical probability that members of each latent class will fall into a unique perfect scale type $(+ + + +, \ − + + +, \ − − + +, \ − − − +,$ or $− − − −)$ is 0.6561.

2. The proportion of all cases falling into perfect scale types, irrespective of latent class from which recruited is found, from the right-hand column of Table 14-1, to be $0.14762 + 0.16218 + 0.16362 + 0.16218 + 0.14762 = 0.78322$. Hence, the proportion of nonscale types is $1 − 0.78322 = 0.21678$.

3. In computing Guttman reproducibility, two nonscale types $(+ + − −$ and $+ − + −)$ must be counted twice. The proportion of cases in these types is $0.00362 + 0.00522 = 0.00884$. The sum $0.21678 + 0.00884 = 0.22562$. The Guttman reproducibility coefficient is $1 − 0.22562/4 = 0.94360$.

4. For ranking respondents by assigning nonscale types to the nearest perfect scale type, Table 14-1 is helpful. It can be used in a number of ways. A simple way is to allocate the nonscale type to the perfect scale type associated with the latent class that has the greatest probability of producing this nonscale type. For example, in Table 14-1, the type $+ + + −$ would be assigned

to Latent Class I. There are five nonscale types whose assignment would be ambiguous by this method $(+ - + +, - + - +, - - + -, + + - -,$ and $+ - + -)$, constituting $0.03258 + 0.03402 + 0.03258 + 0.00362 + 0.00522 = 0.10802$ of all the cases.

Now, let us examine the gains achieved when the H-technique is used. Instead of using one item to determine a particular cutting point, we shall use three items, each with the same theoretical proportion "positive" and

Table 14-2. Probability That Response Patterns Will Be Given by Members of the Classes, and Recruitment (Triplets)

RESPONSE PATTERNS	LATENT CLASS					SUM	PROPORTION OF ALL RESPONDENTS WITH SPECIFIED RESPONSE PATTERNS (SUM ÷ 5)
	II	III	IV	V			
++++	0.892617	0.025713	0.000741	0.000021	0.000001	0.919093	0.183819
+++−	0.025713	0.000741	0.000021	0.000001	0.000021	0.026497	0.005299
++−+	0.025713	0.000741	0.000021	0.000741	0.000021	0.027237	0.005447
+−++	0.025713	0.000741	0.025713	0.000741	0.000021	0.052713	0.010586
−+++	0.025713	0.892617	0.025713	0.000741	0.000021	0.944805	0.188961
−++−	0.000741	0.025713	0.000741	0.000021	0.000741	0.027957	0.005591
−+−+	0.000741	0.025713	0.000741	0.025713	0.000741	0.053649	0.010730
−−++	0.000741	0.025713	0.892617	0.025713	0.000741	0.945525	0.189105
−−−+	0.000021	0.000741	0.025713	0.892617	0.025713	0.944805	0.188961
−−+−	0.000021	0.000741	0.025713	0.000741	0.025713	0.052929	0.010586
+−−+	0.000741	0.000021	0.000741	0.025713	0.000741	0.027957	0.005591
−−−−	0.000001	0.000021	0.000741	0.025713	0.892617	0.919093	0.183819
−+−−	0.000021	0.000741	0.000021	0.000741	0.025713	0.027237	0.005447
+−−−	0.000021	0.000001	0.000021	0.000741	0.025713	0.026497	0.005299
++−−	0.000741	0.000021	0.000001	0.000021	0.000741	0.001525	0.000305
+−+−	0.000741	0.000021	0.000741	0.000021	0.000741	0.002265	0.000453
Σ	1.000000	1.000000	1.000000	1.000000	1.000000	5.000000	1.000000

each with the same probability of "error" as the single item used initially, namely, 10 per cent. We shall assume the errors uncorrelated. Hence, the new contrived item will have four categories, with probabilities as follows:

3 responses without error	$0.9 \times 0.9 \times 0.9 = 0.729$
2 responses without error, 1 with error	$3 \times 0.9 \times 0.9 \times 0.1 = 0.243$
1 response without error, 2 with error	$3 \times 0.9 \times 0.1 \times 0.1 = 0.027$
0 response without error	$0.1 \times 0.1 \times 0.1 = 0.001$
	$\overline{1.000}$

If we decide to call persons who make either two or three positive responses as positive on our contrived item, the latter will have an "error" term of only 0.028, a considerable improvement over our initial error term of 0.1. Here lies the fundamental basis of the theoretical advantage of the new contrived item.

How the advantage actually works out is shown by Table 14-2, which is based on four contrived items (each in turn derived from triplets) with an error of 0.028. The table was computed precisely in the same manner as Table 14-1 except that the error term is 0.028 throughout instead of 0.1.

We can place side by side in Table 14-3 the salient comparisons from the two tables.

Table 14-3

	Conventional Technique Using Four Individual Items	H-Technique: Using Four Contrived Items, Each Based on Triplets of Individual Items
1. Probability that members of each latent class will fall into a unique perfect scale type	0.6561	0.8926
2. Proportion of all cases falling into perfect scale types, irrespective of latent class from which recruited	0.7832	0.9346
3. Guttman coefficient of reproducibility	0.9436	0.9835
4. Proportion of cases which cannot be ranked unambiguously	0.1080	0.0327

A further important comparison is possible by looking at test-retest reliabilities. These can be computed, in each case, by assuming that a respondent does not change in the latent class to which he belongs, but that his scale score on the "first" test does not alter the possibilities of being assigned to various scale scores on the "second" test.[3] The theoretical product-moment correlations between test and retest are as follows:

For scale based on four observed items $r = 0.8085$
For scale using H-technique based on four triplets $r = 0.9565$

The theoretical example discussed has been for a special case where each original item is subject to a 10 per cent error. The situation is generalized somewhat further in Figure 14-1. Assuming, as before, equal errors for all

3. To compute test-retest reliability, response patterns first are grouped and weighted as follows:

				x: weight
$++++$,	$+++-$,	$++-+$		$+2$
$-+++$,	$+-++$,	$-++-$		$+1$
$--++$,	$-+-+$,	$++--$,	$+-+-$	0
$---+$,	$--+-$,	$+--+$		-1
$----$,	$-+--$,	$+---$		-2

Within each latent class, the sums of squares and sums of cross products are computed. For example, on Latent Class I, the frequency for $X = 2$ as seen from Table 14-1 is 0.8019. The contribution toward ΣX^2 is $2^2 \times 0.8019$. Since *within* a latent class, the probabilities of a given response on test X_1 and retest X_2 are independent, the contribution toward $\Sigma X_1 X_2$, made when X_1 and X_2 in Latent Class 1 both equal 2, is $(2 \times 0.8019)^2$. For $X_1 = 1$ and $X_2 = 2$, we have (1×0.1539) (2×0.8019), etc. The process is repeated for each of the five latent classes and the totals for all classes summed for utilization in the conventional formula for Pearson product-moment correlation. (An alternative and more laborious procedure for computing theoretical test-retest reliability, which gives response patterns a separate value based on assigning a separate weight to the frequency within each latent class, yields only slightly different results from the method used above.)

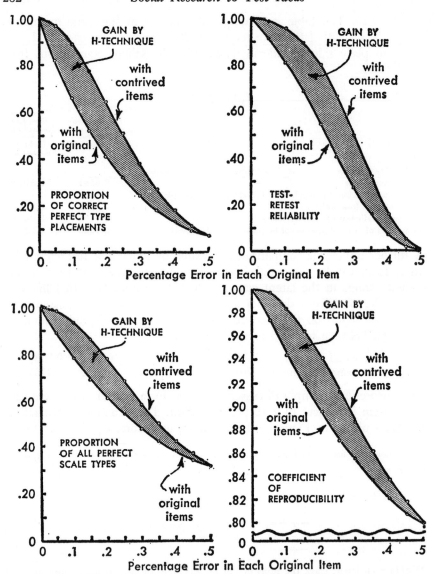

Figure 14-1. *Gain by H-technique for varying amounts of error in the original items.*

four equally spaced items, we can observe in Figure 14-1 the gains expected from the H-technique over the entire possible range of error. Figure 14-1 deserves careful examination, since it demonstrates, on the one hand, that the expected gains are very substantial, and, on the other hand, that the H-technique *cannot be expected to salvage a situation where the original item error is much larger than about 20 per cent.* In other words, the H-technique is definitely not a procedure for lifting oneself with one's own bootstraps.

Earlier in this exposition it was suggested that an original item can be used more than once. One cutting point can be used to contribute toward a given contrived item; another cutting point of the same original item can be used to contribute toward a second contrived item. The theoretical effect on reproducibility, test-retest reliability, etc., appears to be almost the same as when no original item is used more than once. (See Table 14-4 for the special case of equally spaced items with equal errors.) If two original items

Table 14-4. Effect on Reproducibility and Test-Retest Reliability of Using the Same Original Item in Two Different Contrived Items

	COEFFICIENT OF REPRODUCIBILITY		TEST-RETEST RELIABILITY	
	Average Item Error 0.1	Average Item Error 0.2	Average Item Error 0.1	Average Item Error 0.2
Four original items only	0.9436	0.8949	0.8085	0.5443
Four contrived items, each based on three undupli-cated original items	0.9835	0.9415	0.9565	0.7990
Four contrived items, each based on three original items, but with an original item used twice in the pair of contrived items specified:				
Items I and II	0.9830	0.9409	0.9511	0.7777
I and III	0.9836	0.9424	0.9470	0.7845
I and IV	0.9845	0.9456	0.9550	0.7954
II and III	0.9846	0.9457	0.9526	0.7859
II and IV	0.9852	0.9474	0.9547	0.7926
III and IV	0.9861	0.9501	0.9566	0.7982
Four contrived items, each based on three original items but with two original items used twice in the pair of contrived items specified:				
Items I and II	0.9822	0.9397	0.9353	0.7365
I and III	0.9831	0.9420	0.9422	0.7589
I and IV	0.9852	0.9491	0.9529	0.7880
II and III	0.9854	0.9492	0.9405	0.7565
II and IV	0.9864	0.9515	0.9502	0.7845
III and IV	0.9880	0.9572	0.9545	0.7925

are used with different cutting points in the same two contrived items, the reproducibility is substantially unaffected, but the test-retest reliability drops somewhat, depending on which contrived items are involved.

If the original number of items is few, one way of cutting corners might be to use only two original items to form the extreme contrived items I and IV, while using three original items to form the middle contrived items II and III. Contrived Item I would be scored as positive if the respondent is positive on *both* of the original items involved. Contrived Item II would be scored as positive if two out of three of the original items involved were positive; the same with Contrived Item III. Contrived Item IV would be scored as positive if at least *one* of the two items involved were positive. The effect of such an operation is to produce a slightly higher reproducibility than would be obtained if three items were used in each case, but at a small and noticeable cost in lowered test-retest reliability. In the example given above, when the average error in original items is 10 per cent, the use of doublets instead of triplets at the two extremes changes reproducibility from 0.9835 to 0.9888 but cuts reliability from 0.9565 to 0.9298. When the average error is 20 per cent, the use of doublets changes reproducibility from 0.9415 to 0.9597 but cuts reliability from 0.7990 to 0.7630. This kind of result ought to be noted carefully by students of scaling theory because, incidentally, it illustrates one of the dangers in relying on reproducibility alone as a measure of success.

In the examples given, several restrictions were introduced to facilitate computation and exposition. No general mathematical treatment is at present available. Further preliminary theoretical explorations have shown that the assumption of equal error of all items in a triplet is not necessary to obtain a substantial reduction in overall scale error. Moreover, there seems to be no special virtue in the use of three responses to form the new contrived item as in the example cited; more responses should do even better.

One suggested line of inquiry should be explored in greater detail than has been possible as yet. This is to treat a set of individual items making up a given contrived item as contributing to a Lazarsfeld latent dichotomy. (At least four original items probably would be needed to form such a contrived item.) The final cumulative scale would then consist of a series of ordered cutting points, each of which has first been established by latent-dichotomy analysis. Computation might be too heavy to justify this procedure in practice, but its theoretical implications are of much interest.

AN EMPIRICAL EXAMPLE, WITH COMPUTING PROCEDURES

In connection with the Harvard–Air Force research project, 633 officers at six air bases filled out an eleven-item questionnaire designed to order respondents along the single dimension "sensitivity to sanctions."

There are four response categories for each question, which are arbitrarily scored 1, 2, 3, 4, respectively, a score of 1 going to the response intended to indicate the most independent from pressure. As in a conventional item-analysis procedure or in the Guttman Cornell technique, a provisional total score was computed for each person based on his answers to all eleven questions. This total score, together with the individual item responses, was punched on IBM cards.

The remaining machine job, done on an IBM Electronic Statistical Machine, Type 101, required less than four hours, including time spent in wiring a special board. The job also could have been done easily on the more common type of counter sorter, but would have taken more time.

The steps were as follows:

1. Tabulating the correlation tables of each of the eleven items with the provisional total score. These are shown in Table 14-5.

Table 14-5. Responses to Individual Items as Related to Provisional Total (Air Force Data)

PROVISIONAL TOTAL SCORE*	ITEM 1 1	2	3	4	ITEM 2 1	2	3	4	ITEM 3 1	2	3	4
43–44	...	...	...	46	...	...	3	43	...	...	2	44
39–42	...	...	18	23	...	...	9	32	...	3	13	25
35–38	1	4	38	29	2	3	16	51	1	4	36	31
33–34	...	3	59	7	1	2	36	30	...	5	58	6
30–32	...	25	42	5	2	6	37	27	...	19	47	6
28–29	...	43	25	1	1	5	53	10	1	29	33	6
26–27	4	40	21	2	...	11	42	14	5	37	19	6
24–25	3	48	6	1	2	14	37	5	2	38	17	1
21–23	11	59	4	...	...	22	49	3	3	62	8	1
11–20	33	30	2	...	7	28	28	2	31	30	4	...
	52	252	215	114	15	91	310	217	43	227	237	126

	ITEM 4 1	2	3	4	ITEM 5 1	2	3	4	ITEM 6 1	2	3	4
43–44	...	...	2	44	...	...	1	45	...	...	2	44
39–42	1	1	18	21	...	...	7	34	...	2	21	18
35–38	...	9	46	17	...	...	33	39	...	22	38	12
33–34	...	16	49	4	...	3	58	8	1	16	49	3
30–32	2	50	20	...	...	4	62	6	2	49	21	...
28–29	5	61	3	...	1	14	54	...	4	60	5	...
26–27	13	51	3	...	2	26	38	1	13	51	2	1
24–25	23	32	3	...	...	38	20	...	19	35	4	...
21–23	42	32	...	...	1	65	8	...	29	45	...	...
11–20	58	7	...	...	21	40	3	1	58	7	...	...
	144	259	144	86	25	190	284	134	126	287	142	78

	ITEM 7 1	2	3	4	ITEM 8 1	2	3	4	ITEM 9 1	2	3	4
43–44	...	...	...	46	...	...	...	46	...	...	...	46
39–42	...	...	13	28	...	2	10	29	...	...	9	32
35–38	...	11	31	30	2	12	29	29	1	1	40	30
33–34	1	5	54	9	6	6	49	8	1	4	55	9
30–32	...	16	52	4	1	21	45	5	2	10	54	6
28–29	...	22	47	...	4	22	39	4	...	29	37	3
26–27	2	28	35	2	9	31	24	3	2	40	22	3
24–25	1	45	12	...	6	35	17	...	1	40	16	1
21–23	3	66	5	...	7	58	9	...	8	64	2	...
11–20	25	38	2	...	30	32	2	1	38	21	5	1
	32	231	251	119	65	219	224	125	53	209	240	131

	ITEM 10 1	2	3	4	ITEM 11 1	2	3	4
43–44	...	...	...	46	...	...	1	45
39–42	...	...	2	39	...	...	7	34
35–38	...	1	22	49	1	1	39	31
33–34	1	...	51	17	1	2	55	11
30–32	...	2	48	22	1	12	52	7
28–29	...	5	54	10	1	31	34	3
26–27	1	10	44	12	5	41	19	2
24–25	...	19	38	1	2	45	11	...
21–23	1	46	24	3	12	53	8	1
11–20	10	41	13	1	33	32	...	...
	13	124	296	200	56	217	226	134

* Grouped to form class intervals approximating deciles. N = 633.

2. Selecting the cutting points for each item which correlated with the total score high enough to form a fourfold table in which neither "error" cell had a frequency higher than the smaller of the two frequencies on the principal diagonal. For example, if Item I is dichotomized with 3 and 4 combined as positive, we can form from the data in Table 14-5 the following acceptable fourfold table:

	1, 2	3, 4
+	33	267
Provisional score		
−	271	62

From the same item, by dichotomizing with 4 as a positive answer, we can also form an acceptable table:

	1, 2, 3	4
+	18	69
Provisional score		
−	501	45

Also, from the same item, by dichotomizing with 2, 3, 4 as positive answers, another acceptable table is obtained (although it just barely meets the minimum requirements):

	1	2, 3, 4
+	19	549
Provisional score		
−	33	32

In each of the examples, it will be noted, the sum of the errors is well below 20 per cent of the total frequency. If the errors go much above 20 per cent, the item ordinarily should be discarded, although an occasional exception may be tolerated.

3. Ordering all acceptable cutting points from the largest positive to the smallest, as shown in Table 14-6.

4. Selecting sets of triplets to constitute four new contrived items. The original items actually used are indicated in Table 14-6 by Roman numerals, which designate the contrived item they served to form. Thus, Contrived Item I is formed from Original Items 4 and 6 (with categories 2, 3, 4 treated as positive), and Original Item 10 (with categories 3, 4 treated as positive). It will be noted in Table 14-6 that several cuts which met the test of acceptable correlation were not used (designated by †). For example, Items 1, 9, and 11 (with categories 2, 3, and 4 treated as positive) were not used, for two reasons: (1) cutting points so close to the end of the scale were not desired; and (2) it was preferred to use two of the same items (with different cuts) in forming Contrived Item II. The main objective is to select acceptable

Table 14-6. Items and Cutting Points Used in Construction of Contrived Items (Air Force Data)

Item	Positive Response Categories	Frequency Positive	Contrived Item in Which Original Item Is Used
10	2, 3, 4	620	. . . *
2	2, 3, 4	618	. . . *
5	2, 3, 4	608	. . . *
7	2, 3, 4	601	. . . *
3	2, 3, 4	590	. . . *
1	2, 3, 4	581	. . . †
9	2, 3, 4	580	. . . †
11	2, 3, 4	577	. . . †
8	2, 3, 4	568	. . .
2	3, 4	527	. . . *
6	2, 3, 4	507	I
10	3, 4	496	I
4	2, 3, 4	489	I
5	3, 4	418	. . . †
9	3, 4	371	II
7	3, 4	370	. . . †
3	3, 4	363	II
11	3, 4	360	II
8	3, 4	349	. . . †
1	3, 4	329	. . . †
4	3, 4	230	III
6	3, 4	220	III
2	4	217	III
10	4	200	. . . †
5	4	134	IV
11	4	134	. . . †
9	4	131	. . . †
3	4	126	. . . †
8	4	125	IV
7	4	119	. . . †
1	4	114	IV
4	4	86	. . . †
6	4	78	. . . †

* Item at this cutting point does not correlate satisfactorily with provisional total score.
† Item at this cutting point satisfies the criterion of adequate correlation with the provisional total, but was not used in the scale.

items with approximately the same frequency for a given triplet and to space these sets of triplets as evenly as possible over the range.

5. Scoring each individual on each contrived item by calling him positive on a given item if he were positive in either two or three of the component individual responses.

6. Tabulating the sixteen response patterns. Actually operations 5 and 6 were performed together in five minutes by a single pass of the cards through the 101 machine, after a special board had been wired. This would require considerably more time on the older machine, but actually not much more time than is required for a conventional Guttman scale analysis. The sixteen response types are exhibited in Table 14-7.

From Table 14-7 we see that only 45 of the 633 respondents fall into nonscale types. This is an almost unbelievably satisfactory result, as compared with what experience with conventional scales has led us to expect. Because,

Table 14-7. Frequency Assigned to Each Response Pattern by the H-Technique (Air Force Data)

Response Patterns	Frequency
$++++$	92
$+++-$*	1
$++-+$*	1
$+-++$*	22
$-+++$	103
$-++-$*	. . .
$-+-+$*	8
$--++$	157
$---+$	106
$--+-$*	12
$+--+$*	. . .
$----$	130
$-+--$*	. . .
$+---$*	. . .
$++--$*	. . .
$+-+-$*	1
	633

* Nonscale types.

to some extent, artificial restrictions on error are introduced by using more than one cutting point for some of the same items, there is need for caution in reporting a coefficient of reproducibility (just as in the case when trichotomies are used in a conventional Guttman analysis). Even if the computed reproducibility coefficient of 0.982 is a little inflated, a conservative estimate would place it well above 95, since there are only 7 per cent of nonscale types all together.

Because of the high precision with which each cutting point on the cumulative scale is marked off by the H-technique, the rank order of the contrived items, if they are relatively widely spaced, should tend to remain invariant from sample to sample.

A good test of this is provided by sample data made available by the American Telephone and Telegraph Company, which has asked a set of morale questions to respondents in twenty-five different operating units, varying in size from 116 to 963 persons, with an average of 388. A six-step scale based on five contrived items held up in all twenty-five units with only four instances of reversals of rank order of adjacent contrived items out of 100 possibilities, in spite of the fact that we found it impossible to make up conventional scales based on single items without frequent reversals. The average proportion of nonscale types was only 10 per cent (highest among the twenty-five operating units was 15, lowest was 8), and the average coefficient of reproducibility, perhaps slightly overestimated, was 0.98, with no individual coefficient below 0.97. A five-step four-item scale also was constructed by the H-technique, from the same collection of original questions, with even better results. The average proportion of nonscale types was 5 per cent (highest among the twenty-five operating units was 7, lowest was 3). The average reproducibility was above 0.98. The rank order of the contrived items was invariant in all twenty-five units.

The H-technique has been used on other sets of data with equal success, where the original item error, as indicated in the correlation tables with the provisional total score, does not exceed about 20 per cent. Further experience with it may reveal shortcomings not now seen or may suggest better procedures for handling particular steps.

15

□ ☒ □ □ □ *Some Observations*
on Study Design

Of the various essays of which the author has been guilty, none having to do primarily with methodology has been more sought after by students requesting reprints than "Some Observations on Study Design," which originally appeared in the *American Journal of Sociology*. The paper stresses the importance of ideal models of research design as standards toward which we should aspire and from which we must deviate only at our peril. How and why the author's own research, as represented in previous chapters of this volume, falls short of the ideal will be appreciated by many discerning readers. If such a discrepancy challenges a few dedicated research scholars in the younger generation of social scientists to do better, it will have served its highest aim.

As a youth I read a series of vigorous essays in the *Century Magazine* by its editor, the late Glenn Frank. His theme was that the natural sciences had remade the face of the earth; now had arrived the age of the social sciences. The same techniques that had worked their miracles in physics, chemistry, and biology should, in competent hands, achieve equally dazzling miracles in economics, political science, and sociology. That was a long time ago. The disconcerting fact is that people are writing essays just like that today. Of

"Some Observations on Study Design," *American Journal of Sociology*, 40 (January, 1950, pp. 355-361. Copyright 1950 by the University of Chicago.

course, the last two decades have seen considerable progress in social science—in theory, in technique, and in the accumulation of data. It is true that the number of practitioners is pitifully few: only a few hundred research studies are reported annually in sociology, for example, as compared with more than 20,000 studies summarized annually in *Biological Abstracts*. But the bright promise of the period when Frank was writing has not been fulfilled.

Two of the most common reasons alleged for slow progress are cogent, indeed.

The data of social science are extremely complex, it is said. And they involve values that sometimes put a strain on the objectivity of the investigator even when they do not incur resistance from the vested interests of our society. However, an important part of the trouble has very little to do with the subject matter of social science as such but, rather, is a product of our own bad work habits. That is why this paper on the subject of study design may be relevant. So much has been spoken and written on this topic that I make no pretense to originality. But in the course of a little experience, especially in an effort during the war to apply social psychology to military problems, and in an undertaking to nurture a new program of research in my university, I have encountered some frustrations which perhaps can be examined with profit.

A basic problem—perhaps *the* basic problem—lies deeply imbedded in the thoughtways of our culture. This is the implicit assumption that anybody with a little common sense and a few facts can come up at once with the correct answer on any subject. Thus, the newspaper editor or columnist, faced with a column of empty space to fill with readable English in an hour, can speak with finality and authority on any social topic, however complex. He might not attempt to diagnose what is wrong with his sick cat; he would call a veterinarian. But he knows precisely what is wrong with any social institution and the remedies.

In a society that rewards quick and confident answers and does not worry about how the answers are arrived at, the social scientist is hardly to be blamed if he conforms to the norms. Hence, much social science is merely rather dull and obscure journalism—a few data and a lot of "interpretation." The fact that the so-called "interpretation" bears little or no relation to the data is often obscured by academic jargon. If the stuff is hard to read, it has a chance of being acclaimed as profound. The rewards are for the answers, however tediously expressed, and not for rigorously marshaled evidence.

In the Army no one would think of adopting a new type of weapon without trying it out exhaustively on the firing range. But a new idea about handling personnel fared very differently. The last thing anybody ever thought about was trying out the idea experimentally. I recall several times when we had schemes for running an experimental tryout of an idea in the socio-psychological field. Usually one of two things would happen: the idea would be rejected as stupid without a tryout (it may have been stupid, too), or it would be seized on and applied generally and at once. When the provost marshal wanted us to look into the very low morale of the MP's, our attitude surveys suggested that there was room for very much better selectivity in job assignment. There were routine jobs like guarding prisoners that could be given to the duller MP's, and there were a good many jobs calling for intelligence, discretion, and skill in public relations. We thought that the smarter men might be assigned to these jobs and that the prestige of these jobs would be raised further if a sprinkling of returned veterans with plenty of ribbons and no current assignment could be included among them. We proposed a trial program of a reassignment system in a dozen MP outfits for the purpose of comparing the resulting morale with that in a dozen matched outfits which were left untouched. Did we get anywhere? No.

	BEFORE	AFTER	AFTER–BEFORE
Experimental group	x_1	x_2	$d = x_2 - x_1$
Control group	x'_1	x'_2	$d' = x'_2 - x'_1$

Figure 15-1

Instead, several of our ideas were put into effect immediately throughout the army without any prior testing at all.

The army cannot be blamed for behavior like that. In social relations it is not the habit in our culture to demand evidence for an idea; plausibility is enough.

To alter the folkways, social science itself must take the initiative. We must be clear in our own minds what proof consists of, and we must, if possible, provide dramatic examples of the advantages of relying on something more than plausibility. And the heart of our problem lies in study design *in advance*, such that the evidence is not capable of a dozen alternative interpretations.

Basically, I think it is essential that we always keep in mind the model of a controlled experiment, even if in practice we may have to deviate from an ideal model. Take Figure 15-1. The test of whether a difference d is attributable to what we think it is attributable to is whether d is significantly larger than d'.

We used this model over and over again during the war to measure the effectiveness of orientation films in changing soldiers' attitudes. These experiences are described in Volume III of our *Studies in Social Psychology in World War II.*[1]

One of the troubles with using this careful design was that the effectiveness

1. Carl I. Hovland, Arthur A. Lumsdaine, and Fred D. Sheffield, *Experiments in Mass Communication* (Princeton: Princeton University Press, 1949).

of a single film when thus measured turned out to be so slight. If, instead of using the complete experimental design, we simply took an unselected sample of men and compared the attitudes of those who said they had seen a film with those who said they had not, we got much more impressive differences. This was more rewarding to us, too, for the management wanted to believe the films were powerful medicine. The gimmick was the selective fallibility of memory. Men who correctly remembered seeing the films were likely to be those most sensitized to their message. Men who were bored or indifferent may have actually seen them but slept through them or just forgot.

Most of the time we are not able or not patient enough to design studies containing all four cells as in Figure 15-1. Sometimes we have only the top

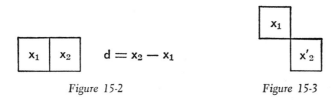

Figure 15-2   Figure 15-3

two cells, as in Figure 15-2. In this situation we have two observations of the same individuals or groups taken at different times. This is often a very useful design. In the army, for example, we would take a group of recruits, ascertain their attitudes, and restudy the same men later. From this we could tell whose attitudes changed and in what direction. (It was almost always for the worse, which did not endear us to the army!) But exactly what factors in the early training period were most responsible for deterioration of attitudes could only be inferred indirectly.

The panel study is usually more informative than a more frequent design, which might be pictured in Figure 15-3. Here at one point in time we have one sample, and at a later point in time we have another sample. We observe that our measure, say, the mean, is greater for the recent sample than for the earlier one. But we are precluded from observing which men or what type of men shifted. Moreover, there is always the disturbing possibility that the populations in our two samples were initially different; hence, the differences might not be attributable to conditions taking place in the time interval between the two observations. Thus, we would study a group of soldiers in the United States and later ask the same questions of a group of soldiers overseas. Having matched the two groups of men carefully by branch of service, length of time in the Army, rank, etc., we hoped that the results of the study would approximate what would be found if the same men could have been studied twice. But this could be no more than a hope. Some important factors could not be adequately controlled, for example, physical conditions. Men who went overseas were initially in better shape

on the average than men who had been kept behind; but, if the follow-up
study was in the tropics, there was a chance that unfavorable climate already
had begun to take its toll. And so it went. How much men overseas changed
called for a panel study as a minimum if we were to have much confidence
in the findings.

A very common attempt to get the results of a controlled experiment without paying the price is with the design that might be as shown in Figure 15-4.

Figure 15-4   Figure 15-5

This is usually what we get with correlation analysis. We have two or more
groups of men whom we study at the same point in time. Thus, we have
men in the infantry and men in the Air Corps and compare their attitudes.
How much of the difference between x'_2 and x_2 we can attribute to experience in a given branch of service and how much is a function of attributes
of the men selected for each branch we cannot know assuredly. True, we can
try to rule out various possibilities by matching; we can compare men from
the two branches with the same age and education, for example. But there
is all too often a wide-open gate through which other uncontrolled variables
can march.

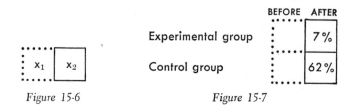

Figure 15-6   Figure 15-7

Sometimes, believe it or not, we have only one cell (Figure 15-5). When
this happens, we do not know much of anything. But we can still fill pages
of social science journals with "brilliant analysis" if we use plausible con-
jecture in supplying missing cells from our imagination. Thus, we may find
that the adolescent today has wild ideas and conclude that society is going
to the dogs. We fill in the dotted cell representing our own yesterdays with
hypothetical data, where x_1 represents us and x_2 our offspring (Figure 15-6).
The tragicomic part is that most of the public, including, I fear, many social
scientists, are so acculturated that they ask for no better data.

I do not intend to disparage all research not conforming to the canons
of the controlled experiment. I think that we will see more of full experi-

mental design in sociology and social psychology in the future than in the past. But I am well aware of the practical difficulties of its execution, and I know that there are numberless important situations in which it is not feasible at all. What I am arguing for is awareness of the limitations of a design in which crucial cells are missing.

Sometimes by forethought and patchwork we can get approximations which are useful if we are careful to avoid overinterpretation. Let me cite an example:

In Europe during the war the army tested the idea of putting an entire platoon of Negro soldiers into a white infantry outfit. This was done in several companies. The Negroes fought beside white soldiers. After several months we were asked to find out what the white troops thought about the innovation. We found that only 7 per cent of the white soldiers in companies with Negro platoons said that they disliked the idea very much, whereas 62 per cent of the white soldiers in divisions without Negro troops said they would dislike the idea very much if it were tried in their outfits (Figure 15-7). Now, were these white soldiers who fought beside Negroes men who were naturally more favorable to Negroes than the cross section of white infantrymen? We did not think so, since, for example, they contained about the same proportion of Southerners. The point was of some importance, however, if we were to make the inference that actual experience with Negroes reduced hostility from 62 to 7 per cent. As a second-best substitute, we asked the white soldiers in companies with Negro platoons if they could recall how they felt when the innovation was first proposed. It happens that 67 per cent said they were initially opposed to the idea. Thus, we could tentatively fill in a missing cell and conclude that, under the conditions obtaining, there probably had been a marked change in attitude.

Even if this had been a perfectly controlled experiment, there was still plenty of chance to draw erroneous inferences. The conclusions apply only to situations closely approximating those of the study. It happens, for example, that the Negroes involved were men who volunteered to leave rear-area jobs for combat duty. If other Negroes had been involved, the situation might have been different. Moreover, they had white officers. One Army colonel who saw this study and whom I expected to ridicule it because he usually opposed innovations, surprised me by offering congratulations. "This proves," he said, "what I have been arguing in all my thirty years in the army—that niggers will do all right if you give 'em white officers!" Moreover, the study applied only to combat experience. Other studies would be needed to justify extending the findings to noncombat or garrison duty. In other words, one lone study, however well designed, can be a very dangerous thing if it is exploited beyond its immediate implications.

Now experiments take time and money, and there is no use denying that we in social science cannot be as prodigal with the replications as the biologist, who can run a hundred experiments simultaneously by growing plants in all kinds of soils and conditions. The relative ease of experimentation in much—not all—of natural science goes far to account for the difference in quality of proof demanded by physical and biological sciences, on the one hand, and social scientists, on the other.

Though we cannot always design neat experiments when we want to, we can at least keep the experimental model in front of our eyes and behave cautiously when we fill in missing cells with dotted lines. But there is a further and even more important operation we can perform in the interest of economy. That lies in our choice of the initial problem.

Professor W. F. Ogburn always told his students to apply to a reported research conclusion the test, "How do you know it?" To this wise advice I should like to add a further question: "What of it?" I suspect that if before designing a study, we asked ourselves, more conscientiously than we do, whether or not the study really is important, we would economize our energies for the few studies that are worth the expense and trouble of the kind of design I have been discussing.

Can anything be said about guides for selecting problems? I certainly think so. That is where theory comes in and where we social scientists have gone woefully astray.

Theory has not often been designed with research operations in mind. Theory as we have it in social science serves indispensably as a very broad frame of reference or general orientation. Thus, modern theories of culture tell us that it is usually more profitable to focus on the learning process and the content of what is learned rather than on innate or hereditary traits. But they do not provide us with sets of interrelated proportions which can be put in the form: If x_1, given x_2 and x_3, then there is strong probability that we get x_4. Most of our propositions of that form, sometimes called "theory," are likely to be ad hoc common-sense observations that are not deducible from more general considerations and that are of the same quality as the observation, "If you stick your hand in a fire and hold it there, you will get burned."

Now in view of the tremendous cost in time and money of the ideal kind of strict empirical research operations, it is obvious that we cannot afford the luxury of conducting them as isolated fact-finding enterprises. Each should seek to be some sort of *experimentum crucis*, and, with rare exceptions, that will only happen if we see its place *beforehand* in a more general scheme of things. Especially we need to look for situations where two equally plausible hypotheses deducible from more general theory lead to the expectation of different consequences. Then, if our evidence supports one and knocks out the other, we have accomplished something.

The best work of this sort in our field is probably being done today in laboratory studies of learning and of perception. I do not know of very good sociological examples. Yet in sociology experiments are possible. One of the most exciting, for example, was that initiated long before the war by Shaw and McKay to see whether cooperative effort by adult role models within a delinquent neighborhood would reduce juvenile delinquency. So many variables are involved in a single study like that one that it is not easy to determine which were crucial. But there was theory behind the study, and the experimental design provided for controlling at least some variables.

It may be that in sociology we will need much more thinking and many more descriptive studies involving random ratlike movements on the part of the researcher before we can even begin to state our problems so that they are in decent shape for fitting into an ideal design. However, I think that we can reduce to some extent the waste motion of the exploratory period if we try to act as if we have some a priori ideas and keep our eyes on the possible relevance of data to these ideas. This is easier said than done. So many interesting rabbit tracks are likely to be uncovered in the exploratory stages of research that one is tempted to chase rabbits all over the woods and forget what his initial quarry was.

Exploratory research is of necessity fumbling, but I think that the waste motion can be reduced by the self-denying ordinance of deliberately limiting ourselves to a few variables at a time. Recently two of my colleagues and myself have been doing a little exploratory work on a problem in the general area of social mobility. We started by tabulating some school records of fifty boys in the ninth grade of one junior high school and then having members of our seminar conduct three or four interviews with each boy and his parents. We had all the interviews written up in detail, and we had enough data to fill a book—with rather interesting reading, too. But it was a very wasteful process because there were just too many intriguing ideas. We took a couple of ideas which were deducible from current general theory and tried to make some simple fourfold tables. It was obvious that, with a dozen variables uncontrolled, such tables meant little or nothing. But that led us to a second step. Now we are trying to collect school records and a short questionnaire on 2,000 boys. We will not interview all these boys and their parents in detail. But, with 2,000 cases to start with, we hope to take a variable in which we are interested and find fifty boys who are plus on it and fifty who are minus, yet who are approximately alike on a lot of other things. A table based on such matched comparisons should be relatively unambiguous. We can take off from there and interview those selected cases intensively to push further our exploration of the nexus between theory and observation. This, we think, will be economical, though still exploratory. Experimental manipulation is far in the future in our problem, but we do hope we can conclude the first stage with a statement of some hypotheses susceptible to experimental verification.

I am not in the least deprecating exploratory work. But I do think that some orderliness is indicated even in the bright dawn of a youthful enterprise.

One reason that we are not more orderly in our exploratory work is that all too often what is missing is a sharp definition of a given variable, such that, if we wanted to take a number of cases and even throw them into a simple fourfold table, we could.

Suppose we are studying a problem in which one of the variables we are looking for is overprotection or overindulgence of a child by his mother. We have a number of case histories or questionnaires. Now how do we know whether we are sorting them according to this variable or not? The first step, it would seem, is to have some way of knowing whether we are sorting them along any single continuum, applying the same criteria to each case. But to know this, we need to have built into the study the ingredients of a scale. Unless we have some ingredients in our data, we are defeated from the start. This is why I think the new interest social scientists are taking in scaling techniques is so crucially important to progress. In particular, the latent-structure theory developed by Paul F. Lazarsfeld, which derives Louis Guttman's scale as an important special case, is likely to be exceedingly useful, for it offers criteria by which we can make a small amount of information go a long way in telling us the logical structure of a supposed variable we are eager to identify. The details of Guttman's and Lazarsfeld's work[2] are likely to promote a good deal of attack and controversy. Our hope is that this will stimulate others to think such problems out still better and thus make their work obsolete as rapidly as possible.

Trying to conduct a social science investigation without good criteria for knowing whether a particular variable may be treated as a single dimension is like trying to fly without a motor in the plane. Students of the history of invention point out that one reason why the airplane, whose properties had been pretty well thought out by Leonardo da Vinci, was so late in development was the unavailability of a lightweight power plant, which had to await the invention of the internal combustion motor. We are learning more and more how to make our lightweight motors in social science, and that augurs well for the future. But much work is ahead of us. In particular, we desperately need better projective techniques and better ways of getting respondents to reveal attitudes that are too emotionally charged to be accessible to direct questioning. Schemes like the latent-structure theory of Lazarsfeld should speed up the process of developing such tests.

I have tried to set forth the model of the controlled experiment as an ideal to keep in the forefront of our minds even when by necessity some cells are missing from our design. I have also tried to suggest that more economy and orderliness are made possible, even in designing the exploratory stages of a piece of research—by using theory in advance to help us decide whether a particular inquiry would be important if we made it, by narrowing down the number of variables, and by making sure that we can classify

2. Samuel A. Stouffer, Louis Guttman, Edward A. Suchman, Paul F. Lazarsfeld, Shirley A. Star, and John A. Clausen, *Measurement and Prediction* (Princeton: Princeton University Press, 1949).

our data along a particular continuum, even if only provisionally. And a central, brooding hope is that we will have the modesty to recognize the difference between a promising idea and proof.

Oh, how we need that modesty! The public expects us to deal with great problems like international peace, full employment, maximization of industrial efficiency. As pundits we can pronounce on such matters, as citizens we have a duty to be concerned with them, but as social scientists our greatest achievement now will be to provide a few small dramatic examples that hypotheses in our field can be stated operationally and tested crucially. And we will not accomplish that by spending most of our time writing or reading papers like this one. We will accomplish it best by rolling up our sleeves and working at the intricacies of design of studies that, though scientifically strategic, seem to laymen trivial compared with the global concerns of the atomic age. Thereby, and only thereby, I believe, can we some day have the thrilling sense of having contributed to the structure of a social science that is cumulative.

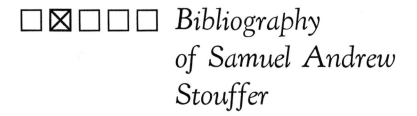 *Bibliography of Samuel Andrew Stouffer*

1930

"An Experimental Comparison of Statistical and Case-history Methods of Attitude Research," an abstract of a Ph.D. thesis, University of Chicago, June, 1930, *Abstracts of Theses*, University of Chicago, 1929–1932, Humanistic Series, 8, pp. 263-270. (See also 1931: Same title.)

"Local Option and Public Opinion," Carroll H. Wooddy and Samuel A. Stouffer, *American Journal of Sociology*, 36, September, 1930, pp. 175-205.

"Note on the Statistical Treatment of Life-History Material," Ruth Shonle Cavan, Philip M. Hauser, and Samuel A. Stouffer, *Social Forces*, 9, December, 1930, pp. 200-203.

1931

"Experimental Comparison of a Statistical and a Case History Technique of Attitude Research," *Publications of the American Sociological Society*, 25, 1931, pp. 154-156. (See also 1930: Same title.)

1933

"Tests of Significance in Applying Westergaard's Method of Expected Cases to Sociological Data," Samuel A. Stouffer and Clark Tibbitts, *Journal of the American Statistical Association*, 28, September, 1933, pp. 293-302. (See also 1951: Same title.)

"Criteria of Differential Mortality," Harold F. Dorn and Samuel A. Stouffer, *Journal of the American Statistical Association*, 28, December, 1933, pp. 402-413.

"A Technique for Analyzing Sociological Data Classified in Non-quantitative Groups," *American Journal of Sociology*, 39, September, 1933, pp. 180-193.

1934

"Problems in the Application of Correlation to Sociology," *Journal of the American Statistical Association*, 29, March, 1934 (supplement), pp. 52-58.

"Sociology and Sampling," (L. L. Bernard, ed.). Part 2, Chapter 16, in *The Fields and Methods of Sociology*, New York: Ray Long and Richard R. Smith, Inc., 1934, pp. 476-488.

"Testing the Significance of Comparisons in Sociological Data," Samuel A. Stouffer and Clark Tibbitts, *American Journal of Sociology*, 40, November, 1934, pp. 357-363.

"Training for Sociological Research," *Sociology and Social Research*, 18, January, 1934, pp. 207-210.

"A Coefficient of 'Combined Partial Correlation' with an Example from Sociological Data," *Journal of the American Statistical Association*, 29, March, 1934, pp. 70-71.

"Fertility of Families on Relief," *Journal of the American Statistical Association*, 29, September, 1934, pp. 295-300.

1935

"Statistical Induction in Rural Social Research," *Social Forces*, 13, May, 1935, pp. 505-515.

"Trends in the Fertility of Catholics and Non-Catholics," *American Journal of Sociology*, 41, September, 1935, pp. 143-166.

S.S.R.C. Monograph Committee on Cort Statistics [1935?], Meredith B. Givens and Samuel A. Stouffer.

1936

"Reliability Coefficients in a Correlation Matrix," *Psychometrika*, 1, June, 1936, pp. 17-20.

"Marriage and Divorce in Recent Years," Samuel A. Stouffer and Lyle M. Spencer, *Annals of the American Academy of Political and Social Science*, 188, November, 1936, pp. 1-14.

"Evaluating the Effect of Inadequately Measured Variables in Partial Correlation Analysis," *Journal of the American Statistical Association*, 31, June, 1936, pp. 348-360. ("Erratum," 31, September, 1936, p. 562.)

1937

Research Memorandum on the Family in the Depression, Samuel A. Stouffer and Paul F. Lazarsfeld, New York: Social Science Research Council, Bull. 29, 1937.

1938

"Problems of the Bureau of the Census in Their Relation to Social Science," Section 7 in *Research—A National Resource, I. Relation to the Federal Government to Research*, Report of the Science Committee to the National Resources Committee. Washington, D.C.: United States Government Printing Office, November, 1938, pp. 195-231.

1939

"Recent Increases in Marriage and Divorce," Samuel A. Stouffer and Lyle M. Spencer, *American Journal of Sociology*, 44, January, 1939, pp. 551-554.

Contribution to "New Light on Old Health Problems," *Proceedings* of the 17th Annual Meeting of the Milbank Memorial Fund, March, 1939, 91 pages. Discussant of Robert E. Chaddock, "The Changing Status of Group Differences in Fertility,"

1940

"Intervening Opportunities: A Theory Relating Mobility and Distance," *American Sociological Review*, 5, December, 1940, pp. 845-867. [See also Part 7 of Chapter 8, "Social Change" (Lyle W. Shannon, ed.) in *Readings in General Sociology* (Robert W. O'Brien, ed., Palo Alto, Calif.: Pacific Books, 1947, pp. 512-514 (excerpts).]

"Radio and the Printed Page as Sources of News," Chapter V (pp. 214-235), and "For Further Details . . .," Chapter VI (pp. 263-272), in *Radio and the Printed Page* by Paul F. Lazarsfeld. New York: Duell, Sloan and Pearce, 1940.

1941

"How a Mathematician Can Help a Sociologist," *Sociometry*, 4, February, 1941, pp. 56-63. (Read before a joint session of the Institute of Mathematical Statistics and American Sociological Society, Philadelphia, December, 1939.)

"Notes on the Case Study and the Unique Case," *The Prediction of Personal Adjustment* (Paul Horst, ed.). New York: Social Science Research Council, Bull. 48, 1941, pp. 240-249. (See also *Sociometry*, 4, November, 1941, pp. 349-357.)

1942

"A Sociologist Looks at Communications Research," in *Print, Radio, and Film in a Democracy* (Douglas Waples, ed.), pp. 133-146. Chicago: University of Chicago Press, 1942.

1943

"Social Science and the Soldier," in *American Society in Wartime*, Charles R. Walgreen Foundation Lectures (William Fielding Ogburn, ed.). Chicago: University of Chicago Press, 1943, pp. 105-117.

1944

"Negro Population and Negro Population Movements: 1860–1940, in Relation to Social and Economic Factors." Manuscript deposited in the Schomburg Collection of the New York Public Library (one of four volumes of studies made in connection with *An American Dilemma*, by Gunnar Myrdal, 1944).

1946

"Government and the Measurement of Opinion," *Scientific Monthly*, 63, December, 1946, pp. 435-440.

1947

"United States Methodological Research in Public Opinion," *Proceedings of the International Statistical Conferences*, 3, 1947, pp. 532-544.

"Sociology and Common Sense," *American Sociological Review*, 12, February, 1947, pp. 11-12. (Discussion of Presidential Address, American Sociological Society, read at Chicago, December, 1946, by Carl C. Taylor.)

1948

"Sociology and the Strategy of Social Science," paper read before the American Association for the Advancement of Science, September 16, 1948. (See also the debate between Samuel A. Stouffer and Percy Bridgman, April 20, 1948; and 1950: Same title.)

"Studying the Attitudes of Soldiers," *American Philosophical Society Proceedings*, 92, November, 1948, pp. 336-340. (Read February 6, 1948, at the Symposium on Research Frontiers in Human Relations.)

1949

"Evidence Pertaining to Last-minute Swing to Truman," Samuel A. Stouffer and Duncan
MacRae, Jr. Chapter X in *The Pre-election Polls of 1948* by Mosteller, Hyman,
McCarthy, Marks, and Truman. New York: Social Science Research Council, Bull. 60,
1949, pp. 251-262.
"Social Science and the Study of Social Attitudes," American Association of Advertising
Agencies, Thirty-first Annual Meeting, The Greenbrier, April, 1949, pp. 5-12.
Selections in *The Polls and Public Opinion* (Norman C. Meier and Harold W. Saunders,
eds.). New York: Henry Holt & Co. [pp. 11-19, "Basic Social Science Research"; pp.
36-39, by Kenneth W. Spence, Samuel A. Stouffer, Robert R. Sears, and Walter A.
Shewhart, "Cooperative Research in the Social Sciences"; pp. 207-214, by Leslie G.
Moeller, Archibald M. Crossley, George H. Gallup, Paul F. Lazarsfeld, and Samuel
A. Stouffer, "The SSRC Committee Report" (The Iowa Conference on Attitude and
Opinion Research, sponsored by the State University of Iowa, Iowa City)].
"A Study of Attitudes," *Scientific American*, May, 1949, pp. 11-15. (See also 1951: Same
title.)
"An Analysis of Conflicting Social Norms," *American Sociological Review*, 14, December,
1949, pp. 707-717.

1950

"Sociology and the Strategy of Social Science," *Centennial*, Collected Papers Presented at
the Centennial Celebration, Washington, D.C., September 13-17, 1948, pp. 14-19
(Subhead: Sciences of Society). Washington, D.C.: American Association for the
Advancement of Science, 1950. (See also 1948: Same title.)
"Some Afterthoughts of a Contributor to 'The American Soldier,' " in *Continuities in
Social Research: Studies in the Scope and Method of "The American Soldier"*
(Robert K. Merton and Paul F. Lazarsfeld, eds.). Glencoe: The Free Press, 1950,
pp. 197-211.
"Some Observations on Study Design," *American Journal of Sociology*, 40, January, 1950,
pp. 355-361.

1951

"An Empirical Study of Technical Problems in Analysis of Role Obligations," Chapter 5
in *Toward a General Theory of Action* (Talcott Parsons and Edward Shils, eds.).
Cambridge: Harvard University Press, 1951, pp. 479-496. (See also "Role Conflict
and Personality," below.)
"Standardization of Rates When Specific Rates Are Unknown," *Handbook of Statistical
Methods for Demographers* (preliminary edition) by A. J. Jaffe. Washington, D.C.:
United States Government Printing Office, 1951, pp. 56-58.
"Tests of Significance in Applying Westergaard's Method of Expected Cases to Sociological
Data," reprinted in *Handbook of Statistical Methods for Demographers* by A. J.
Jaffe (preliminary edition) Washington, D.C.: United States Government Printing
Office, 1951, pp. 65-70. (See also 1933: Same title.)
"Role Conflict and Personality," Samuel A. Stouffer and Jackson Toby, *American Journal
of Sociology*, 56, March, 1951, pp. 395-406. (Included in Chapter 5 of *Toward a
General Theory of Action*.)
"A Study of Attitudes" in *The American Soldier*, The University of Chicago Round Table,
no. 692, July, 1951. Also discussion. (See also 1949: Same title.)

1952

"Conflicting Roles and Leadership," Chapter 12 in *Problems in Social Psychology: An
Interdisciplinary Inquiry* (J. E. Hulett, Jr., and Ross Stagner, eds.). Urbana: Uni-

versity of Illinois Press, 1952, pp. 136-139. (Paper presented at the Allerton Conference on Social Psychology, held at Robert Allerton Park, Monticello, Illinois, December, 1950.)

"A Technique for Improving Cumulative Scales," Samuel A. Stouffer, E. F. Borgatta, D. G. Hays, and A. F. Henry. *Public Opinion Quarterly*, 16, pp. 273-291. (See also 1954: Same title.)

"Trends in Public Opinion Polling since 1948 and Their Probable Effect on 1952 Election Predictions" (Analysis), in *Proceedings, 1952 Invitational Conference on Testing Problems*, pp. 70-74. Princeton, N.J.: Educational Testing Service, 1952.

1953

"Measurement in Sociology," *American Sociological Review*, 18, December, 1953, pp. 591-597.

1954

"1665 and 1954," *Public Opinion Quarterly*, 18, Fall, 1954, pp. 233-238. (Presidential Address, American Association for Public Opinion Research, Asbury Park, N.J., April 24, 1954.)

"A Technique for Improving Cumulative Scales," Chapter 17 in *Sociological Studies in Scale Analysis* by Samuel A. Stouffer, Matilda W. Riley, John W. Riley, Jr., and Jackson Toby. New Brunswick, N.J.: Rutgers University Press, 1954, pp. 372-389. (See also 1952: Same title.)

Report by a Faculty Committee, *The Behavioral Sciences at Harvard*, June, 1954.

1955

"Social Forces That Produce the 'Great Sorting,'" in *The Great Sorting*, College Admissions, College Entrance Examination Board, No. 2, 1955. (Paper delivered at Arden House, October 23, 1954.)

"Needed Research on the Tolerance of Nonconformity," Proceedings of the American Philosophical Society, 99, August, 1955, pp. 239-243. (Read before the American Philosophical Society, in Philadelphia, April 21, 1955.)

1956

"Sociological Theory and Public Opinion Research," *Transactions of the Third World Congress of Sociology*, 8, August, 1956, pp. 306-312.

1957

"Quantitative Methods," Chapter 2 in *Review of Sociology, Analysis of a Decade* (Joseph B. Gittler, ed.). New York: John Wiley & Sons, Inc., 1957, pp. 25-55.

1958

"Sociological Factors Favoring Innovations," Chapter 7 in *Consumer Behavior, Research on Consumer Reactions* (Lincoln M. Clark, ed.) New York: Harper & Brothers, 1958, pp. 52-60.

"Karl Pearson—An Appreciation on the 100th Anniversary of His Birth," *Journal of the American Statistical Association*, 53, March, 1958, pp. 23-27.

"Changes in Living Patterns," paper presented at a forum, *Your Customer in a World of Change*, sponsored by E. I. du Pont de Nemours & Co., Wilmington, Del.

1959

William Fielding Ogburn, 1886–1959, printed memorial service, June, 1959, by R. Wendell Harrison, Quincy Wright, Samuel A. Stouffer, and Philip M. Mauser, pp. 9-13.

1960

Foreword to *Social Problems in America,* by Harry C. Bredemeier and Jackson Toby. New York: John Wiley & Sons, Inc., 1960.

"Intervening Opportunities and Competing Migrants," *Journal of Regional Science,* 2, Spring, 1960, pp. 1-26. (See also paper read at the American Sociological Society, September, 1956.)

Books

1949

The American Soldier: Studies in Social Psychology in World War II. Princeton: Princeton University Press. Volume I: *Adjustment during Army Life,* by Samuel A. Stouffer, Edward A. Suchman, Leland C. DeVinney, Shirley A. Star, and Robin M. Williams, Jr. Volume II: *Combat and Its Aftermath,* by Samuel A. Stouffer, Arthur A. Lumsdaine, Marion Harper Lumsdaine, Robin M. Williams, Jr., M. Brewster Smith, Irving L. Janis, Shirley A. Star, and Leonard S. Cottrell, Jr.

1950

Experiments in Mass Communication: Volume III of *Studies in Social Psychology in World War II,* by Carl I. Hovland, Arthur A. Lumsdaine, and Fred D. Sheffield. Princeton: Princeton University Press. *Measurement and Prediction:* Volume IV of *Studies in Social Psychology in World War II,* by Samuel A. Stouffer, Louis Guttman, Edward A. Suchman, Paul F. Lazarsfeld, Shirley A. Star, and John A. Clausen. Princeton: Princeton University Press.

1955

Communism, Conformity, and Civil Liberties. New York: Doubleday & Company, Inc.

 *Index*

DATE DUE